AMERICA IN THE 21ST CENTURY

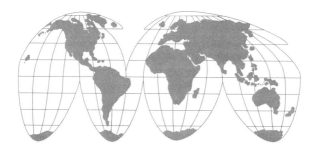

AMERICA IN THE 21ST CENTURY

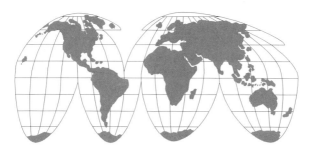

CHALLENGES AND OPPORTUNITIES IN FOREIGN POLICY

EDITED BY

KUL B. RAI
SOUTHERN CONNECTICUT STATE UNIVERSITY

DAVID F. WALSH
SOUTHERN CONNECTICUT STATE UNIVERSITY

PAUL J. BEST
SOUTHERN CONNECTICUT STATE UNIVERSITY

PRENTICE HALL, UPPER SADDLE RIVER, NEW JERSEY 07458

Library of Congress Cataloging-in-Publication Data

America in the 21st century: challenges and opportunities in foreign
   policy/edited by Kul B. Rai, David F. Walsh, Paul J. Best.
      p.   cm.
   Includes bibliographical references and index.
   ISBN 0-13-570961-X (pbk.)
      1. United States—Foreign relations—1989–   2. United States—
   Foreign relations—1989–   —Forecasting.   I. Rai, Kul B.
   II. Walsh, David F.   III. Best, Paul J.
   E840.A617   1997
   327.73'009'049—dc20   96-41017
                                                                    CIP

Editorial/production supervision, interior design,
   and electronic page makeup: Kari Callaghan Mazzola
Editorial director: Charlyce Jones Owen
Editor-in-chief: Nancy Roberts
Acquisitions editor: Michael Bickerstaff
Editorial assistant: Anita Castro
Cover design: Wendy Alling Judy
Buyer: Bob Anderson

This book was set in 10/12 New Baskerville by Big Sky Composition
and was printed and bound by Courier Companies, Inc.
The cover was printed by Phoenix Color Corp.

© 1997 by Prentice-Hall, Inc.
Simon & Schuster/A Viacom Company
Upper Saddle River, New Jersey 07458

Printed in the United States of America
10 9 8 7 6 5 4 3 2 1

ISBN   0-13-570961-X

PRENTICE-HALL INTERNATIONAL (UK) LIMITED, *London*
PRENTICE-HALL OF AUSTRALIA PTY. LIMITED, *Sydney*
PRENTICE-HALL CANADA INC., *Toronto*
PRENTICE-HALL HISPANOAMERICANA, S.A., *Mexico*
PRENTICE-HALL OF INDIA PRIVATE LIMITED, *New Delhi*
PRENTICE-HALL OF JAPAN, INC., *Tokyo*
SIMON & SCHUSTER ASIA PTE. LTD., *Singapore*
EDITORA PRENTICE-HALL DO BRASIL, LTDA., *Rio de Janeiro*

CONTENTS

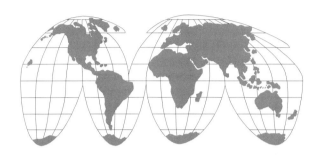

PREFACE

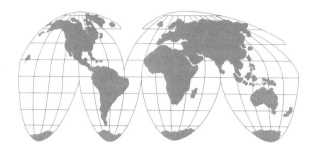

This volume is an examination of U.S. foreign policy in the post-Cold War period, in particular of the direction it is likely to take in the twenty-first century. The sudden end of Communism and the Cold War was not anticipated, with very rare exceptions, by either the policy makers or the scholars in the United States or in any other country. These two events in a sense caught American policy makers off guard and created new challenges and opportunities for the United States.

With the collapse of Communism and the dismemberment of the Soviet Union, the United States emerged as the sole superpower of the world. The United States not only possesses the most sophisticated nuclear and conventional weapons and has the best trained military forces in the world, but also its economy is the single most influential. As a result, U.S. global responsibilities have increased in both the military and economic areas. Even more so than during the Cold War, the United States is now responsible for maintaining peace in the world and for approving and conducting any collective military action that may become necessary. Although Russia, France, Britain, and China are world military powers, the United States is indisputably the military leader and guardian of peace on the globe. This alone presents challenges and opportunities that require a careful review.

While the economies of most countries in the world were connected to the U.S. economy during the Cold War, their links to the latter have further increased, in part due to the growing global interdependence, but equally important, due to the newly-gained status of the United States. Russia, the legal successor state to the former Soviet Union, is now dependent on the United States and other Western countries for its economic recovery.

Although fluctuations in the economy of any major developed country have an impact on the economies of other countries, the magnitude of such an impact is most widely felt in the case of changes in the U.S. economic situation. The world's increased economic links to the United States have a significant influence on the growth of the U.S. gross domestic product and the living standards of this country's people. It is imperative, therefore, that U.S. leaders face up to new challenges, with ingenuity as well as boldness, and exploit the opportunities to the greatest advantage of the American people.

Our focus in this study is on U.S. foreign policy toward different regions of the world. The global revolution in transportation and communications and the rise of the integrated world market have brought countries closer, and there is indeed a growing emphasis on globalization. However, while the United States does need to continually review its global perspectives on economic and foreign policy, the world regions will remain foremost in the formulation and implementation of the U.S. policy.

This book contains chapters on the U.S. policy toward Western Europe, "East Europe," East Asia, South Asia, Latin America, the Middle East, and Africa. In addition, two introductory chapters—one on the changing nature of the international system and the other on the history of the American policy from a regional perspective during the Cold War—are included. In order to make the writing consistent, the following major headings are used in most of the chapters: "Historical Background"; "U.S. Interests, Challenges, and Opportunities"; "Policy Options: Pros and Cons"; and "Policy Recommendations for the Twenty-First Century."

The contributors to this work are faculty members from three of the four campuses of the Connecticut State University—Southern, Central, and Eastern—and are predominantly political scientists. (One is from the department of history.) All have published in their areas of specialization.

ACKNOWLEDGMENTS

The editors gratefully acknowledge the assistance of the Connecticut State University Research Grants Committee and Faculty Development Office at Southern Connecticut State University in the preparation of this manuscript. We wish to thank Jean Polka, the Secretary of the Political Science Department at the university, for her endless hours of work on the manuscript, expert word processing skills, and cheerful attitude in meeting deadlines. We also thank Mrs. Kathleen Walsh, without whose help some of the chapters would not have been completed.

Kul B. Rai wishes to express appreciation for the assistance of Paul Holmer of Southern Connecticut State University Library in obtaining books, articles, documents, and other materials through the interlibrary loan network.

The editors wish to dedicate this volume to H. G. Peter Wallach—a friend, teacher, and scholar—who passed away suddenly while this volume was in preparation.

CONTRIBUTORS

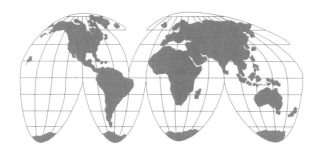

Kul B. Rai, Ph.D. University of Rochester (1969), is professor and chairman of the department of political science at Southern Connecticut State University. He is a co-author of three books, *Governing Through Turbulence* (1995), *Politics in Three Worlds* (1985), and *Political Science Statistics* (1973), and a co-translator of another, *Politics Among Nations* by Hans Morgenthau, into Hindi (1976). Dr. Rai has published articles in scholarly journals in the United States, Europe, and India, notably in *International Organization, Polity, Comparative Political Studies, Journal of Peace Research,* and *Indian Journal of Politics.* He served as president of the Northeastern Political Science Association in 1990–1991.

David F. Walsh, Ph.D. University of Connecticut (1975), is professor of political science at Southern Connecticut State University. He is a co-author of two books, *Governing Through Turbulence* (1995) and *Politics in Three Worlds* (1985). Dr. Walsh is a frequent participant in professional conferences and specializes in Western European political economy.

Paul J. Best, Ph.D. New York University (1965), is professor of political science and coordinator of Central/East European and Eurasian Studies at Southern Connecticut State University. He is a co-author of two books, *Governing Through Turbulence* (1995) and *Politics in Three Worlds* (1985), and has published articles in several scholarly journals, most notably *The Polish Review* and the *Journal of European Economic History.* Dr. Best served as Managing Editor of *The Polish Review* for twenty-three years (from 1969 to 1992).

James R. Cobbledick, Ph.D. Fletcher School of Law and Diplomacy, Tufts University (1965), is professor of political science at Eastern

Connecticut State University. A former U.S. Foreign Service Officer, he is the author of *Choice in American Foreign Policy* (1973).

H. G. Peter Wallach, Ph.D. University of Connecticut (1973), was professor of political science at Central Connecticut State University until his untimely death in 1995. A noted scholar on German politics, he was the author or co-author of five books.

Ta-Ling Lee, Ph.D. New York University (1965), is professor of history at Southern Connecticut State University. He is a co-author of seven books on China, the latest of which is *The Bamboo Gulag* (1994).

James W. Dull, Ph.D. Columbia University (1981), is professor of political science at the University of New Haven and an adjunct professor of international relations and foreign policy at Southern Connecticut State University. He is the author of *The Politics of American Foreign Policy* (1985).

Ghassan E. El-Eid, Ph.D. University of Nebraska (1988), is associate professor and chairman of the department of political science at Central Connecticut State University. He specializes in the Middle East.

Walton L. Brown, Ph.D. University of Michigan (1982), is associate professor of political science at Central Connecticut State University. She has published articles in *The Presidential Studies Quarterly*, *Latino Encyclopedia*, and *Business and Society Review*, and a chapter in *Notable Black American Women* (1994).

INTRODUCTION

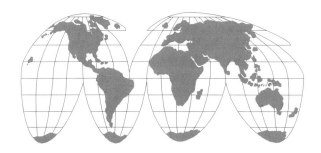

AMERICA IN A WORLD IN TRANSITION

DAVID F. WALSH AND KUL B. RAI

"The old world is dead. The future lies with those who can resolutely turn their back on it and face the new world with understanding, courage, and imagination."[1] These words, written by an eminent historian more than fifty years ago, during World War II, are once again applicable to international relations. At the end of the twentieth century, the international system is in a state of transition, as the scope and rapidity of change reach breakpoint, historic proportions.[2] Unlike the period of the 1940s, however, which witnessed the violent changes brought about by competing nations in World War II (and culminating in the onset of the Cold War), the changes of the last three decades have been driven by complex scientific, technological, social, and political factors that no existing international paradigm seems entirely adequate to explain. These changes have been of two varieties: short-term and long-term developments.

In the short term, the most important manifestations of these most recent changes have been those developments associated with the end of the Cold War—the reunification of Germany, the demise of the Soviet Union, and the transition of the former soviet states from state socialism to capitalism and democracy. These events, which occurred with startling rapidity between the mid-1980s and the early 1990s, permanently altered the configuration of world power and brought an end to the postwar era of international relations. The post–World War II era had been dominated by the Cold War competition between the United States and the Soviet Union and by the resulting bipolar division of much of the world into the rival Western Alliance and Soviet bloc. The Cold War was characterized by a remarkable stability in

1

international politics. For more than four decades, the global competition between the United States and the Soviet Union dominated the international arena and justified the leadership of each superpower over its respective allies. As the accounts of statesmen and scholars document, the leadership of the superpowers, for a time, amounted to hegemony, absolute dominance, and supremacy over the rules governing military, political, and economic behavior within their respective spheres of influence. The Cold War was a worldwide competition that ultimately impacted every region of the world and most of the world's states. Regional conflicts were exploited by the superpowers to advance their interests, and economic and political relationships were interrupted or fostered according to the alliances of the states involved. Even states that had previously attained the status of regional powers were reduced by the overwhelming military dominance of the superpowers to the role of Cold War surrogates, dependent on foreign military and economic aid.

In extreme cases, states themselves were divided by the Cold War conflict, as were Germany, China, Korea, and Vietnam, but the majority of states also found their international identities determined by their Cold War affiliations. Despite efforts to escape these bipolar constraints through declarations of "nonalignment" or the development of policies independent of the superpowers, such as France's *de facto* withdrawal from NATO under Charles de Gaulle, most states found their foreign and defense policies under the dominant influence, if not outright control, of one of the superpowers. With the events of 1989–1991, the Cold War pattern of international politics came to a sudden and unexpected end. As the twenty-first century approaches, the former bipolar pattern of politics has given way to new and more complex relationships, the Soviet Union has been replaced by a number of successor states, the economic and political leadership of the United States has been challenged by other advanced industrial states, and new and different security concerns have arisen.

If short-term changes reversed the international pattern of the last forty-five years, longer term developments, driven by scientific and technological innovations of the last three decades (that were built upon earlier findings), have begun to transform the basic relational parameters upon which traditional international politics have been based. In particular, innovations in electronics, microelectronics, computer science, global radio and television, and transportation have altered basic economic and political roles and relationships around the globe. Two developments have already had an important transforming influence. *First*, in the international economic issue–area, technological advances in communications, new production technologies, and transportation have given rise to truly global patterns of investment, production, and consumption that have replaced older, largely national ones. These developments, often referred to as the shift to the global market, have revolutionized economic relationships throughout the international system.[4] Some states have lost their economic advantages, new industrial locations have been established, and trade patterns have been altered by the existence of regional economic organizations like the European Union. In addition, the globalization of economic activity has increased the power of private actors, including transnational corporations, investors, and currency speculators, whose decisions now impact the economic well-being of the citizens of even the most powerful states. In the context of the global market, economic power now seems more important than military power, and the new openness, fluidity, and volatility that have accompanied globalization have greatly increased the importance and contentiousness of trade and other economic relations.

Second, states as institutions now find their authority threatened by new political movements committed to two different goals—the establishment of supranational organizations above the state and support for subnational ethnocultural identities that sometimes demand secession from existing states.[5] The movement toward supranational authority has most commonly taken the form of support for regional economic organizations, like the European Union, that have the power to regulate important social and economic activities within the member states. Although motivated in part by the desire to achieve practical economic advantages, supranational institutions also reflect commitment to the values of the new culture of global capitalism, loyalty to one's firm, and the pursuit of economic profit above all else. This culture now competes with the traditional values of patriotism and support for one's state. Subnationalism develops from the desire of groups within an existing state to liberate themselves from current political or cultural constraints and, in some cases, to establish a new state that will allow the true expression of their ethnocultural identity. Strong subcultural movements can be found in states at all levels of development, including advanced industrial states. Subnational movements are proliferating in all regions of the world. Both supranational and subnational groups are sustained by contact and communications between like-minded people, and the availability of instantaneous media coverage and global communications have been important factors in the growth of these movements.[6]

The changes that have become apparent at the end of the twentieth century have produced an international environment of extreme complexity and fluidity. The number of international actors has increased, new economic and environmental issues have been added to the international agenda, and the increasing globalization of economic and social activities has produced an unprecedented interdependence among actors. These transformations have created uncertainty at both the international and the state levels. Viewed from the level of the international system, the end of the Cold War and the emergence of the new patterns of economic competition have contributed to a redistribution of power among states, including the eclipse of the former Soviet Union as a superpower, the rise of trading nations in Europe and Asia (especially Germany and Japan), and the end of American economic hegemony. The configuration of power in the postwar era has broken down and a new distribution has emerged. The future configuration of power is of crucial importance because the most powerful state or states will determine the rules and relationships of the world order of the twenty-first century. Presently, however, it is impossible to predict which states will win the global economic competition, to what extent economic power will replace military power, or the exact extent of America's decline and whether a new state will replace the United Sates as a world hegemon. It is also unclear what security arrangements will be needed to promote peace in the post–Cold War era, and whether any effective security measures can be devised to deal with regional crises, such as the one in the former Yugoslavia. In sum, at the end of the twentieth century, both the actors and the structures of the international system are in a state of flux. It is clear that new rules and institutions must be devised for all three areas of international politics—the security issue-area, the international economic issue-area, and the ecological issue-area—but it is unclear which actors will be positioned to determine the rules and what these rules will be.

The new international conditions have also had a profound impact at the state level, and states in some regions of the world have experienced revolutionary changes. In Eastern and Central Europe, the end of the Cold War, the strategic withdrawal of the Soviet Union from this region, and the subsequent disintegration of the Soviet Union itself produced the end of the authority of Communist regimes and the deconstruction of foreign and defense policies in place for the last forty-five years. At present, the outcome of the difficult transition to democracy and capitalism remains unclear, and the proliferation of subnational groups and ethnocultural violence threatens the territorial integrity of several post–Communist states, including the chief successor state to the Soviet Union, Russia. It is clear, however, that the transition process and the reorientation of foreign and defense policies in these states will not produce a uniform outcome or a common timetable for integration into the Western European political and economic system.

The states of the West were also profoundly affected by the end of the Cold War and the demise of the Soviet Union. Although a welcomed development, the end of the Cold War deprived the West of a common enemy and the need for joint security cooperation among Western nations. In the ensuing political vacuum, the Western states were required to reorient their foreign policies, redefine their roles in the world, and reallocate foreign policy resources. The Western European states contiguous to the post–Communist countries face special problems, including an influx of refugees, increased crime, and demands for large-scale economic aid for the transition process. In a more general sense, relations among the Western states were altered because the removal of the common Soviet threat resulted in a de-emphasis on national security and political cooperation and a corresponding emphasis on economic and trade issues on which significant differences existed, especially between the United States and Japan. The common front against Iraq in the Gulf War of 1991 masked these differences for a short time, but the reality remained that the triangular economic competition among the United States, Japan, and the European Union was a contest of "the highest stakes" that is likely to produce the hegemonic state or states that will lead the world in the twenty-first century.[7]

The globalization of economic activities also altered relations among international actors in every region of the world, but the effect has been extremely uneven. Adjustments to the global market have been most pronounced in the regions at the core of the world economy—North America, East Asia, and Europe. In the case of Western Europe and its European Union, fifteen states interact in a single economic market and are committed to the goal of a single currency by the turn of the century. As the dominant power in its hemisphere, the United States organized the North American Free Trade Agreement (NAFTA) with Canada and Mexico, while Japanese transnational corporations have organized and linked the markets of East Asia through investments and the establishment of corporate subsidiaries. In the regions on the periphery of the world economy, however, lower economic capacities, limited access to finance, and reduced trade opportunities have placed severe constraints on economic adjustment strategies.[8] However, even in most of these regions, the trend toward greater preoccupation with economic power and economic issues is clear.

The United States, despite its dominant position in the postwar era, has also been forced to reassess its role in the world and to confront the task of constructing a post–Cold War foreign policy. At both the public and private levels, the rise of the global market and the end of the Cold War have been historic turning points and have served as catalysts for an amorphous national debate that has included both foreign and defense policy issues, with a special emphasis on foreign economic policy. Typical of the transformation of American politics in domestic areas, the debate on America's role in the world has been characterized by the advancement of a large number of diverse theories, issues, and positions, as think tanks and single-issue lobbies of every description have become involved in the process.[9] As one source has noted, the United States is now urged by the world community to pursue a plethora of foreign policy objectives, including the advancement of democracy, human rights, civil liberties, equality before the law, protection of minorities, self-determination, an orderly world, international law, environmental protection, curtailment of arms trade, the prevention of nuclear proliferation, and many other causes without careful regard for the inherent conflicts and trade-offs involved in these rival concerns.[10]

The current debate on "American economic decline" is also in large part a reaction to the apparently reduced significance of America's military power and to the increased economic competition from other advanced industrial states. The theme of "the end of American economic hegemony" is a widely discussed issue, yet its meaning is fiercely debated. A wide variety of conflicting interpretations have been offered to explain America's current place in the world economy, including the following: Given its combined military and economic power, America remains the likely world leader of the twenty-first century; the rise of Japan and Western Europe as economic powers reflects the success of America's postwar policies and represents a return to economic normalcy; America's economic decline relative to Japan and Western Europe has laid the groundwork for a possible future challenge to American supremacy in military and security areas; and America's decline is absolute and irreversible and will likely parallel the decline of Great Britain at the beginning of the twentieth century. Many conflicting prescriptions have also been offered as measures to improve America's competitive position, including less government involvement in the operation of the domestic market and in foreign trade, more government intervention in the domestic market in the form of an Asian-style industrial policy, a new trade policy, the expansion of NAFTA, and a reorientation of America's economic activity toward Asia.

While at one level the post–Cold War dialogue sought to identify a new grand strategy for the United States to replace the principles of global containment and multilateral economic openness, it also included a reassessment of American policies toward the individual regions of the world.[11] Given the scope and suddenness of change in areas such as Central and Eastern Europe and Eurasia, and the unevenness with which global trends have impacted the various regions, such considerations were inevitable. The regional reassessment was also driven by concern for the national budget deficit and the desire to allocate America's foreign policy resources more effectively through careful identification of American interests in each region. In the initial months after the events of 1989–1991, optimistic assumptions were advanced regarding the prospects for political and economic reforms in the former Soviet bloc countries, the opportunity for an American military withdrawal from Europe, the avoidance of armed aggression in the new world order, and the end of the need for foreign intervention in sub-Saharan Africa. These predictions were soon confounded by ethnocultural conflict within the former Soviet Union, the disintegration of the former Yugoslavia into barbarous civil war, the Iraqi invasion of Kuwait, and the need for humanitarian intervention in Somalia. Such events made clear that any reassessment of America's regional interests would require careful analysis of the history, content, and likely future course of relations with each region, as well as a clear understanding of the pattern of recent political and economic changes within each region. As a recent work has argued, such a study of regional change reveals a picture of great variation rather than a common model of a globalized, peaceful society.[12]

In the following volume, U.S. relations with seven regions are analyzed. The regions covered are Western Europe; East Europe; East Asia; South Asia; Latin America; the Middle East; and Africa. In each of these surveys, special attention is given to the opportunities and constraints confronting American foreign policy in each region as we approach the twenty-first century. In addition, to provide a context for the regional studies, two additional chapters are included—one surveying the recent changes in the international system and the other providing a review of U.S. involvement in the Cold War from a regional perspective. The individual chapters are summarized below.

In Chapter 1, David Walsh discusses the evolution of the international system in the last three decades. Long-term changes resulting from the spread of new technologies, the most important change being the rise of the global market, and short-term changes associated with the end of the Cold War have combined to end the postwar era of international politics. The collapse of the Soviet Union and the relative decline of the United States vis-a-vis its main economic rivals have destroyed the bipolar configuration of power on which the postwar era was based. The international system has now entered a transitional phase that will probably last twenty to thirty years, and perhaps significantly longer, before the emergence of a new and clear configuration of power and the definition of a new world order. The current transitional environment is characterized by extreme complexity, including pronounced regional differences, as major global trends have penetrated various regions unevenly. While the triangular economic competition among the United States, Japan, and the states of the European Union is currently the most important international contest, other important contemporary issues exist. Other challenges include the need to construct post–Cold War security arrangements, the need to develop new rules and institutions in the area of international economic relations, and the need for increased cooperation to protect the biosphere.

In Chapter 2, James Cobbledick examines American policy in the Cold War from a regional perspective. This chapter provides a broad analysis of how and why the United States incrementally formulated a worldwide containment policy toward international communism at the end of World War II, a policy which would last for forty-five years. At the center of the American engagement was the perceived Soviet threat to the interests and values of the United States and other non-Communist societies. After an initial brief exposition of the broad reasons for the sources of Soviet–American tension, the chapter analyzes the beginning of the Cold War and its concentration in Europe. With the outbreak of the Korean War, superpower competition expanded to encompass the entire globe. This expanded competition is dealt with on a regional basis. The regions include East Asia, the Subcontinent of South Asia, the Middle East, sub-Saharan Africa, and Latin America. The purpose of this chapter is to provide an integrated, historical background to all the following regional studies that deal with United States policy in the post-Cold War era.

Throughout the twentieth century America's relationship with Western Europe has been of critical importance to both parties. In Chapter 3, H. G. Peter Wallach reviews this relationship in the postwar era and critically analyzes contemporary trends in U.S. relations with individual states and with the European Union. In the first two decades after World War II, European states accepted the reality of American hegemony, and two American-dominated institutions—the North Atlantic Treaty Organization and the General Agreement on Tariffs and Trade—served as linchpins for Atlantic cooperation. Despite growing European independence in the 1960s resulting from the success of the European Economic Community and the subsequent onset of detente, the Western Alliance continued as a strong and effective force until the end of the Cold War. With the disappearance of the Soviet bloc, both parties recognized the need to restructure the relationship. In the economic issue-area competition between the United States and the European Union is intense, but the recent conclusion of the Uruguay Round of GATT demonstrated that tough bargaining can also produce agreement. Military cooperation in the Gulf War, and, belatedly, in Bosnia, has also documented the continued effectiveness of the Atlantic Alliance. In sum, Wallach argues that Western Europe and the United States have constructed a model of cooperation, international integration, and economic-oriented competition.

In Chapter 4, Paul Best reviews American policy toward "East Europe." The collapse of the Soviet Union and Yugoslavia in the early 1990s created an unprecedented situation in the world. From nine former "East European" political entities, twenty-seven have emerged. Where there was formerly one political bloc, the Soviet bloc (plus Yugoslavia and Albania), we can now discern seven geographic and political areas of concern to U.S. planners. These seven areas are the Russian Federation (Eurasia), East Europe outside Russia (Ukraine, Belarus, Moldova), the Baltic States (Estonia, Latvia, Lithuania), the Caucasuses (Georgia, Armenia, Azerbaijan), Central Asia (Kazakhstan, Kyrgyzstan, Uzbekistan, Turkmenistan, Tajikistan), East Central Europe (Poland, Czech and Slovak Republics, Hungary), and Southeast Europe (Romania, Bulgaria, Macedonia, Albania, Serbia, Bosnia, Croatia, and Slovenia). Old monolithic "East Europe" is gone, and each of the emergent areas and countries represents new and unique challenges and opportunities for the United States in the twenty-first century. The complex problems of the fractured "East Europe" will be of concern in U.S. diplomatic efforts well into the next century.

In Chapter 5, Ta-Ling Lee considers American policy toward the two East Asian giants—China and Japan. In the twenty-first century, the United States will have exciting new opportunities in the vibrant region of East Asia but will also face new challenges from these two giants. With both countries, the United States has gone through a bittersweet history of enmity and friendship, love and hate. China, a traditional friend and an ally in World War II, became a bitter enemy during the Cold War era, and relations were not normalized until the late 1970s. Japan, a defeated enemy, benefited enormously from the subsequent benevolent U.S. occupation to become a major democratic power and bulwark against communism in the region. In the post–Cold War era, major issues in Sino-American relations include regional security, trade, human rights, and Taiwan, while trade, mutual defense, and nuclear nonproliferation stand out as the most pressing issues between Tokyo and Washington. These issues do not lend themselves to quick solutions; rather, they must be handled with patience and vision, balancing perceived short-term national interests with enduring moral principles. Above all, moderation and cooperation, rather than confrontation and hostility, should guide policy formulation.

In Chapter 6, Kul B. Rai examines American policy toward India and Pakistan, the South Asian rivals. During the Cold War period, American policy toward South Asia, particularly India, was often ambivalent and marked by ups and downs. Although the United States became deeply involved in this region on several occasions, it never gained much influence. The end of the Cold War and the occurrence of another significant event—the acquisition of nuclear-weapons capabilities by India and Pakistan—present new challenges and opportunities for the American policy makers. The liberalization of economies in South Asia and its vast market of over a billion consumers have become enticing to American corporations for investment and trade. An even more compelling concern for the United States in the late twentieth century, which will last well into the next century, is the possibility of a nuclear war between India and Pakistan. This concern has been aggravated by the growing power of religious fundamentalists in both countries and the seemingly unresolvable conflict in Kashmir.

In Chapter 7, James Dull analyzes the transition and potential transformation in Latin America resulting from changes in the international system. After nearly two centuries of the Monroe Doctrine, American hegemony, and the absence of a serious foreign threat to the Western hemisphere, U.S. foreign policy in the Americas is changing. In the face of vast changes in the global and hemispheric systems, Latin America is more important than ever to the national interests of the United States. One result is the search for a partnership between Latin America and the United States reflected in contemporary U.S. foreign policy. Whether this partnership will continue into the next century is not certain, but the underlying interdependence between the Americas is beyond dispute.

In Chapter 8, Ghassan El-Eid reviews U. S. policy toward the Middle East since World War II and considers the future of this policy into the next century. He constructs a conceptual framework to help identify the major determinants of America's policy toward the region by analyzing domestic politics, the decision-making process, economic variables, geopolitical considerations, and personality traits of American presidents. Furthermore, he discusses five distinct phases in America's Middle East policy, encompassing the years 1945–1948, 1948–1967, 1967–1974, 1974–1990, and 1990–present. The key questions that El-Eid seeks to answer pertain to the challenges and opportunities facing Washington in the Middle East and the policy options available as we approach the twenty-first century. Regional conflicts, religious extremism, intense nationalism, dwindling resources, and the proliferation of weapons of mass destruction are other challenges facing the United States in this region. In the ninth and last chapter, Walton Brown considers American policy toward Africa. U.S. policy toward Africa during the twentieth century has been determined by its relationship with its European allies and its Cold War geostrategic policy of containment of the Soviet Union. The end of the Cold War created the opportunity and necessity for the United States to redefine its interests and reformulate its policy goals in Africa. Brown discusses how the end of the Cold War and the end of the Soviet Union have altered the definition of U.S. interests in the international system, particularly in Africa. She then analyzes strategies and instruments of American policy toward Africa. She also examines challenges, prospects, and opportunities that will affect U.S. post–Cold War African policy. The chapter concludes with a discussion of policy options and recommendations for the twenty-first century.

NOTES

1. E. H. Carr, cited in J. C. H. Blom and W. ten Have, "Making the Netherlands? Ideas about Renewal in Dutch Politics and Society during the Second World War," in *Making the New Europe: European Unity and the Second World War*, M. L. Smith and P. M. R. Stirk, eds. (New York: Pinter Publishers, 1990), p. 98.
2. This thesis is discussed by James Rosenau, *Turbulence in World Politics: A Theory of Change and Continuity* (Princeton, NJ: Princeton University Press, 1990), pp. 68–87.
3. Ibid., pp. 10–20.
4. See Peter Dicken, *Global Shift: The Internationalization of Economic Activity*, 2nd ed. (New York: Guilford Press, 1992).
5. Rosenau, *Turbulence in World Politics*, pp. 7–26.
6. Ibid., pp. 373–387.
7. The term "the highest stakes" is employed by Sandholtz, et al., in *The Highest Stakes: The Economic Foundations of the Next Security System*, Wayne Sandholtz, et al., eds. (New York: Oxford University Press, 1992).
8. For a discussion of this theme, see Barbara Stallings, ed., *Global Change, Regional Response: The New International Context of Development* (New York: Cambridge University Press, 1995).
9. For this theory of American politics, see David Ricci, *The Transformation of American Politics: The New Washington and the Rise of Think Tanks* (New Haven: Yale University Press, 1993), pp. 103–123, 182–207.
10. James Schlesinger, "Quest for a Post–Cold War Foreign Policy," *Foreign Affairs* 72, no. 1 (1973): 19.
11. Kenneth A. Oye, "Beyond Postwar Order and New World Order: American Foreign Policy in Transition," in *Eagle in a New World: American Grand Strategy in the Post–Cold War Era*, Kenneth A. Oye, Robert J. Lieber, and Donald Rothchild, eds. (New York: HarperCollins, 1992), p. 5.
12. Hans-Henrik Holm and Georg Sorensen, "Introduction: What Has Changed?" in *Whose World Order? Uneven Globalization and the End of the Cold War*, Hans Henrik Holm and Georg Sorensen, eds. (Boulder, CO: Westview Press, 1995), pp. 11–15.

CHAPTER 1

THE INTERNATIONAL SYSTEM IN TRANSITION

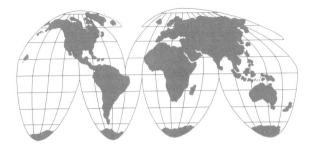

THE NEW ENVIRONMENT OF FOREIGN POLICY

DAVID F. WALSH

CONTINUITY AND CHANGE IN THE INTERNATIONAL SYSTEM

The international system is always subject to two contradictory sets of pressures—one favoring continuity, the other leading to change. Continuity, the preservation of existing systemic characteristics, is usually associated with the following conditions: a clear distribution or hierarchy of power among international actors; patterned and predictable relations between major states and other types of actors; similar foreign policy goals and diplomatic styles among major states; common principles, rules, and norms of international behavior; and a stable number of international actors. Much of the history of international relations in the modern era is concerned with attempts by the most powerful states to develop international institutions, rules, and norms, known collectively as regimes, to facilitate the achievement of their foreign policy objectives. In a recent example, after World War II the United States supported the development of such institutions as the International Monetary Fund (IMF), the International Bank for Reconstruction and Development (IBRD—the World Bank), and the General Agreement on Tariffs and Trade (GATT) as part of its program to construct a liberal international economic regime. This regime, known as the Bretton Woods system, reduced the barriers to trade and other international transactions and allowed the United States to exploit its economic and technological superiority in exchanges with other countries.

Since 1648, a succession of major states have sought to dominate international politics through the construction of regimes and the imposition of particular conceptions of "world order." Since 1740, nine distinct "system-periods," "international systems," or "world orders" have existed, each with a unique configuration of power and a major state or group of states structuring the new regime.[1] These systems experienced varying degrees of success and stability, but in each successive century their duration has grown shorter.[2] Regardless of the degree of stability, such systems are always temporary, and at any point in time states or other international actors exist that embrace different conceptions of world order and seek to establish alternative international regimes. Even in their most stable periods, such systems never consist of static or fixed hierarchies and relationships, but rather consist of elements in a state of temporary "dynamic equilibrium."[3] The most important factor in their viability and maintenance is the presence of a dominant or hegemonic actor with both the power and the will to maintain the existing conception of world order against all challenges.

Pressures for change in the international system can develop at either the international or the domestic level. At the international level a wide range of political, economic, and ecological factors can alter the balance of power and undermine existing regimes. The emergence of new actors, the spread of revolutionary ideologies, changes in the structure of alliances, mass migrations, the development of new technologies, or the scarcity of vital national resources are but some of the factors with the potential to undermine an existing system or world order. At the domestic level, changing conditions in the state structure, government, or society can produce the same result. For example, nationalist conflicts in Austria-Hungary before 1914 weakened the structural integrity of that state and contributed to the onset of World War I; the Nazi assumption of power within the German government in 1933 doomed the world order established by the Treaty of Versailles, which ended WWI; and changing attitudes toward foreign policy, work, and personal achievement within British society contributed to the erosion of Britain's international position at the beginning of the twentieth century.

Since developments at international and domestic levels have a mutually determinative effect, the international system is always experiencing incremental, or small-scale, change.[4] Even in a short time span, the relative power of states may be affected by the outcomes of international crises, yearly trade figures, domestic political events, and the performance of domestic economies. In addition, nonstate actors, such as international movements, subnational political groups, and transnational corporations, can also act as catalysts for incremental change. The decade of the 1970s demonstrated that an array of terrorist groups, international cartels, and international movements could force limited changes in some forms of international behavior and temporarily alter rules and procedures of regimes governing such areas as trade and immigration.

At critical periods in history, however, major changes have occurred in the international system that have transformed basic political relationships, terminated established patterns of political behavior, and permanently altered the characteristics of the international system. Such changes qualify as "historic," "breakpoint," and "qualitative in nature" because they produce a fundamental and permanent restructuring of the international system.[5] It is at such times that one "world order" or "international system" ends and the transition toward a new system begins. International actors find themselves in a new environment in which previously accepted rules, identities, and policies become increasingly irrelevant. Of course, such changes never occur at a single moment in time, but in most cases become increasingly apparent over a period of years, or more commonly, decades. As one source has argued, such periods express the effects of accumulated social change over time, and there are always significant variations in the speed and intensity with which the changes impact the various regions of the world.[6] Transition periods are always accompanied by widespread speculation from governmental, political, and scholarly sources about the characteristics and meaning of the next world order, including prescriptions for future regimes to address what are perceived to be the most serious global problems.

POLITICAL CHANGES IN THE 1980S AND 1990S

At the end of the twentieth century, the international system has once again experienced historic, breakpoint change and the breakdown of the pre-existing world order. In the 1970s, 1980s, and 1990s a series of complex, multidimensional changes have transformed the existing political relationships and established patterns that had prevailed since the end of World War II, a period of nearly forty-five years. The result has been the end of the so-called "postwar system" and the onset of a transitional period that most observers believe will last at least twenty to thirty years until the new world order becomes clear. To an unusual, perhaps unprecedented, degree, the changes that transformed the postwar system were unexpected, sudden, decisive, and broad in scope. In the twenty-five months between November 1989 to December 1991, the international security issue-area was changed forever by the end of the Cold War, German reunification, and the demise of the Soviet Union. Not even the governmental participants in these events were prepared for such outcomes.

Likewise, developments associated with the growth of the global market have also decisively altered the temporal, spatial, and locational factors in the international economic arena. Although these changes began to manifest in the 1960s, their full impact on the hierarchy of economic power was not recognized until the late 1970s. As has been recently argued, the new flexibility in the global economic hierarchy is the result not only of the maturation of individual states (e.g., Japan and the states of the European Union), but also of the implementation of new technologies in production, travel, and communications and the impact of the operation of transnational corporations on individual states.[7]

Combined with innovations in communications and telecommunications and the trends toward regionalization and decentralization they have spawned, the changing conditions of the 1980s and 1990s produced a fundamental shift in the balance of world power. This power shift will inevitably lead to the restructuring of regimes in the most important areas of international relations—national security, trade, immigration, foreign aid, and environmental protection. The process of regime restructuring has already begun.

TECHNOLOGY: THE CATALYST FOR CHANGE

The changes in the international system at the end of the twentieth century were primarily the result of the global revolution in technology, which has increasingly affected economic, social, and cultural development. Especially important were innovations in electronics, microelectronics, biotechnology, and industrial materials and production techniques. These, in turn, spawned new skills and attitudes and affected global organizational patterns. Although many of the basic technologies that had the most profound impact had been in existence for some time, further refinements from the 1960s on and their mass availability in the 1980s and 1990s served to invalidate the postwar political and economic patterns. In the most obvious example, the development of new industrial materials, new production technologies, and the revolution in microelectronics, telecommunications and computer science made possible the globalization of the world economy, and with it the challenge to American economic hegemony from Japan, the European Union, and several Newly Industrializing Countries (NICs). Even the collapse of the Soviet Union must ultimately be attributed to the fact that, from the 1980s on, Soviet society was unable to absorb relevant innovations in microelectronics, lasers, and the use of new industrial materials.[8]

It seems clear that in historical perspective the last half of the twentieth century will prove to be one of the most significant periods of technological change in human history. The revolution in technology has already brought about the end of the postwar era and driven the international system toward greatly increased interdependence, a new division of labor, a new global economy, a new global society, and a new conception of security, which places emphasis on economic power and competitiveness. Although their exact parameters are as yet unclear, these technological transformations will continue and will determine the new environment of foreign policy making in the twenty-first century. Even states as powerful as the United States, the hegemon of the postwar era of international politics, will be compelled to formulate and implement foreign policy in a changing and uncertain context.

THE END OF THE POSTWAR ERA

A proper understanding of the current transformation of the international system requires a review of the specific changed relationships that caused the end of the postwar era. For purposes of analysis the complex, multidimensional changes will be discussed under four headings: (1) the end of the Cold War, (2) the decline of American hegemony, (3) the globalization of economic activity, and (4) the onset of global turbulence.

THE END OF THE COLD WAR

The Cold War was the most important factor in the development of the postwar system. From the end of World War II until 1990, the superpower competition between the United States and the Soviet Union created a bipolar division of the world that became the dominant organizational pattern in world politics. Efforts by Third World countries and, later, by Islamic states to establish a third, independent bloc proved of little significance. Each superpower fostered the development of a bloc or alliance of states and created military, political, and economic institutions through which it dominated bloc policies. Since the Cold War conflict centered on the control of Europe, particularly of Germany and Poland, that continent was divided along geographic and political lines—Soviet satellite states of Central and Eastern Europe on one side and the Western European allies of the United States on the other. While the core states of both alliances were primarily European, Japan became an integral member of the Western alliance, and the People's Republic of China, a Communist state but a political rival of the U.S.S.R., assumed a position of strategic importance in Soviet foreign policy calculations. Both blocs also had minor allies in Asia, Africa, and Latin America, the geographic periphery of the Cold War conflict.

The Cold War fostered a clear link between national power and purpose.[9] This link manifested in the form of a crude geopolitics—projecting one's own global power and influence to achieve world leadership while containing one's adversary—and a narrow, excessively militarized conception of national security.[10] On both sides of the Cold War divide, superpowers and their core state allies sought to win this ideological, diplomatic, military, and economic competition and to impose their model of politics and society on the rest of the world. Beginning in the 1960s, the bipolar constraints loosened somewhat as the member states of both blocs achieved some independence in a few policy areas. However, the Cold War patterns demonstrated remarkable stability and continuity until the mid-1980s. These patterns shaped international politics in several ways: (1) the Cold War legitimated American leadership of the Western alliance; (2) the need for solidarity against the Soviet threat contained economic disputes among the western allies;[11] (3) the Cold War legitimated Communist party rule in the states of the Soviet bloc, including the U.S.S.R.; (4) within the Soviet bloc, the coercive power in the party-dominated state was used to forcibly integrate all elements of society, including ethnic and nationality groups; (5) regional conflicts were exploited by both superpowers and regional issues were subordinated to superpower foreign policy goals; and (6) with certain notable exceptions, nuclear deterrence contained the number and intensity of conventional wars.[12]

By the 1980s the Soviet Union found itself in a technological time warp. The Soviet economy had failed to make the transition from heavy industry to high levels of mass consumption and, more importantly, had been largely excluded from the technological revolution in microelectronics, industrial materials, lasers, and other areas that was underway in the more advanced western states.[13] In the context of nuclear deterrence and Mutual Assured Destruction (MAD), this technological backwardness increased the danger of strategic and military vulnerability. In addition, it was clear that the Cold War competition was exhausting Soviet resources and the country's standard of living was unacceptably low. By the mid-1980s, the failure of the planned economy and the dismal social realities confronting the Soviet leadership convinced it to seek an end to the Cold War and to undertake a major program of domestic reform. This program, symbolized by the concepts of *glasnost* (political openness) and *perestroika* (restructuring of the economy), was originally intended to reform the communist system. The new environment of reform unleashed a variety of dynamic societal forces, however, including renewed nationalism among the various ethnic groups constituting the Soviet state. Following a failed coup by Communist hardliners, reform elements outlawed the Communist party. On December 8, 1991, the Soviet Union was officially ended and the Commonwealth of Independent States, a confederation of the newly independent countries, was proclaimed. By the end of the month, eleven successor states had joined the confederation.

The unexpected events of 1988 through 1991 revolutionized world politics. The distribution of world power was decisively altered by the breakup of the Soviet Union, as that state lost superpower status. The end of the Cold War not only signalled the conclusion of the forty-five-year conflict between the United States and the U.S.S.R., but also the end of the seventy-year crisis in the European state system that had begun before World War I.[14] The Soviet withdrawal from Central Europe made possible the reunification of Germany and the general reordering of Europe in a political and spatial sense. The successor states of the former U.S.S.R. and the former Soviet satellites of Central and Eastern Europe began the transformation to democracy and capitalism, some even seeking membership in western political and economic institutions. The end of the Cold War also had profound effects that were not immediately apparent in the rush of events of 1989 to 1991. The agenda of world politics was altered as the value of military power declined and the importance of economic power increased, a process that one source has called the global transition from geopolitics to geoeconomics.[15] New agenda issues, such as assisting the former Communist states in the consolidation of democracy and the transition to capitalism, also developed. Finally, the end of the Cold War deprived both the United States and Russia, the most powerful Soviet successor state, of the rationale for leadership of their allies. In this sense, the Cold War had fostered integration, policy coordination, and superpower hegemony within each bloc. The collapse of the Cold War system, however, contributed to the general global trends of devolution, decentralization, disintegration, and the rise of previously suppressed nationalism.[16] The disintegration of the former Yugoslavia and the chaos in several areas of the former Soviet Union stand as testimony to these trends.

THE DECLINE OF AMERICAN HEGEMONY

The postwar era has often been referred to as America's "half century" because of the dominant role played by the United States in world politics. In both relative and absolute terms, few nations, if any, have experienced the disproportionate power possessed by the United States at the end of World War II. American hegemony was based on a monopoly of atomic weapons (until 1949), possession of approximately one half of the world's gold and convertible currencies, and an economy that accounted for nearly one half of the world's GNP in 1945.[17] As a victor in World War II, champion of anticolonialism and leader of democratic-capitalist states, the United States also enjoyed unrivaled moral authority in the regions outside of the Soviet sphere. American power and influence were further inflated by the fact that the states of Western Europe and Japan, its natural rivals for markets and political influence, had been temporarily reduced in status by the catastrophic effects of World War II. This was true even of the victorious states—Britain and France. In the artificial and largely unprecedented conditions of the immediate postwar period, the western world possessed one superpower but no states of "great power" rank.

In the period from 1945 to the mid-1970s, the United States used its power and influence to fashion a strategy for containment of the Soviet Union that ultimately helped to produce the end of the Cold War, to develop the Bretton Woods system of economic liberalization, and to promote the economic and political recovery of the states of Western Europe and Japan. No other nation could claim an equal role in shaping world politics. Two factors were crucial in the establishment of American hegemony: (1) a clear consensus existed among governing elites and the general public supporting the goal of global leadership, and critics of the policy were successfully marginalized; and (2) unlike the Soviet Union, which resorted to force, the United States maintained its alliance system and the Bretton Woods regime by offering military assistance, foreign aid, and trade concessions which included access to American markets. In short, the United States fostered integration in the western world by providing benefits in excess of the adjustment costs incurred by states participating in the American-sponsored system.[18]

The decade of the 1970s revealed both the limits of American power and the erosion of American dominance across several areas of international politics. In the military-strategic issue-area, the attainment of nuclear parity by the Soviet Union deprived the United States of the use of nuclear brinksmanship, and the failure to achieve its objectives in Vietnam, despite the fact that three administrations had defined the conflict as a test of America's credibility, contributed further to the erosion of its power and influence.[19] Equally important, domestic disillusionment with the costs of the Vietnam conflict and the fallout from the political defeat there contributed to the end of the consensus on America's international role. Over the next two decades, diverse, pluralistic interests asserted themselves in the national debate over foreign policy, testifying to the growing tension between domestic and foreign policy priorities. This tension intensified with the end of the Cold War. In the economic issue-area, by the 1970s the American economy came under pressure as Japan, Germany, and later several Newly Industrialized Countries (NICs) of East Asia successfully employed advanced technologies and new production techniques in the growing competition for world market shares. Although the pattern of regime change varied from one area to another (for example, trade, money, and oil), beginning in the late 1960s the United States began to seek protection from the impact of economic interdependence.[20] America's relative economic decline became apparent in its growing deficits in three areas: trade, the current accounts balance and the federal budget, and in the declining rates of domestic savings and investment.

In the 1980s the Reagan administration sought to bolster American hegemony through a policy of remilitarization, which committed $1.5 trillion to military spending (8 percent of the GNP).[21] Also, the states of Western Europe and Japan continued to sustain their high rates of growth through the profits from exports to the United States which were paid for by deficit spending and borrowing abroad.[22] Regardless of their other results, these policies aggravated the trade and budget deficits, and by 1985 the United States was forced to seek a devaluation of the dollar and to ask for the cooperation of its allies in programs to stimulate their economies in order to help redress America's trade deficit. With these developments, the era of economic hegemony gave way to one in which the United States, still powerful and capable of leadership, required the assistance of its major allies in bearing the economic and political costs of maintaining existing regimes. This new relationship was clearly illustrated in the Gulf War of 1991, in which the United States organized and led the military coalition that liberated Kuwait, but in which Japan, Germany, Saudi Arabia, and Kuwait were persuaded to pay most of the financial costs of the military operation.

The end of the Cold War produced intense speculation about America's future role in the world, and a wide range of interpretations were presented. Some sources argued that the unexpected demise of the Soviet Union had enhanced the power of the only remaining superpower and that the interna-

tional system would evolve toward a unipolar structure. Another major interpretation argued that the United States had suffered a decline in its relative
power, and that this decline was due mainly to the natural recovery of states
like Germany and Japan, which were now prepared to resume their historic
international roles. This outlook assumed a slow transformation toward a multipolar world but stressed that, at present, the United States was the only country that could claim superpower status in both the military-strategic and international economic issue-areas. A third interpretation maintained that the
United States, like Great Britain before it, had become a victim of "imperial
overreach" and would ultimately be replaced by another hegemon that would
determine the characteristics of the next world order.[23] Finally, a wide array of
theories were developed that argued that America's future role, yet undeter-
mined, would depend on the degree of success of efforts at domestic reform
in such areas as economic performance, education, savings and investment,
and control of the public debt. Although America might be past its peak of relative power, a variety of future power trajectories were still available to it.[24]

As the end of the twentieth century approached, the United States
remained the most important global actor. America's foreign policy behavior
and domestic political outcomes will continue to have profound effects on
the global political order in the foreseeable future. The future path of
American power will be a major determinant of the speed and nature of
international structural change.

THE RISE OF THE GLOBAL ECONOMY

In no area was the impact of technology greater than in the transformation
of the international economy. In the last half of the twentieth century, but
especially since the 1970s, a variety of scientific and technological innovations
made possible the increasing globalization of economic activity. These innovations included new production technologies, new industrial materials, flex-
ible production methods, renewable energy, lasers, and, most important,
developments in microelectronics, computing power, and telecommunications that transformed the speed, quantity, and quality of information flows
and made possible near-instantaneous linkages.[25] These new technologies
facilitated not only the international spread of economic activity, an old phenomenon, but the actual integration of economic functions across diverse
geographic areas producing fundamentally different patterns of production
and consumption. Transnational Corporations (TNCs), particularly those
from the United States, Japan, and Western Europe, were the most important
agents in arranging the prerequisites of transnational economic integration,
including channeling international capital, creating transnational production systems, identifying new foreign markets, and arranging international
distribution. The movement of capital was itself facilitated by the new information and communication technologies that made possible instant international transactions and innovations such as computerized program trading.

In addition, the institutions of the Bretton Woods regime created an environment that favored liberalization and made the imposition of currency controls in the advanced industrial states impossible.

By the 1980s the new international economy, commonly referred to as "the global marketplace," displayed a number of new characteristics:

1. The hypermobility of financial capital and production facilities to maximize profits without regard to national borders
2. The end of the national economy as the sole building block of the world economy and the emergence of the global market as its rival[26]
3. Growing economic interdependence in production and capital markets
4. The rapid transmission of economic effects across national borders, including internationally transmitted "shocks"
5. Increased competition for world markets in both tradable goods and services
6. The emergence of a new division of labor based on the capacity to create and process knowledge, rather than the location of natural resources for cheap labor[27]
7. A dramatic increase in the number of international business mergers and acquisitions and in the volume of foreign direct investments (FDI) and speculative movements of capital (for example, currency speculation and rentier income)[28]
8. Uneven integration into the global economy across states and regions
9. Growing global inequality between the core areas of the information economy and the peripheral areas, particularly the so-called "Fourth World," the poorest of the less-developed countries (LDCs)

Since the impact of the new technologies steadily increased, these trends intensified with each successive year.

The globalization of the world economy had profound effects on states, international regimes, and regional organizations. For the political leaders of states, the developments at the end of the twentieth century created new problems and vulnerabilities. A wide range of domestic economic conditions within the home states of transnational corporations remained important factors in their ability to compete successfully in the global marketplace. These included the state of the infrastructure, the quality of the education system, fiscal policies affecting government spending and taxation, monetary policy and interest rates influencing exchange rates, the success of industrial policy, the ability of the state to establish its currency as an international exchange medium, and the relative political strength of the state in multilateral economic organizations such as the World Trade Organization, which establish the rules of world trade. In addition, occasional resorts to force, most notably the United States-led liberation of Kuwait and its oil resources, have been of great significance to TNCs in specific sectors. However, at the end of the Cold War, precisely the time at which national power came to be measured more in economic terms than in military ones, states found themselves increasingly vulnerable to economic decisions made by foreign and private sources. For example, decisions by private investors to shift funds to foreign markets, by corporations to reduce local content in their products, or by TNCs to entirely relocate production facilities to low-wage areas all have the potential to aggravate domestic unemployment. Similarly, the adoption of protectionist policies by rival states or their use of high interest rates and tight money policies to lure away investors can also have a major negative effect on a state's economy.

In the period after 1973, the collective effects of globalization contributed to an economic environment of uncertainty, instability, and rivalry.[29] The end of fixed exchange rates for currency and the onset of fluctuating rates after 1972, the OPEC oil price increases of 1973 to 1979 which dramatically increased industrial production costs, and the increased competition for markets (resulting, in large part, from the new technologies that negated previous market advantages) all contributed to the new environment of economic insecurity. From 1973 until 1980, each of the major industrial states, Japan and Germany excepted, experienced lower rates of growth, increased unemployment, and increased business failures. Despite the diminished capacity of states to control the economic environment, insecure electorates turned to their governments for economic protection. The result, in many cases, was government charges of "unfairness" and "social dumping" against competitor states and the imposition of neomercantilist policies that employed a variety of nontariff barriers to exclude foreign goods from the domestic marketplace.[30] In addition, the development of regional trade groups, including the expansion of the European Union and the creation of the North American Free Trade Agreement (NAFTA), was part of a defensive reaction to the rising levels of competition. From the 1970s on, these actions reversed the general trend of trade liberalization that had prevailed since the creation of the Bretton Woods system.

At the end of the twentieth century, it is premature to proclaim either the end of the nation-state or the end of the domestic economy of the nation-state as a result of economic globalization. However, it appears clear that the nature of competition between states has changed from conflict over land and natural resources to one over market shares in the world economy.[31] Given the existence of 35,000 large TNCs with a total stock of $1,700 billion in foreign investment, it is equally clear that the state must now share authority over the economy and society with these entities.[32] For the twenty-first century the ongoing scientific and technological revolution promises greater consumer choice and still higher profits, but it also foretells the continuing transformation of the international economic issue-area.

THE ONSET OF GLOBAL TURBULENCE

In addition to the political and economic changes associated with the end of the Cold War and the globalization of the world economy, the passing of the postwar system was also marked by an even more fundamental transforma-

Rise of non state Actors

tion. Beginning in the decade of the 1960s, the international system experienced growing complexity, density, and dynamism—three conditions associated in the international relations literature with the model of political turbulence.[33] *Complexity*, an inordinate number of international actors with a high degree of interdependence between them,[34] was largely the result of the proliferation of nonstate actors, such as transnational corporations, subnational political groups, and supranational political organizations (groups seeking to replace the authority of the state with regional or global authority). *Dynamism* refers to the extensive variability in the goals, behavior, and political styles of these nonstate actors, while *density* characterizes the crowded political environment, so thick with different types of actors that interactions among them cause disturbances throughout the international system.[35] In this environment of hyperturbulence, the disturbances caused by the unprecedented degree of interdependence among so many different types of international actors created powerful forces for change. By the 1990s, new international structures had formed, particularly at regional levels, states were under simultaneous attacks from subnational and supranational forces, and the relationship between ordinary citizens and traditional sources of authority had been transformed.

The most important factor in the development of turbulence was the revolution in communications and information technology. The diffusion of global radio and television, satellite transmissions, the international spread of electronic media, and the availability of personal computers served as catalysts for change in three ways. First, global radio and television provided citizens in every state with messages from around the world, including those hostile to existing state authorities. In earlier periods, state authorities had enjoyed a monopoly over the means of communication or had been able to electronically interdict such messages. In the era of the "Global Village," however, states lost control of their communications space and were exposed to unprecedented flows of foreign ideas. The daily television transmissions from the West into the former German Democratic Republic doubtless played an important role in the demands for political and economic change that swept that region in 1989. In general, communist party elites and the systems of state socialism were unable to survive the test of comparison with their counterparts in the West.[36]

Second, the unprecedented flow of communications served as a vehicle of transmission for both the "world culture" of high-technology business, on which the global economy is based, and for the transmission of traditional, subnational, and regional cultures, including antimodern and fundamentalist religious creeds.[37] Both types of cultural messages contributed to the growth of new, nonstate actors which competed with states for loyalty and support. Supranational groups, forming around the identity of global high technology and the emerging issues of the global economy, sought to replace the authority of the state with regional or global organizations and regulations. Thus, their efforts in the international system sought to advance the processes of integration, centralization, and unification. At the opposite end of the cultural spectrum, subnational groups with primary loyalties to communities within existing states sought increased autonomy or outright secession. Their presence contributed to the processes of devolution, fragmentation, and disintegration. The disintegration of the former Soviet Union and the former state of Yugoslavia stands as testimony to the strength of the subnational movements.

For the first time since the dawn of the nation-state era in the seventeenth century, a clear division, or bifurcation, of the international system occurred in which a multi-centric system of nonstate actors existed alongside the traditional state-centric structure of territorial states.[38] Of course, the multi-centric system is itself divided between forces advocating supranational centralization and those seeking international fragmentation and subnationalism.

Finally, developments such as near-instantaneous global news reports and the mass availability of personal computers helped to transform the relationship between ordinary citizens and their governments. These resources provided the general electorate with information that was previously the reserve of governments. Dramatic events from the Lenin Shipyard in Gdansk to Tiananmen Square in Beijing testify to the emergence of "powerful people" with an enhanced ability to "connect to world politics," question authority, and challenge habitual models of political behavior.[39] This increase in political skills stimulated the proliferation of political groups of all types and led to increased popular interest in international issues in general and in the state's conduct of foreign affairs. This interest in international affairs also contributed to the emergence of a variety of demands and special interest agendas, including advocacy of increased global environmental regulation, human rights enforcement, and population control.

Driven as it was by irreversible technological and scientific developments, turbulent change intensified as the twentieth century reached its end. Subnationalism or religious fundamentalism continued to pose a serious challenge to the authority of the central state in countries as diverse as Canada, India, Egypt, Algeria, Rwanda, the former Czechoslovakia (which became two states, the Czech Republic and the Slovak Republic, in 1993), and most of the successor states of the former Soviet Union. As a force for change, the transforming relationship between cultural pluralism and the nation-state became one of the central political dramas of the times.[40] In addition, the norms and values of the culture of global capitalism also became an increasingly important influence on nation-state behavior. Policies of liberalization, privatization, and deregulation (which, in some cases, meant re-regulation by international or regional organizations, such as the World Bank or European Union) documented the influence of global business. Even within the state-centric sphere, states came increasingly to accept the logic of economic power over military power, interdependence, and nonviolence. In addition, states confronted increasingly complex foreign policy trade-offs between often incompatible economic and national security goals. These developments gave rise to widespread speculation that the concept of the national security state had been replaced by the new model of the trading state.

The conditions of global turbulence stood in sharp contrast to those of the 1940s and 1950s when international political patterns were stable and coherent, and one national security issue, the Cold War, dominated the international agenda. While it is clear that these postwar conditions will not return, it remains unclear to what extent the new dynamics of political turbulence will transform existing international political patterns.

THE INTERNATIONAL SYSTEM IN TRANSITION

As the most important processes of the late twentieth century, the end of the Cold War, the decline of American hegemony, the growth of the global market, and the onset of global turbulence functioned as "exits" or pathways from the postwar international system. The rapid and largely unexpected acceleration of these events undermined the existing hierarchy of global power, transformed previously dominant relationships, and rendered irrelevant the rules of the bipolar system. But the exit from the postwar system did not signal the entry or movement into a new world order, and by the early 1990s it became clear that the international system had entered a transitional period that would last at least twenty to thirty years, and possibly much longer. From the perspective of the present, several alternative "futures," or international orders, appear possible, but none is certain. The characteristics of the next world order will be determined in small, incremental stages through the results of global economic competition, through the dynamics of choice in foreign policy decision making, and by the conduct of relations between major actors. In short, a proper understanding of the current international system requires not only an assessment of the present distribution of power and the existing relationships between actors, but also an analysis of trends in four areas:

1. The growth of regional cooperation and integration in several geographic areas as it relates to world economic competition
2. The relations between regional economic blocs, especially the European Union, the states of the North American Free Trade Agreement (NAFTA), and Japan and the states of East Asia
3. The domestic political developments in the major states that are likely to affect their economic and foreign policy decisions
4. The movement of new or previously less important issues to the forefront of the international political agenda (for example, the environment and immigration)

In the current transitional period, the most important developments have occurred at the regional level and have involved individual states, groups of states, and regional organizations. Especially important have been regional efforts to develop economic adjustment strategies to address the effects of global economic change. Since important developments have occurred at the regional and subnational levels and are not confined to the level of the state, the transitional international system cannot be understood solely through the lens of "politics among nations."

ECONOMIC COMPETITION: THE NEW STRATEGIC TRIANGLE

In the initial years of the transitional period, the most important responses to global economic change have occurred at the regional level in North America, Western Europe, and East Asia. The dominant economic powers in these regions—the United States, Germany, and Japan, respectively—have molded economic adjustment strategies and promoted regional economic integration. The economic competition among these regions, which has replaced the Cold War as the most important international contest, has two interrelated dimensions. First, at the private or societal level, the contest is to determine which states and regions will provide the best, highest value-added products in such industries as microelectronics, biotechnology, telecommunications, civilian aviation, robotics and machine tools, computers and computer software, and the new "materials-science industries."[41] Dominance in these industries assures the highest profits for business and the world's highest standard of living for the general population. Economic success is dependent on a wide range of factors, including the following: investment in equipment, infrastructure, and research and development; the organizational skills of business; and the efficiency of governmental, educational, and business institutions.[42]

At the second level, that of the state, the trilateral competition centers on two issues, one of immediate concern and the other of long-term significance. Of immediate concern is the issue of how the burdens of sustaining the world economy and providing for military defense should be divided among the emerging regional blocs.[43] In the postwar international system, when the Soviet Union existed as the common enemy, a general consensus prevailed among the states of the West regarding burden sharing. The United States possessed both the will and the ability to contribute disproportionately to the defense of the free world and to the recovery of other capitalist economies. In turn, at least until the 1960s, Japan and the states of Western Europe willingly accepted American leadership and coordinated their economic and military policies with those of the United States. Since the 1980s, confronted with the emergence of two ascending economic rivals, as well as growing trade and budget deficits, the United States has sought a more equitable distribution of the cost of defense and pressured Germany and Japan to stimulate their economies so that their consumers can buy more products from the United States. Of longer-term significance is the issue of which states or blocs will make the rules governing trade, finance, and investment in the twenty-first century.[44] The power to decide the rules of future economic regimes will belong to the states or blocs that possess the world's largest economy and control major international institutions, such as the World Bank, IMF, and the newly created World Trade Organization (WTO). For this reason, trade disputes with the potential of establishing leadership precedents have become increasingly contentious, and rule-making institutions are treated as arenas for the advancement of bloc interests.

By any standard, the economic competition among the three regional superblocs is safer and more beneficial to the world community than the Cold War conflict, which it replaced. The Cold War was a zero-sum conflict that consumed enormous resources and always involved the possibility, however remote, of nuclear catastrophe. By contrast, the current economic competition permits cooperative as well as conflictual strategies and does not involve the likelihood of war between the advanced industrial states. In addition, by promoting efficiency, innovation, and competition, it has contributed to increased productivity and higher standards of living. Despite this, however, economic losses in the forms of unemployed workers and failed businesses are real, and the outcome of superbloc economic competition is likely to be the major determinant of the hierarchy of power in the next world order. Further, the competition is taking place in a complex and rapidly changing environment, which presents great challenges to the participants. The application of recent scientific and technological innovations to industry and business has negated traditional competitive advantages in most market sectors. This has been clearly evident in the demise of traditional industries in the United States and Western Europe. In addition, the continuing "telecommunications-computer-transportation-logistics revolution" has permitted not only the globalization of economic activity but also the development of a world capital market.[45] In sum, these changes have increased access to investment capital, made it easier for industries in poor countries to export to rich countries, and made possible the relocation of production facilities from the richest states to peripheral areas.[46]

An additional factor contributes to the degree of complexity: In no other issue-area is the bifurcation of the international system between private and state-centric activities more evident. In the current environment of state deregulation and market-dominated policies, private entrepreneurs and business leaders will play a decisive role in the degree of competitiveness of each state. In addition to traditional diplomatic competition conducted by states, state-societal arrangements in the form of rival models of capitalism have become crucial variables in international competition. The competing models are derived from different historical legacies, societal structures (more open or closed societies), and cultural attitudes, as well as from fundamentally different relationships between the public and private sectors and between business and labor.[47] Not only do the different models of capitalism create different preferences regarding the rules of trade, finance, and investment, but they also lead to different levels of competitiveness across various economic sectors. It is often these economic realities that underlie trade conflicts between the United States, Japan, and the states of Western Europe.

The outcome of the trilateral superbloc competition is likely to be the most important factor in determining the shape of the next world order. The conflict is currently being waged by superblocs of roughly equal economic power, each with unique assets that make it difficult to predict future developments. The prevailing relationship in the economic issue-area has been aptly described as "nonhegemonic interdependence," an unstable situation in which participants seek to improve their economic conditions by convincing others to downgrade theirs (for example, voluntary quotas or stimulating their economies to consume more imports), or by creating new institutions to contain conflict.[48] Certainly, if one bloc were to emerge the clear victor, the leading state of that bloc would emerge as the hegemon of the twenty-first century, but a state of rough parity may persist and reinforce the tendency toward a multipolar system. Beyond this, the basic nature of the relationship among the three blocs, that is, the structure of world capitalism, will have a major effect on the structure of the international system.[49] One scenario is that a single global system of cooperation and free trade will be imposed on all states as interregional economic flows increase faster than intraregional ones contained within North America, Western Europe, or Asia.[50] An alternative scenario, assuming the absence of a hegemonic state able to make new rules for the world economy, is that capitalist competition will lead to the development of three competing blocs tending toward neomercantilism and protectionism and divided by different models of capitalism and intense, head-to-head competition in the same industries.[51]

Both domestic and international factors will influence which scenario ultimately prevails. At the domestic level, the attitudes of political elites toward protectionist and neomercantilist solutions to national economic problems will be a critical factor. Another important variable will be the willingness of private groups to change longstanding patterns of business behavior that are objectionable to trading partners. As a case in point, Japanese market structure and corporate culture have been contentious issues in the United States–Japanese economic relationship. At the international level, diplomatic skills, particularly the ability to craft compromises on trade and other issues that are acceptable to all parties, will be significant. Equally important will be the capacity of international organizations like the World Trade Organization, which succeeded the GATT in 1995, to manage international conflicts as they arise. Since most of the existing institutions were created to deal with the unique economic conditions of the postwar era, successful conflict resolution will require the creation of some new institutions.

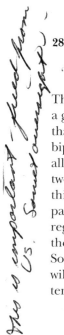

SECURITY IN THE TRANSITIONAL SYSTEM

The end of the Cold War transformed the international security issue-area to a greater degree than it did any other dimension of world politics. For more than forty years the prevailing international security regime had been the bipolar military balance between the two superpowers and their respective allies. Because of their relative power positions, the security policies of the two superpowers had pervasive influence throughout the world, and security thinking was dominated by the East–West concepts of nuclear deterrence, parity in the correlation of forces, and spheres of influence.[52] In addition, regional conflicts were exploited and used by the superpowers to advance their own narrow interests. The end of the Cold War and the demise of the Soviet Union created an entirely new political and military environment that will ultimately require the construction of a new international security system.[53] The new environment included the following five changed conditions:

1. Major actors were resituated in the hierarchy of military and political power.

2. The primary focus of international competition shifted from the military to economic and technological competition.[54]

3. Regional conflict patterns assumed increased importance, and regional powers gained increased opportunity for local initiatives.

4. New security issues emerged, which acted as catalysts for the development of regional security regimes.

5. A new conception of security was developed, emphasizing both common and comprehensive security.[55]

In addition, despite the removal of the Cold War issue from the international agenda, several new challenges to world peace emerged. These included ethnocultural violence in the former Soviet Union and the states of Eastern Europe, renewed regional rivalries in several areas, tensions associated with increased immigration, and the potential for conflicts resulting from trade tensions among the advanced industrial states.

The conflict in the former Yugoslavia and the Gulf War of 1991, which involved Iraq and the coalition of states led by the United States, rapidly dispelled any illusion that the events of the last decade or the spread of global technology would produce a sudden end to international violence. As in the international economic issue-area, the security system that will eventually govern the transitional international system and the next world order will be determined by the relative power of individual states, the nature of economic and political relations among the major states, and the degree of acceptance of competing conceptions of security.

ECONOMIC FOUNDATIONS OF THE SECURITY SYSTEM

Because of the obvious relationship between economic and technological strength and military capabilities, the economic competition among the United States, Japan, and the states of Western Europe has critical security implications and will be a major factor in shaping the next world order's security system. After World War II, the United States gained the power to construct the security system in the West because the nuclear security umbrella made possible by America's nuclear technology was indispensible to the other Western states. Similarly, the size of the American economy and its industrial and technological leadership in most fields justified American dominance of the western trading system. The economic changes that have occurred since the 1970s, however, especially the relative decline of the United States and the rise of Japan and Germany to the status of economic superpowers, have created the foundations for a new and different security system.[56] By the 1990s Japanese industrial investment surpassed that of the United States, America's technological leadership in major sectors was severely threatened, and America evolved from the world's largest creditor to the world's largest debtor. In addition, recent initiatives in Western Europe have enhanced the competitive position of the European Union (EU) in both economic and political relations. The achievement in 1992 of the integrated internal market under the Single European Act, common programs for collaboration in high-technology industries, and the signing of the Treaty on European Union (Maastricht Treaty) were important milestones in the evolution of the EU's international position. The Maastricht Treaty was especially important since it provided a framework for possible future common policies in foreign policy and defense.

Overall, the powerful new industrial and technological capabilities in Western Europe and Japan have created the foundations of a possible new security system in which those actors would play a major, determinative role.[57] Of course, such a development would require sufficient national will or sense of purpose and the assumption of new security responsibilities in the form of specific defense strategies. In the postwar system, Germany and Japan were "contained" within the American-sponsored alliance system that provided both countries with cheap solutions to their defense problems and subjected them to the processes of integration, cooperation, and negotiation.[58] In addition, antimilitaristic and pacifistic attitudes remained strong within the general populations of both countries. Through 1995, neither Germany nor Japan displayed a sustained interest in assuming a role of international responsibility in the security field. Despite the new questions of national identity and purpose in the post–Cold War era, Germany and Japan have remained "civilian powers," primarily oriented toward enhancing the material well-being of their citizens through economic growth.[59]

Despite the restraint displayed by Germany and Japan in the initial stage of the transitional international system, neither state is permanently immune to change, and strong international forces, especially their economic and technological capabilities, exist that could impel them toward a greater political and military role. From the perspective of the mid-1990s, the trends in economic competitiveness could produce several alternative scenarios:[60]

1. A system of mutual interdependence with U.S. leadership could continue producing a pattern of "managed multilateralism" (cooperation between major states) which would serve U.S. interests. This is a preferred scenario for the United States in the post-hegemonic period since vital U.S. interests would be respected and the principles of free trade and stable finance will be strengthened. At present, a system of managed multilateralism persists because Germany and Japan choose not to pursue a new system by articulating autonomous security interests and objectives.

2. A system of regional coexistence could emerge. In this instance the multipolar economic system would produce a multipolar security system with the American, European, and Asian regions each having the political capacity and technical and industrial foundations for independent action and distinct regional security regimes. This security system would reflect the trend toward the regionalization of the world economy, and Europe and Japan would escape the constraints of U.S. influence in their regions.

3. A system of regional mercantilism could develop. Economic relations would be increasingly dominated by the logic of competition, protectionism, and the concept of "taking the economic offensive," while conceptions of security would diverge and cooperation would lessen.[61] This scenario is most likely to occur in the context of the continued decline of the United States in both military and economic categories. In such a closed and protected economic environment, the United States could become increasingly dependent on other states for the technology necessary to maintain its military, thus creating new patterns of dependence and autonomy in the security area less favorable to American interests.

In the current transitional system, the contest for economic and technological superiority has important implications for the evolution of the security system. As in the case of international economics, a period of at least twenty to thirty years will be required before the direction of that evolution becomes clear.

Regional Disparities: Threats to the Peace   In the current transitional international system, the processes of economic and cultural globalization are uneven, and several regions have experienced reverse processes of devolution, deintegration, and ethnocultural violence. In addition, the end of the Cold War did not have a uniform effect in every region. In some regions conflicts from the Cold War era have persisted, as on the Korean Peninsula, while in others, previously suppressed regional conflicts have emerged to create new risks to the peace. Viewed from the system level, there is currently greater diversity among regions than at any time since World War II, and new zones of peace and new zones of conflict have emerged simultaneously.[62]

Soviet Successor States and the States of Eastern Europe   With the end of the Soviet Union, the fifteen successor states confronted the difficult transitions to democracy and capitalism, the fury of ethnocultural violence, and threats of secession. The plight of Russia, the strongest of these states, illustrates the current environment of complexity and instability. Viewed from a military perspective, Russia now has all of the nuclear arsenal of the former Soviet Union and is therefore an important actor in the strategic-military area. Viewed from an economic perspective, however, the country appears destined to be relegated to the semiperiphery of the world economy.[63] In addition, the Russian Federation confronts a legitimacy crisis, with twenty-two small, indigenous ethnocultural groups having proclaimed their sovereignty by 1993.[64] Contemporary Russian leaders also confront a host of other foreign policy constraints, including the following: the need to function as leader of the Commonwealth of Independent States; the existence of twenty-six million ethnic Russians outside the borders of the Russian state; regional conflicts on Russia's borders; security problems resulting from the decision of medium and small border states to seek membership in NATO; the rise of Islamic militancy in some areas; and a growing economic dependence on international organizations and western sources that seem unwilling to meet Russia's perceived needs.[65] While at present Russia seems focused on regional security problems in the area of the former U.S.S.R., a resurgence of xenophobic nationalism and new episodes of expansion and imperialism cannot be ruled out. The majority of other successor states also confront ethnocultural conflicts and threats to their territorial integrity from secessionist groups.

The states of Eastern Europe also face a difficult political and economic transition. Legacies of government alienation and economic stagnation remain from the era of state socialism in every state. In addition, with the end of Communist-party control, traditional ethnocultural and regional rivalries re-emerged to claim a number of early casualties. Between 1991 and 1995, the state of Yugoslavia disintegrated into barbaric ethnic violence that threatened to spread to neighboring states. In 1993 Czechoslovakia split into the Czech and Slovak Republics. At least nine ethnic groups remain divided by borders.[66] Given the history of the region and the weakness of existing governments, the specter of possible ethnic and nationalist violence is a serious concern. On the positive side, Poland, Hungary, and the Czech Republic appear comparatively well situated to complete the transitions to democracy and the market economy.

East Asia and South Asia East Asia and South Asia reflect two different legacies of the Cold War. In East Asia a regional balance of power among the United States, China, the Soviet Union, and Japan has existed since the Cold War era. The balance was developed in the context of big-power competition, in which each state has sought to promote its influence while countering the interests of others.[67] In addition, there are two regional military powers, North Korea and South Korea, that were important components of rival alliances during the Cold War. In the contemporary setting, stability is by no means assured, and a number of potential issues exist that could destabilize the region. These include United States–Chinese enmity over economic and human rights issues; armed conflict between the two Koreas; the further disintegration of Soviet successor states, creating power vacuums; hostile reactions to Japan's economic hegemony in the region; Chinese political instability; regional conflicts involving smaller Asian nations; and unresolved border disputes in a number of states.[68] Two broad processes seem likely to determine the mix of conflict and competition:

1. Security roles in the region are in a state of transition and the survival of existing alliances, such as that between the United States and Japan, will require the adjustment of military, economic, and political contributions.

2. The rise of the trans-Pacific economy, including cross-national alliances of labor and capital, will confuse security relations and subject Asian societies to strong pressures for change.[69]

For the immediate future, the strategic environment in East Asia remains complex and potentially volatile in a region characterized by extreme diversity and a multiplicity of rivalries.

In South Asia, a region of seven extremely diverse countries, the end of the Cold War has been accompanied by a reduction in the involvement of outside states and a strengthening of traditional security patterns. South Asia is dominated by India, which has historically sought to establish hegemony in the region. India's pursuit of hegemony has been opposed by China and Pakistan. China, India, and Pakistan have Asia's first, second, and third largest militaries, respectively. Since the 1950s, India and Pakistan have fought three major wars, and India and China were engaged in a brief border war in 1962. Recent Indian-Pakistani relations have been characterized by meaningful dialogues and cooperative bargaining, as well as by competition, but a risk of nuclear war persists because both states are capable of deploying small nuclear forces.[70]

North-South Relations   No discussion of security would be complete without reference to the growing economic and social gap between the advanced industrial states at the core of the global economy, the so-called North, and the less-developed countries (LDCs) on the periphery of the economy, the political South. Since the 1970s the economic gap between the two groups of states has continuously widened, and the disparity between the wealthiest and poorest people within most southern states has also grown. With the end of the Cold War and the growth of the global market, the advanced industrial countries have unprecedented power in relation to the states of the South.[71] (The NICs of East Asia, which have left the periphery and have developed strong industrial economies, stand as the major exception.) Despite the increased military capacities of some Third World states, several conditions in the global economy have worked to the disadvantage of the South. Foremost among these are the declining importance of low-cost labor in high-technology production, instability in the prices of natural resources and commodities, and declining interest in much of the South as a sight for foreign direct investment (FDI).[72] The states of the North have sought to exploit their advantage in both bilateral relationships and through multilateral agencies like the International Monetary Fund and World Bank by establishing political as well as economic conditions for financial assistance.[73] These conditions include such broad areas as arms expenditures; human rights; the imposition of multiparty democracy and the rule of law; greater government accountability; transparency (openness) in decision making; reduced government social spending; and liberalization of markets.[74]

While it is popular in the North to proclaim the global trends toward democracy and economic liberalization, the imposition of these conditions has exacerbated social and political tensions in many of the states of the South. In the present transitional system, some LDCs have sought an association with more advanced economies, as did Mexico in joining the United States-dominated NAFTA, but such a decision involves loss of sovereignty in foreign and economic policy making.[75] Given the current absence of a clear model of development and any commitment from the North to a massive program of international aid, much of the southern periphery is likely to remain unstable and a potential site for domestic violence, civil war, and international conflict. The prospects for security in the South are further complicated by the lack of a strong consensus in the developed states on the advisability of multilateral peacekeeping efforts by the United Nations or other organizations. The growing ambivalence came in the wake of the costly U.N. missions in Somalia and Bosnia, which were unable to fully achieve their objectives.

NEW IDEAS AND NEW ISSUES IN THE TRANSITIONAL SYSTEM

Following the sudden and recent end of the postwar era, the new environment of the transitional system opened space for the development of new conceptions of international security and world order. The changed conditions have also given rise to new international issues with the potential to remake the world political agenda. Whether these concerns constitute the framework of the next world order is presently unclear, but ideas once institutionalized—such as state sovereignty, the balance of power, and hegemony—have provided the foundations of previous epochs of world order.[76] Since every era of international politics is shaped by the interaction of objective conditions and subjective perceptions, these new ideas bear careful examination.

With the end of the Cold War, a new, expanded definition of security has been advanced as a substitute for bipolarism and spheres of influence. In place of the narrow focus on the military security of states, the new conception seeks to expand the definition of security in four ways:[77]

1. The concept of security is extended downward from a focus on the security of states to a concern for the security of individuals and groups, frequently referred to as "common humanity."
2. The definition of security is extended upwards, beyond the level of the state, to include the security of the supranational physical environment (that is, the earth's environment or biosphere).
3. The concept of security is extended horizontally to include not just the military area, but also political, economic, social, and environmental matters.
4. The political responsibility for ensuring security is extended in every direction to include international organizations, states, regional and local governments, and even private actors.

At first consideration these new ideas may seem excessively abstract and idealistic, but they do accurately reflect the objective conditions present in the current transitional system. Above all, the state is no longer the only actor in contemporary global society and must compete with subnational groups, transnational corporations, and other actors. There is a growing incongruence between the ever-increasing mobility of persons, things, and information and the static structure of the nation-state.[78] One source has recently argued that this incongruence extends to several areas, including the operation of the global economy and the structure of the state, ecological systems and political boundaries, and ethnic and religious identification and loyalty to one state.[79]

Further, many of the new issues that have become part of the international political agenda have developed from the openness of the post-Cold War international system. These include such concerns as immigration, international terrorism, international crime (especially the sale of narcotics and nuclear materials), global communications, technology transfers in sensitive areas, weapons sales, and human rights as different cultures increasingly confront one another. The end of the immediate threat to world peace posed by the Cold War also permitted consideration of other long-term threats to human welfare, above all environmental problems. The study of these problems was aided by the general advance of scientific and technological methods over the past three decades.

THE ECOLOGICAL PARADIGM

Revelations between the 1960s and 1980s regarding deforestation, acid rain, the "greenhouse effect," and depletion of the ozone layer have given rise to a new conception of world politics that assigns top priority to the need for global management of the world environment.[80]

Two critical problems have been identified: (1) global climate changes resulting from the warming of the earth's atmosphere; and (2) threats to the viability of soil, water, and forests as habitats to sustain life.[81] In addition, specific environmental disasters, such as the nuclear accident at Chernobyl in the former Soviet Union (1986), the release of lethal gas in Bhopal, India

(1984), and the general degradation of the environment in Eastern Europe from the era of state socialism, have called attention to the irresponsibility of governments and private groups in the industrial states. Since environmental issues involve complex and interrelated problems, local and national programs are useful. However, the ecological paradigm places emphasis on the need for systematic and binding international environmental regimes.[82] Currently, two contradictory trends can be identified in the environmental issue-area. First, since 1972 a series of international conferences and commissions have sought to present and legitimate the ecological paradigm and its new agenda. They have also documented the failure of states to deal effectively with both global pollution, such as of the seas and oceans, and environmental degradation within the borders of individual countries. Various agencies of the United Nations, including the United Nations Environmental Program (UNEP), the World Commission on Environment and Development (the Brundtland Commission of 1987), and the Earth Summit in Rio de Janiero in 1992, have issued scientific reports, legal declarations containing new legal concepts, normative statements, international conventions, and treaties that form the foundations of several different international regimes.[83] These regimes include such areas as the Law of the Sea, ozone protection, and others. On the other hand, the concern for state sovereignty, fear that new models of development would impact the lifestyles of millions, and the inability of weaker states to enforce any environmental laws have combined to render the existing international environmental regimes weak and largely voluntary. As one source has recently argued, environmental agreements abound with nonbinding targets, weak sanctions, caveats, qualifications, and escape holes.[84]

The elevation of the environmental paradigm to the top of the international political agenda would involve a complete transformation of the nature of international politics. In the current transitional international system, it is unclear how extensive that transformation will be or to what extent international authority will supplant that of the state in this issue-area.

THE STATE IN THE TRANSITIONAL SYSTEM

Viewed from the perspective of the state, the expanded conception of security and the ecological paradigm are part of a larger debate on the future position of the state itself in the international system. It is generally accepted that in the current "global society" the state must compete for power and influence with other actors, such as regional organizations, transnational corporations, and subnational groups. Beyond this, however, some sources have argued that the state is now obsolete and that the era of state dominance of international politics, which began in 1648, is coming to an end. Numerous arguments have been advanced to support this position, but most such theories focus on three points:

1. The growth of neoliberal thought and of the global economy has weakened the state while increasing the power of transnational business groups and supranational organizations, especially regional trading blocs like the European Union.[85]

2. Individual states are no longer able to solve the most pressing social problems, including security, environmental protection, economic security, and ethnocultural expression.

3. The dual processes of globalization and subnational disintegration within the borders of states have rendered the concept of state sovereignty irrelevant. (According to the doctrine of state sovereignty, the state possesses united and indivisible power and recognizes no source of authority above it.)

Proponents of the view that the state is obsolete also argue that contemporary international relations can no longer be viewed as the competition between states for power and influence in an anarchical international environment—the so-called "realist critique."[86] Instead, they see increasing interdependence and cooperation among a host of actors, of which the state is only one. The main attribute of the state, the possession of military power, is now less important than economic power, and economic power is primarily acquired by private transnational corporations. Several recent studies have described the state as subverted, defective, and hollow.[87]

The state, the concept of sovereignty, and the state system are artificial constructs that are now more than three centuries old. As man-made structures, they will not last forever, and the state system will eventually be replaced by something else. It is uncertain, however, if the current transitional international system constitutes the beginning phase of the end of the era of state dominance. States currently remain the most important actors in the international system, and if the decline or breakup of some states can be documented, primarily in the periphery or the South, the process has not occurred uniformly throughout the international system. States like Germany and Japan have emerged in the post–Cold War era with enhanced power and influence. The same can be said of the Asian NICs and several postcommunist states of Eastern Europe. In addition, the competition between states and other types of actors is not without precedent. Major religions and messianic revolutionary movements, such as fascism and communism, competed with states for human loyalty in earlier periods, and lost. In describing the current international system as transitional in nature, the fluidity of existing relationships between actors is recognized. It will take at least twenty to thirty years, and perhaps as long as a century, to determine the future status of the state in the next world order.

NOTES

1.   Richard N. Rosecrance, *Action and Reaction in World Politics: International Systems in Perspective* (Boston, MA: Little, Brown and Company, 1962), pp. 1–14.

2.   Henry Kissinger, *Diplomacy* (New York: Simon & Schuster, 1994), p. 806.

3.   Saul B. Cohen, "Geopolitics in the New World Era," in *Reordering the World: Geopolitical Perspectives on the 21st Century*, George J. Demko and William B. Wood, eds. (Boulder, CO: Westview Press, 1994), p. 19.

4.   See Theodore Geiger, *The Future of the International System: The United States and the World Political Economy* (Boston, MA: Unwin Hyman, 1988), pp. 2–5.

5.   For a discussion of the dynamics of change, see James N. Rosenau, *Turbulence in World Politics: A Theory of Change and Continuity* (Princeton, NJ: Princeton University Press, 1990), pp. 67–90.

6.   Ferdinand Brendel, cited by Hans-Henrik Holm and Georg Sorensen, "Introduction: What Has Changed?" in *Whose World Order? Uneven Globalization and the End of the Cold War*, Hans-Henrik Holm and Georg Sorensen, eds. (Boulder, CO: Westview Press, 1995), p. 1.

7.   Cohen, "Geopolitics in the New World Era," p. 23.

8.   For a discussion of economic backwardness in postcommunist states, see W. W. Rostow, "Eastern Europe and the Soviet Union: A Technological Time Warp," in *The Crisis of Leninism and the Decline of the Left: The Revolution of 1989*, Daniel Chirot, ed. (Seattle: University of Washington Press, 1991), pp. 60–73.

9.   Zaki Laidi, "Power and Purpose in the International System," in *Power and Purpose after the Cold War*, Zaki Laidi, ed. (Providence, RI: Berg Publishers, Ltd., 1994) pp. 8–9.

10. Richard Ullman, "Redefining Security," in *Global Dangers: Changing Dimensions of International Security*, Sean M. Lynn-Jones and Steven E. Miller, eds. (Cambridge, MA: The MIT Press, 1995), pp. 16–25.

11. Laidi, "Power and Purpose in the International System," p. 7.

12. Ibid., p. 7.

13. Thomas D. Lairson and David Skidmore, *International Political Economy: The Struggle for Power and Wealth* (New York: Harcourt Brace Jovanovich College Publishers, 1993), p. 162.

14. For a discussion of this thesis, see Bruce Cumings, "The End of the Seventy-Years' Crisis: Trilateralism and the New World Order," in *Past as Prelude: History in the Making of a New World Order*, Meredith Woo-Cumings and Michael Loriaux, eds. (Boulder, CO: Westview Press, 1993), pp. 9–25.

15. Edward N. Luttwak, "From Geopolitics to Geo-Economics," in *The National Interest* 20 (Summer 1990): 17–23.

16. Thomas J. McCormick, *America's Half-Century: United States Foreign Policy in the Cold War and After*, 2nd ed. (Baltimore, MD: The Johns Hopkins University Press, 1995), pp. 242–243.

17. For a discussion of the position of the United States in the postwar world economy, see Geiger, *The Future of the International System*, pp. 9–20.

18. Ibid., pp. 3–7.

19. Kenneth A. Oye, "The Domain of Choice: International Constraints and Carter Administration Foreign Policy," in *Eagle Entangled: U.S. Foreign Policy in a Complex World*, Kenneth A. Oye, Donald Rothchild, and Robert J. Lieber, eds. (New York: Longman, 1979), p. 5.

20. Robert O. Keohane, *After Hegemony: Cooperation and Discord in the World Political Economy* (Princeton, NJ: Princeton University Press, 1984), p. 15; see also pp. 135–182.

21. McCormick, *America's Half-Century*, p. 217.

22. Geiger, *The Future of the International System*, p. 112.

23. Kennedy's thesis is presented in Paul Kennedy, *The Rise and Fall of the Great Powers: Economic Change and Military Conflict from 1500 to 2000* (New York: Random House, 1987), esp. pp. 514–535.

24. For a discussion of the debate on American power in the contemporary inter-

national system, see Charles F. Doran, "Quo Vadis? The United States' Cycle of Power and its Role in a Transforming World," in *Building a New Global Order: Emerging Trends in International Security*, David Dewitt, David Haglund, and John Kirton, eds. (New York: Oxford University Press, 1993), pp. 12–39.

25. Vincent Cable, "The Diminished Nation-State," in *What Future for the State, Daedalus*, American Academy of Arts and Sciences, vol. 124, no. 2, Spring 1995, p. 26.

26. John Agnew, *The United States in the World-Economy: A Regional Geography* (New York: Cambridge University Press, 1987), p. 87.

27. Martin Carnoy, Manuel Castells, Stephen S. Cohen, and Fernando Henrique Cardoso, *The New Global Economy in the Information Age* (University Park: Pennsylvania State University Press, 1993), p. 6.

28. Ingomar Hauchler and Paul M. Kennedy, eds., *Global Trends: The World Almanac of Development and Peace* (New York: A Development and Peace Foundation Book, 1994), pp. 218–220.

29. For a discussion of this period, see John Agnew and Stuart Corbridge, "The New Geopolitics: The Dynamics of Geopolitical Disorder," in *A World in Crisis? Geographical Perspectives*, R. J. Johnston and P. J. Taylor, eds. (Cambridge, MA: Basil Blackweel, Inc., 1988), pp. 266–288.

30. Cable, "The Diminished Nation-State," p. 25.

31. Susan Strange, "The Defective State," in *What Future for the State, Daedalus*, pp. 55–56.

32. Ibid., p. 59.

33. For the best presentation of this model, see Rosenau, *Turbulence in World Politics*, pp. 1–66.

34. Ibid., pp. 59–62.

35. Ibid., pp. 7, 61–62.

36. For a discussion of the importance of the communications media in modern politics, see Rosenau, *Turbulence in World Politics*, pp. 315–388.

37. Hauchler and Kennedy, *Global Trends*, pp. 346–347.

38. See Rosenau, *Turbulence in World Politics*, pp. 101–108.

39. Ibid., pp. 334–335.

40. Crawford Young, "The Dialectics of Cultural Pluralism," in *The Rising Tide of Cultural Pluralism, The Nation-State at Bay?* Crawford Young, ed. (Madison: The University of Wisconsin Press, 1993), p. 4.

41. Lester Thurow, *Head to Head: The Coming Economic Battle among Japan, Europe, and America* (New York: Warner Books, 1993), p. 30.

42. Ibid., pp. 23–24.

43. For a discussion of this issue, see Jeffrey E. Garten, *A Cold Peace: America, Japan, Germany, and the Struggle for Supremacy* (New York: A Twentieth Century Fund Book, 1993), p. 162.

44. Ibid, pp. 169–189.

45. Thurow, *Head to Head*, p. 16.

46. Ibid., p. 16.

47. Jeffrey A. Hart, *Rival Capitalists: International Competitiveness in the United States, Japan, and Western Europe* (Ithaca, NY: Cornell University Press, 1992), pp. 1–35, esp. 5–7.

48. Barbara Stallings and Wolfgang Streeck, "Capitalism in Conflict? The United States, Europe, and Japan in the Post–Cold War World," in *Global Change, Regional Response: The New International Context of Development*, Barbara Stallings, ed. (Cambridge, MA: Cambridge University Press, 1995), p. 67.

49. Ibid., p. 69.

50. Ibid., pp. 70–71.

51.   Thurow, cited by Stallings and Streeck, "Capitalism in Conflict?" pp. 71–72.
52.   Paul R. Viotti, "International Relations and the Defense Policies of Nations: International Anarchy and the Common Problems of Security," in *The Defense Policies of Nations*, 3rd ed., Douglas J. Murray and Paul R. Viotti, eds. (Baltimore, MD: The Johns Hopkins University Press, 1994), pp. 6–13.
53.   Wayne Sandholtz, Michael Borrus, John Zysman, et al., *The Highest Stakes: The Economic Foundations of the Next Security System* (New York: Oxford University Press, 1992), pp. 3–5.
54.   Ibid., pp. 3–5, 197–205.
55.   Robert C. Johansen, "Building World Security: The Need for Strengthened International Institutions," in *World Security: Challenges for a New Century*, Michael T. Klare and Daniel C. Thomas, eds. (New York: St. Martin's Press, 1994), pp. 374–375.
56.   See Sandholtz et al., *The Highest Stakes*, pp. 7–52; see also Charles W. Kegley, Jr., and Gregory Raymond, *A Multipolar Peace? Great Power Politics in the Twenty-first Century* (New York: St. Martin's Press, 1994), pp. 166–211.
57.   Ibid., pp. 10–11, 46–48.
58.   Hanns W. Maull, "Germany and Japan: New Civilian Powers" in *Foreign Affairs* 69, no. 5 (Winter 1990–1991): 96–97.
59.   Ibid., pp. 102–106.
60.   These scenarios are identified by Sandholtz et al., *The Highest Stakes*, pp. 10–11 and Kegley and Raymond, *A Multipolar Peace?* pp. 169–180.
61.   Ibid., p. 168.
62.   Holm and Sorensen, "Introduction," p. 15.
63.   Vladislov M. Zubok, "Russia: Between Peace and Conflict," in Holm and Sorensen, *Whose World Order?* p. 105.
64.   Ibid., p. 106.
65.   Ibid., pp. 107–109.
66.   Jonathan Dean, *Ending Europe's Wars: The Continuing Search for Peace and Security* (New York: The Twentieth Century Fund Press, 1994), p. 114.
67.   Thomas A. Drohan, "East Asia and the Pacific: The Security of a Region," in Murray and Viotti, eds., *The Defense Policies of Nations*, p. 340.
68.   James Chace, *The Consequences of the Peace: The New Internationalism and American Foreign Policy* (New York: The Twentieth Century Fund Press, 1992), pp. 335–344.
69.   Drohan, "East Asia and the Pacific," pp. 334, 342.
70.   Stephen E. Montgomery, Jr., "South Asia: The Security of a Region," in Murray and Viotti, eds., *The Defense Policies of Nations*, pp. 459–461.
71.   Geoffrey Hawthorn, "The Crises of Southern States," in *Contemporary Crisis of the Nation State?* John Dunn, ed. (Cambridge, MA: Blackwell Publishers, 1995), p. 130.
72.   Holm and Sorensen, "Introduction," p. 16.
73.   Hawthorn, "The Crises of Southern States," p. 131.
74.   Ibid., pp. 131–136.
75.   Ibid., p. 143.
76.   For a discussion of the importance of ideas and beliefs, see Judith Goldstein and Robert O. Keohane, "Ideas and Foreign Policy: An Analytical Framework" in *Ideas and Foreign Policy: Beliefs, Institutions, and Political Change*, Judith Goldstein and Robert O. Keohane, eds. (Ithaca, NY: Cornell University Press, 1993), pp. 8–13.
77.   Emma Rothschild, "What Is Security?" in *The Quest for World Order, Daedalus*, pp. 54–55.
78.   Seyom Brown, *New Forces, Old Forces, and the Future of World Politics: Post-Cold War Edition* (New York: HarperCollins College Publishers, 1995), p. 244.

79. Ibid., p. 244.
80. Albert Legault, "Conclusion: Towards the Twenty-First Century," in Dewitt, Haglund, and Kirton, eds., *Building a New Global Order*, p. 405.
81. For a discussion of these points, see Hauchler and Kennedy, *Global Trends*, pp. 278–304.
82. Ibid., p. 275.
83. Andrew Hurrell, "A Crisis of Ecological Viability," in Dunn, ed., *Contemporary Crisis of the Nation State?* pp. 150–152.
84. Ibid., p. 152.
85. For a discussion of this point, see Vivian A. Schmidt, "The New World Order, Incorporated: The Rise of Business and the Decline of the Nation-State," in *What Future for the State, Daedalus*, pp. 75–85.
86. For a defense of the realist critique, see Raymond Aron, "The Anarchical Order of Power," in *The Quest for World Order, Daedalus*, pp. 27–52; see also Hedley Bull, *The Anarchical Society: A Study of Order in World Politics* (New York: Columbia University Press, 1977).
87. See Susan Strange, Vincent Cable, and Chris Hann, "Subverting Strong States," in *What Future for the State, Daedalus*, pp. 23–54, 133–154.

CHAPTER 2

AMERICAN POLICY
IN THE COLD WAR

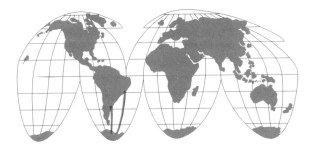

A REGIONAL APPROACH

JAMES R. COBBLEDICK

With the end of World War II there was an ambivalence to American foreign policy. On the one hand, the American people wanted to "bring the boys home" and concentrate on peacetime internal activities, thereby leading to a rapid demilitarization of the enormous military capability produced during World War II. It was also clear, however, that the United States, as the most productive society in the world and virtually unscathed by the war, was the only world power that had the capability to bring some kind of order and stability to the war-torn world. The United States had assumed occupying positions in Germany, Japan, and South Korea and proceeded to extend economic aid on a bilateral basis to Europe and Asia. The United States hoped that with this bilateral economic assistance the devastated economies would recover and an internal balance of power would emerge in Asia and Europe. The United States also hoped that the wartime unity of the Big Three could continue after the war and that the Security Council of the new United Nations would serve as a focal point for the "Great Powers" to cooperate and achieve international stability. The necessary harmonization of security interests did not occur, and within months tensions between the Soviet Union and the United States began to emerge.

Before discussing specific tension points and the evolving policy options adopted by the United States, a brief review of the fundamental sources of tension that lasted for forty-five years between these two powers is necessary. The basic ideologies of the two superpowers were at opposite ends of the political spectrum. The United States was grounded in the political ethos of the enlightenment in which individual self-worth, free political choice, and limited state power were fundamental. Community based on individual liberty and freedom, including religious freedom, wherein policy choices would be made through the interplay of peacefully competing interests would be the framework of a democratic society. The Soviet Union, based on Marxism-Leninism, asserted the power and effectiveness of the collectivity, that is, the proletariat controlled and directed by the state. Individual needs would be achieved through collective action, with the state being all powerful with unlimited means, including coercion, to achieve a command society. Democratic centralism, in which commands flowed from the top down, either from an individual, Stalin, or the Politburo, would direct society, and the individual would have no check on state policy directives. With the command society as the basic organizational framework, inevitably the state owned and controlled all resources, modes of production, and distribution of goods: A planned economy was the hallmark of Bolshevism. In contrast, the United States had a decentralized economy based on the principles of the market mechanism, that is, supply and demand. In reality, the United States evolved into a mixed economy, but the dominant and leading edge of the economy would be the private sector. The two fundamentally different ways of organizing society would permeate and vie for influence in all regions of the globe.

Of concern for both great powers were the relative productive capabilities of each society. Neither society had confronted another society of such scale—the Soviet Union, stretching across the northern land mass of Eurasia for eleven time zones, and the United States, stretching from the Aleutians to the North Atlantic dominating the core of North America. The United States had come out of the Second World War as the preeminent world power, and the Soviet Union had become the strongest single Eurasian power. Of particular concern to both powers was the actual or potential relative military capability that ensued from their respective economies. The United States had produced an enormous military machine during the Second World War and, although demobilizing much of its conventional military capability after the war, retained a nuclear monopoly. The Soviet Union had created vast land armies that had defeated the Nazis on the Eastern European front and had struck decisively against Japan in Manchuria and Korea. The Soviet Union had not demobilized its armies as the West had done at the conclusion of the Second World War. The demonstrated military power of both countries evoked fear in the rival capitals.

Most important, the relative positioning of these two powers had been radically altered after 1945. The United States and the Soviet Union traditionally were located at opposite ends of the northern temperate zone. Their one point of contiguousness, the Bering Strait, never had become a prime center of tension due to the arctic weather conditions. Through all of Russian and American history, intervening powers—England, France, and Germany in Europe and China and Japan in Asia—had been their primary centers of interest. The expansion of two of those powers, Germany and Japan, had produced the Grand Alliance during the Second World War. By the conclusion of the war, much of Japan had been destroyed by American bombs, China was weak and descending into civil war, and in Europe, Nazi Germany was in ashes and dismembered, France had been defeated and occupied, the British Empire was disintegrating and internally was exhausted. The Red Army had swept through Eastern Europe and held an occupying position in the center of Europe. Stalin not only proceeded to install Communist regimes in Eastern Europe, stretching from the Baltic to Bulgaria, but also had assisted Mao in Manchuria and created a Communist regime in the northern half of the Korean peninsula. The United States had broken free of its own confines in North America and acquired an occupation zone in Austria, southern Germany, and West Berlin, involved itself in the attempted economic stabilization of Western Europe and was the prime occupying presence in South Korea and Japan. In effect, the intervening powers had collapsed, the balance of power had been fundamentally altered, and the new antagonists were contiguous at the opposite ends of Eurasia. The United States had moved into position in Japan and Germany, two powers that had endangered Russia through the first half of the twentieth century.

A series of events in 1946 and 1947 precipitated the fundamental change in American foreign policy that led the United States to long-term involvement outside North America. Lack of agreement over the future of Germany, the communization of Eastern Europe, Russian reluctance to withdraw its forces from northern Iran, the possible Communist victory in the Greek Civil War, and Soviet pressure to force open and possibly control the Turkish Straits all sounded alarm bells in Washington. Great Britain had signaled it could no longer pursue its traditional policy of the containment of Russia from Greece to the Khyber Pass. The gravest consequences were also feared if national communist parties came to power in France and Italy because of the slow rehabilitation of those two societies.

The United States was unwilling to permit the possibility that Stalin, through Communist victories, could gain control of a majority of European resources, thereby gaining a hegemonic position in Europe. To preclude such an eventuality, the United States initially adopted George Kennan's basic thesis.[1] Kennan viewed the Soviet Union in a fundamentally defensive position and assumed that it would not use direct military force beyond its current power periphery. The essential threat to the non-Communist world was the disintegration of societies due to the enormous destruction of the war. To contain Communist influence linked to Moscow, the United States need not use American armed forces but rather must address the fundamental reason for the growth of communism by offering economic assistance to its allies for economic recovery. In line with the Kennan analysis, the Truman Doctrine was announced, in which American military and economic aid was extended to the anti-Communist forces in Greece and Turkey. To all of Europe the United States offered massive economic assistance through the

Marshall Plan. The onus for the division of Europe fell squarely on the Soviet Union when Stalin refused the Marshall Plan and would not allow the Eastern European satellites and Czechoslovakia to accept such aid. Stalin feared America's economic capability and its potential to undermine Moscow's control of Eastern Europe. At the heart of the European issue was the question of Germany. Control over Germany would provide Washington or Moscow a dominant position in Central and Western Europe. Thus, a divided Europe meant that the key power of Germany would become divided along with its former capital, Berlin.

With the ensuing division of Europe along the Iron Curtain, the circumstances for long-term U.S. engagement were established. The Iron Curtain shifted in 1948 when Marshal Tito of Yugoslavia, to avoid becoming a Soviet satellite, split with Moscow. To bolster Tito's resolve against Stalin, the United States granted economic and military assistance to Belgrade. In return, Russian supplies flowing through Yugoslavia to the Greek Communist forces dried up, and the anti-Communist Greeks proceeded to win that civil war. American assistance to Yugoslavia indicated that the United States was willing to work with communist regimes that broke with Moscow and checked Soviet hegemony in Europe. The United States, therefore, would encourage a policy of Communist polycentrism, and Yugoslavia was the opening wedge in that policy. That principle was invoked in 1969 when the United States condemned the possibility of a Soviet attack on Communist China.

To overcome any isolationist tendencies that might inhibit American resolve in resisting Communist expansion across a line stretching from Turkey to Scandinavia, the Truman administration developed an anti-Communist theme that would coalesce much of the American public behind its containment policy. It was the fear of atheistic, coercive communism that became the glue that would cement together much of American opinion and society. There was danger in such a strongly stated theme, and this was exhibited after Mao's victory in China with the emergence of McCarthyism. To organize the American government for such a long-term engagement with the Soviet Union, the National Security Act was passed in 1947, which included the creation of the Central Intelligence Agency (CIA). George Kennan, head of the State Department's Policy Planning Staff, was concerned that American democracy was not equipped to sustain a long peacetime engagement with authoritarian communism. Democracy, he and others believed, was best organized to handle domestic affairs, not foreign problems that required perseverance, diplomatic secrecy, and, at times, immediate action. A poorly informed, less interested public opinion, acting through a divisive Congress, was ill-equipped to persevere in such a long-term struggle. Kennan's answer in such a democratic setting was to have foreign policy formulated and executed by an elite. Such a formula would have to be America's response to counter the perceived advantages of an authoritarian system that could organize and mobilize resources on an unlimited basis, unencumbered by public opinion.

Kennan's elite formula persisted until the Vietnam imbroglio when American opinion became more fractured, reflecting the pluralistic nature of our society. Nevertheless, the openness, private incentives, market mechanism, and democratic polity of the United States withstood the four-decade challenge that ultimately proved authoritarianism less able to initiate internal change and revitalize society to respond to new technologies. But this outcome could not be foreseen at the beginning of the Cold War.

Reacting to the American initiatives of the Marshall Plan and Truman Doctrine, Stalin attempted to complete the creation of his sphere of influence in Eastern Europe. Internal and external pressure was brought to bear to create a Communist regime in Prague. Many in Western Europe worried if a similar fate awaited them; and then Stalin, with the overt use of force in closing overland autobahn traffic, began the Berlin blockade. Many in Washington, including Secretary of State Dean Acheson, now argued that Russia was exhibiting its traditional militaristic, expansionist character and that, for Western Europe's protection, the United States needed to develop more than an economic response. Acheson argued that there must be a military component to America's containment policy. To that end, the North Atlantic Treaty Organization (NATO) was created in 1949.[2] NATO initially was an American nuclear umbrella placed over Western Europe, including the newly created West German Republic.

Divisive events accelerated as the Soviet Union, far sooner than expected, exploded its first nuclear device in August 1949 (thereby precipitating the American development of a thermonuclear weapon), mainland China fell to Mao's Communist revolution, and, within months, Moscow and Beijing concluded a security treaty. Monolithic, militant Eurasian communism was not only threatening Europe but also Asia. When the Korean War started the United States worried that it was a prelude to a military move in Europe. To increase the credibility of American resolve in Europe, the conventional arming of Western Europe began in earnest with the deployment of four United States divisions to West Germany. In addition, the Western Europeans at the Lisbon Conference agreed to begin a large-scale conventional build up, and Greece and Turkey were added to NATO. With the death of Stalin in 1953 there may have been a window of opportunity for slowing down the unrestrained militarization of Central Europe when the Soviets withdrew from their military bases in Finland and their occupation zone in Austria, and a united, neutral Austria was created. Such an option was posed for Germany. Nevertheless, John Foster Dulles pressed ahead with the incorporation of West Germany into NATO; Russia's response was to create the Warsaw Pact, including the militarization of East Germany. Kennan, fearing that the accelerating militarization of Central Europe could lead to a hair trigger war situation, proposed, in 1957, a military disengagement policy for Central Europe, but Washington ignored this proposal.

The United States, while by far the strongest power in the world, did not want to remain solely responsible for pursuing the policy of containment. The United States wanted the restoration of the European economies in order that they could increasingly assist it in the containment of communism. The United States, looking at West Europe as a whole, did not want Europe to emerge with small-scale competing national economies; the United States, therefore, encouraged the West Europeans to move toward economic integration. The aim was the so-called "dumbbell theory" in which two large economic entities—one in North America, the other in West Europe, linked by NATO—would emerge to successfully counter Soviet power in Europe. In providing Marshall Plan assistance, the United States began this process by encouraging the Europeans to look at Western Europe as a whole in requesting and receiving aid on a regional, comparative advantage basis. The Europeans, feeling squeezed between the two superpowers, began a rapid series of regional initiatives. The success of the European Payments Union (EPU) and the European Coal and Steel Community led in 1957 to the creation of the inner six Common Market (France, Italy, West Germany, Belgium, The Netherlands, and Luxembourg).

Great Britain, resisting integration into Europe, reacted by creating a Free Trade Zone with Scandinavia. The British represented a fundamental dilemma for the United States. The British still retained many extra-European responsibilities, and the United States encouraged the British to cooperate with it in areas of traditional British interest. To that end, the United States helped the British acquire a nuclear capability so that the British would feel they continued to have the power to be a major player on a worldwide basis. The United States, however, fearing French political instability, did not provide similar nuclear assistance to France; the French, therefore, proceeded to develop their own nuclear *force de frappe*. Despite encouraging the British to remain involved in the outer world, within Europe the United States wanted Great Britain to join the continent. Great Britain, along with some of the other members of the Free Trade Zone, finally did enter the Common Market from 1973 through 1975, but continued to resist deepening European integration. In the Iberian Peninsula, the United States developed an independent security relationship with Franco's Spanish government, but after democratic revolutions swept both Spain and Portugal in the mid-1970s, both countries joined the Common Market. The United States encouraged the economic integration of Western Europe even though, by the 1980s, the Common Market became an economic competitor. Of concern to the United States was Europe's growing protectionism, led by France, that could precipitate a protectionist response within the American economic community.

When the United States lost its nuclear delivery monopoly with the launching of Sputnik in October 1957, the policy of massive retaliation in response to any act of Soviet aggression in Europe was thrown in doubt. In order to buy time before a massive strategic nuclear exchange between the superpowers occurred, the Americans implored the Europeans to build up their conventional military power. The Europeans resisted the American entreaties, for political, financial, and strategic reasons, even though the second Berlin crisis, which began in 1958, had intensified with the building of the Berlin Wall in 1961. Even though the Berlin crisis receded shortly after the Cuban Missile Crisis, the Americans still persisted in urging the Europeans to rearm within NATO. To enhance American nuclear credibility in Europe, the United States proposed the Multilateral Force (MLF) in which disguised merchant ships carrying strategic nuclear weapons would be manned by multinational crews, including West Germans. The Soviets opposed any possibility of the Germans gaining a finger on this nuclear trigger; to win Soviet acceptance of the Nuclear Non-Proliferation Treaty, the MLF proposal was dropped. Clearly, for the United States NATO was not just a way of thwarting Soviet power in Europe; it was also a means of preventing an independent German military power from being created—particularly the creation of any kind of independent German nuclear capability. These series of negotiations also revealed that the Soviets agreed with the United States that nuclear proliferation beyond the existing nuclear powers must be contained. In 1965, the two powers even offered India a mutual nuclear guarantee through the Security Council to deter India from matching China's nuclear program. India declined the offer.

One interpretation of the October 1962 Cuban missile crisis is that Khruschev wanted to negotiate the West out of West Berlin in return for the removal of Soviet missiles in Cuba. Moscow was responding to the fundamental change in the relation of military power between the superpowers after Sputnik by attempting to tidy up its Eastern European sphere of influence, particularly its position in East Germany. President Kennedy's hard-line response in imposing the Cuban blockade and forcing the withdrawal of Soviet missiles, which threatened the American strategic deterrent in the Rocky Mountains, meant that the division of Europe established in 1949, when the United States was the sole superpower, remained intact.[3] Amazingly, while other portions of the world became increasingly more fluid from 1962 until 1989, Europe strategically remained sharply divided until the collapse of the Berlin Wall in November 1989. An anomaly to this rigid division of Europe occurred in 1967 when Secretary of State Dean Rusk announced a NATO protective screen over Yugoslavia. Rusk was responding to Soviet pressure on a potentially post-Tito Yugoslavia, although Tito was to live for another ten years. In 1975, when Secretary of State Henry Kissinger was concerned about a Communist success in revolutionary Portugal, the Russians were deterred from making any move of assistance to the Portuguese Communists. Throughout the Cold War the Soviets made no major move west of the Iron Curtain.

At the Yalta Conference in February 1945, the United States, acknowledging the westward tide of the Red Army in Eastern Europe during the final stages of the war, accepted Stalin's assertion that Russia had a special zone of influence there. Hence, the coerced communization of Poland and other

Eastern European societies was not effectively challenged as Europe became divided in 1949. The Eisenhower administration voiced a roll back policy in Eastern Europe after 1953, but when no effective action was taken in 1956 to assist the Hungarian rebellion, which was being crushed by Soviet forces, the roll back option died a quiet death. The United States did nothing to assist the Czechs during the Dubchek spring of 1968 or the Polish Gdansk worker rebellion in 1970. It did, however, encourage the Romanians in their struggle to develop a somewhat independent foreign policy from Moscow and to resist Soviet attempts to keep Romania an agricultural entity. In hindsight, the Helsinki Agreement of 1978, whereby the Soviets agreed to respect human rights and to allow the monitoring of their policies in Eastern Europe, was of historic significance. While the Soviets reneged on many provisions of the agreement, the principle of respect for human rights was enunciated and that legitimized the political ferment that swept Eastern Europe in the following decade. When the Solidarity Movement emerged in Poland after 1980, the United States provided covert financial and communications equipment assistance, while the movement undermined Communist party control of Poland. Although the Soviets threatened to intervene militarily in Poland, the fact that they did not, being increasingly bogged down in Afghanistan, signaled Soviet reluctance to militarily crush non-Communist movements in Eastern Europe. The United States welcomed Gorbachev's announcement in early 1988 that he would not move Soviet troops out of their barracks to preserve Eastern European Communist regimes. Very quickly, the coercive Communist regimes collapsed, and the division of Europe, established forty years before, ended.

Throughout the entire Cold War, the United States and the Soviet Union were involved in an action-reaction syndrome that produced a largely unrestrained arms race. Being more economically and technologically advanced than the Soviet Union, the United States was first to develop most new weapons systems and technologies, with the exception of Sputnik. Throughout this era the Soviet Union was basically in a catch-up position, developing nuclear, sea, and air power to counter the superiority of the Americans. The Soviets had conventional military predominance at the center of Europe and along the northern periphery of the Middle East. While attempting to build up anti-Communist military power along the Soviet periphery, the West's ultimate defense against Soviet conventional superiority was strategic and tactical nuclear weapons. After Sputnik, the United States sought to diversify its strategic launch systems and to make them more invulnerable. As the nuclear triad of land, sea, and air systems developed, special emphasis was placed on the Poseidon, later Trident, undersea launch systems. The Soviets, particularly after the Cuban missile debacle, moved to match the American delivery capability, and in 1971 President Richard Nixon acknowledged that the Soviet Union had become a true world military power and that both sides had achieved a MAD position, that is, Mutual Assured

Destruction. Major public opinion and diplomatic wrangles occurred over the competitive positioning of weapons systems in Europe. In the 1980s, President Ronald Reagan held firm to his pledge to send Pershing missiles to West Germany to match improved Soviet nuclear capability in Eastern Europe. The increasing cost and danger of the militarization of Central Europe led to the first move toward a disengagement policy when the Intermediate-Range Nuclear Force (INF) treaty was negotiated and theater nuclear weapons were withdrawn by both sides from Central Europe.

In the 1950s John Foster Dulles' policy for the escalation of a competitive arms race was based on the presumption of superior American economic capability that would force the smaller Soviet economy into bankruptcy. However, the increasing Soviet discovery and exploitation of resources and the accelerating industrialization of the Soviet sphere precluded his hoped-for result. The Soviets, of course, with a far smaller economy, had to allocate a far higher percentage of their GNP to defense. Three decades later, the Reagan administration based its military build-up policy on the Dulles thesis. The Soviet economy finally was stretched beyond its productive limits, especially when it was challenged by the enormously costly Star Wars proposal. Even the United States was feeling the strain of Cold War expenditures. The possible expenditure of hundreds of billions of dollars on the new proposal caused many in the United States to look askance. More importantly, Star Wars was a challenge to the basic principle of MAD, the ascendency of the offense in the nuclear era. Even if an effective Star Wars capability had been developed, the rival side, thinking its counterforce capability thwarted, might launch a first strike while it still retained that capability. Throughout the Cold War the United States always posited that the Soviet Union would be the initiator of a nuclear war. The Soviets, however, had the same fear in reverse.

Until the Cuban Missile Crisis, there had been an unrestrained arms race, but after that crisis both sides looked down the nuclear tunnel and recoiled from the actuality of a nuclear war. Both sides wanted a nuclear deterrence, but a nuclear exchange would produce mutual suicide. Therefore, to contain the nuclear genie, a series of agreements began to be reached. First, hot-lines connecting Moscow and Washington were established so that verbal communication would be faster than missiles to avoid an unintended policy mistake. With the wheat deal (1963) Kennedy helped to keep Khruschev in power for two more years; it was in America's interest to have a Soviet leader in power who had looked down the tunnel and respected the nuclear danger. Throughout the remainder of the Cold War the emergence of any new leader in either capital was a matter of concern until it became manifest that there remained mutual respect for the danger of nuclear weapons. President Reagan's "Evil Empire speech" was of particular concern until he softened his stance. The Non-Proliferation Treaty of 1968 pledged the superpowers and encouraged other existing nuclear powers not to disseminate military nuclear technology to non-nuclear nations, and that treaty called on all non-nuclear nations to commit to a non-nuclear status. In the Space Treaty of 1967, the United States and the Soviets agreed not to militarize space and, specifically, not to test, store, or transport nuclear weapons to extraterrestrial bodies, such as the moon. Thus, the consequence of the race to the moon was limited before it was actually reached. With both powers achieving even greater depths in their submarine technology, to avoid the construction of nuclear launch sites on the ocean floor, the Seabed Treaty of 1971 was negotiated, which banned any positioning of nuclear sites at the bottom of the ocean.

None of these agreements, however, limited the nuclear arms race or the introduction of new delivery systems. When detente deepened during Nixon's administration, the Strategic Arms Limitation Treaty (SALT I) was successfully negotiated in 1971, thereby preserving the offensive nature of MAD. This agreement placed restrictions on the construction of new Anti-Ballistic Missile systems (ABMs) and a minimal start was made to limiting launch systems. As the number and variety of launch systems blossomed in the 1970s, SALT II was negotiated in 1975, but never ratified by the United States Senate. In this agreement outer numerical limits were placed on most launch systems in each other's triad, but the new cruise missiles were not included.[4] Cruise missiles increasingly became the delivery system of choice during the 1980s. In the latter stages of the Reagan Administration and in the Bush era, a series of arms control and disarmament talks—the Strategic Arms Reduction Treaty (START) round—were initiated with the aim of limiting both powers' overkill capability.

ASIA

Mao's communist victory on the mainland of China in 1949 was a major blow to the American postwar Asian policy of having a friendly, united, modernizing Nationalist China, led by Chiang Kai-shek, to check the southerly flow of Soviet power in Asia. The possibility of an internal Asian balance of power was thrown in doubt, especially with the Sino-Soviet Security Treaty of March 1950, which created a monolithic Communist military configuration stretching from the Elbe River in the center of Europe to the Pacific Ocean. With American-Asian policy in disarray, in January 1950 Secretary of State Dean Acheson redrew America's security sphere off the mainland of Asia, thereby reducing our ties to the Nationalist regime that had retreated to Taiwan. South Korea was also excluded from the new sphere of influence, and Stalin, assuming a vacuum of power had emerged south of the 38th parallel, moved to fill the vacuum by having the North Koreans (a Soviet creation) move to unify the Korean peninsula by force. Immediately, the Truman Administration, reversing its decision of six months earlier, reintroduced American forces under United Nations aegis into South Korea. This multinational U.N. action, led by General Douglas McArthur, not only ejected the

Communist forces from South Korea, but after the Inchon landing attempted to unify all of Korea. China, fearing the northward flow of American power toward the newly unified Communist mainland, introduced its own forces, and a long, drawn-out war lasted until March 1953.[5] The Truman administration successfully limited the Korean War to the narrow Korean peninsula, not allowing it to spread into China proper, even though that decision required the removal of a recalcitrant General McArthur. With the death of Stalin and the Eisenhower threat of the use of nuclear weapons if a peace was not successfully negotiated, an armistice was finally achieved.

While the Cold War had primarily been contained to Europe until 1949, the communization of China and the North Korean attack spread the superpower competition to all regions of the globe. The United States proceeded to draw lines around the entire Communist world so that there would be no misreading of American intentions as had occurred on the Korean peninsula. The policy of containment became global. A Pacific offshore island arc was created, stretching from the Aleutians to Australia and New Zealand (ANZUS). Included in this security sphere was a new ally, Japan with Okinawa, Taiwan (the United States reentering the Chinese Civil War), the Philippines, the Pacific Trust Territories, and the lone North Asian mainland commitment, South Korea. To replace the French and the British in Southeast Asia and the Subcontinent, the Southeast Asia Treaty Organization (SEATO) was created, encompassing Pakistan, Thailand, and the Philippines. To fill the vacuum of former French Indo-China, by separate protocol Laos, Cambodia, and Vietnam below the 17th parallel received U.S. security assurances. SEATO was the least viable security arrangement because so many nations in the region, including the two major states of Indonesia and India, did not join the alliance. Filling the containment gap between Turkey and Pakistan in the Middle East, the Baghdad Pact was created; in 1958, with the withdrawal of Iraq, the pact was renamed the Central Treaty Organization (CENTO) with special emphasis placed on the security of Iran. The United States now had worldwide responsibility in containing the one-third of mankind under communism, and the realistic means of fulfilling such an enormous military commitment around the Eurasian continent was the policy of massive nuclear retaliation. As in Europe, the United States believed an Asian internal balance of power was not achievable, and, fearing a Moscow-dominated Communist hegemony, had moved into Asia and the northern tier of the Middle East to create an externally achieved balance of power.

The United States did not want to remain alone in resisting Asian communism. As in Europe, our policy was to provide a shield behind which non-Communist Asian nations would develop, prosper, and grow to check Communist expansion. The most obvious anti-Communist asset in the Far East was Japan. Before the Cold War had permeated Asia, the American occupation reforms had aimed to create an unarmed, modernizing, democratic Japan that would not constitute any future military threat to its neighbors.

Civil rights, including women's rights, liberal arts education, land redistribution, economic decentralization, labor unionization with the right to strike, and open elections with universal suffrage were instituted. The United States opened up its market and resources to the Japanese economy. With the coming of the Cold War to Asia, American policy shifted to create Japan as an anti-Communist bulwark in East Asia that would be economically self-sustaining and tied to the United States militarily. The occupation terminated when the peace treaty was signed in 1951, with Japan becoming an unarmed ally protected by American military forces and limited to a weak, internal Self-Defense Force. Japan, therefore, could devote all its energy and resources to reconstruction and the development of a technologically modern, export economy with access to non-Communist resource basins and markets.

The internal social, educational, and political reforms took root in Japan because a majority of the Japanese recognized that these reforms best served their interests. After 1960 the Japanese political system became stabilized with Liberal Democratic Party dominance, within a multiparty system that basically accepted these reforms. Japan concentrated on an export-driven economy with government direction and assistance, and by 1963 it was able to post its first trade surplus with the United States. As American involvement escalated in Asia with the introduction of American power into former French Indo-China, the United States began to encourage Japan to revise its interpretation of Article 9 of its constitution and build up its self-defense forces. To that end the United States returned Iwo Jima and Okinawa to Japanese sovereignty, suggesting that Japan begin to take increasing conventional responsibility for their own defense. The Japanese public and government were reluctant to rearm significantly or to alter their very successful demilitarized stance toward the world. A ceiling of 1 percent of the GNP was placed on defense expenditures, so that a slow, incremental conventional military build-up occurred with strategic nuclear defense remaining in the hands of the Americans.

With the United States devoting a significantly higher percentage of its GNP to defense, by the 1970s and 1980s Japan was steadily able to develop export products that could significantly penetrate segments of the American market. Major American industries, for example, auto, TV, and communications, became engulfed or threatened by Japanese imports. Trade tensions emerged as Americans, while providing Japan with security, perceived Japan as creating a nonlevel trading field in which Japan remained protectionist toward many American exports. The nature of the world was changing even before the end of the Cold War. We had encouraged the Japanese to rebuild and become an anti-Communist bulwark in the Far East. While the Cold War had become essentially stalemated until 1989, a new, nonmilitary challenger of our own making had emerged to endanger American productivity and markets (internal and external). American attention was moving away from a single-minded focus on the Soviet threat by the mid-1980s.

With respect to Communist China, as a result of the Korean War the United States developed an extremely antagonistic stance. American policy treated the two Communist giants differently: The Soviet Union was to be militarily contained but to be gradually, hopefully, integrated into the community of nations; China, on the other hand, was not only to be militarily contained but also isolated from the international community, thus forcing Beijing toward Moscow. The United States encouraged the international community to follow its lead in having no diplomatic relations with the mainland, imposing an economic blockade on trade of a declared outlaw for intervening against U.N. forces on the Korean peninsula, and denying it the Chinese seat in the United Nations. In re-entering the Chinese civil war by signing an alliance with Taiwan, the United States placed itself in a position to intervene if the mainland Chinese government ever moved to finish the civil war. In 1955, when the first Quemoy-Matsu Crisis emerged, the United States moved naval forces to within three miles of the mainland to signal its intent to prevent Communist aggression against these Nationalist-held islands. A similar American response came in 1958 when the crisis re-emerged, and the threat of massive retaliation once again forced the Chinese to stand down. American policy was determined that communism, Chinese or otherwise, would not extend its perimeter in Asia.

In the early 1960s when the position of the anti-Communist regime in South Vietnam began to weaken, the United States made a decision to stop the southerly spread of communism.[6] Policy makers believed that if South Vietnam fell, other small Southeast Asian nations would fall like a line of dominos. Vietnam also became linked to the Berlin crisis because America's credibility to resist communism had been undermined ninety miles off our shore at the Bay of Pigs. To enhance our credibility, especially to deter the Soviets from misreading American intentions in the Berlin crisis, the United States acted to shore up the Saigon regime. Nevertheless, the South Vietnamese situation continued to deteriorate, and by 1963 the arguments for continued American involvement increasingly revolved around containing the southward expansion of Chinese Communist influence. After our Korean experience, the United States did not want another war with China and therefore respected Chinese declared limits that American ground forces should not proceed north of the 17th parallel and North Vietnamese agriculture should not be destroyed by bombing the crucial levee system of North Vietnam. Thus, war was avoided between the United States and China, but the limitations placed on American power preserved the "privileged sanctuary" of North Vietnam and provided the base from which, despite the introduction of half a million American troops and massive air power, the North Vietnamese were able to press southward to complete victory by 1975.

The Sino-Soviet schism that had emerged in 1960 continued to intensify and, as ideological and strategic linkages dissolved, more traditional animosities between the two Communist giants resurfaced. In 1964, China exploded its first nuclear device, but quickly thereafter China descended into chaos with the beginning of the Cultural Revolution in 1966. The Soviet Union, now fearing a nuclear-armed society south of its 4,500 mile border with China, contemplated military intervention to strip China of its nuclear capability. In March of 1969 when the Soviets asked the United States what our policy would be to such a Soviet intervention, the new Nixon administration replied that it would condemn the Soviet action. With this reply a new chapter in American-Chinese relations began to unfold as the United States once again moved into a semiprotector position to mainland China. The Korean War era had receded. Now Communist China would be used to check Soviet power in Asia, and the United States worked with the Sino-Soviet schism to create an internal Asian balance of power. The earlier assumption of monolithic Eurasian communism that underlay our involvement in Vietnam was scuttled, and thus an American withdrawal from Vietnam was strategically possible.

With this fundamentally altered strategic situation in Asia, American policy under Nixon-Kissinger changed very rapidly. The United States concurred with an overwhelming majority of the United Nations in 1971 to have the Communist Chinese replace the Nationalists within the United Nations. The Nationalists, who had represented China from 1945 until 1971, rejected the policy option of creating a sovereign, independent Taiwan and quietly left the United Nations. The Nationalist government continued to insist that Taiwan was an integral part of China. Kissinger flew to Beijing in 1971 to open direct American-Chinese negotiations, which led to President Nixon's visit in 1972. The culminating document of that visit was the Shanghai Communiqué, in which the United States agreed that since both Chinese governments believed that Taiwan was a part of China, a solution to the question of Taiwan's relationship with the mainland would be left to the two Chinese governments, as long as violence was avoided. Thereupon a slow normalization of Chinese-American relations began, as Soviet power expanded in the 1970s after the American debacle in Vietnam. The United States began to play its China card by allowing China access to American and Western technology, finance, education, and administrative skills. The United States had returned to its 1945 China policy in relation to the Soviet Union; instead of Nationalist China checking power in Asia we would deal with a Communist Chinese regime. As the United States was withdrawing from the Far Eastern Asian mainland, with the exception of South Korea, it moved into an external balancer position to help deter a possible Soviet attack on China. When Deng Xiaoping was in the United States in 1978, he proposed a Chinese-American military alliance. Deng feared the Soviets might strike to wipe out China's strategic nuclear capability before it developed the range to reach European Russia and thereby achieve a genuine nuclear deterrence against the Soviet Union. The United States rejected Deng's proposal, instead wishing to retain the flexibility of an eternal balancer with more limited involvement. President Carter did, however, finally recognize the Beijing regime with an exchange of ambassadors. Because the Communists would not reciprocate diplomatically unless the recognizing power accepted the Beijing regime as the government of all of China, the United States withdrew its diplomatic personnel from Taipei and concomitantly terminated its alliance with Taiwan.

As long as Beijing feared a possible Soviet attack, it remained in a special protective relationship with the United States. By the mid-1980s when China achieved the missile range to reach European Russia, thereby gaining an effective nuclear deterrent, China altered its dependent stance with the United States and returned to a more independent worldwide diplomatic stance. The United States continued to encourage and support Deng's internal economic, educational, religious, and cultural reforms to integrate China into the international community and to open up investment and trade opportunities for American business. In 1979 the United States granted China Most Favored Nation (MFN) trading status to assist China in its modernization by allowing it more open access to American markets. The trading relationship steadily grew until Deng's crackdown on the pro-democracy demonstrators in Tiananmen Square in 1989. While Deng continued the modernization of the Chinese economy by favoring the emergence of the private sector and its integration into the world economy, he continued to assert unity through Communist party authoritarian rule. The ruling authorities did not want to emulate the Soviet Union's fate. The Tiananmen Square events posed great difficulty to the United States, however, which favored Deng's economic reforms but also desired the emergence of a more open Chinese political system that respected human rights.

Although the United States had come to emphasize its relations with mainland China, it still retained a meaningful relationship with Taiwan. The United States continued to sell defensive weapons to Taipei; Beijing's objections to this were minimal until the break-up of the Soviet Union, since it did not want the Russians to replace the Americans in Taiwan. Brezhnev had said that the Russians would like to occupy any warm seat left in Asia by the retreating Americans after the fall of Saigon. While Taiwan became a steady customer for American defensive conventional weapons, the primary relationship with the United States became economic. The Japanese had developed Taiwan's economic infrastructure during their fifty years of occupation, the island experienced minimal bombing during World War II, and with American economic aid in the 1950s, the economy had flourished to the point that, in 1965, Taiwan became the first country to have its American foreign aid terminated. By the 1980s Taiwan had become one of the Pacific Rim's Tigers, and it had accumulated a large surplus in its trade with the United States. Mainland China had seen Taiwan become a Chinese economic success story with essentially an authoritarian regime. By the late 1980s, however, the mass of Taiwanese citizens successfully began to open up the political system and use the electoral mechanism for legislative representation. The Americans supported the opening of their political system, and both governments were appalled by the Tiananmen Square massacre. Hence, the United States and Taiwan are watching closely to see how Communist China treats the Hong Kong political system when the British withdraw in 1997. Although ties are slowly linking Taiwan to the mainland, the future of Hong Kong within China could in part determine Taiwan's relations with the mainland.

South of China, in Southeast Asia, the withdrawal of the American forces (1972) and the fall of the Saigon regime (1975) provided a "warm seat" into which the Soviets flowed as they sent their military southward in Asia. Vietnam felt it needed the Soviets' assistance for its newly unified state because it feared a traditional Chinese sphere of influence policy in the region. The Communist Khmer Rouge had won the civil war next door in Cambodia. The Chinese, hoping to gain a satellite in Cambodia, supported the Khmer Rouge in its efforts to halt the spread of Vietnamese-Soviet influence; the Vietnamese responded by attacking and conquering most of Cambodia. The United States, by maintaining a linkage with Thailand through the weakened SEATO alliance, assisted anti-Communist guerrillas in Cambodia while the Chinese supported the remnants of the Khmer Rouge. Implicitly, the United States and China moved to preserve the independence of Thailand against Vietnamese pressure. While Vietnam had captured enormous stockpiles of American weapons and possessed a victorious army, it became bogged down in Cambodia, and that quagmire drew away resources from the sputtering Vietnamese economy.

The once feared domino theory, which in part drew the United States into Vietnam, did not materialize. Instead Thailand, Malaysia, Brunei, Singapore, Indonesia, and the Philippines formed a regional organization, the Association of Southeast Asian Nations (ASEAN), which helped develop and coordinate new policies that were to spur the modernization of their economies. By the 1980s, led by the "new Tiger," Singapore, the economies of this region, with the exception of the Philippines, expanded rapidly, as Southeast Asia became one of the fastest developing regions in the world. Trade with the United States grew concomitantly. With the deterioration of the Soviet economy in the 1980s, after 1988 the Soviet Union lessened its economic and military support to Vietnam and eventually withdrew its naval forces from Camranh Bay. Vietnam, seeking a protector from China, which had attacked it in 1979, invited the United States back into Camranh Bay, but the United States rejected the offer. America did not want to repeat its past involvement error; in fact, the United States distanced itself from Vietnam, excluding all trade, economic, and diplomatic relations until the MIA question was resolved. Strategically, by the end of the Cold War the United States had pulled back from the mainland of Asia with the exception of its continued military presence on the Korean peninsula and a nominal presence in Thailand. The United States defense perimeter once again was offshore with

American power in a broad arc from the Aleutians, Japan (the key alliance), Guam, and the Pacific Strategic Trust Territories, the Philippines (but with hostility to American bases at Clark Field and Subic Bay growing), and Australia. The United States security policy had finally responded and incorporated the emergence of an internal Asian balance of power into its policy.

THE SUBCONTINENT

Until the communization of China and the Korean War, the United States had never been involved in the Subcontinent, as it was considered a British preserve. With Mao's victory in 1949, however, the new emergent democracy in India became a major model option for Asia, and American foreign aid began to flow to India in that year. The United States wanted a stable democratic India, and to that end India became a major recipient of foreign aid, primarily in the form of food aid to help feed India's burgeoning population. In 1965, President Johnson extended massive food shipments to India to prevent large-scale starvation, even as the American engagement was deepening in Vietnam. Thereafter, with the coming of the Green Revolution's dramatic increase in food production to Southern Asia, India moved toward food self-sufficiency, and American food aid declined. At the security level, the outbreak of the Korean War induced the United States to seek anti-Communist allies in Southern Asia. Secretary of State John Foster Dulles (of the Eisenhower Administration) asked the Southern Asians to view their security on a North-South axis, that is, to view the Communist giants of China and the Soviet Union as their primary security threats. India's Premier Nehru did not accept such an analysis. He would not link India to the West when India had so recently freed itself from the British Crown. India wanted an unarmed, neutral, nonaligned policy, which included peaceful relations between the two most populous Asian countries, China and India. Pakistan, less secure and newly separated from Hindu India, accepted the American offer to receive American economic and military assistance and joined both SEATO and CENTO. India became nervous as Pakistan's armed forces were re-equipped with American arms, for the question of partitioned Kashmir remained unsettled. India worried that Pakistan considered its primary security axis not on a North-South axis but on an East-West axis. Thus, India armed itself sufficiently to protect its western border with Pakistan.

India's minimally armed, nonalignment policy was placed under severe stress as a result of China's building a road across Indian-claimed Ladakh to supply its forces in suppressing the Tibetan peoples' rebellion against the imposition of Chinese Communist rule. In the middle of the Cuban Missile Crisis, war broke out between India and China over the Ladakh region, and it quickly spread to the Assam region of Northeast India. The Indian military was ill prepared to fight the Soviet-equipped Chinese forces. Although India was not a member of SEATO, the United States moved elements of its 7th Fleet into the Bay of Bengal and temporarily extended an air cover guarantee over Northern India to deter the Chinese from using their airplanes positioned on the Tibetan plateau. India feared that its policy of nonalignment would be undermined by its dependence on Western military assistance, but it was able to preserve nonalignment when the Soviets switched sides and also offered India military aid against China. The Sino-Indian war ended India's policy of minimal militarization, as it initiated a large-scale arms build up to counter Chinese power in the Himalayas. The Soviet Union became the primary supplier of weapons to India, as India distrusted America's siding with China against the Soviet Union after 1969 and its arming of its subcontinent adversary, Pakistan.

When war broke out between India and Pakistan over Kashmir in 1965, contrary to the agreed-upon limitations on the use of American military equipment against India, Pakistan propelled its American-equipped tank forces against India.[7] The use of American equipment greatly inflamed the Indian government and its people against the United States, even though we were supplying massive food assistance to India. The Soviet Union reaped the benefits of its policy when India defeated Pakistan, and five years later India and the Soviet Union signed a special Treaty of Friendship. The Nixon administration perceived this treaty as significantly weakening India's nonaligned Cold War policy and moved the United States into an anti-Indian policy when war once again erupted in 1971 between Pakistan and India. A secessionist movement had emerged among the Bengali people of East Pakistan, and the Pakistan army of West Pakistan moved to suppress the Bengali rebellion with American-supplied munitions. To deter the massive flight of Bengalis into the Calcutta region of India, India mobilized its army along the East Bengali border. To dissuade India from intervening, the United States once again moved elements of its 7th Fleet into the Bay of Bengal. The Indians, nevertheless, successfully intervened in East Bengal and established the conditions for severing East Bengal from West Pakistan to create the independent state of Bangladesh. India had become militarily dominant on the subcontinent.

American policy had made the Indians distrustful and wary of the United States, but Soviet overplaying of its hand and India's increasing ability to build its own weapons reaffirmed its neutral policy. Pakistan withdrew from SEATO when Saigon fell, but its CENTO membership became useful when Soviet forces invaded Afghanistan in 1979. Pakistan became a conduit for American weapons to the Afghans, although some of these weapons were diverted by the Pakistan military to strengthen its forces opposite India. India initially took a low key approach to the Soviet incursion in Afghanistan, quietly urging the Soviets to withdraw, but when the Soviets persevered, New Delhi began to lean toward Washington and to sign arms deals with the United States until Gorbachev withdrew Soviet forces in 1989. As a consequence of this episode and India's need for American technology, capital, and trade, by the end of the Cold War American-Indian relations were more positive. The warming of American-Indian relations was also assisted by the loosening of American ties with Pakistan. The Soviet withdrawal from Afghanistan and the breakup of the Soviet Union undercut Pakistan's strategic worth, and Pakistan's drive for a nuclear capability linked to the increasing tension in Kashmir moved the United States to view Pakistan as a proliferation problem.

THE MIDDLE EAST

This region, extending from Morocco to Iran and encompassing numerous nations with varied competing interests, became an area of extreme complexity for the United States. Until the end of the Second World War it was considered within a European sphere, but as the French and British withdrew, the United States was slowly drawn in for a multiplicity of reasons. Our interests in the Middle East included the following:

1. "Freedom of the Seas" through the choke points and waterbodies of the region
2. Access to trade, investment opportunities, and resources, especially oil
3. Preservation of regimes amenable to American and Western interests
4. Limiting the influence of regimes hostile to Western interests
5. Resisting any transnational movement or national expansion hostile to Western interests
6. Containment and limitation of Soviet encroachment and influence in the Middle East
7. Preservation of the state of Israel

These numerous American interests in such a complex region invariably produced many overlapping and, at times, contradictory policies.

"Freedom of the Seas," one of the oldest and most primary of American foreign policy principles, was a major factor for engaging American power in the region. As British naval strength declined in the Mediterranean, the United States introduced the powerful 6th Fleet, which throughout the Cold War buttressed and legitimized American resolve in the region. The United States sought to maintain access through the choke points of Gibraltar, the Suez Canal, the Straits of Tiran, the Straits of Hormuz, and the water bodies of the Mediterranean, Red Sea, Arabian Sea, and the Persian Gulf. When President Abdul Nasser of Egypt nationalized the Suez Canal and permitted the upgrading of Soviet presence after each Israeli victory—especially the Suez Crisis in 1956 and the Six-Day War in 1967—the United States tried vigorously to weaken the Soviet presence. When Egypt's Soviet option for defeating Israel was proven to be nonviable, with the result of the Yom Kippur War (1973), the United States, through protracted negotiations that lasted through three American presidencies, achieved the Camp David agreement of 1978 wherein Egypt tied itself to the United States and the West.[8] Earlier in 1967, when the United States wavered on the principle of "Freedom of the Seas," it lost control of the situation. When Nasser threatened to blockade the Straits of Tiran and deny Israeli access from its southern port of Elat down the Gulf of Aquaba to the Red Sea, the United States did not immediately fulfill its guarantee to Israel for its access through the Straits of Tiran. The Israelis, therefore, unilaterally launched an attack on Egypt, which led to their victory in what became known as the Six-Day War of 1967. In the Persian Gulf region, the United States encouraged the British to remain as long as possible, but with Britain's pull-out from Aden, Oman, and the Gulf Sheikdoms in 1971, the United States slowly established a minimal naval presence at Bahrain.

When the victorious regime of the Ayatollah Khomeini in Iran precipitated the American-hostage crisis in 1979, the United States sent major naval forces to the Arabian Sea. The situation became very touchy as the Soviets anchored a cruiser in the middle of the Straits of Hormuz. After the great tension of the helicopter rescue attempt, the Soviets withdrew the cruiser. Later during the 1980s when the Iran-Iraq War intensified and threats to international shipping became more prevalent, the United States established a larger, more permanent naval presence in the Gulf to maintain access through that water body. Clearly, by the end of the Cold War the United States had moved to fill the vacuum created twenty years earlier by the British withdrawal.

Initially the American interest in the development and preservation of international access to the important oil reserves of the Middle East was made to assist the economies of Western Europe and non-Communist Asia. By the early 1970s, when America was no longer self-sufficient in oil, the United States itself was increasingly drawn in for its own energy needs. To this end, the United States attempted to keep in power regimes that were amenable to Western access to oil. When the Mossadegh regime emerged in Iran in 1953, the United States covertly moved to reinstall the Shah. With oil profits as the basis of wealth for the Shah's military forces after 1973, the United States even encouraged Iran to increase the price of oil. The United States wanted Iran to fill the vacuum in the Gulf left by the disengaging British, but that policy reached a dead end when the Shah fell from power and the revolutionary fundamentalist government, which viewed the United States as a Satanic force, turned hostile to the United States.

The country with the greatest oil reserves, Saudi Arabia, became of prime interest to the United States. To counterbalance the surrounding British power, in 1933 the Saudis invited in American oil engineers and used American involvement to deter any nearby threat. As the importance of Saudi oil reserves and production increased during succeeding decades, the United States was more than willing to continue in that capacity. Throughout the

Cold War the United States moved to keep the Soviet Union at bay, particularly when it gained a foothold in South Yemen (Aden) and supported civil war in Oman. In 1961 when the new Baathist regime in Iraq threatened Kuwait (a precursor to the 1990 crisis), the United States supported the British when they sent in troops to prevent an Iraqi incursion. Such an Iraqi move would implicitly endanger Saudi Arabia. Between 1962 and 1968, when Soviet-equipped Egypt became engaged in the Yemeni civil war in order to gain a foothold on the Arabian peninsula, the United States strenuously supported Saudi Arabia in assisting the conservative forces in the Yemeni hills. When the Shah's regime in Iran fell, the United States developed the concept of a rapid development force, which could be flown to preconstructed sites in Saudi Arabia, since the Saudi government would not allow the permanent stationing of foreign troops within its borders. When two anti-western regimes, Saddam Hussein of Iraq and the Ayatollah regime of Iran, became embraced in a deadly war (1980–1988), the United States pursued a balanced policy to make sure that neither side would gain a clear victory, thereby gaining the capability to endanger Saudi Arabia. After that war the United States, wishing to gain influence in Baghdad, placated Saddam Hussein too much, and miscalculations as to American intentions were made that precipitated the Kuwaiti crisis of 1990.

Beyond Saudi Arabia and Kuwait the United States moved to support any government in the Middle East, usually moderate and conservative, which was amenable to American interests. Assistance was extended to Turkey (a strategic, emerging democracy); the monarchies of Morocco, Jordan, and the United Arab Emirates; Iraq (until the military coup of 1958); Libya (until 1969); the Shah's regime in Iran; Tunisia; the military regimes of Sadat and Mubarak in Egypt; the Sudan (until the rise of the fundamentalists); and the Lebanese democracy. The United States inserted Marines into Lebanon in 1983 as part of a multinational western force to provide security for the beginning of the resurrection of a unified Lebanese state. The American withdrawal of its forces after major loss of life tragically permitted the continuation of the multifaceted civil war in Lebanon, resulting in the country's continued occupation and dismemberment by foreign forces.[9]

In the past forty years, as anti-Westernism has risen in the Middle East, a series of governments have increasingly developed policies hostile to American and Western interests. Quadhafi's government in Libya supported a vast array of anti-western measures, which ultimately provoked an American military response after major acts of terrorism were attributed to that regime. Algerian support of the Polisario rebels in former Spanish Sahara, claimed and occupied by Moroco, produced American assistance to King Hussein's Moroccan government. Syrian President Assad's intransigence on a whole range of issues, including the Camp David Agreement and the Lebanese crisis, evoked an American response.

Beyond specific regimes, the United States has been opposed to any transnational Arab grouping or national expansion that would produce a larger entity that could threaten American interests. President Nasser's United Arab Republic (UAR 1958–1969) posed a clear threat to many of our interests in the region; fortunately for the United States, that attempt at transnational union was thwarted when Syria regained its sovereignty in 1961. Colonel Quadhafi of Libya tried to form a series of larger, transnational Arab political links that could have harmed Western interests but all of them dissolved in the shifting political winds sweeping the region. Fertile Crescent Baathism (a form of Arab Socialism), in concept very similar to Nasserism, projected a major ideological opportunity for Arab unity, but the two Baathist regimes—Syria and Iraq—have been locked in their own protracted struggle. Each of these regimes has asserted its own national expansionist doctrines. The United States has opposed both the concept of Greater Syria, incorporating major segments of Lebanon and northern Jordan, and Saddam Hussein's expansion of Iraq into the major oil-rich regions of Iran and Kuwait. U.S. opposition has also been directed against the exporting of Iran's fundamentalist revolution throughout the Middle East.[10] By limiting the growth of regimes hostile to Western interests and supporting regimes amenable to our interests, the United States implicitly has pursued a continual policy of balkanization within the region.

In early 1950, as Soviet-American competition spread around the entire communist Eurasian periphery, the United States tried to continue Great Britain's policy of totally excluding Russian influence from the Middle East. The United States attempted to create a Middle East NATO (CENTO), embracing all the newly independent states in an anti-communist alliance. Nasser of Egypt was positively inclined to join until the United States refused to provide Egypt with ten divisions worth of conventional weapons: The United States feared their potential deployment against Israel. With Nasser leading many Arab states into a nonaligned policy, Russia was first to penetrate the region with the Czech arms deal with Egypt in 1955. When the United States withdrew its offer of assistance for the construction of the Aswan Dam, the Soviet Union filled the gap by assisting in its construction. Pursuing a policy of total opportunism to increase their influence and diminish American-Western influence, the dual approach of arms transfers and economic assistance became the Soviets' primary mechanism for entry into the Middle East. Middle East regimes were always wary of dealing with atheistic, expansionist communism, and they always turned to the West and the United States first to counter the demonstratively superior armed might of Israel. When they were unsuccessful in receiving weapons from the West, after 1955 countries increasingly turned to the Soviet arms option; thereafter, Moscow was able to sign a whole series of agreements with the following regimes: Nassar's Egypt, Quadhafi's Libya, anti-French Algeria, Sudan, Baathist Syria, Saddam Hussein's Iraq, and even Jordan. Along with the arms transfers came economic aid, particularly to oil-deficient Syria. The existence of a powerful

Israel, increasingly buttressed by the United States with resulting Arab unease, became the primary motivation for Arabs turning to Moscow. The Soviets were opportunistically willing to deal with any kind of Arab government. They were only able to implant one communist regime in the Middle East, however; Marxist South Yemen existed precariously until 1990.

Each time the Soviets made a Middle-Eastern advance, the U.S. reactivity moved to counter that incursion. As a result, both superpowers were unable to establish any kind of sphere of influence below CENTO. Caught in an action-reaction syndrome, both superpowers were sucked on opposite sides into a multitudinous array of local struggles, each trying to deny the other advantage. The danger of such a vacuum of power sucking the two powers into dangerous confrontation occurred on the fifth day of the Yom Kippur War, when the United States went to a level of nuclear alert to deter the Soviets from sending nuclear forces to Egypt. As Israeli forces moved westward, crossing over the Suez Canal, Moscow moved into a protecting position to keep Israel's forces from advancing on Cairo and the Nile River. Although less serious than the Cuban Missile Crisis, this short-lived nuclear confrontation profoundly influenced both superpowers' nuclear policy in the Middle East. In the immediate threat the Soviets never did insert nuclear forces with supporting conventional power into Egypt, and the United States itself worked assiduously to limit the westward advance of Israeli forces. From then on both superpowers, no matter how involved on opposite sides of various crises in the Middle East, made sure their competition did not escalate to a nuclear confrontation. Thus both the dangerous American helicopter rescue attempt in Iran and the extremely volatile Iran-Iraq War were defused of nuclear implications.

The final major American interest in the Middle East, the preservation of the state of Israel, became increasingly important to the United States during the Cold War era. Even before the announcement of Israel's independence in May 1948, U.S. congressional resolutions and American support for the United Nations Partition Plan of 1947 were evidence of special American interest in the victims of the European holocaust. During Israel's fight to maintain independence, private American financial assistance was crucial, and American support for Israel's admission into the United Nations was a necessity. During the election of 1948 American support for Israel became an important part of that campaign, and ever since American support for Israel has been an integral part of the internal American political fabric. Israel has by far become the largest recipient of American private and public assistance in the entire world.

In 1950, when the West still held an arms transfer monopoly, Great Britain, France, and the United States agreed that they would control their flow of arms into the Middle East so that the existing internal balance of power would not be upset, and especially that Israel would not be endangered by neighboring Arab States. That principle has remained a key feature of American arms transfers ever since, and our adherence to that policy provided an eventual opening for the transfer of Soviet arms to Israel's neighbors. Until the Six-Day War of 1967, France and Great Britain were the primary arms suppliers to Israel, but with Israel's resounding victory in that war, both Western European countries diminished their military support. When Israel became seriously endangered during the first days of the Yom Kippur War of 1973, the United States rushed to fill the gap and ever since has remained overwhelmingly the primary external weapons source for Israel, including an enormous stockpiling of weapons in Israel for any future eventuality. As Saudi security became threatened by ensuing events in Iraq and Iran in the 1970s and 1980s, American arms flowed into Saudi Arabia, but with tight limitations on the types of weapons and their deployment in Saudi Arabia, so that Israel would not be threatened. The United States attempted to separate the militarization and tension of the Gulf region from the tension of Israel with its neighbors in the eastern Mediterranean.

From 1950 until 1973 the United States attempted to pursue an even-handed policy between Israel and its Arab neighbors. The United States opposed the joint Israeli, British, and French attack on Nasser's Egypt during the 1956 Suez crisis and negotiated the Israeli withdrawal from the Sinai peninsula by sponsoring the creation of the U.N. peacekeeping force in the Eastern Sinai (1956–1967) and guaranteeing Israel's passage through the Straits of Tiran, thus deterring any future Egyptian blockade. When the United Nations suddenly withdrew the Sinai force in May 1967 and the United States hesitated in upholding its Straits of Tiran guarantee (the United States was fully embroiled in the Vietnam quagmire), Israel took its security into its own hands and went on to win a resounding victory against Egypt, Jordan, and Syria. The potential bittersweet fruits of the victory, that is, the Sinai, Gaza Strip, West Bank, and Golan Heights, were all occupied by Israel, but the United States consistently made it clear that it would not recognize the permanent annexation of any of these territories to the state of Israel. This policy placed the United States in opposition to the Likud coalition government's (Begin and Shamir) policies of incorporation of the latter three territories.

When Israel was gravely endangered during the initial phases of the Yom Kippur War, the United States rushed military assistance to it to prevent any possibility of an Egyptian-Syrian breakthrough. Kissinger and Nixon, however, did not want a total Israeli victory, as had occurred in 1967, which had led to Israeli overconfidence and intransigence: By controlling the flow of arms and diplomatic pressure, the United States did not allow a total Israeli victory in 1973. Egyptian military units remained east of Suez. The military impasse established the conditions for a compromise on the Sinai, which ultimately led to the Camp David Agreement of 1978. Israel withdrew, the Sinai was demilitarized, a U.N. presence was reinserted, buttressed by American-manned sensor devices, and Egyptian-Israeli relations moved toward normalization. The insertion of the U.N. peacekeeping presence, successfully deployed in the Sinai from 1956–1967, became a significant option for the United States around Israeli's borders. The U.N. presence was established in the Golan Heights as part of a withdrawal agreement, but a too-small U.N. force was placed in Southern Lebanon. It was not large enough to separate the warring parties, deter the Israeli attack of Beirut in 1982, or to secure the volatile southern Lebanon-Israeli border region. The continued Soviet arming of Syria throughout the remainder of the Cold War maintained high tension in the region even though the United States had established an alliance relationship with Israel. The Middle East, to the end of the Cold War, remained a very dangerous zone of the American-Soviet competition.

SUB-SAHARAN AFRICA

This region, located the furthest away from both superpowers, remained on the periphery of the Cold War as the antagonists concentrated their energies and attention on areas of more immediate concern. The United States signaled its unwillingness to become directly involved when the Congo Crisis erupted in 1960, as the Belgians too quickly exited the Congo and it descended into chaos. The United States supported the multilateral approach of the United Nations by largely financing the twenty-thousand-man U.N. force, composed of neutral military forces, to re-establish internal order and territorial unity. When the U.N. operation was withdrawn in 1964, the United States supported the Mobutu regime with economic and military assistance. This regime remained in power throughout the remainder of the Cold War.

In West Africa, where the British and French had prepared those societies more successfully for independence, the United States essentially left that region to European influence. The United States remained neutral throughout the Nigerian Civil War (Biafra, 1967–1970) and left the Libyan incursion across the Sahara into Chad to be handled by the French. The new East African nations of Kenya, Uganda, and Tanzania were left to the British.

In the Horn of Africa (Ethiopia and Somalia), close to the Middle East at the southern end of the Red Sea, the fall of Haile Selasse's pro-Western regime in 1975 and its replacement by a Marxist regime in Addis Abbaba, produced a deepening reactive American engagement. With Cuban forces assisting the Ethiopian government in its attempts to suppress the rebellion in Eritrea on the Red Sea coast and the Somali rebellion in the Ogadan desert, the United States reversed its policy toward the formerly pro-Russian Marxist government in Somalia.[11] When the Cuban-Ethiopian forces successfully suppressed the Somalia rebellion in the Ogaden and threatened Somalia itself, the United States diplomatically came to the support of Mogadishu. When the Soviets had gained a base in South Yemen and were constructing another base on an Ethiopian island in the southern Red Sea off the coast of Eritrea, the

United States actively considered constructing a base in Berabera, Somalia. The United States finally settled for port rights in Mombasa, Kenya. With the Somalia border respected, the United States allowed the Eritrean-Ethiopian struggle to remain essentially an internal affair.

Simultaneously with the fall of the Haile Selasse regime in Ethiopia, the last European Empire in Africa collapsed. The Portuguese had fought with American NATO equipment for many years; the United States had needed the Portuguese Azores as a touchdown point for its supply line to the Middle East. But by the mid-1970s their fight had exhausted them and revolution had come to Lisbon. Marxist regimes emerged in both Angola and Mozambique, and both these societies descended into civil war. The United States did not engage itself in Mozambique on the Indian Ocean, but the tribal struggle in Angola became of great concern. The Marxist forces in Luanda, with significant Soviet support, won the initial phase and formed a government. The United States moved to support the southern tribes under Savimbi, and during the ongoing struggle significant Cuban forces entered the fray in support of the Marxist government. Although the Cuban troops ultimately departed, the ferocious struggle continued throughout the Cold War with significant superpower support. At one point even South African forces fought in support of the anti-Luanda rebels.

The country of greatest ultimate concern was South Africa, with its great resources, investment opportunities, and its strategic position at the tip of Africa. Apartheid was imposed in 1948 by the Afrikaners, and while the Americans morally condemned apartheid, the United States maintained a hands-off policy in pursuit of its strategic and economic interests. As anti-apartheid pressure increased in the international community, especially within the United Nations, the United States agreed to an arms transfer ban but opposed efforts to pressure the Pretoria government with economic sanctions. President Carter, through his U.N. representative Andrew Young, took a firmer stand with his support of human rights, but his successor, President Reagan, initially returned to the traditional American stance on apartheid.

During the 1980s, as international pressure intensified, the Reagan administration developed a dual policy; while maintaining its traditional policy toward the internal situation within South Africa, the United States encouraged South Africa to disengage its involvement from its newly independent northern neighbors, which under European rule had earlier provided a protective buffer. The South Africans were covertly active in the Mozambiquen civil war, had militarily engaged Luanda's forces in southern Angola, and had resisted U.N. resolutions to move South-West Africa (Namibia) toward self-determining status. By 1992, with American encouragement, South Africa had disengaged from all three neighbors.

Overcoming a Reagan veto, in 1986 the U.S. Congress passed a series of economic sanctions and encouraged American investors to review their involvement in South Africa. A worldwide move to pressure South Africa economically, the increasing willingness of the African National Congress (ANC) to resort to violence, the collapse of totalitarianism in East Europe, and the ensuing retreat of Soviet activity from Africa induced President De Klerk to revolutionize Pretoria's policy by freeing Nelson Mandela and beginning negotiations for the peaceful emergence of black majority rule.

WESTERN HEMISPHERE

The vast regions south of the United States had been, until President Franklin Roosevelt's noninterventionist policy, divided into two spheres: (1) the Caribbean and Central America, in which the United States had repeatedly intervened and (2) the large landmass of South America, in which the United States wanted friendly economic and political relations but had never directly inserted American forces. In 1948, at the beginning of the Cold War, the United States lined up on its side all the nations in both regions through a reinvigorated Organization of American States (OAS) and the Pact of Bogota. To the north, Canada became firmly aligned through its membership in NATO and its integrated involvement in North American defense through NORAD.

In South America the United States wanted continued access to natural resources, the maintenance of trade and investment opportunities, and the elimination of any regime, especially Marxist, that might undercut U.S. interests and at worst align itself with the Communist bloc and Moscow. South America traditionally experienced alternating cycles of dictatorship and democracy, and, as these cycles continued to unfold in South America, the United States lessened its emphasis on encouraging democracy out of fear that the early phase of a democratic era might allow the political left to emerge and form a government through the ballot box that could endanger the United States, particularly at the security level. As a consequence, the United States developed close ties with the military in most South American countries and was more than willing to work with them to suppress the left wing of the political spectrum. The United States supported the Brazilian military when it unseated the Goulart government in 1965 and covertly worked to undermine the Allende government in Chile and to permit the repressive Pinochet regime to emerge and tie Chile to the West. The United States remained quiet as the military fastened its hold on Argentina, although we did side with Great Britain when the military government in Buenos Aires attempted, by military force, to annex the Falkland (Malvinas) Islands. Immediately after the British victory, the United States encouraged both sides to settle the long-term future of those islands through diplomacy. As part of the Monroe Doctrine the United States had always supported the decolonization of the New World, but when it appeared that Cheddi Jagan (a Marxist) might come to power when British Guiana became independent, the United States fiscally supported the British to remain for several years past their original withdrawal date to preclude that possibility. The United States assisted local forces in the Andean countries of Peru and Bolivia in preventing any left-wing guerrilla forces acting under the tutelage or influence of Che Guevara's concepts of revolution from seizing power by force. The United States, nevertheless, supported the democratically elected government of Betancourt in Venezuela in the 1960s to provide a democratic model for Latin America to counter Castro's Cuban communism.

In Central America and the islands of the Caribbean, however, the American engagement became more complex as the Cold War unfolded. To keep these countries aligned with the United States and to dissipate their fear of the "Colossus of the North," the United States attempted to maintain a non-interventionalist policy. However, when the Castro government moved to the left and began to align itself with the Soviet bloc, the United States initiated the ill-fated Bay of Pigs invasion. When that invasion ran into trouble, the United States refused to directly involve U.S. forces. The resultant loss of American credibility in Khruschev's eyes led the Soviet leader to risk the insertion of Soviet missiles into Cuba. The basic U.S. policy of not allowing any fundamental security threat to emerge south of its borders produced President Kennedy's naval quarantine with the threat of American invasion and the quick removal of Soviet missiles. The United States, however, agreed not to invade Cuba, and thus Castro's Communist regime was allowed to survive, bolstered by extensive Soviet economic and military assistance. To weaken the Cuban economy and to isolate it from the rest of the hemisphere, all subsequent American presidents maintained an economic embargo on Cuba's economy, thus forcing Cuba to rely economically on the Communist bloc.

The United States did not want the possibility of any domino effect to emerge. When instability emerged next to Cuba in the Dominican Republic, the United States reversed its noninterventionist stance and sent in troops to maintain a non-Communist government in 1965. When Castro's influence was rising in neighboring Grenada in 1982, the United States invaded to the same effect. However, American public opinion under the influence of the Vietnam syndrome limited the Reagan administration's options when the Sandinistas came to power in Nicaragua. Instead, a variation of the Bay of Pigs option was devised whereby the U.S. trained, armed, and supported the anti-Communist Nicaraguan contras as they attempted to destabilize and overthrow the Marxist regime in Managua.[12] When leftist forces made substantial gains in the El Salvadorean civil war, the United States became deeply engaged to prevent their victory. The United States stood aside when a ruthless military imposed its brand of stability in neighboring Guatemala. When vociferous anti-American sentiments emerged in Panama in the 1970s, to prevent a continuing direct clash of American forces in the Canal Zone with Panamanians, President Carter negotiated a new Panama Canal Treaty that would incrementally abolish the Canal Zone, return that territory to

Panamanian sovereignty, phase out most American bases, but still provide for exclusive American security for the Canal. Under the rubric of curtailing Panama's General Noriega's drug operations, his growing anti-Americanism, and his covert links with Cuba, the United States military intervened in December 1990 to install a government more amenable to U.S. interests, particularly since the administration of the Canal is to be turned over to the Panamanians in 1999. Clearly, with the exception of Cuba, the United States has once again become a policeman preserving its interests within its traditional sphere of influence in Central America and the Caribbean.

CONCLUSION

The Cold War era of 1947 to 1990 represented a remarkable period in American history, as the United States became engaged, on a worldwide basis, in establishing alliances in the Western hemisphere and around the Eurasian periphery of the Communist world. In the nonaligned, less-developed portions of the world—Southern Asia, the Middle East, and Sub-Saharan Africa—the United States had matched Soviet penetrations in an action-reaction syndrome so that neither side gained decisive advantage. National security became the overriding theme of American foreign policy and was achieved through unilateral or multilateral alliance action. The universal security mechanism of the United Nations, based on unanimous great power action through the Security Council, was a dead letter because of the lack of great power harmony on security interests. A United Nations peacekeeping presence had been inserted into the Congo, around selected Israeli borders and into the dangerous Cyprus situation, but the United Nations had been ineffective in the major superpower confrontations. With the fall of the Berlin Wall, the withdrawal of Soviet forces from Eastern Europe, and the ultimate demise of the Soviet Union, the great competition that had dominated the post-World War II era had come to an end. All kinds of possibilities, a greater variety of policy mechanisms, and new problems would emerge to provide challenges and opportunities for the new post-Cold War era, which will be examined in succeeding chapters.

NOTES

1. George F. Kennan, *Memoirs* (Boston, MA: Little, Brown & Co., 1967), Chapters 13–19.
2. Dean Acheson, *Present at the Creation: My Years in the State Department* (New York: Norton, 1969).
3. Graham T. Allison, *Essence of Decision: Explaining the Cuban Missile Crisis* (Boston, MA: Little, Brown & Co., 1971), Chapters 1–2.
4. Richard Smoke, *National Security and the Nuclear Dilemma* (Reading, MA: Addison-Wesley, 1985).

5. Irving L. Janis, *Groupthink*, 2nd ed. (Boston, MA: Houghton Mifflin Co., 1982), Chapter 3.

6. David Halberstam, *The Best and the Brightest* (New York: Random House, 1969).

7. John G. Stoessinger, *Why Nations Go to War* (New York: St. Martin's Press, 1985), Chapter 5.

8. Henry Kissinger, *Years of Upheaval* (Boston, MA: Little Brown, 1982), Chapters 11, 13, and 18.

9. Roy R. Anderson, Robert F. Seibert, and Jon G. Wagner, *Politics and Change in the Middle East* (Englewood Cliffs, NJ: Prentice Hall, 1993), Chapters 11–13.

10. Gary Sick, *All Fall Down* (New York: Penguin Books, 1986).

11. Gerald Bender, James Coleman, and Richard Sklar, eds., *African Crisis Areas and U.S. Foreign Policy* (Berkeley and Los Angeles: University of California Press, 1985).

12. Kenneth M. Coleman and George C. Herring, *The Central American Crisis* (Wilmington, DE: Scholarly Resources Inc., 1985).

CHAPTER 3

AMERICAN POLICY TOWARD WESTERN EUROPE AND THE EUROPEAN UNION

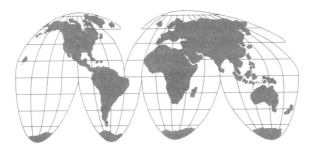

H. G. PETER WALLACH

In a remarkable improvement over past patterns, Western Europe and the United States have constructed a model for international integration and economy-oriented competition. Though Americans now lament the loss of the stable and dependent market they helped create after World War II, the arena for competition is one they defined. It is based on economic goals rather than diplomatic zones and problem solving rather than polarization. On such broad issues as world order, democratic forms of government, and human rights, U.S. and Western European values are similar. The frictions of today largely concern methods for dealing with particular problems close to the European sphere of influence. With economics now the major area of contention, competing economic priorities are the major source of conflict.

Advancing, yet complicating, relationships between the two regions are two coalition structures. The North Atlantic Treaty Organization (NATO),[1] established by the United States to combat the Soviet bloc, is now being refocused to deal with a post–Warsaw Pact world.[2] The European Union does not include the U.S., but it is the major economic linkage among fifteen Western European nations.[3] On a secondary level, negotiations around the General Agreement on Tariffs and Trade (GATT),[4] replaced by the World Trade Organization in 1994, have been a focus of contention, and the Helsinki Accords, or Conference on Cooperation and Security in Europe,[5] raise major questions about support for Eastern Europe.

Cultural traditions, governing institutions, and social practices have established the foundation for mutual understanding between the United States and Western Europe. Within the American democracy, the high immigration of

Europeans has played a major role in sustaining linkages. But natural competitiveness and independent efforts to dominate new markets promote conflict. In addition, each area, North America and the European Union, strives to protect local producers while opening markets in the other region. This is currently ameliorated by joint competition with Asian producers but promises to take a new turn when Eastern European markets are open.

Today, one of the most complex and vexing issues in the United States-Western European relationship concerns how to deal with the former Soviet bloc nations and the former Yugoslavia. Their military potential, the rise of nationalism, and the general confusion in the East challenge both European Union and U.S. policy in new ways. Beyond the differences over the former Communist states, political competition regularly arises around visions of a new world order, the nature of economic relationships, and the future of the welfare state. Americans have traditionally been more individualistic and more optimistic than Europeans. In the political arena, however, it is possible that Western Europe and the United States are becoming even more like one another. In the elections of the mid-1990s, such issues as the role of "big government," the nature of the "social safety net," and the future of established tax systems have been similarly debated on both sides of the Atlantic.

HISTORICAL BACKGROUND

Although George Washington's farewell warning about entanglement in European affairs dominated U.S. policy until World War II, the present relationship represents a rejection of that concept. The Monroe Doctrine was a warning to Europeans to stay out of the American hemisphere. The U.S. naval fleet, ordered by President Theodore Roosevelt in 1907 to sail around the world, announced the growing power of this relatively new nation. Involvement in World War I established that the United States could, if it chose to, influence affairs abroad. In a sense, Woodrow Wilson's recommendation of a League of Nations and Fourteen Points for settling the First World War demonstrated U.S. willingness to guide Europe toward peace. But the unwillingness of the American people and Congress to follow the Wilson suggestion meant a withdrawal into isolation.

This all changed at the end of World War II. The technological, human, and productive superiority of the United States, demonstrated by the outcome of the war, was immediately challenged by Josef Stalin's Soviet Union. By 1947 it was clear that cooperation between the Soviet and non-Soviet world would not continue, and by 1949, with the explosion of a Russian atomic bomb in Siberia, the Cold War was well underway.

The United States met the increased belligerency of the Soviet Union with an aggressive policy of anti-communism and containment of the Soviet Union. Successful containment required the demonstration of economic and political reasons for citizens to support the West, not just superior military prowess. The Marshall Plan provided aid for rebuilding European industry.[6] The Truman Doctrine established a defense zone.[7] Containment of communism and of the Soviet Union became first principles of U.S. policy, and, under the supervision of Great Britain and the United States, the West Germans organized a democratic government that could be a model to the East.[8]

The return of sovereignty to Austria, Germany, and Italy became a major aspect of European policy. The issue was never as absolute for Italy as for the German-speaking countries. After June of 1943, Italy joined the fight against the Nazis, and Franklin D. Roosevelt, facing a re-election campaign in the heavily Italian districts of the Northeast, promised support for the post-war nation. This support included economic aid, which was soon delivered. The peace treaty that followed in 1947 restricted Italian military involvement and placed certain responsibilities on Great Britain and the United States, but allowed Italian self-governance to continue. By 1947 the Soviet threat was clear, and in Italy there was the additional threat of rising support for the National communist party.[9] Austrian sovereignty was complicated, like that of Germany, by a four-power division of the nation. Although an Austrian government had been established in 1946, only the easing of tensions with the Soviet Union during the mid-1950s provided an opportunity for a peace treaty. In return, Austria was required to pursue a policy of neutrality in the Cold War competition between the Western Alliance and the Soviet Union.[10]

The unification of Germany and the final end of occupation took more than forty years, until 1990. By 1949 the two Germanys were already flashpoints of the Cold War. Each side had encouraged establishment of a government that would give its allegiance in the fight against the other. The fuse had begun to burn when economic unification of the British and American sectors, through the issuance of a new currency, led the Russians to impose a blockade on Berlin. The airlift that resulted not only saved the democratic forces in the city, but also the western reputation for reliability. Great Britain and the United States then promoted the establishment of the Federal Republic of Germany (FRG), often referred to as West Germany, while demanding such democratic guarantees as a Constitutional Court. Communist East Germany, which was officially the German Democratic Republic (GDR), became a major economic force in the Soviet bloc. Neither Germany carried out a foreign or military policy until the United States, persuaded by the Korean War, encouraged West Germany to do so. Nevertheless, until May 27, 1968, the three western powers maintained the right to take over German sovereignty in case of emergency.[11] In the meantime, each German government achieved stability. In the GDR, stability was realized only after the government erected the Berlin Wall in 1961 to keep citizens from leaving. Since NATO and the Warsaw Pact enmeshed the two Germanys in institutions controlled by the superpowers, the neighbors of Germany, who had lived through a century of invasions, had also become more secure.[12] In addition, the West German constitution, the Basic Law, did not allow military engagement without NATO involvement, and in the East, GDR forces were not used to put down revolts by citizens in other Soviet satellites. In a Europe threatened by nuclear destruction, NATO was a major force for stability. Not only did it provide a united front against the Soviet threat, but it also kept political conflicts between member states to a minimum. NATO also served as a community of joint responsibility to which all American presidents committed themselves. At the same time, at those moments when Greece and Turkey threatened each other or Britain and France took belligerent stances in the Middle East, NATO was a major vehicle for American attempts to maintain order. Even France, which occasionally demonstrated opposition to the United States by acting independently of NATO, found a need to form coalitions with individual countries within the alliance. Austria, Finland, Sweden, and Switzerland, on the other hand, never joined NATO but could act in the knowledge that a major counterforce to the Soviet Union was at hand. NATO was the most important element in the U.S. policy of containment.[13]

As a defense organization, NATO established a military link among European nations. Beyond the military occupation that France, Great Britain, and the United States shared in Germany, NATO provided an opportunity for joint training, joint development of weapons, and the spread of North American technology. Officers of all member nations had reason to meet regularly, while political leaders maintained constant contact. Ultimately, the recognition of joint values among NATO members proved to be as important as the common security measures.

Other educational, cultural, and economic group linkages were also important. The Fulbright program, for instance, brought future leaders to the United States to study and observe, while giving American students the opportunity to become acquainted with Europeans.[14] At various times U.S. orchestras traveled abroad, labor union leaders were encouraged to establish sound relations with their counterparts in other countries, and political parties provided training opportunities for European candidates.

The early postwar request of the British for "trade, not aid" indicated that no matter how much richer the United States was than Europe, the Marshall Plan could only be a stopgap measure.[15] The machinery and other capital goods sent to Europe under the plan would lie fallow if European nations had no market for the resulting products. Germany demonstrated the need for economic support through the actions of its workers. Although the United States, under the wartime Morgenthau Plan, considered keeping Germany economically weak, it found workers there voluntarily going to their old factories and rebuilding them.[16] When these workers then remained without employment, they voted for Communist candidates.[17] Against an ideology emphasizing economic exploitation and disparity, it was obvious that the best antidote was economic security. The American aid program, sparked by the Truman Doctrine promise to commit money in the battle with communism, was thus continued with instruments of trade that overcame the limits of protective tariffs.

The process of European economic integration proved to be the most important factor in the postwar reconstruction of Western Europe. The economic unification of Europe was hardly a new idea.[18] Through customs unions it had been an element uniting the German states before 1870 and providing for Swedish centralization two centuries earlier. After the war the first catalyst for Western European economic integration was the American-sponsored Marshall Plan, formally known as the European Recovery Program. The plan was announced in 1947 and in 1948 the Organization for European Economic Cooperation (OEEC) was created to administer it. By the time of its completion in 1951, the plan and the OEEC had helped to solidify the Cold War after Moscow forbade the participation of its satellites.[19] More positively, it provided a forum for continental cooperation on the distribution of American aid and the future of Europe. Over the next six years trade among the Western European nations doubled, and the balance of trade with the United States improved. The experience was obviously a success.[20] In 1950, however, the OEEC faltered, as a customs union was proposed, and Britain indicated that it would not participate in such a project. In the spring of 1950 the Schumann Plan was developed in France. Agreed to in 1951, it provided for a common market in the important coal and steel industries. The members were the six countries that would later form the Common Market: France, West Germany, Italy, Belgium, The Netherlands, and Luxembourg. Within five years their combined steel production would increase 42 percent, while that in Great Britain would languish.[21] The lesson was obvious. As the result of a treaty signed in Rome, the European Economic Community (EEC) was established on the first day of 1958.

American policy had been fundamental to European affairs throughout the 1950s. In 1950, Dwight D. Eisenhower, the U.S. general who had commanded the European victory in World War II, became head of NATO. In 1952 he would become President of the United States. He strongly supported European development and integration. In the words of his Secretary of State, John Foster Dulles, victory in the Cold War required "closing the Franco-German breach that has for a century caused the West to war with itself, and expend its vigor in internecine strife."[22] This led him, at the end of the 1950s, to promote a Western European Union that would control any adventurism by Germany.[23] This union would have been a defense community focused against the East.

There was little positive response to the Dulles proposal, but many of the goals were reached nevertheless. In 1958 Charles de Gaulle had become President of France, and Konrad Adenauer was in his last term as Chancellor of West Germany. As the decade of the 1950s ended they became friends. De Gaulle wanted France to dominate European affairs, as independently of

Great Britain and the United States as possible. Adenauer was promoting the idea that a Germany enclosed in a strong European structure would be constrained from belligerence.[24] Although not always jointly, they were able to play off each other's inclinations to promote support for a united Europe, even if it did not include Britain.

It is interesting to note that when President Kennedy arrived in Europe as an untested statesman, de Gaulle was able to use the opportunity to provide European strength in efforts to stand up to the Soviets.[25] This led Adenauer to believe de Gaulle would be the force that could prevent any potential softening of American support for Western Europe against the Soviets.[26] The establishment of the Berlin Wall in 1961 gave Germans special reason to worry about American resolve and American reasons to reassess their policy toward Europe. One result was increased independence from the United States by Germany, while another was a greater effort at cohesiveness by the Europeans.[27]

A business argument for furthering European unity was also gaining force, that through European economic integration multinational firms would become big enough to compete with such American giants as General Motors. Within the European Economic Community, progress toward elimination of national customs barriers and the creation of a common external customs barrier that would raise money for the EEC bureaucracy moved quite steadily until 1965. At that point DeGaulle vetoed further progress toward supranationalism. Whatever the dismay at DeGaulle's opposition to integration, it could not hide the increasing economic success of the Market. In the United States the success of Volkswagen, Mercedes, Philips, and Shell (Royal Dutch Shell) in marketing their products demonstrated the competitiveness of the once-dependent European economies.

On the diplomatic front, de Gaulle's stance provided an extraordinary opportunity for the Nixon-Kissinger foreign policy, which continued into the Ford administration. A student of the "balance of power" conventions established during the Congress of Vienna (1815), Henry Kissinger strove to keep as many world forces in play as possible, especially when he could influence their relationships. He extricated the United States from the Vietnam War by establishing a triangular diplomacy with the Soviet Union and China, and he promoted special relationships that would surround the Communist nations while involving them in detente.[28] Kissinger's policies produced some loss of cohesiveness among the western nations and permitted the implementation of independent initiatives by the Western Europeans. The most important was West German Chancellor Willi Brandt's "Ostpolitik." It provided initiatives toward East Germany that would ultimately promote a united Germany. The friendship treaties with Poland, Hungary, and other eastern nations that followed not only strengthened ties between those nations and the West, but also provided some guarantee that Germany would not be able to unite within its pre-World War II borders that now lay within eastern nations.[29]

By the mid-1970s, economic growth had slowed and was providing less impetus to the European integration movement. Neither the world nor the European Community (EC), as it came to be known, was continuing the surge of previous years. In the United States this brought Ronald Reagan to power, in 1981, while in Europe it made Jacques Delors President of the European Commission in 1985. Subsequent events gave a spur to world growth. The United States borrowed money to lower taxes, increase military spending, and encourage business growth, while the rest of the world found investment in the United States worthwhile. Once the oil crisis of the mid-1970s was over and the value of money was again a result of free-market actions, the lethargy of the 1970s revealed that new competition was growing in Asia. For the EC this provided an impetus to compete as a continent. Jacque Delors persuaded the community to establish programs for scientific and technological collaboration. He also rejuvenated the drive toward a single market. By the end of the decade, agreement to eliminate most customs barriers by the last day of 1992 was reached as part of the Single European Act (SEA) of 1985 (proposed in 1985 and completed December 31, 1992). As a result, goods and labor could easily cross borders between community members.[30] The SEA was the final nail in the coffin of the European Free Trade Association (EFTA), which had been formed as a competitor to the EC in 1959. It was weakened when Great Britain and Denmark joined the Common Market in 1973, foundered once again as Portugal and Spain left for the EC in 1986, and was further reduced when Eastern European nations spurned it in the early 1990s.[31] In 1994, Sweden, the wealthiest per capita member of EFTA, voted to join the EC. By the end of 1994 only Norway and Switzerland, as a result of referenda, stood against a solidly united economic community of all the Western European nations.

In one sense, the widening of EC membership made trade negotiations simpler for the United States. There were fewer countries to negotiate duties with, trade rules became similar, and the increasing size of multinational corporations meant greater cohesiveness in various industries. However, efforts to encourage agricultural exports to Europe produced a trade war in the late 1980s, and the Uruguay round of GATT negotiations demonstrated that the states of the European Community were not always united. In 1993, after it had negotiated special concessions with the Commission of the EC, the United States found that further deliberations would have to be undertaken with France because that country was ready to veto the EC agreements reached two years earlier.

In the meantime, a new organization that brought together the states of the Western Alliance, including the United States, and the states of the Soviet bloc was formed in 1975 in Helsinki, Finland. The Conference on Security and Cooperation in Europe helped to reduce East-West friction by (1) recognizing the borders established at the end of the Second World War and requiring advanced notification of military maneuvers, (2) promoting economic cooperation between East and West, and (3) expressing strong support for human rights. While it left implementation to follow-up meetings, it assured the Soviet Union that it need not fear a war begun by the West and provided Americans with the belief that human rights transgressions by their enemies would be acted upon.[32] The full impact of the organization only became evident as the Soviet Empire declined.

The decline and ultimate demise of the Soviet bloc presented the United States and Western Europe with new opportunities and challenges. The success of the Solidarity movement in Poland in the early 1980s and Gorbachev's policy of reform in the U.S.S.R. contributed to the rapid collapse of the Communist regimes throughout the Soviet bloc by 1989–1990. The break in the Berlin Wall in November 1989 became a portent of coming events. By the time the East Germans voted to join the West in the March 1990 election, open requests for a broadening of the Helsinki accords and acceptance of former Warsaw Pact nations into NATO had been articulated. West German Foreign Minister Genscher even agreed with many Warsaw Pact officials that the Helsinki Agreements might provide a framework for the new Europe.[33] Although such suggestions provided no direct advantage for the Eastern European nations, they became instrumental in gaining acceptance for the unification of Germany by the Four Powers, the United States, Soviet Union, United Kingdom, and France, and the neighbors of the two Germanys. Chancellor Helmut Kohl had established the reliability of Germany within NATO and the EC to argue that fear of unification was unjustified. NATO, after acknowledging that the potential for major conflict had been reduced, went on to suggest that effective pan-European security measures could be developed through the Helsinki process.[34] NATO and Germany ultimately rejected the creation of a demilitarized Central Europe, as briefly demanded by the Soviet Union, but they acknowledged that it would be inappropriate for NATO troops to be stationed in the former GDR. In addition, Gorbachev persuaded Kohl to make Germany a nuclear-free zone. The final negotiations, whereby the occupation powers declared an end to World War II, included stipulations that Germany would also be free of biological and chemical weapons. With strong support from the Bush administration, Germany was thus allowed to unify.[35]

The events of 1989 through 1991 required a redefinition of NATO. By the end of 1990 even the Soviet Union was undergoing upheaval. In the West there was now discussion of what President Bush called "The New World Order." In the East an immediate desire for economic benefits and security from attack manifested. The events of 1989 through 1991 had the effect of assuring the world that Germany could be controlled, but what role would NATO have regarding other European problems?[36] Some answers are still developing and others gained focus during the Bosnian crisis, but as unrest and upheaval grew in the former Soviet bloc, supporters of NATO became convinced that its continuance would be necessary.

The European Community was now faced with the question of how far to expand and what actions to take regarding the applications for membership from the East. First, it accepted Austria and Finland, which no longer needed to worry about Soviet demands for neutrality. Switzerland, Sweden, and Norway also reconsidered membership in light of the advantages of the newly expanded EC area. Several post-Communist states also articulated the desire to join. However, since states of the former Soviet bloc had just begun the transition to capitalism, they were offered no more than candidacy for future membership. A harder question was how to set standards of capitalist development for determining when to accept these nations in the future.

By the early 1990s, the worldwide recession, including rapidly rising unemployment, had reached Europe. The question of progress by the EC was now complicated by political considerations resulting from local economic difficulties. In 1993 the tacit agreement on maintaining exchange rates between European currencies, commonly referred to as currency bands, broke down and national economic pressures threatened to tear the Community apart. For most of the previous decade, European currency bands had remained stable because of agreements that central banks would prevent them from varying outside of the accepted limits. Any other changes were reached by mutual agreement, and the whole spiral was allowed to vary against gold and the U.S. dollar. In late 1993 Great Britain and Italy broke from this agreement. The result suggested further havoc as the price of the dollar fluctuated against these currencies more than 15 percent. Some control was soon re-established, but the latest efforts to further European unity through monetary convergence were now in question.

The Maastricht Treaty, formally the Treaty on European Union, which began in 1993, was in theory the most important measure yet undertaken in the process of integrating Western Europe. Unlike the Single European Act of 1985, which was confined to the removal of barriers to free trade, the Maastricht Treaty included provisions for the European Union to become both an economic and monetary union as well as a political union. These provisions established institutional frameworks for future cooperation in the following areas: (1) the creation of a common central bank and a common currency by 1999, thus increasing the Union's influence over macroeconomic policy; (2) law enforcement and judicial matters, such as immigration and asylum; (3) common foreign and security policy making (CFSP) on issues on which members unanimously desire such a procedure; and (4) the possible future development of a common defense policy, in which the Western European Union would have an important role. In addition, in an effort to accomplish institutional reform, the powers of the European Parliament were expanded, the budget process was revised, and citizens of the Union were given new residence and voting rights.

In recognition of the importance of the Maastricht Treaty, the institutions of the EC were absorbed within the new framework, and the name of the organization was changed from the European Community to the European Union (EU). The Maastricht Treaty clearly represented the first efforts by the Western Europeans to collectively confront the new conditions of the post-Cold War world and to prepare the EU to assume a greater role in world affairs in the future. However, this ambitious project engendered considerable internal opposition, especially from Great Britain and Denmark, which won the right to opt out of some programs. The worsening crisis in the former Yugoslavia also quickly illustrated the difficulty of forging a common foreign policy.

The secession of several states formerly comprising Yugoslavia and their subsequent efforts to expand their authority challenged both NATO and the European Union. The effort to gain support for a united policy within the EU was complicated by the fact that the victims of the most violent campaigns in Bosnia were Muslims, and thus not within the normal European religious majority. Keeping one's hands off was thus the inclination of many, but governmental leaders were afraid that nationalistic violence would spread. Various efforts at a united policy were attempted. Hans Dietrich Genscher, for instance, had Germany recognize some of the new states in order to mobilize the EU to take action. The United States, on the other hand, strove to remind the European states that it was their responsibility to solve the problem. All plans, however, lacked the force to make them work. Ultimately, some success was achieved with a U.N. force, but when the United States strove to make this force more powerful, the Europeans, especially the French government, maintained that this was a European problem and sought to retain the political initiative. Although most European nations joined in the U.N. effort to force Iraqi troops from Kuwait in 1991 in "Desert Storm,"[37] the difficulty of achieving policy consensus increased as the problem shifted closer to the area of the European Union.

An issue on which common ground has been found is that of the development of the East, the post-Communist states presently undergoing the transition to democracy and capitalism. Western Europe and the United States, within the "Group of Seven" (G-7)[38] and outside it, have determined that economic development in Russia and its former satellite states must be supported if stability is to be created there. Through the Agency for International Development (AID), the United States promotes training programs, seminars on capitalism, and contacts between a variety of private groups. U.S. immigrant groups and religious societies also play a significant role, one that is rarely matched by other European nations. Although the United States has not always kept loan and investment commitments, along with Germany it has been the major investor in the states of the former Soviet bloc. Despite these achievements, many European businesspeople fear that not enough is being done, while American and European political leaders have expressed concern that current investment may be insufficient to produce Eastern stability.

As the world approaches the twenty-first century, Western European political stability and economic cooperation seem assured. The European Union stands as testimony to the success of America's postwar policy of reconstruction, and recent American efforts to construct a free trade area with Canada and Mexico can be viewed as recognition of the economic accomplishments of the EC and EU. The North American Free Trade Agreement demonstrates that the European Union is on the right track, and a reduction in the number of competitors certainly has an advantage. However, the size of the European Union, especially the potential size once Eastern European nations join, poses formidable obstacles to successful management and governance in the future. For those who believe democracy and competition work best when there are not too many large players, these problems seem especially challenging. Similarly, the argument that large bureaucracies stifle initiative raises concern about the impact of a world dominated by trade agreements between major trading blocs. Viewed from a political perspective, the American alliance with Europe seems entirely positive. Whatever the minor differences concerning the Gulf War or the Bosnian crisis, there is fundamental agreement among citizens on both sides of the Atlantic. Attitudes prevail supporting peace, mutual defense, common initiatives to prevent any dangerous international conditions from developing, and support for democratic politics throughout the world.[39] Together such values provide few headlines, but they constitute a framework for mutual cooperation and security.

U.S. INTERESTS, CHALLENGES, AND OPPORTUNITIES

Contemporary relations between Western Europe and the United States demonstrate that even in victory frustrations and challenges can develop. For those with a perspective firmly rooted in the power politics of the state, the rise of an integrated Europe with some supranational features is a defeat. Yet there is victory insofar as a former enemy, communism, has been vanquished. The reality is that Western Europe and the United States, along with Japan and other alliance partners, have demonstrated how productive and beneficial a peaceful and democratic world can be. In the process they have changed the shape of national competition, proven the benefits of firm alliances, and demonstrated the advantages of large free-trade markets. For some Americans, however, who have been forced to bear the adjustment costs of increased economic competition from Europe and elsewhere, the rise of the global market has brought new concerns about economic scarcity. Such is the case with the unemployed autoworker in Michigan, the hard-pressed farmer in Nebraska, or the New York banker, as the dynamics of competition continually change their economic playing fields. They are voters who may support isolationism at the moment when their jobs are threatened. On the other hand, they are also persuadable when working for an export-oriented employer or reminded, as Lufthansa did during a "fly American" effort of the 1950s, that many foreign firms buy most of their capital goods in the United States. The voters who are not as easily persuaded are those who dislike new imports from abroad or neighbors they cannot quite understand or who just want to protect a way of life they have become accustomed to. One of the challenges of any foreign policy decision maker, especially when there is massive economic restructuring, is accommodating the demands of such domestic interest groups. The American interest groups that most strongly support pro-European policies represent industries that gain advantages from the global market, consumers who have more choices, and the "hyphenated Americans" who still identify with the nations of their heritage.

Between the pro-isolation and pro-European positions, there is a vast array of groups that identify with a particular economic, cultural, or political interest. Investors, traders, ideologues, and travelers all have reason to support certain types of policies toward Europe. Some fear too much power for any one nation and simply want effective competition for the United States. Others find competition conducive to originality and productivity. Another perspective trumpets openness among all nations and the decline of all national or regional boundaries. World government is the goal of still other groups. All of these interests influence foreign policy, especially policy toward Europe, and collectively constitute the political environment of U.S. policy toward Western Europe.

As a united economic bloc, the European Union is currently a formidable economic actor. Less than one half the size of the United States, it represents a population 50 percent larger. It is thus potentially more important as a market and producer, but, as Ford, General Motors, IBM, and foreign companies have demonstrated, it is not a purely European producer. Although the United States is technically outside the market, it still has significant clout within it. Great Britain, Germany, and Italy, which have sizable trade with the United States, frequently look out for American interests, and the Market is generally aware that the United States is its best partner in any disputes with Asian producers. When Margaret Thatcher was British Prime Minister (1979–1990), Great Britain was especially helpful in the ongoing U.S. complaint about EC subsidies to agriculture in France and other EC countries. The Dutch, Belgians, and British have significant investment in U.S. commerce. The Irish are dependent on the United States for the creation of specific new industries. Even Switzerland, though not a member of the Union, has established a banking web that ties European and U.S. financial fortunes together. The languages, cultures, educational systems, religious values, and psychology of Europeans are especially close to those of the United States. The two sub-continents have been drawn together by the fight against communism and victories over dictatorships. The standard of living in both parts of the world is relatively similar. So there is every reason for increased cooperation.

Despite the factors promoting increased cooperation between the United States and the EU, important competitive elements also exist. Where economic competition is rife, it is often more important to emphasize those differences than to emphasize similarities. During the GATT and NATO negotiations of the 1990s, several issues divided the United States and the EU, including the subsidies to farmers, concern for the success of Russian capitalism, the problem of refugees, events in such world trouble areas as the Middle East, and the role of individual governments in the GATT negotiations. The issue that unites the United States and Europe, especially within the NATO framework, is foreign policy outside Europe. Except for Germany, which was constrained by its constitution, European members of NATO took direct part in the Gulf War.[40] They have also worked together on advancing peace between Israel and her neighbors, pressuring Serbia for a peaceful solution in Bosnia, and aiding Eastern Europe. Although Great Britain sometimes pursues independent initiatives, France focuses on North Africa, and Germany is heavily involved east of its borders, when united action is necessary the members of NATO are usually ready to cooperate. The perpetual problem is communication. When the United States strives to be the independent leader, or a European politician takes action without consultation, there are predictable complaints. In several cases, U.S. presidents, soon after coming to office, have made policy pronouncements that created irritation in Western European capitals.

The forty years of experience as a united force against the Soviet bloc has established a firm foundation for political and military cooperation between the United States and the states of Western Europe. When called upon in an emergency these nations can be expected to act together. The question is what they will do when there is not quite a full crisis and when there is time and space for differences. On such occasions the Europeans sometimes wait for American leadership, especially when their differences could become divisive within Europe. But what they fear even more than a lack of leadership by the United States is undependability. Because of the volatility of American politics and the growing reluctance of American voters to risk lives or money, there is a sense that the United States may not fulfill its commitments or may remove itself from a crisis. Europeans understand their politics may not seem sufficiently relevant to Midwesterners or groups in Congress. So they point to President Johnson's hesitancy about being involved in their problems or the American indecisiveness over Bosnia.[41] Especially troubling has been the promise of President Clinton to provide $400 million to Russia, which has never been fulfilled.

In the few years since the collapse of the Soviet Union, a major problem has been the lack of well-defined foreign policy goals. Not only did President Bush fail to explain his "New World Order," but President Clinton has taken a position of increased support for piecemeal attention to human rights issues despite the fact that he has not had the political support to carry this out. In effect, Europe and the United States are agreed that capitalism needs to be advanced in Russia, but neither has the will nor the available resources to find a means to accomplish this.[42] Complicating this lack of policy is the shock therapy approach to correcting Soviet deficiencies that does not take into account the inevitable transition problems in passing from communism to capitalism.[43] In facing this task, and in relating to Europeans on such issues Henry Kissinger writes:

> ...America's dominant task is to strike a balance between the twin temptations inherent in its exceptionalism: the notion that America must remedy every wrong and stabilize every dislocation, and the latent instinct to withdraw into itself. Indiscriminate involvement in all the ethnic turmoil and civil wars of the post-Cold War world would drain a crusading America. Yet an America that confines itself to the refinement of its domestic virtues would, in the end, abdicate America's security and prosperity to decisions made by other societies in faraway places and over which America would progressively lose control.[44]

He goes on to write, "What America must master is the transition from an age when all choices seemed open to a period when it can still accomplish more than any other society if it can only learn its limits."[45] Most such studies of American foreign policy in the post-Cold War period emphasize the point that U.S.-Western European cooperation is essential. However, such commentaries cannot provide simple answers for addressing the fact that, as an ally, Western Europe possesses both interests in common with the United States and unique economic and political interests independent of the United States.

A major element of complexity in the U.S.-Western European relationship develops from the presence of political interests in the United States. Once common ideology is laid aside, Americans of European national origin constitute an especially interested population. For most Western European nations, this is a sizable number. For Middle Eastern and North African nations, however, the numbers are minuscule, and of Eastern European countries only Hungary, Poland, and Russia[46] have sent over five hundred thousand emigrants to the United States since 1820.[47] U.S. policy toward Europe is also susceptible to the same pressures as any other U.S. policy, with the caveat that American interest groups often have linkages with European counterparts. For instance, leaders of the Republican Party frequently consult with neoliberals in Europe, and Democratic Senator Joseph Biden once used a speech from the Labour Party leader in Great Britain, Neil Kinnock. In addition, labor unions, corporate boards, universities, and banks all have solid relations with their opposite numbers throughout Western Europe. The result is that the politics of the United States is often reflected in, and is a reflection of, politics in Europe.

Nowhere is the interdependence between American and Western European societal structures more apparent than in the economic sphere. Not only are banks and corporations global in nature, but the ebb and flow of economic currents usually engulf all advanced industrial nations simultaneously. Thus, the problems of slowed growth and global competition have affected both the United States and Europe at the same time. It is especially evident that when the U.S. economy contracts, all countries selling in that market are affected, and, where those countries buy from the United States, the state of their economies has an impact on the American market. On the functional level, banks, employers, and service providers have to make decisions based on economic conditions in Western Europe and elsewhere. This makes them part of special interest groups that want U.S. foreign policy to achieve specific outcomes in the economic issue-area. Bankers want loan repayments facilitated, writers want copyrights protected, singers want to be able to collect for their performances abroad, and product liability rules can be a major factor in the readiness of a seller to enter one market or another.

The greatest challenge to any policy maker is unifying sufficiently large numbers of such groups to gain support for a particular approach. When a threat to the availability of energy arises, which happened at the time of the Gulf War, this is relatively simple. Difficulty occurs with the more subtle issues. Although a standardized measurement system like the metric system promotes interchangeability of parts, should it be promoted if it prevents innovation or the ability to protect the uniqueness of a specialized product in the United States? Should local banks be protected so national and international ones do not deprive small producers of loans? Are international environment projects more positive than national or local ones? These examples demonstrate that in the United States and in Europe there are overlapping, centrifugal, and centripetal pressures. At the same time integration is progressing, there are efforts to return some authority to the states or towns, or, in Europe, to the regions.[48] The United States is thus confronted with the challenge of whether to focus on the whole of Europe, the European Union, or on specific states and regions. The whole is usually a simpler unit to deal with, but the tactic of using one part against the other, or simply getting what one wants where it can be negotiated, certainly has advantages. The United States has long promoted a "United States of Europe" because of the standard commercial regulation and reduced feuding that it would produce. Now it faces the question of how much unity is best. A policy based on narrow American interests would favor exactly the degree of unity and the combination of commercial structures that will favor this country. But this is antithetical to some of our long-range interests. We also seek to promote democracy, and we must allow the Europeans the right to determine the nature of their own economic and political institutions.

Of course, the United States has not refrained from attempts to influence the development of European institutions. From the perspective of America's political and military relationship with Europe, NATO remains the most important institution. Defense Secretary William Perry has recently expressed the view that NATO is so important that the European Union should only admit members who are also members of NATO. In his opinion, if a nation that is not a member of NATO becomes a member of the European Union, the United States will be committed to defend it although we will have little influence over that nation.[49]

POLICY OPTIONS: PROS AND CONS

Recommendations like that of Defense Secretary Perry are an expression of American national interest that the European Union is unlikely to receive well. For understandable reasons any option that seems to constrain the decision making of the Union will meet with resistance. This is also true of suggestions that push the Union toward unwelcome initiatives or infer U.S. dominance of Europe. Yet it can hardly expect the United States not to express and strive to further its own national interests. Within the United States there have even been occasional debates over whether it is worth cooperating with such a potentially strong competitor. Regardless of the nature of the domestic discussion, however, the problem for the United States is that NATO, a defense-oriented organization, is the only important institution of European integration in which North American states retain membership. Thus, there are three practical questions that underlie any discussion of U.S. relations with a united Western Europe:

1. To what degree should U.S. policy be carried out through multilateral institutions rather than with individual countries?
2. Assuming the importance of NATO, what should the new definition of the North Atlantic Treaty be?[50]
3. Should new structures of interactions between Washington and Western Europe be established?

Some degree of negotiation with individual countries will certainly continue unless Europe becomes so cohesive that this is impossible. As the process of European integration continues, however, the United States regularly finds it must negotiate with the European Union, and sometimes through the organs of NATO.

The defense orientation of the North Atlantic Treaty Organization is only one of the problems in making it the fundamental arena for U.S.-Western European negotiations. The United States has, in recent years, systematically persuaded European nations that they must assume more of the responsibility for and cost of their own defense. As a result, it is hardly surprising that the Europeans feel increasingly independent of the United States. In addition, the Maastricht Treaty formally authorized another institution, the Western European Union (WEU), to implement European Union decisions in the defense area. For the first time since World War II, the leadership of NATO in defense policy making is no longer assured. The

Europeans now possess an institution, somewhat analogous to the still-born European Defense Community, that gives them, in theory, the capability to undertake security measures independent of NATO and the United States. Should the WEU undertake such action, it is unclear whether the Union would expect NATO's help when the United States and Canada are not directly involved in a particular situation. The bigger danger for the United States is that it will become increasingly irrelevant to the European security process. Should the United States not strive to work cooperatively with its allies, they could marginalize it. This does not mean Europe would become a military competitor, but the United States would lose influence. On the other hand, some argue that this loss of influence may be just what the United States needs. It could give the United States greater opportunity to concentrate on domestic affairs or on nations with more critical problems.[51]

One solution, as country negotiations are replaced by Union negotiations, is the creation of new structures that involve the United States. Although "America's leaders have generally stressed motivation over structure,"[52] the structural isolation inherent in the singular focus on NATO leaves the United States unable to move economic and human rights issues. Werner Weidenfeld, a German professor who strives to strengthen relations between his country and the United States, calls for institutionalized means by which the United States and the European Community can work together on economic and Third World issues.[53] Although GATT is a trade organization to which the European Union and the United States both belong, it does not address problems unique to those areas. It is interesting to note that the U.S.-led North Atlantic Free Trade Agreement may provide a model for the European Union on problems of economic disparity that it may soon face. NAFTA is the only free trade agreement between Third World nations and advanced industrial states. Unlike the European Union, NAFTA does not include the financial supports that Ireland, Portugal, and Spain have been receiving. If it is successful, it may provide an appropriate example for Eastern European membership in the Union.

Additional institutional linkages with Europe, such as the new World Trade Organization, may also prove to be important in resolving problems associated with economic competition. Not that they will eliminate such competition, even if that should be desirable, but they can provide clear rules and the means for channeling competition in ways that will avoid misunderstanding and prevent economic competition from spilling into other areas. Regardless of whether the United States and Europe develop such institutional linkages, intense competition in certain economic sectors is certain to continue, driven by those desiring employment or profit from individual industries. Should the cooperative methods fail or prove unsatisfactory to domestic forces, the United States has another card worth playing. It can play its Asian and North American partners off against those in Europe. With a Pacific policy, as well as an Atlantic one, the United States has the advantage of automobile, electronics, and agricultural industries well-positioned in both markets and with the capacity for trade across both oceans. If handled in a sophisticated manner, this card can provide a win-win situation for the American economy.

In a new twist on the old American pattern, the technique of playing human rights off against economic benefits also has potential now that Eastern Europe is in the picture. The human rights appeal always had the by-product of furthering free competition by limiting government control of economic activities. This aided American investors who strove to gain a foothold in target nations. In the competition for European markets, similar human rights pressure on newly capitalistic nations of Eastern Europe may provide opportunities for smaller U.S. investors. The Helsinki Accords, which involve the United States, are a prime mechanism for human rights initiatives that will also benefit economic growth. Once Eastern European economies are more firmly established, the Helsinki process can be used as a mechanism for further opening markets. This has the potential of reducing any protectionism that might be engendered in these states or in the European Union as a result of their membership.

The United States has also always promoted competitiveness because that means fewer monopolies within the EU. Differences among business units have always meant a potential gain for American entrepreneurs. If the Union becomes less vigilant about anti-trust actions as some member countries would like, the United States will be disadvantaged. In principle, any national deregulation or limitation on restrictive national practices will also enhance the potential for U.S. investment profits.[54] Further, the United States has lobbied to change the EU rule requiring 80 percent of government purchasing from member countries so that the market will be opened to the United States.[55] On a larger scale, as long as the U.S. policy is interested in fractionation within the EU it promotes federalism.

The effort to change internal EU markets for the benefit of U.S. industries is not a one-way street. The Union has also sought to open certain U.S. markets. For instance, it finds the state-oriented banking system difficult to enter and would prefer that stock market investment be combined with bank investment the way it is in Europe. Should government procurement be opened up in Europe, reciprocal rights will also be expected here.[56] Even in the absence of such reciprocal rights, European firms are investing in the United States because of two clear advantages—the size of the U.S. market and the comparative freedom firms have in employing and unemploying workers. Corporate restructuring is severely limited in Germany, Sweden, and the Netherlands due to rules protecting employees. Thus, the new factories that Mercedes, BMW, and Volvo are building within the United States provide these firms with added flexibility. European corporations also find research and development cooperation with the United States an effective antidote against Asian challengers. In 1991 the government of the south German state of Baden-Wurttemberg offered her sister state, Connecticut, joint research and customized forefront technology development as a defense against "generic" electronic goods from the Far East.[57] Two years later the same two states were undertaking discussions about exchanging training and organizational information for promoting a technologically advanced workforce.[58]

Focus on two specific sectors provides perspective on some of the potential advantages and problems in European Union-U.S. economic relations. First, Airbus, the European aircraft consortium, has overtaken Boeing in new orders since 1989. Although their planes are sometimes powered by Pratt and Whitney engines and always include numerous American parts, they directly challenge recent U.S. hegemony in this field. The U.S. complaint about Airbus is that it has benefited from over $13.5 billion of government subsidies. Europeans answer that U.S. government military orders have provided a kind of subsidy to Lockheed and Boeing. Some American manufacturers now ask whether they should also demand more government help in gaining equal access to world markets.[59] Secondly, agriculture raises similar problems. It is highly subsidized in Europe with support to local residents who do not want to be dependent on foreign producers in case of war or other catastrophe. Moreover, every large European nation, and even such small nations as the Netherlands, has sizeable areas with agrarian populations. In 1967 the EC established the Common Agricultural Policy (CAP) to guarantee food supplies, improve productivity, and ensure a fair standard of living for farmers. This is a program that export-oriented American farmers resent. Because this policy was costing the EC over $50 billion by 1990, European Union negotiators were willing to make modifications in it during the GATT negotiations. However, as we have already noted, France disputed parts of the resulting agreement. The CAP has now produced such large surpluses and provoked so many environmental complaints that additional international pressures have developed to change it. In the future West European special access to East European markets may replace the CAP as the major competitive obstacle facing U.S. farmers.[60]

In both the aviation and agricultural areas, and in many others, the United States and the European Union negotiate openly and are well aware of each other's political interests. Since both share joint values and common historical perspectives, they have found it productive to negotiate rather than fight. But an additional reason exists for the current level of cooperation—competition from Japan. Confronted with this competition, the European Union has tried to establish protective barriers that will prevent a Japanese victory in the automotive and electronics fields such as the one that the United States suffered in the mid-1980s. Under some circumstances such protectionism could also be directed against the United States. Fortunately, the Uruguay round of GATT provided a process for addressing these issues. It included an arrangement for open access to markets, enforced by international institutions, which was ultimately supported by both the United States and Europe.

POLICY RECOMMENDATIONS FOR THE TWENTY-FIRST CENTURY

The interdependence of products, markets, and investments, no matter where they are situated, requires an open-market policy by the United States. Markets closed in retaliation or protective fervor by the United States can only engender similar actions elsewhere. American barriers to trade from other countries may simply give competitor nations the opportunity to experience a technology or a style of life that we ourselves do not enjoy. If the United States is truly interested in establishing a "level playing field," two outstanding opportunities are at hand. The Uruguay Round of the GATT and its follow-up negotiations provide the general means for overcoming protection by competitor nations and include an enforcement mechanism that involves all members acting against an infringing nation. The major problem for the United States in this procedure is that it takes more than one nation to ask for implementation of corrective measures against overly protective practices. Here the second opportunity becomes pertinent. The United States will need friends who can help it in such enforcement complaints. This will become most relevant if a particular nation targets the United States alone for its protective trade practices. As long as the United States has friends with similar values and economic interests, it will have allies in this process. Should friendship not suffice, it is building a network of states in an open-trade consortia that will allow it to play one competitor nation against another. Thus, the recently concluded North American Free Trade Agreement, the Pacific trade agreement that is now under consideration, and any new linkages that can be established with the European Union can only be beneficial to American interests.

In the future, relations with the EU will depend both on traditional bilateral relations with member countries and newly established fora for working with the European Union. This means the United States must have strong offices, preferably a recognized linkage organization, in the Council of Europe and the European Parliament (both in Strasbourg) and representation to the European Commission centered in Brussels. These offices will need to integrate the responsibilities of the U.S. Agriculture, Commerce, Labor, and State Departments, as well as the U.S. Treasury. At the same time they will need to identify long-term interests that can be supported by a number of U.S. administrations. This will overcome the "divided tongues" phenomena that sometimes confounds U.S. policy and fosters inconsistency in our stance toward Europe.

In the U.S. relationship with the former Communist states of Eastern Europe and Eurasia, additional factors come into play. The United States must have a clear and decisive policy that will support the transition to democracy, maintain the peace, and encourage a free-trade order. If Russia, Kazakhstan, or Ukraine threatens its neighbors or the world, it will have to be brought to order, fought militarily, or effectively integrated into a pan-

European economic and security system. The latter condition was the goal of Western policy in the early post-Cold War years, but economic support for the project has waned in the wake of the world recession and the international restructuring of economic forces. Whether that will change if a more positive economic climate is achieved is unclear. So one must consider the possibility of constraining the threat. For this purpose the well-established coalition of NATO is ideal. It unites the nations facing potential threats and commands extensive resources. Any such threat will increase the power of NATO and strengthen the alliance between North America and Europe. Should all the post-Communist nations develop peacefully and become members of the European Union, the United States could also feel itself threatened by such a vast grouping of states. It can prepare for this scenario by establishing a direct relationship of its own with the states of the former Soviet bloc. This means it must continue to expand the financial, educational, and cultural programs it carries on in these states. Such an expansion will mean that when those nations join the Union they will do so with cognizance of U.S. interests and an understanding of the advantages of maintaining U.S. support.

None of these solutions will necessarily help the workers and industries currently impacted by world competition. A policy that only protects threatened groups, if it were possible, would probably not preserve benefits for the whole. The United States needs positive domestic policies to promote education, investment, and human resource development that will guarantee its competitive position in a variety of fields. Such domestic policy can only make international policy more effective.

NOTES

1. The Organization, established in 1949, includes Belgium, Canada, Denmark, France, Germany, Greece, Iceland, Italy, Luxembourg, The Netherlands, Norway, Portugal, Spain, Turkey, the United Kingdom, and the United States.
2. The Pact of Soviet bloc nations formed in 1955. It included Albania, Bulgaria, Czechoslovakia, East Germany, Hungary, Poland, Romania, and the U.S.S.R.
3. Belgium, Denmark, France, Germany, Great Britain, Greece, Ireland, Italy, Luxembourg, The Netherlands, Spain, and Portugal were joined by Austria, Finland, and Sweden in 1995.
4. Originally established in 1948, the General Agreement on Tariffs and Trade, now absorbed within the World Trade Organization, was the world's largest organization striving to limit customs barriers between nations.
5. This 1975 Agreement between thirty-seven nations, supporting the Soviet bloc and the West, guaranteed borders and respected national sovereignty within the United Nations Charter.
6. In a June 5, 1947 speech at Harvard University, Secretary of State George Marshall proposed a comprehensive recovery plan for combatting hunger and poverty in wartorn Europe. U.S. aid would help the re-establishment of productive capacities. The Soviet Union suggested this would enslave the continent and prevented the possibility of involvement by Soviet-occupied countries.

7. Truman established an aid program for Greece and Turkey to help "free peo-
    ple defend themselves against the spread of communism."

8. Under the policy of containment, as developed by George Kennan, the United
    States would stop the spread of communism beyond the borders of nations it
    then ruled.

9. Norman Kogan, *A Political History of Postwar Italy* (New York: Frederick A.
    Praeger, 1966).

10. Walter Laquer, *Europe since Hitler: The Rebirth of Europe* (New York: Holt, Rinehart
    & Winston, 1970), pp. 386–387.

11. Alfred Grosser, *Germany in Our Time: A Political History of the Postwar Years* (New
    York: Praeger Publishers, 1970).

12. Christian Graf von Krockow, *Die Deutschen in Ihrem Jahrhundert* (Hamburg:
    Rowohlt, 1990).

13. George F. Kennan, *Memoirs: 1925–1950* (Boston, MA: Little-Brown & Co., 1967),
    Chapter 15.

14. The program, named after Senator James William Fulbright, provided a means
    for foreign countries to pay their debts to the United States in educational
    opportunity, rather than cash. They could spend the money locally to support
    American students and scholars, or they could support their own citizens'
    efforts to learn in the United States.

15. The ultimate sum committed was over $12 Billion.

16. In 1944, while World War II was still in progress, Secretary of the Treasury
    Morgenthau proposed Germany be kept permanently weak by being divided
    and being prevented from developing large industries.

17. In many of the largest coal and steel cities of the Ruhr Valley, Communists dom-
    inated the city councils after the first postwar elections.

18. Richard N. Coudenhove-Kalergi, *Crusade for Pan-Europe* (New York: G.P.
    Putnam's Sons, 1943).

19. Walter Issacson and Evan Thomas, *The Wise Men: Six Friends and the World They
    Made* (New York: Simon & Schuster, 1986), p. 416.

20. Laquer, *Europe since Hitler*, p. 130.

21. Ibid., p. 133.

22. John Foster Dulles in a memorandum entitled "United States Foreign Policy,"
    May 16, 1954, DP, White House Memoranda Series, as quoted by Richard D.
    Challener in "The Moralist as Pragmatist: John Foster Dulles as Cold War
    Strategist," in *The Diplomats, 1939–1979*, Gordon A. Craig and Francis L.
    Lowenheim, eds. (Princeton, NJ: Princeton University Press, 1994), p. 145.

23. Challener, "The Moralist as Pragmatist," p. 155.

24. Paul Weymar, *Adenauer*, Peter de Mendelsohn, ed. and trans. (London: Andre
    Deutsch Limited, 1957), pp. 508–524.

25. Don Cook, *Charles DeGaulle: A Biography* (New York: Putnam Publishing, 1983),
    p. 356.

26. Gordon A. Craig, "Adenauer and His Diplomats," in *The Diplomats, 1939–1979*,
    Gordon A. Craig and Francis L. Lowenheim, eds. (Princeton, NJ: Princeton
    University Press, 1994), p. 221.

27. Frank A. Ninkovich, *Germany and the United States* (Boston, MA: Twayne
    Publishers, 1988).

28. Henry Kissinger, *Diplomacy* (New York: Simon & Schuster, 1994).

29. Ibid., pp. 735–737.

30. Derek W. Urwin, *The Community of Europe: A History of European Integration since
    1945* (London: Longman Group, 1991).

31. David P. Lewis, *The Road to Europe* (New York: Peter Lang, 1993), pp. 280–291.

32. Francis L. Loewenheim, "From Helsinki to Afghanistan: American Diplomats

and Diplomacy, 1975–1979," in *The Diplomats, 1939–1979*, Craig and Lowenheim, eds., pp. 629–664, esp. 630.

33. Hans Dietrich Genscher, "German Responsibility for a Peaceful Order in Europe," in *Germany and Europe in Transition*, Adam Daniel Rotfeld and Walther Stutzle, eds. (Oxford: Oxford University Press, 1991), pp. 20–29.

34. H. G. Peter Wallach and Ronald A. Francisco, *United Germany: The Past, Politics, Prospects* (Westport, CT: Praeger, 1992), pp. 69–74.

35. Ibid., pp. 73–77.

36. Peter H. Merkl, *German Unification in the European Context* (College Park: Pennsylvania State University Press, 1993).

37. Paul Gordon Lauren, "The Diplomats and Diplomacy of the United Nations," in *The Diplomats, 1939–1979*, Craig and Lowenheim, eds., pp. 459–496.

38. At regular intervals, often every three months, the governmental leaders and heads of the Central Banks of Canada, France, Germany, Italy, Japan, the United Kingdom, and the United States meet.

39. Within the United States, political leaders are careful to assure that common initiatives do not impinge on national politics or U.S. national sovereignty. This is one of the reasons U.S. politicians are careful in entering any treaty obligations.

40. Germany helped fund the war.

41. Since Johnson was focused on the Vietnam War, he rarely paid attention to other international problems. One result was that after President Nixon took office, Henry Kissinger made a point of indicating Europe would again be a focus of attention.

42. Paul Krugman, "Europe Jobless, America Penniless," *Foreign Policy* 95 (Summer 1994): 19–34.

43. Georgi Arbatov, "Euraisa Letter: A New Cold War," *Foreign Policy* 95 (Summer 1994): 90–104.

44. Kissinger, *Diplomacy*, pp. 832–833.

45. Ibid., p. 834.

46. Ukrainians, Georgians, and other nationalities included with Russia during the Soviet period are included in these figures.

47. U.S. Immigration and Naturalization Service, as compiled in *The World Almanac and Book of Facts: 1993*, p. 397.

48. In Europe there is a long history of certain kinds of cross-national regional cooperation. For instance, the Scandinavian countries cooperate on Lapland policy, which deals with nomadic residents who largely live north of the Arctic circle. The German Land of Baden-Wurtemmberg, the Swiss Canton of Basel, and French Alsace are cooperating on joint projects. Not far away, the relevant portions of contiguous Austria, Italy, and Switzerland are establishing a joint organization.

49. Discussion at Freedom Forum conference in Washington, D.C., November 10, 1994. Televised on C-Span.

50. Michael J. Collins, *Western European Integration: Implications for U.S. Policy and Strategy* (New York: Praeger Publishers, 1992).

51. Stanley R. Sloan, "U.S.-West European Relations and Europe's Future," in *Europe and the United States: Competition and Cooperation in the 1990s*, Glennon J. Harrison, ed. (Armonk, NY: M. E. Sharpe, 1994), p. 171.

52. Kissinger, *Diplomacy*, p. 833.

53. Werner Weidenfeld, "Jenseits des selbstverstandlichen: Europa und USA brauchen einen Neubeginn," *EuropaArchiv* 48, no. 13/14 (July 25, 1994): 366.

54. U.S. International Trade Commission, *The Effects of Greater Economic Integration within the European Community on the United States* (USTIC Publication 2269, 1991).

55. Raymond J. Ahearn, "U.S. Access to the EC-92 Market: Opportunities, Concerns, and Policy Challenges," in *Europe and the United States*, Harrison, ed., pp. 177–192.
56. Ibid., pp. 188–190.
57. October 11 meeting with Connecticut legislators in the Economics Ministry of Baden-Wurtemmberg in Stuttgart.
58. November 1–10 in Hartford, Connecticut.
59. John W. Fischer, "Airbus Industry and Subsidy in the European Context," in *Europe and the United States*, Harrison, ed., pp. 214–228.
60. Charles E. Hanrahan, "European Integration: Implications for U.S. Food and Agriculture," in *Europe and the United States*, Harrison, ed., pp. 229–238.

CHAPTER 4

AMERICAN POLICY
TOWARD "EAST EUROPE"

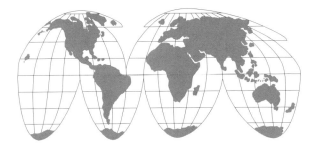

PAUL J. BEST

INTRODUCTION

When Europe was included in the bipolar international regime of the post-World War II era, it was fairly clear to observers what was "East" and what was "West." West Europe consisted of the European Economic Community (today the EU), most of whose member-states were also allies of the United States in the North Atlantic Treaty Organization (NATO). The West also included a few technically neutral states—Austria, Finland, Sweden, and Switzerland—which were clearly in the liberal democratic free-enterprise/capitalist economy camp. Eastern Europe included all of the constituent republics of the Soviet Union plus its allied Communist party-ruled states of Poland, German Democratic Republic, Czechoslovakia, Hungary, Romania, and Bulgaria. In the same grouping was the Federal Republic of Yugoslavia, an independently ruled Communist state consisting of the republics Slovenia, Croatia, Macedonia, Montenegro, plus Serbia along with its two autonomous regions of Kosovo and Vojvodina. The Albanian Socialist Republic was also included in East Europe.

In the 1990s, however, "East Europe" had fractured into twenty-seven separate states, in seven regions, each state proclaiming sovereignty. The listing of these "successor states" in the process of "transition" includes the following: from the former U.S.S.R., the Russian Federation (two-thirds of the Soviet Union and the officially U.N.-recognized successor to the U.S.S.R.); outside of the Russian Federation but in the eastern part of Europe, Moldova, Ukraine, and Belarus (the latter two states inhabited by East Slavs, closely related to Russians); and in the Caucasus, historically, Christian Georgia and Armenia plus Moslem Azerbaijan. Also from the U.S.S.R. comes Central Asia, which includes the Turkic Moslem states of Kazakhstan, Uzbekistan, Kyrgyzstan, Turkmenistan, and Persian-speaking Tajikistan.

On the eastern edge of the former U.S.S.R., bordering on the Baltic Sea, are Estonia, Latvia and Lithuania. All three are of western cultural background. Estonia and Latvia have a Lutheran religious inheritance while Lithuania is Roman Catholic. All three were independent in the interwar period (1918–1939), but were annexed by the Soviet Union in 1940, lost to Germany 1941–1944, and regained by the U.S.S.R. in 1945.

In the eastern part of Central Europe, Poland is again independent (its previous twentieth-century independence was in the interwar years of 1918–1939) while the German Democratic Republic (GDR) has been absorbed into the Federal Republic of Germany. Czechoslovakia, however, has split into independent Czech and Slovak Republics. Hungary, Romania, and Bulgaria have reasserted their independence. Yugoslavia has, like the U.S.S.R., disintegrated into its constituent units in the following fashion: Slovenia and Croatia are separate states along with Macedonia, while Bosnia-Herzegovenia fell into a tripartite civil war among Moslems, Orthodox Serbs, and Catholic Croats—although it is internationally recognized as a single independent state. Rump Yugoslavia includes the former Yugoslav republics of Serbia and Montenegro. Albania concludes the list of post-Communist states of former "East Europe." We now have twenty-seven countries where formerly we had nine, three times as many. How then have things changed? What is "East Europe" now? Can we continue to use political terminology from the Communist era that is no longer true for the twenty-first century? The answer is—no, we cannot use the blanket term "East Europe" anymore. Therefore, let us look at the redefinition of Europe east of the European Union.

Europe is a peninsula of the Eurasian landmass. The Arctic Ocean is on the North, the Atlantic Ocean on the West, and the Mediterranean Sea is to the south. The eastern border of Europe, however, is not all that clear. Where does Europe end and Asia begin? The answer to that is arbitrary: Russian geographers in the nineteenth century decided that the Ural Mountains would be the frontier between Europe and Asia, and rivers flowing west, south, and north from the Urals would be considered to be within Europe, while rivers flowing from the east side of the Urals would be considered to be wholly within Asia. In this sense, the Russians identified a line in the Ural Watershed as the Europe/Asia continental divide.

The problem with this is that it works geographically but it does not work for culture, religion, and nationality. Clearly, the dominant element of the former Russian Empire, the former Soviet Union, and today's Russian Federation is the East Slavic Russian people (to be precise, "Great Russian" people as opposed to the two other East Slavic Peoples, the "Little Russians" (Ukrainians) and "White Russians" (Belarusians)) whose historical culture and religion springs from Greek-Byzantium and Orthodox Christianity. The Russians in modern times have dominated territories from the Carpathian mountains in Central Europe on the west to the Chukchi and Kamchatka peninsulas and the Pacific Ocean on the east (and even temporarily on into Alaska from 1741 to 1867).

This great north Asian Russian dominated area can be referred to as Russia or Eurasia. The Central Asian area of Muslim Turkic and Iranian peoples that was part of the Russian and Soviet Empires is now putatively independent with the collapse of the Soviet Union, although still heavily influenced by Russia.

Returning to Europe west of the Urals we must further subdivide the continent between *historic West Europe* (that area of Roman civilization and culture, using the Latin Alphabet, of Roman Catholic or Protestant religious inheritance, and which felt the invigorating influence of the Renaissance, Reformation, and Enlightenment) and *historic East Europe* (the area of Greek-Byzantine influence and Eastern Orthodox christianity that uses the Cyrillic alphabet for East Slavic languages and was subject to Ottoman Turkic Moslem pressures and that did not undergo the Renaissance, Reformation, and Enlightenment).

It is clear that the political "East Europe" of 1945–1990 is not the same as the historical East Europe, for the Baltic states of Estonia and Latvia (Lutheran and Latin Alphabet), and Roman Catholic Lithuania, and, in Central Europe, Poland, the Czech and Slovak Republics, Hungary and, in Southeast Europe, Slovenia and Croatia and parts of Bosnia plus eastern Germany (the former GDR area) were clearly West European despite being under Communist control for forty-five years. The point is that the political term "East Europe" in use during the Communist era is no longer valid. However, we do recognize that there exists a zone of conflict between historical East and West Europe ("Zwischen Europa," in German), which has its origin all the way back to the rise of Greek and Roman civilization in the fourth century B.C. and the separation of the Roman Empire into eastern and western parts in the fourth century A.D. Later, the Byzantine Empire and its successor, the Ottoman Empire, Imperial Russian Empire, Austro-Hungarian Empire, Sweden, Poland, and Germany fought to control this zone. This middle zone can be referred to today as East Central Europe, the Baltic Region, and Southeast Europe.

Armenia and Georgia, of "Oriental" Christian heritage (a Christianity related to but not the same as Orthodox Christianity, that is, Christianity that developed outside the borders of the Byzantine Empire) in the Caucasus region are sometimes included as an additional part of Europe, especially since they have, in modern times, depended on Orthodox Russia for support against their Moslem enemies, and in the past had been under Byzantine influence, but not control.

Samuel P. Huntington of Harvard University reminded the world about what we have said above in the seminal article "The Clash of Civilizations" which he wrote for the journal *Foreign Affairs* in 1993. In this article he argued, among other things, for the recognition of the perennial struggle between historic Roman-Western Europe and Byzantine-Eastern Europe, a struggle that has reasserted itself in the post-Communist period. Beyond that, discussing as he does the whole of the globe, he draws attention to the historic Islamic-Christian clash that has been resurrected in the Balkans, the Caucasus, and to a lesser extent, Central Asia.[1]

HISTORICAL BACKGROUND

The United States is essentially an outgrowth of West European populations, cultures, and religions and is an inheritor of the Renaissance, Reformation, and Enlightenment. Before its independence in 1776, the North American colonies can be said to have had no foreign policy of their own. Afterwards, until the end of the Civil War, the United States was little interested in Europe east of Germany. Poland had been gobbled up by its neighbors by the end of the eighteenth century, while the rest of the area was dominated by the Russian, Austro-Hungarian, and Ottoman Empires. Only with the influx of Baltic, Central, Southeast, and East European immigrants did the United States even begin to notice the existence of the peoples there. Relations with the Russian Empire, however, were quite good, and it even was thought that Russia supported the North during the Civil War: After that war Russia rather quickly sold off the Alaska territory to the assertive United States in 1867.

World War I, however, drew the United States into the Baltics, Central, Southeast, and Eastern Europe as part of America's support of its "Kith and Kin," France and Great Britain, against Imperial Germany. Since Russia was a cobelligerent of the Western allies of the United States, so too the United States became allied with Russia and supported it.

When in 1917 the Russian regime collapsed and along with it the Eastern Front of the war, a war the United States was just entering, the way for a German victory on the Western Front appeared to be open. The United States became greatly alarmed and, following the British and French lead, landed troops in accessible Russian ports. This "allied intervention" soon brought the United States into conflict with the new Bolshevik-Communist government that overthrew the provisional government and claimed the Russian Empire as its inheritance.

Much has been written about the U.S. role in the intervention, which lasted almost two years past the end of World War I (the last U.S. troops withdrew from Soviet territory in 1920).[2] Suffice to say that the United States withdrew into practical isolation until December 7, 1941, but the Bolshevik-Communists viewed the U.S. actions from 1917 to 1920 as part of a conspiracy of Western capitalist powers (including Japan) to "strangle the Bolshevik

baby in its cradle," something for which the Communists never forgave the
United States.

In fact, while the United States officially loathed Bolshevik excesses, it
was little concerned with that area of the world and only wished to prevent
Bolshevik infection into the United States itself. While it is true Franklin
Roosevelt recognized the Communist government of the Soviet Union in
1933, this had little effect on U.S. policy toward the U.S.S.R. since, during the
1930s, there really wasn't much of a U.S. foreign policy at all.

In regard to the Baltic states, East Central, and Southeast Europe,
Woodrow Wilson was given credit for the emergence of independent Poland,
Czechoslovakia, and Yugoslavia upon the break-up of the German, Austro-
Hungarian, and Russian Empires, based on his famous "Fourteen Points,"
which included the idea of national self-determination of the peoples of
Europe.[3] While Wilson's "points" did sound quite stirring, they had little prac-
tical effect other than to encourage the Balts (Estonians, Latvians,
Lithuanians), West Slavs (Poles, Czechs, Slovaks), and South Slavs (Yugoslavs)
to fight for their independence.

Between 1939 and 1941, when the U.S.S.R. was an ally of Germany and
when Poland, which the United States fancied as an American client in
Central Europe, was crushed between the Soviet Communists and the German
Nazis, the United States maintained an aloof posture, while still aiding Great
Britain as much as President Roosevelt dared, given the U.S. political climate.
In 1941, when the United States was drawn into World War II, real U.S. interest in the Baltic region, Central, Southeast, and East Europe began, an interest that would be of paramount importance to the United States for the next
fifty years! The U.S.S.R.'s erstwhile ally Nazi Germany attacked it on June 22nd
and nearly drove the Communists to defeat by December of that year. At the
same time that the *Wehrmacht* was knocking on the gates of Moscow, the
Japanese were preparing to attack the United States at Pearl Harbor in the
Hawaiian Islands. Several days after the Japanese attack Hitler declared war on
the United States and America was in the thick of World War II.

The government in Washington, faced with a two-front war, chose to
fight Hitler first: The battle with Japan was relegated to a secondary place. The
United States Lend-Lease program, already in effect with Great Britain, was
rapidly expanded to include the U.S.S.R. and, because a collapse of the
U.S.S.R. could easily tip the war in Hitler's favor, Roosevelt ordered "in March
1942 ... that material promised to Stalin was to be delivered ahead of all other
commitments including the requirements of American armed forces."[4]

The U.S.-Soviet alliance of World War II was an alliance of necessity. No
one who cared to look thought that the Soviet Union was a democracy (and,
in fact, the more one looked the more one realized that the U.S.S.R. and Nazi
Germany were the evil twins of the same mother—totalitarianism), but at least
it was the enemy of our enemy and thus could be an ally. To be sure, many in
the West convinced themselves that "Uncle Joe" Stalin was a benevolent

nationalist who could be counted on to support a peaceful democratic world after the war. For these people, the shock was great when the United States and U.S.S.R. became involved in a forty-five-year Cold War after the defeat of Germany and Japan.

The clash between the West (the United States and its allies in Western Europe, Australia, New Zealand, Japan, South Korea, and Taiwan) and the East (the U.S.S.R. and its allies) that defined the postwar period is sometimes described by revisionist historians as an avoidable fight. Some writers think that if the West had only somehow accommodated the Soviets, had calmed Communist fears, then the world would have been a happier and safer place.

This writer feels, however, that this is a false view. To be sure, mistakes, even major ones, were made, but the overall picture appears to show that irreconcilable ideological differences and Soviet expansionist policies made the confrontation nearly unavoidable.

The end of the second (or third if you count the Napoleonic Wars) great European civil war brought two powers peripheral to Europe, the United States and U.S.S.R., into conflict on a global scale in a struggle for global hegemony. Besides asserting power as all great nations have historically done, the Soviet Union also claimed to be the leading ideological force in the world. According to Marxism-Leninism, the Soviet state was the greatest advance humankind had ever made. It was the first state to enter into the highest possible stage of human social development, socialism-communism. The Soviet Union was not only the pathfinder for the human race, but it also had the right and the duty to assist other nations along the road to social progress—to communism.[5] The United States, on the other hand, espoused liberal democracy and free-market capitalism, the antithesis of all that the Soviet Union's socialism-communism stood for.

As a result, the United States saw to it that the so-called Tri-Lateral area—West Europe, the United States and Canada, and Japan (plus Australia, New Zealand, the Pacific Islands, and, after the outbreak of the Korean War, South Korea)—was protected as the core of the West. The Soviet Union protected all its own territories plus East, Central, and Southeast Europe and the anomalous Cuba in the Caribbean Sea. The West and the East faced each other in gridlock in the very center of Europe along the "Iron Curtain." They also fought each other in Latin America, Asia, and Africa.[6]

During the period from May 7–8, 1945 (the end of World War II in Europe) to December 25, 1991 (the date of the final and definitive dissolution of the Soviet Union), bilateral United States and U.S.S.R. relations went through several distinct periods.

The *first period* was between the end of the World War II and Winston Churchill's famous Fulton, Missouri, speech on March 5, 1946. In this speech Churchill urged containment of the Soviet Union by the West by acting to thwart Soviet expansionism. It was a period of increasingly souring relations.[7]

The *second period*, between 1946 and March 5, 1953 (the death of Stalin), was the time when the Cold War began in earnest and deepened into the greatest chill it ever had. The Iron Curtain did form in the center of Europe, although not precisely from Stettin in the north to Trieste in the south as Churchill stated. Poland, Hungary, Romania, Bulgaria, Yugoslavia, and Albania were forcibly communized (although by the middle of 1948 Yugoslavia and Albania had departed the Soviet Communist camp, but not communism itself). By 1950 the Soviet occupation zone of the divided Germany was formed into a socialist state called the German Democratic Republic (GDR), and the peculiar situation of Berlin, the capital of prewar Germany, divided as it was into four occupation zones, but resting within the borders of the GDR, was a source of constant strife. From June 1948 to May 1949 the Soviet Union blockaded the land routes (road, rail, and water) to the Berlin occupation zones of France, Britain, and the United States, precipitating a major crisis. Later, in November 1958, Nikita Khrushchev, the then leader of the Soviet Union, threatened the West with war if it didn't leave the city. In 1961 a Wall (Die Mauer) was constructed all around West Berlin, the political entity encompassing the three Western occupation zones, to prevent East Germans from seeking refuge there. The collapse of this great Wall in November 1989 signaled the beginning of the end of communism in Germany.[8]

The *third period*, between March 1953 and the end of 1955, was one of relative quiescence, an interlude, when the Soviets felt uncertain. It was during this time that the Korean War was concluded in an Armistice and the Austrian State treaty was signed, ending the allied occupation of Austria and effectively neutralizing that country.

The *fourth period*, encompassing Nikita Khrushchev's consolidation of power in 1955 to his fall in 1964, was one of nearly a decade of Soviet activity on a global scale. Besides the aforementioned Berlin crises, Khrushchev projected Soviet power outward in an attempt to destabilize and cow the capitalist world. Particularly frightening to the West were the Soviet advances in military technology. "On ... October 4, 1957, the Soviet Union ... launched the world's first artificial satellite ... [n]amed 'Sputnik' [which traveled at] eighteen thousand miles per hour. More significant ... was the powerful booster rocket ... for it indicated Soviet capability of sending a powerful weapon at high speeds to targets within a four thousand mile radius."[9] Fears that Soviet ICBM's (Intercontinental Ballistic Missiles) would soon be deployed, an act that could decisively alter the world's balance of power in favor of the U.S.S.R. (the so-called "Missile Gap" of the 1960 Kennedy-Nixon U.S. presidential campaign), were further enhanced by Soviet nuclear weapons testing. This testing concluded with the greatest round of nuclear explosions ever made by human beings, in 1961 and 1962, including the detonation of a device of perhaps fifty million megatons.[10]

Ideologically speaking, both Khrushchev, in 1961 at the 22nd Congress of the Communist Party of the Soviet Union, in his notion of overtaking and surpassing the West, and Mao Zedong, in 1957, when he bluntly stated, "There are two winds in the world today—the East Wind and the West Wind.... I think the characteristic of the situation today is the East Wind prevailing over the West Wind," indicated that communism would take over the world, and soon.[11] In the end, however, and especially after the Cuban missile crisis, Nikita Khrushchev endangered and angered the Soviet "Nomenkaltura" (the ruling class) who got rid of him in 1964.

The *fifth period*, 1965 through 1985, is known in the former Soviet blocs as that of the "Stagnation" (zastoi). Leonid Brezhnev was the General Secretary of the Central Committee of the Communist Party of the Soviet Union, from October 1964 until his death in November 1982. He was succeeded by the short-lived General Secretaryships of Yuri Andropov (Nov. 1982–Feb. 1984) and Konstantin Chernenko (Feb. 1984–March 1985). These three leaders are generally treated as one during this twenty-year period of detente with the United States. Detente was characterized by a tacit agreement not to fight face-to-face: The two superpowers struggled in Indo-China, Africa, Latin America, and Afghanistan without direct confrontation. It was an international relations regime understandable and acceptable to both sides.[12]

The *sixth and final period* of post World War II U.S.-Soviet relations was dominated by two men, Mikhail Gorbachev of the U.S.S.R. and Ronald Reagan of the United States. In this period Soviet leaders came to a realization that the tremendous cost of the arms race was so burdensome that it could no longer be borne.[13] Ronald Reagan planned to, and to a certain extent did, spend the U.S.S.R. into destruction. Realizing that the United States was overwhelming the Soviet Union in military technology, Mikhail Gorbachev attempted to scale down the arms race while planning to reinvigorate both the Soviet economic and political systems. He was successful in reaching the first goal but disastrously unsuccessful in the second and third ones.

Mikhail Gorbachev launched his peace (Novoye Myshlenie—"new thinking") campaign soon after he came to lead the U.S.S.R. in 1985. He authorized a multilanguaged, world-distributed edition of speeches and interviews wherein he called for new thinking in international relations.[14] He clearly understood the tremendous weight the Soviet military burden placed on his country; a cost never completely and satisfactorily calculated, but that can be roughly estimated as the following:

	U.S.	U.S.S.R.
Gross Domestic Product	100%	40% or 60% of U.S. GDP
Average Annual percent of GDP expended on arms	6.5%	30% or 50% of U.S.S.R. GDP

Whether one takes the conservative 40 percent rate for the Soviet relation to U.S. GDP or the liberal 60 percent rate and whether one uses the 50
percent of 40 percent or 30 percent of 60 percent rates, the costs were obviously ruinously suffocating to the U.S.S.R.[15] Thus Gorbachev decided to end
the Cold War decisively. In 1987, the United States and the U.S.S.R. signed the
INF treaty (Intermediate-range Nuclear Forces), which eliminated a whole
class of nuclear weapons in the European theater, that is, over a thousand
short to medium-range (500–1,000 kilometer striking distance) missiles in
Central Europe and 1,600 intermediate-range ballistic and cruise missiles
(1,000–3,000 kilometer striking distance). These weapons were to be, and
were, destroyed under monitored conditions.[16] A second treaty, Conventional
Forces in Europe (CFE), settled the confrontation between NATO and
Warsaw Pact forces in Central Europe.[17] The Warsaw Pact dissolved itself in
1992.

Finally, in July 1991, a Strategic Arms Reduction Treaty (START)
reduced the number of strategic launch vehicles (airplanes and various types
of missiles and warheads) on both sides to a relatively low level. (With the collapse of the U.S.S.R., Russia became the official nuclear successor state and
nuclear weapons stationed in Ukraine, Belarus, and Kazakhstan were turned
over to Russia for redeployment or destruction).[18]

In the areas of *Perestroika* (reconstruction—that is, economic change)
and *Glasnost* ([political] openness), Gorbachev got contrary results. He apparently intended to reform the political system first and then the economy, just
the opposite of the more successful example of the People's Republic of
China. In the process of reform, Gorbachev unleased forces he could not control. One observer entitled his book on the Soviet Union's fall, the *Torrents of
Spring*,[19] another *The Walls Came Tumbling Down*.[20] Nationalisms sprang up, the
system was undercut, and the Soviet Union collapsed.

Perhaps a short digression into Gorbachev's internal problems is in
order since these problems will have a direct bearing on U.S.-Russian relations
in the twenty-first century. Mikhail Gorbachev inherited a system in crisis in
1985. A rapid decline in the economy was quite apparent—the Soviet Union,
despite its claims to the contrary, had failed to develop a dynamic economic
system—and it had failed to deliver the goods to the consumer. Heavy-handed
authoritarians in a bureaucratic system gone wild (the state apparatus was
responsible for practically everything) appeared irreformable. Another problem was the truth of communist "errors" and "distortions" was seeping out,
while the clear neo-class structure of a dominant *nomenklatura* ruling group
was quite open for all to see. Widespread corruption in ruling circles was also
well known—the system was certainly in "General Crisis."[21] Beyond that, industrialization in the U.S.S.R. (and other Communist states) had brought about
an ecological crisis of gigantic proportions, including an actual overall decline
in life expectancies.[22]

A general analysis of why Gorbachev failed includes failure to attempt real reform until 1988 and then only in fits and starts; failure to maintain domestic support while "Gorbomania" developed in Western countries; a nearly nonexistent domestic nationality policy; emphasis on political reform and de-emphasizing social and economic reform, thus not creating a support base of satisfied consumers (like that which Deng Xiaoping created in China); not keeping the military satisfied; and, finally, Gorbachev's image, to the Soviet man-in-the-street, of a leader more interested in foreign acclaim than domestic affairs.[23]

Thus, on August 19, 1991, a group of close Gorbachev associates tried to overthrow him, and for a few days, they appeared successful. On August 21, Gorbachev returned to power, but he was politically weakened and could hold on only until December 25, 1991, when, having been overtaken by events, he resigned as President of the now nonexistent U.S.S.R.

U.S. INTERESTS, CHALLENGES, AND OPPORTUNITIES

The Soviet Union is dead, communism (at least of the old variety) is dead, "East Europe" is dead—where do we go from here?

The United States was forced, kicking and screaming, onto the world scene in December, 1941. It stayed there in fear of being overrun by the Russian and Chinese communists or being bombed into ashes by Soviet ICBMs or being annihilated in chemical and germ warfare attacks. The lesser fears were that the U.S. economy would be surpassed by a superior socialist one or that the West would be squeezed out of markets and barred from raw materials by advancing Communist hordes. But none of this has happened—so now what should be done?

Certainly, a return to pre-1941 isolationism could be dreamed of, but unfortunately the military and political events of the last forty-five years preclude such a policy. Like the Genie that got out of the bottle but couldn't be convinced to get back into it again, we cannot get nuclear weapons and their delivery systems to return to non-existence. The United States cannot retreat from the world; it is stuck with it and it with us. The developments of the most bloody of centuries, the twentieth century, cannot be undone—one must live with them and go onward.

What interests does the United States have in the former Eurasian Communist areas? The answer is many. To begin with, a substantial part of the U.S. population has roots in that area of the world—the Kith and Kin argument. Beyond that, in the global struggle for markets, the United States cannot safely ignore over three hundred million people who sooner or later might develop the buying power to purchase U.S. products. Scientific developments in that area of the world have not been small in the past and, while not significant presently, they could be in the future. The United States needs information exchanges and ties with the former Communist area. Raw materials are of special interest to U.S. industry, especially the petroleum available from Central Asia, Azerbaijan, the Russian Arctic, Siberia, and the Far East. Concern for the development of a liberal democratic and free market system is not just altruism since the United States can ill-afford a revival of the Cold War with a neo-Soviet state in Eurasia.

The principal challenge to the United States today is to develop successful policies that will foster good relations with all of the twenty-seven post-Communist states of the former "East Europe." The challenge includes fostering the growth of a cadre of U.S. experts who understand the complexities of the post-Cold War era—complexities, that, having been repressed for 50 to 75 years, have sprung forth in sometimes violent ways.

The challenges to a globally engaged United States are great but the opportunities are greater. If the United States is able to successfully navigate the shoal-filled waters of the immediate post-Communist years, it could reach the shore of enduring friendship and cooperation with not only nations of Western heritage in the Baltic area, East Central Europe, and Southeast Europe, but also with the nations of Eastern Europe and the Caucasus plus Central Asia—a result that could be beneficial to all.

A failure to act could very easily produce hatred, fear, the rise of a new anti-U.S. power(s) in former Communist areas and, in a worst case scenario, war.[24]

POLICY OPTIONS: PROS AND CONS

OPTION 1: WITHDRAWAL FROM THE FORMER COMMUNIST EUROPEAN AND EURASIAN AREAS

This option is not feasible since, as stated previously, in the "U.S. Interests, Challenges, and Opportunities" section, the United States cannot withdraw from the world and, especially in the case of Russia, cannot ignore the possibility of a renascent rival.

OPTION 2: MINIMAL CONTACT

Letting the situation develop as it will, naturally, is also a nonfeasible option since, as will be seen following, such a choice cannot be applied to the whole area in any case.

OPTION 3: SUBSTANTIAL ENGAGEMENT TO SUPPORT LIBERAL DEMOCRATIC AND FREE MARKET FORCES

This is a very feasible option. Open support of political democracy, open loans and financial aid, open technical assistance, free exchange of knowledge, open investment, and open exchange of scholars and scientists would foster an appreciation by all concerned. Covert activity should be of the absolute last resort, especially in the former Soviet area where people were trained for sev-

eral generations to hate, fear, and distrust westerners, who were seen as con-
spiratorial enemies bent on the destruction of their system.

OPTION 4: MAXIMUM ENGAGEMENT

This is not a likely scenario because, while the United States may have "won"
the Cold War, it is in no position to try to rebuild whole economies and
nations, much less project military force into the region. The use of maximum
pressure, including that of the military, could only be in case of a threat to the
most vital interests of the United States and its allies or to their very existence.
Nuclear war breaking out in Eurasia, loss of fissile materials, loss of control of
bacteriological or chemical weapons, threats, and actual attack upon NATO
frontiers are the only reasons to exercise Option 4. Otherwise too high a profile by the United States and the West in former Communist areas might be
misunderstood and resented.

POLICY RECOMMENDATIONS FOR THE TWENTY-FIRST CENTURY

In a review essay entitled "Can History Stop Repeating Itself?" concerning Paul
Kennedy's book *Preparing for the 21st Century*, Gerard Piel notices that "Hardest
to decipher [of the whole world Kennedy discusses] are the futures of the erstwhile U.S.S.R. and its former buffer states in Eastern Europe."[25] The former
Soviet area is suffering from a triple crisis: nationalism, a bad economic system, and weak political structures.[26] Robert Heilbroner, in reviewing the same
book, entitles his essay "The Worst Is Yet to Come."[27] Let us hope this is not
true and, in order to assist policy makers, let us make some recommendations
for the twenty-first century.

RECOMMENDATION 1

Follow Option 3 as previously outlined, engage the successor states and governments, assist wherever possible, be open, don't be pushy or moralistic,
don't act with a superiority complex.

RECOMMENDATION 2

Treat each of the seven areas mentioned following and each successor state
individually, realizing that each has its own unique history, culture, religious
heritage, and interests.

RECOMMENDATION 3

Recommendations for Northern Eurasia (the Russian Federation) The
Russian Federation is the legal successor of the U.S.S.R., possessing its nuclear
weapons, most of its conventional armed forces, its permanent seat on the
U.N. Security Council, and two-thirds of the former Soviet territory. In the loss
of influence in the Russian Federation, the United States has the most to lose.

While a smaller Russia emerging as a rival or an enemy is not as bad as the existence of the huge Soviet bloc, such an outcome is to be avoided as much as possible.[28] Russia is nearly twice as large as the United States with about 150 million inhabitants. Its climate much more resembles that of Canada than the United States. It is a federation made up of about 85 percent Russians and, obviously, 15 percent non-Russians.[29] The main Russian-inhabited area is divided into provinces (Krais or oblasts) plus two cities, Moscow and Saint Petersburg, of "Federal Importance." There are also twenty-one autonomous units within the Federation called republics, one autonomous province, and ten smaller national districts where the non-Russian nationalities have an official home although, in many cases, Russians are a majority in those areas, too.[30]

Russia is the most dangerous and delicate of successor states and also the most important. The nationality question is frequently written about in the scholarly and popular press, especially concerning the war in the Chechnya where a non-Slavic population of Moslem heritage battled in the 1990s to separate from the Russian Federation.[31] It is possible that Moslem peoples within Russia could join with Moslems outside the Federation's borders to create very considerable problems for Russia. In reaction to this, Russian nationalistic fever has risen. The recommended policy for the United States is to support Russia within her current borders while encouraging Russia's leadership to satisfy, as much as possible, non-Russian aspirations within the Federation.

Another major problem for Russia is that of Russians living in nearby successor states, the so-called "near abroad." Upwards of 25 million Russians now live outside Russia. Russia recognizes as a citizen everyone living in Russia as of November 28, 1991, those living outside the country who were born on Russian territory, or those who are descended from at least one parent born in Russia.[32] Obviously, any state seeks to protect its citizens and equally obviously this gives Russia a lever in relation to other successor states.[33] U.S. policy should be to recognize Russian interests in ex-Soviet areas but only insofar as repatriation of Russians to the motherland and not as an excuse for meddling in other countries' internal affairs.

A third major problem the United States must face with Russia is a military one and this includes the enlargement of NATO, continuing dismantlement of nuclear weapons, and reaching CFE treaty limitations. Here, the United States should pursue NATO expansion to encompass all the historically western states, including the three Baltic republics, East Central European states (see following), Slovenia, and, eventually, Croatia in Southeast Europe. This must be done in such a way as to salve Russian sensibilities but not in such a way as to give Moscow a veto on NATO activities.[34] This could be achieved by encouraging Russia's full participation in the OSCE (Organization for Security and Cooperation in Europe), NACC (North Atlantic Cooperation Council), NATO's "Partnership for Peace" program, the

Council of Europe, and all other parts of the Pan-European cooperation regime. We recommend that Russia also be admitted to the G-7 political and economic organization as a full member and 8th (G-8) partner. It is simply better to have Russia in the regime than outside of it as a troublemaker.

In regard to Russia's other domestic problems, one can only agree with former president Richard Nixon, who recommended the following:

1. Creation of a "U.S.-led organization to spearhead Western Aid Efforts"
2. Acceleration of aid to Russia's agriculture
3. Establishment of "enterprise funds" to help economic reform
4. Expanded "educational and information exchange programs"[35]

RECOMMENDATION 4

In regard to the three non-Russian successor states geographically in the eastern part of Europe—Ukraine, Belarus, and Moldova—we recommend that the United States simply have normal relations with Moldova and that the predominant interest of Romania be recognized, since Moldovians are Romanians and, at some time, the two states will probably unite. In regard to Belarus, it appears that the low-level of distinct Belarusian national feeling, the high number of ethnic Russian inhabitants, and the historic fear of the West, especially Poland and Lithuania, will cause Belarus to gravitate toward and unite with Moscow, something over which the United States can have very little influence.

Ukraine is another matter: In a broad sense we may say Ukraine is pulled both East and West. Eastern Ukraine, with a heavy majority of Russian speakers who can identify either as Russians or Russo-phone Ukrainians, look to Moscow, while Western Ukrainians, for historic and religious reasons, look West. The United States should support the Ukrainian government as much as possible in order to encourage Ukrainian independence and in the very long run its possible accession to NATO.

RECOMMENDATION 5

The three Baltic states, Estonia, Latvia, and Lithuania, clearly belong in the West and the United States, which never ceased its recognition of Baltic independence during the period in which these states were forced republics of the U.S.S.R., should continue to support them. Finland can take the lead in Finnic Estonia as can Sweden in Latvia and Lithuania. Poland should be discouraged from being too aggressive toward the latter, especially in regard to the Polish minority in Lithuania and in regard to historic claims to Lithuania's capital, Vilnius. NATO and EU membership should come very early in the twenty-first century to these states. The Kalingrad Oblast (Province)—the remains of war booty taken from Germany—should be turned into a free trade zone and a Europort (all European seaport) for the greater area (Poland, Lithuania, Belarus, Ukraine, and Russia).

RECOMMENDATION 6—CAUCASIA

In view of the far distant geographical location and the caldron of Christian-Moslem hatreds, the United States should tread very lightly in relation to Armenia, Georgia, and Azerbaijan. Settlement of border disputes within Georgia between Christians and Moslems (Abkhazia and South Ossetia) and the dispute between Azerbaijan and Armenia over Nagorno-Karabakh should be encouraged, but the United States cannot and should not get too involved. Russia, which has its problems with non-Russian Moslem populations on the north slope of the Caucasus will continue to be the dominant foreign power there in the twenty-first century.

RECOMMENDATION 7—CENTRAL ASIA

U.S. interests in Central Asia are limited to raw materials and support of its secular, though Moslem, ally, Turkey. Kazakhstan, Uzbekistan, Kyrgystan, and Turkmenistan are inhabited by Turkic peoples related to the Turks of modern Turkey but separated from them by history and geography. It would seem that secular states similar to Turkey with good relationships with the West would be the best for the United States. Support of Turkish help for such an outcome should be the goal for the United States in the twenty-first century. Tajikistan is a bit of a different matter, since Tajiks are related to peoples in Afghanistan and Iran and speak a version of Persian. Further, Russia has a sort of "peace-keeping" force there that probably will remain in place for a long time. Given border disputes and ethnic conflict in Central Asia, the United States would do best to tread lightly and act indirectly.

RECOMMENDATION 8—EAST CENTRAL EUROPE

Poland, the Czech Republic, Slovakia, and Hungary have historically always been part of Western civilization—using the Latin alphabet, being of Western Christian heritage and having taken part in all West European historical developments especially the Renaissance, Reformation and Enlightenment. They should be taken into NATO and the European Union before the beginning of the twenty-first century—period. U.S. influence should push toward that goal.

RECOMMENDATION 9—SOUTHEAST EUROPE

Southeast Europe will continue to be the tinder box of Europe in the twenty-first century as it was in the twentieth. Romania, with its desire to eventually absorb Moldova, is quiet now but carryover from the Communist regime, plus conflict with Hungary over Hungarian ethnic elements in the Carpathian mountains within Romania, will be causing destabilization for decades to come. Bulgaria suffers from conflict over its domestic Turkish minority as well as tension in relation to the potential revival of the claim that Macedonians are Bulgarians—in case Macedonia should fall into conflict. Macedonia has symbolic and ethnic difficulties with Greece (flag style, name, and "slavo-phone Greeks"). Another major source for internal struggle is the 20-40 percent Albanian ethnic minority. If Bulgaria, Serbia, or Albania were to assert their claims, a terrible new Balkan War could ensue. The United States should work to prevent this from occurring but certainly not get directly involved until an opportune moment arrives such as happened in Bosnia, with the signing of the Dayton peace treaty.

Albania, the poorest country in Europe, is encumbered by Greek claims to a portion of its southern region ("Northern Epirus" to the Greeks). The Kosovo autonomous region of Serbia, where there is upwards of 90 percent Albanian population, is also a source of tension, as is the large and fairly compact Albanian population in Macedonia. Other than economic aid and peacekeeping assistance, the United States should stay clear of the fray.

The former Yugoslavia presents a mixed picture. Slovenia in the north is the most likely candidate for NATO and EU membership, while Croatia, if it settles its Bosnian adventure, would be another.

As far as Bosnia is concerned, it will not survive long into the twenty-first century. After the Implementation Force (IFOR) of NATO withdraws in accordance with the Tripartite Croat-Serb-Moslem peace treaty, the Serbian part will undoubtedly join Serbia, and the Croat part and the Moslem area may find itself standing alone as a mini-state or in confederation with Croatia. This latter outcome should be encouraged by the United States if the anticipated final disintegration does occur.

Serbia, with its autonomous provinces of Vojvodina and Kosovo, should be encouraged to be satisfied with its union with Montenegro and to curtail its expansiveness. Serbia should not be high on the list of priorities for economic and or political support since it was the principal instigator of the recent Bosnian war and it could yet cause considerable problems in the Balkans in the twenty-first century.

CONCLUSION

To repeat and summarize, the collapse of the Soviet Union and Yugoslavia in the early 1990s created an unprecedented situation in the world. From the former nine East European political entities, twenty-seven have emerged. Where there was formerly one political bloc, the Soviet one (plus Yugoslavia and Albania), we can now discern seven geographic areas of concern to the U.S. planners. These seven areas are Eurasia (the Russian Federation), East Europe outside Russia (Ukraine, Belarus, Moldova), Baltic States (Estonia, Latvia, Lithuania), Caucasia (Georgia, Armenia, Azerbaijan), Central Asia (Kazakhstan, Kyrgyzstan, Uzbekistan, Turkmenistan, Tajikistan), East Central Europe (Poland, Czech and Slovak Republics, Hungary) and Southeast Europe (Romania, Bulgaria, Macedonia, Albania, Serbia, Bosnia, Croatia, and Slovenia). Old monolithic East Europe is gone, and each of the successor regions and countries represents new and unique challenges and opportunities for the United States in the twenty-first century. The complex problems of the fractured East Europe will be a problem for U.S. diplomats well into the next century.

NOTES

1. For a full discussion on this issue, see Samuel P. Huntington, et al., *The Clash of Civilizations? The Debate: A Foreign Affairs Reader* (New York: Council on Foreign Relations, 1993).
2. Karl W. Ryavec, *United States-Soviet Relations* (New York: Longman, 1989), p. 32.
3. Norman Davies, *God's Playground: A History of Poland, Volume II: 1795 to the Present* (New York: Columbia University Press, 1982), p. 387.
4. Donald W. Treadgold, *Twentieth Century Russia*, 7th ed. (Boulder, CO: Westview Press, 1990), p. 349.
5. Any good textbook on *Marxism-Leninism* will give details of this *weltanshauung* (world view).
6. For a short discussion on the origin of the Cold War, see David MacKenzie and Michael W. Curran, *A History of Russia, the Soviet Union and Beyond*, 4th ed. (Belmont, CA: Wadsworth Publishing Co., 1993), pp. 701–708.
7. Adam B. Ulam, *Expansion and Coexistence: The History of Soviet Foreign Policy, 1917–1967* (New York: Praeger Publishers, 1968), p. 424.
8. A Berlin chronology is available in *Berlin: Outlook* (Berlin: Informationszentrum, 1992), pp. 5–22.
9. Walter LaFaber, *America, Russia, and the Cold War: 1945–1984*, 5th ed. (New York: Alfred Knopf, 1985), p. 195.
10. Ulam, *Expansion and Coexistence*, p. 664.
11. LaFaber, *America, Russia, and the Cold War*, p. 199.
12. See Adam B. Ulam, *Dangerous Relations: The U.S. and the Soviet Union in World Politics—1970–1982* (New York: Oxford University Press, 1983) for an excellent analysis of most of this period. For a negative view, consult Richard Pipes, *U.S.-Soviet Relations in the Era of Detente* (Boulder, CO: Westview Press, 1981).
13. Paul Kennedy, *The Rise and Fall of the Great Powers* (New York: Vintage Books, 1987), p. 442.
14. Mikhail S. Gorbachev, *A Time for Peace* (New York: Richardson & Steirman, 1985).
15. See Henry Rowen and Charles Wolf, eds., *The Impoverished Superpower: Perestroika and the Soviet Military Burden* (San Francisco, CA: Institute for Contemporary Studies, 1990).
16. Coit Blacker, *Hostage to Revolution: Gorbachev and Soviet Security Policy, 1985–1991* (New York: New York Council on Foreign Relations, 1993), p. 184.
17. Ibid., p. 184.
18. Ibid., pp. 184–185.
19. Jonathan Adelman, *Torrents of Spring: Soviet and Post-Soviet Politics* (New York: McGraw-Hill, 1995).
20. Gale Stokes, *The Walls Came Tumbling Down: The Collapse of Communism in Eastern Europe*, 2nd ed.(New York: Oxford University Press, 1995).
21. Richard Sakwa, *Gorbachev and His Reforms: 1985–1990* (Englewood Cliffs, NJ: Prentice Hall, 1990), pp. 41–52.
22. Murray Feshbach and Alfred Friendly, *Ecocide in the USSR: Health and Nature under Seige* (New York: Basic Books, 1992).

23. Adelman, *Torrents of Spring*, pp. 232–234.

24. See Manus Midlarsky, et al., eds., *From Rivalry to Cooperation: Russian and American Perspectives on the Post-Cold War Era* (New York: Harper Collins, 1994) for further discussion on this issue.

25. Gerard Piel, "Can History Stop Repeating Itself?" *Scientific American* (July 1993): 114–117.

26. Paul Kennedy, *Preparing for the Twenty-First Century* (New York: Random House, 1993), pp. 228–254.

27. Robert Heilbroner, "The Worst Is Yet to Come," *The New York Times: Book Review*, February 14, 1993, p. 1.

28. Further discussion on this issue can be found in Daniel Yergun and Thane Gustafson, *Russia 2010 and What It Means for the World* (New York: Vintage Books, 1995).

29. Data from Minton Goldman, ed., *Global Studies: Russia, the Eurasian Republics, and Central/Eastern Europe*, 5th ed. (Guilford, CT: Dushkin Publishing Group, 1994).

30. *Constitution of the Russian Federation* (in Russian, 1993), in Chapter 3, "Federal Structure," Article 65 lists all the provinces, republics, and districts.

31. "How Many Other Chechnyas?" *The Economist*, January 14, 1995, pp. 43–45.

32. N. I. Marysheva and I. O. Khlestova, *The Legal Position of Russian Citizens Abroad: Questions and Answers* (in Russian) (Moscow: "Yurist" Publishers, 1994), p. 3.

33. "Europe: Russians in Ex-Soviet Republics," *The Economist*, December 10, 1994, p. 55.

34. "Russia and NATO: Moscow's Foreign Policy and the Partnership for Peace," Briefing paper of the "Commission on Security and Cooperation in Europe," Washington, D.C., May 1994.

35. Richard Nixon, "The Time Has Come to Help," *Time*, January 13, 1992, p. 23.

CHAPTER 5

AMERICAN POLICY
TOWARD CHINA AND JAPAN

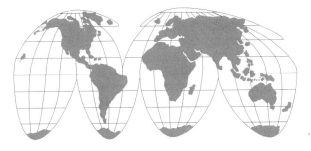

THE EAST ASIAN GIANTS

TA-LING LEE

HISTORICAL BACKGROUND

CHINA

In a real sense, U.S. relations with China predate the founding of the republic. Five years before George Washington was inaugurated as the first president in 1789, a Yankee clipper, properly named *Empress of China*, was half-way
around the globe calling at Canton. China trade by then had already become
a highly lucrative business for many European powers, particularly Great
Britain, and America was anxious to be a part of the action. Trade continued
to develop and by the time of the Opium War in 1839–1842, the United States
overtook the Dutch, the Portuguese, and the Spaniards, having developed a
trading interest in China second only to Britain among western powers.
Although the volume of business was to remain small for a long time to come,
the huge market in China never failed as a lure, then and now.

Before long, merchants out to make a profit were joined by Protestant
missionaries, who went to China to save "godless" souls. With the best of
intentions, missionaries, many with medical training, ventured to the inland
areas far from the coast to work among the teeming peasants, providing badly
needed services while at the same time hoping to win their souls. Merchants
and missionaries thus constituted the two most important constituent groups
whose interests the U.S. government had to serve. And they, in addition to a
small number of diplomats and consular officials stationed mainly in coastal
cities, were to become the main sources of information on China and the
Chinese through a continuous stream of communications on the conditions

in the field. Their voices carried weight with Washington and when they returned home, either in retirement or on business, their impact would invariably be felt in the community. So a special relationship with China, with both material and spiritual content, began at an early date.

The determination to pursue the dual objectives—commercial interest and the spread of Christianity—eventually led to the famous Open Door policy at the turn of the twentieth century, when other western nations and Japan threatened to partition China by claiming their respective "spheres of influence." The United States refused to acknowledge the claims of the other powers and insisted on leaving the Chinese door open so that everybody who did not have a foothold in China could come to trade and preach (including the United States). The Open Door policy, through its noble call for respecting Chinese territorial integrity and sovereignty, has since acquired a moral significance. In time, it became the cornerstone of U.S. China policy, to which successive leaders and diplomats would unfailingly pay lip service, whether the high moral principles read into it could be lived up to or not.

Upholding Chinese territorial integrity and sovereignty in the face of ambitions concerning China by other imperialist powers was a difficult task to accomplish, requiring both will and power that the United States did not always possess. U.S. policies toward China, therefore, wavered between idealism and pragmatism, at times producing conflicting results. However, with occasional lapses, such as the anti-Chinese immigration policy in the 1880s, the United States has taken the moral high ground in its relations with China, striving to live up to its widely popular image among the Chinese of being the least "imperialist" among the Western powers having an interest in China. This was particularly true during World War II, when the United States became the most important ally of China, which was fighting desperately to resist Japan's aggression. With the help of compassionate missionaries and a sympathetic press, a vast amount of goodwill was generated in the United States for the heroic and suffering Chinese people. This helped to further enhance the image of America in the minds of the Chinese as a bounteous land with generous people, an image that was not far off the mark. This image of America grew out of a comparison with most other countries that professed an interest in China in the last two hundred years.

During World War II, China, which bore the brunt of the Japanese attack, was led by Chiang Kai-shek, whose Nationalist Party controlled the government. The Chinese Communist Party under Mao Zedong was a guerrilla force, fighting both the Japanese and the Nationalists in north China. As China's ally, the United States supported the Chiang Government, which was war-weary and corrupt. At the end of the world war in 1945, full-scale civil war broke out between the Nationalists and the Communists who, through fast expansion in the last years of World War II, were able to field a seasoned fighting force a million strong. The United States tried unsuccessfully to broker a peace between the two sides. It continued to help Chiang Kai-shek intermittently until late 1949, when Chiang fled to Taiwan and Mao proclaimed the birth of the People's Republic in Beijing's Tiananmen Square on October 1, to the cheers of millions.

Quite apart from ideological reasons making capitalist America a mortal enemy of a Communist China, Washington's siding with the Nationalists during the civil war years would not bode well for friendly relations with the new government. As it turned out, there were more than two decades of unrelenting enmity between Washington and Beijing. The remote possibility that the Truman administration might have been able to formulate a new China policy along pragmatic lines was dashed to pieces by the Korean War in June 1950. China's sending of nearly a million "volunteers" to fight against U.S. soldiers, who were under the aegis of the United Nations, further deepened the enmity between the two. By the time the Korean War was over, with heavy casualties on all sides, China was condemned as an aggressor by a U.S.-dominated United Nations, and Taiwan, which Beijing saw as a renegade province to be taken over, was militarily allied with Washington through a Mutual Defense Treaty.

Despite the looming presence of mainland China under the effective control of the Communists, the United States continued to champion the cause of the Republic of China on Taiwan, treating it as the legitimate government of all China. Cold War considerations were so overpowering that this position was faithfully adhered to for two decades by both Republican and Democratic administrations. At the United Nations, the annual ritual of fighting over the "China representation" issue was led by the United States, thwarting Beijing's desire to replace Taiwan in the General Assembly and, more importantly, in the Security Council.

The 1960s was a period when the United Nations experienced phenomenal growth, when many newly independent former colonies joined the world body, which deprived the United States of the automatic majority it had enjoyed for two decades. As more and more members favored Beijing's representation, Washington began to see the handwriting on the wall. In 1971, Beijing was voted in to take the China seat and the delegation from Taiwan was expelled. When the vote was announced despite the last minute effort mounted by the U.S. representative, Ambassador George Bush, many delegates from pro-Beijing nations literally danced in the aisles of the General Assembly hall.

As it turned out, what happened at the United Nations was nothing compared to what was already going on in utter secrecy: Bush's superiors, President Nixon and his national security adviser Henry Kissinger, were completing a strategic switch of historic proportions. A Republican President who built his reputation as a hard-line anti-Communist, Nixon was about to visit Beijing, a visit, in Nixon's words, that was to "change the world." The weeklong visit came close to doing just that. The texture of the bipolar Cold War was changed forever. Instead of a Washington-Moscow balance of terror,

Beijing was now added to the U.S. side to tip the balance, leaving the Soviet Union vulnerable and thus more willing to compromise.

The "opening to China" began a new chapter in Sino-American relations, which was enthusiastically embraced, once again, by both the Republican and Democratic administrations. What started as a bold first step by Nixon in 1972 was eventually completed by Jimmy Carter, when the relations with the People's Republic were "normalized" in 1979. In an official communiqué, the United States formally "acknowledged" that there is only one China, that Taiwan is a province of China, and expressed the hope that the Chinese on both sides of the Taiwan Straits will resolve their differences by peaceful means.

Sino-American relations, after an estrangement of three decades, were finally restored at the official level and slowly at the unofficial level, as well. The first decade following the normalization of relations saw rather cautious moves on both sides, still constrained by Cold War necessities. The subsequent economic reform in China and the collapse of communism elsewhere, notably in the former Soviet Union and Central and Eastern Europe, hastened the pace of the development of a closer relationship between the United States and China.

Trade, which was nonexistent during the decades of estrangement and negligible through the mid-1980s, exploded, reaching a two-way volume of well over $30 billion in 1993, more than $40 billion in 1994, and $60 billion in 1995. China now stands as the sixth largest trading partner of the United States. American investors are among thousands of foreign companies that have invested billions of dollars in assets and services in China, constituting an important part of the Chinese economy. Cultural exchanges thrived and military cooperation continued into the post-Cold War era, with only a temporary setback as a result of the Tiananmen Massacre—the mass killing of students demonstrating for democracy in Tiananmen Square in 1989.

As the United States is looking to the twenty-first century, bracing for the challenges of developing constructive relations with a nation widely assumed to be destined to greatness, a reminder may be in order. Despite its phenomenal economic growth in recent years, the People's Republic of China remains a self-proclaimed socialist country ruled by a one-party dictatorship with an unenviable human rights record. The likelihood of a sudden change in China *a la* the former Soviet Union is not great. In the foreseeable future and into the twenty-first century, as China becomes stronger in its own right, the United States should expect many of the familiar problems inherent in dealing with independent and powerful nations in any age.

JAPAN

When Commodore Matthew Perry with his fleet of black ships arrived in Yokohama Harbor in 1853 and again in 1854, little did he realize that he had opened up a relationship that was to become one of the most important ones between the two nations a mere century and a half later. Neither the United States nor Japan was a particularly outgoing nation at that time. Japan, in the last decades of the more than 250-year-old Tokugawa Shogunate, was tenaciously clinging to its proclaimed seclusionist policies, despite increasing pressure from the outside for an opening. The United States was experiencing growing pains as a nation, with the divisive controversy over slavery consuming the energy and attention of the people. There was only incidental interest in trade with Japan—the lure, then as now, was in China—and there were occasional incidents involving alleged mistreatment of shipwrecked crew members of American fishing vessels operating off the coast of Japan. It was to address these rather minor problems and to probe a vague prospect of trade that Perry was sent on his mission by a government that was still a long way from viewing itself as a Pacific power.

The ensuing decades were times of momentous change in both countries. From the mid-1860s on, Japan was to go through one of the most important periods in that nation's history. For some thirty years, Japan was totally immersed in the Meiji Restoration, a thorough-going modernization drive to transform Japan from a medieval feudal state into a modern nation. It was not until the mid-1890s, when the Meiji Restoration was completed, that Japan began to make its first major venture beyond its borders, in the Sino-Japanese War of 1894–1895.

Interestingly, there was a parallel series of events in the United States during the same period. After the gathering storm of the late 1850s came four years of bloody Civil War, which did not end until 1865. The end of the killing on the battlefield was followed by a much longer period in which the nation, divided between the victorious and the vanquished, groped for a viable way of living together. Whether it was the punitive Reconstruction, the wound-healing "let alone" years of the 1870s, the subsequent birth of the New South, or indeed the overall post-Civil War effort at national economic development characterized by some as the "Era of the Robber Barons," national attention had unmistakably turned inward.

The first venture abroad by the United States did not take place until 1896, in the Spanish-American War, which coincided with Japan's first post-Meiji foreign war, the first Sino-Japanese War of 1894–1895. The Spanish-American War had profound implications in terms of America's future role in Asia, for it was at the end of that war that the United States acquired the Philippines from the defeated Spain. The Philippines was the first and only U.S. colony in Asia. In a sense, that signaled the beginning of the U.S. involvement in Asia as a global power with a vested interest in that part of the world.

As far as United States-Japan relations were concerned, the next milestone was Theodore Roosevelt's successful brokering of a peace between Japan and Russia, ending the Russo-Japanese War in 1905. That war was fought on Chinese soil and near Chinese territorial waters over spoils mainly in Manchuria, a mineral-rich territory in China's northeast. It not only marked the ascendancy of Japan as a great power, but also confirmed the United States as an interested party in Asian affairs.

From that time on, the development of United States-Japan relations would continue mainly as a function of Sino-Japanese relations. More precisely, in the next several decades, U.S. policy toward Japan would move along a zig-zag path of trying to contain Japan's ambitions toward China and beyond. No consistent pattern is discernible; indeed from time to time, the United States appeared to alternate its course between resistance and tolerance. For example, Washington championed the moral cause, with Secretary of War Henry Stimson's famous nonrecognition policy toward the puppet "Manchukuo" created by the Japanese militarists in China in 1931. But as Japan's aggression intensified in the ensuing years, Washington kept up the well-known sale of scrap iron to Japan through the 1930s, which had the effect of bolstering Japan's war machine. All that, of course, was to be changed overnight by the attack on Pearl Harbor on December 7, 1941. The United States was now in full-scale war with Japan, bringing the conflict to an end with atom bombs in August 1945.

In the immediate postwar years, the United States played the role of a benevolent occupation power, giving Japan a "blood transfusion" to turn it from a devastated enemy to a grateful friend. A different occupation power, say a U.S.S.R., could conceivably have produced a totally different Japan with profound consequences. It is true that the general Cold War environment, the emergence of Communist China and, in particular, the exigencies of the Korean War to a large extent dictated American policy toward Japan in the decades following World War II. However, one cannot overemphasize the plain fact that the conscientious efforts at helping to rebuild Japan politically and economically (rather than punishing a former enemy) contributed enormously to Japan's quick recovery and growth as a modern and democratic nation. To prevent the revival of militarism, the American-dictated new Constitution of Japan was to contain the famous clause renouncing war as an instrument of national policy. As a corollary of this "no-war" Constitutional provision, the United States agreed to extend the nuclear umbrella over Japan, assuring Japan's security through the signing of a mutual defense treaty. Not having to devote a big chunk of its national resources to the military, Japan was able to concentrate on economic development, achieving recovery and prosperity in quick succession. In other words, the economic prosperity was made possible because the United States shouldered Japan's defense burdens. As Japan became the second largest economy in the world, enjoying a growing trade surplus with the United States, it is only natural that questions would be raised on whether the assumptions on which U.S. policies toward Japan have been based since the end of World War II are still valid. If these assumptions are no longer valid, then new policies based on new assumptions must be developed and implemented in the days to come. With this in mind, we now turn to an examination of the specific issues involved in

U.S. relations with China and Japan in order to explore the range of challenges and opportunities in the future.

U.S. INTERESTS, CHALLENGES, AND OPPORTUNITIES

From the above historical background, we can see that the United States has, during the past two centuries, developed a wide range of interests in East Asia. Some interests have been actively sought by the United States, such as trade. Other interests have accrued by virtue of international forces and the developing role of a great power, such as U.S. security concerns in the region.

To begin with, as the strongest nation in the post-Cold War era, the United States has an undeniable responsibility of world leadership. It is in this capacity that the United States will help shape the new world order. Critics may regard this type of Pax Americana as inherently arrogant, but few can deny the simple fact that the United States is truly the only superpower in the world today and will remain so well into the next century.

In the new world order, the Western Pacific rim will figure prominently as the world's most vibrant region. In the interest of global stability, the United States has legitimate concerns about promoting and maintaining regional stability and peace in East Asia, where China and Japan are the two largest powers. With one-fifth of the world's population and nuclear weapons, China simply cannot be left out of any meaningful global or regional security framework envisioned by the United States. China's cooperation and participation are imperative. With economic and political changes, China represents unlimited opportunities for the United States in the future. As the second largest economy in the world and likely to remain so for some time to come, Japan has become closely linked to the United States in an increasingly interdependent global economy. One-third of all vehicles on U.S. highways are made by Japanese companies (some in the United States), and Japanese cameras and television sets are mainly responsible for bringing the world to our living rooms. Developing new relationships with China and modifying old relationships with Japan both present great challenges for the United States.

Opportunities in American relations with China and Japan should be seen in the larger context of East Asia as a whole. With China as an engine and a lead player by virtue of its immense size, and with Japan's technology and sophistication and with the unabated energies of the "little dragons," the world community can expect the rise of a Pacific century in the next 100 years, much in the same way the Industrial Revolution ushered in the European century in the past. The savings rate in East Asia is three times as high as in the United States. Asia's share of the world's investable capital has more than doubled in the past decade. And East Asian countries are the world's main growth markets for airplanes, cars, cellular phones, and construction equipment. Taking the region as a whole, trade with the United

States, although still highly significant, is decreasing in relative importance, as trade among Asian countries continues to grow. Japan, for example, sends twice as large a share of its foreign investment to Asia as it did a decade ago. It has as large a trade surplus with the rest of Asia as with the United States.[1] The ascendancy of East Asia only underscores the importance of the region as a place of new challenges and vast opportunities for the United States in the twenty-first century.

In a larger sense, U.S. interests, challenges, and opportunities in East Asia, with special reference to China and Japan, to a great extent require an unending process of adjustments between different cultures. These adjustments proceeded at a rather slow pace in the past, but began to pick up speed by the middle of this century, as the world fast became a global village. While technological advances have shrunk the world, our minds, however, have not kept pace with the changes. In an age when our interests, from trade to security to environment, are defined in global terms, our minds are still confined by national and cultural boundaries. Shaped by material and spiritual forces over thousands of years, the distinctiveness of Chinese or Japanese culture is not likely to disappear soon, so a mutual understanding of them is essential when defining our interests, envisioning the opportunities and meeting the challenges ahead in our relations with China and Japan. As we search to define our leadership role in the new world order, we need to keep in mind how Japan and China have blended the old and the new in the past, in their respective quests for modernization, and the ways in which the process will continue in the future.

CHINA

Major issues in U.S.-China relations are regional security, trade, human rights, and Taiwan. Regional security is obvious. As the largest country in the region, China is the leading player in Asian politics and good relations with her neighbors are a prerequisite to regional stability. Because of her power, China's role in solving any regional security problem is also important. Hence, as long as a U.S. presence is considered essential as an anchor in East Asian regional security, it is clear that the United States must involve the People's Republic in dealing with issues concerning regional security. The alarm over North Korea's nuclear capability is a case in point. As a long-time ally and principal supporter during the Korean War, China has always been in a position to have its impact felt in Pyongyang. With the collapse of the Soviet Union, her other patron, North Korea is increasingly isolated with few friends left in the world. China is thus the only remaining "socialist" nation that can exert considerable influence on Pyongyang, particularly at this crucial juncture of power transfer from the long-time dictator, the late Kim Il-sung, to his son, Kim Jong Il. Any U.S. accommodation with Pyongyang on the nuclear issue, to be meaningful, will need Beijing's blessing, if not cooperation. Conversely, if Beijing shows unqualified support for Pyongyang, refusing to exert a moderating influence, it will only foster a hard-line attitude on the part of the new North Korean leadership.

The immense opportunities for U.S. trade in China have always been a lure for businesspeople, dating back to the days of Yankee clipper ships. Earlier in the twentieth century, before China entered the age of electricity, the fondest dream of American business was perhaps best expressed by Standard Oil, which hoped to put a drop of oil in every oil lamp in China. That dream was rekindled at the end of summer 1994 by the visit to Beijing by Ron Brown, U.S. Secretary of Commerce. With twenty-four chief executives of top Fortune 500 corporations in tow, Brown naturally wanted to see the U.S. business cash in on the opportunities in the fast-growing economy of China. One member of the Brown mission, John E. Bryson, head of South California Edison Company, reportedly gasped in awe at the electricity needs there in the coming years. "This is the largest power market in the world," he declared.[2]

Billed as "business diplomacy," Brown's mission was supposed to bring about improvements in human rights conditions in China through trade. However, initial signs pointed exactly in the opposite direction. Just before the arrival of the Brown mission, police detained a number of political dissidents, apparently to prevent them from speaking to the visitors about the dismal human rights situation in China. Should the United States simply turn the other way, pretending not to see flagrant human rights violations? Or should the United States uphold moral principles at the expense of trade? Herein lies one of the great challenges in future relations with China.

In early summer 1994, soon after President Clinton "delinked" human rights from trade, he was praised by many who speak for American business interest. No less than two former secretaries of state, Henry Kissinger and Cyrus R. Vance, both now consultants to major U.S. corporations, hailed the President's "difficult but correct decision" in extending the "Most Favored Nation" (MFN) trading status to China and in decoupling that status from the objective of promoting human rights in China. The resulting "new China policy," they argue, will better serve both American interests and those of peace and stability in Asia. Pursuing better relations with Beijing is not a favor that America is bestowing upon China, since America and China need each other in their mutual search for regional stability. America needs China's cooperation on any number of major issues, ranging from dealing with North Korea to the proliferation of advanced weapons technology to threats to the environment. They, therefore, praised the President for placing legitimate human rights concerns in the "broader context of overall relations."[3]

Not mentioned is the fact that the United States has abandoned the use of trade as leverage, which has produced results in the past. For example, each year when the Congressional debate on renewing the MFN approached, Beijing would release selected political dissidents from prison. Presumably, Beijing can now jail political dissidents with impunity, without fear that the all-important trade with America will be adversely affected. This appeared to be exactly what happened during the Brown visit. From the standpoint of U.S. foreign policy, these are troublesome implications. It would seem that an amoral foreign policy is decidedly against the grain of American ideals and values. Besides, one might point out the obvious inconsistencies: Wasn't it the economic pressure from America that helped end apartheid in South Africa? Why not the same economic pressure on China for the same lofty cause of human rights?

Of the major issues, the Taiwan problem is the most intractable. For it not only involves U.S. relations with Taiwan, but also directly affects the future course of U.S.-China relations. The challenge to the U.S. government is simply this: How can the United States simultaneously maintain friendly relations with two parties that have been mortal enemies for half a century?

The root of the problem goes back to the days of World War II and the subsequent Cold War years, as we discussed in the earlier section. After the normalization of relations with China in 1979, Washington did not "abandon" its long-time ally, the Nationalists on Taiwan. Instead, a tacit understanding was apparently reached with Beijing about Taiwan and its 20 million people, who had no desire to live under Communism. The upshot of the understanding was the Taiwan Relations Act, passed by Congress soon after diplomatic relations were finalized with Beijing. Billed as "domestic" legislation, the Act redefined relations with Taiwan as "unofficial," and everything from weapons sales to trade, from visa procedures to cultural exchanges, must be done on an "unofficial" basis. A charade was thus begun.

Under the arrangement, apparently tolerated by Beijing, the American Embassy in Taiwan became known as the "American Institute in Taiwan," while the Embassy of the Republic of China (Taiwan) in Washington changed its name to the incomprehensible "Coordination Council for North American Affairs." Both, incidentally, were fully staffed by career diplomats who would temporarily "retire" from diplomatic service in order to serve in the "unofficial" capacity. No Taiwan officials were allowed into U.S. government offices and negotiations had to be conducted, literally, in restaurants or motels.

At a time when it was weak and its voice unheard in the international arena, Taiwan could do little but swallow the indignities. However, by the late 1980s, Taiwan managed to turn itself into one of East Asia's four little dragons (along with South Korea, Hong Kong, and Singapore) with phenomenal economic growth, earning international recognition and respect. Since the death of President Chiang Ching-kuo (Chiang Kai-shek's son) in 1988 and the succession of Lee Teng-hui, a native of Taiwan and an economist with a Ph.D. from Cornell University, political liberalization quickened its pace alongside economic growth, making Taiwan an example for other developing nations to follow.

Taiwan's new international status is especially clear in terms of trade with the United States. The two-way trade volume stood at well over $30 billion in 1993, almost the same as that of China, which is 200 times its size and 50 times its population. Moreover, the trade is much more profitable for the United States, for Taiwan buys twice as much from the United States as does China, amounting to $16 billion compared to China's $8 billion in 1993. Put another way, the United States suffers an annual trade deficit of over $30 billion with China, but only a negligible amount with Taiwan. The two-way trade with Taiwan reached $50 billion in 1995, and the deficit remained negligible.With its newly acquired sense of pride, it is only natural that Taiwan demands some respect from others, including the United States. However, any move to upgrade relations with Taiwan would invite strong opposition from Beijing, which regards such moves as an insidious attempt to split up China by fostering Taiwan independence. The problem is further complicated by the fact that there is indeed an independence movement on Taiwan, championed by a formidable opposition party, the Democratic Progressive Party.

The long-awaited review of U.S. policy toward Taiwan, the first since the normalization of relations with China in 1979, was made public in early September 1994. As expected, there was no radical change of policy. Washington was clearly walking a tight rope, trying to balance between China's sensitivity and Taiwan's economic importance. So the result of the policy review was a modest one: Government officials can now have mutual visits and Taiwan's diplomatic office in Washington has been renamed the "Taipei Economic and Cultural Representative's Office."[4] After the announcement was made, neither Beijing nor Taiwan was happy. Beijing severely criticized Washington for interfering in China's internal affairs, while Taiwan was disappointed that the United States did not go further.

China has never renounced the use of force if Taiwan declares independence. Given the nationalistic goals of unifying China—under Mao as well as under Deng—this should not be seen as an empty bluff, for it is entirely within Beijing's ability to do so. On the other hand, Taiwan, as a fledgling democracy, can do little to check the growth of the opposition that has been gaining support in recent elections. Should the Democratic Progressive Party gain power, a formal declaration of independence from China should not be ruled out. If Beijing decides to carry out its threat to use force, the consequences would be disastrous. Open hostility across the Taiwan Straits would indeed be a nightmarish prospect to contemplate. Considering this, the challenge to the United States in the years to come is how to exert a moderating influence on the Chinese under two political regimes, enabling them to continue living in peace.

JAPAN

Some twenty-five years ago, the late Japanese novelist and nationalist Yukio Mishima expressed deep worry that material success, western style, would destroy Japan's traditional values. Japan would become wealthy and astute, but "inorganic, empty, neutral-tinted," Mishima wrote.[5] Mishima eventually committed ritual *hara-kiri* in despair. But twenty-five years later, the Japan he feared would be totally Westernized has not yet been swallowed up by McDonald's and Coca-Cola. Rather, a new generation of Japanese youth have "domesticated" rock music and blue jeans. Modernization did not mean westernization after all, as many people today have come to understand. Japan has modernized spectacularly, giving the world many opportunities, yet it has not become another Great Britain, or a mini-United States. Japan in so many ways remains very "Japanese" today, and yet it has unmistakably become an integral part of the global village.

Japan appears to be at a crossroads today, as the factors responsible for Japan's spectacular post-World War II economic growth begin to fade: hierarchical society giving way to growing individualism, corrupt long-ruling Liberal Democratic Party toppled by young reformists, copying Western technology giving way to much more difficult original ideas, an export-driven economy to be increasingly dependent upon domestic consumption.[6] Change is in the air in Japan, to be sure, but the West is also changing, and the convergence need not be toward either direction. The future is far more complex than the earlier dichotomy of East and West perceived romantically by Rudyard Kipling: "East is East, and West is West, and never the twain shall meet."[7] One needs to appreciate the complexities of the results of social change and economic growth in this shrinking world. For those who are responsible for the formulation of U.S. policy toward Japan, this is of particular importance.

For a long time before World War II, the general assumption that modernization and Westernization were synonymous was not seriously challenged. After all, progress in the post-Industrial Revolution world was led by Western nations as other nations struggled to follow the same path, seemingly toward a set of common goals. It was thought that the West must have found the universal laws governing all endeavors to achieve common goals. To a considerable extent, U.S. foreign policy is still under the influence of this type of thinking. It enables the United States to think in universal terms while, in fact, it more often represents a culturally self-centered attitude that can skew one's vision and produce bad policies.

It is interesting to note that in the past ten years, while American ties to China have grown closer, there has been a steady decline in American trust and friendliness toward Japan. This remarkably consistent pattern is shown in thirty different polls series.[8] The reasons for this are not hard to find: Japan appears less important as an ally now that the Cold War is over, and Japan is accumulating a large trade surplus with the United States. Through the late 1980s, American fear of Japan spread as Japanese manufacturers visibly invaded American markets with cameras, television sets, and, above all, automobiles. The fear deepened by the early 1990s, when Japanese companies bought American icons such as Columbia Pictures, Pebble Beach golf course, and Rockefeller Center in New York. It was further helped along by Hollywood, in such movies as Michael Crichton's *Rising Sun*, which portrayed Japanese investment as a threat to America. Japan-bashing became a popular game, and unemployed Detroit auto workers took to smashing Toyotas and Nissans before TV cameras to show their resentment. Lost to the public mind is the simple fact that Japanese investment in the United States is behind that of Great Britain, Canada, and even the Netherlands, and yet there has been no public outcry against any of those nations.

Seen from a different perspective, however, things may look quite different. In late 1994, the American economy was surging while Japan remained in a lengthy recession. The flood of Japanese investment has already dwindled to a trickle and many investments made with the much-appreciated *yen* in the go-go years, particularly in real estate, have turned out to be disastrous. According to one estimate, between 1986 and 1993 the Japanese lost more than $300 billion on American bonds, property, and other financial assets.[9] Even the much maligned trade surplus can be seen partially as a result of the *yen's* rise against the dollar, not of real trade flows; because measured in *yen*, the surplus is actually falling.

As the American economy improves, Japan as an economic threat seems to be fading in the public mind. Indeed, according to Michael Armacost, former ambassador to Japan, the days of talking about the secret of Japanese corporate management are gone. The once seemingly invincible Japan, Inc. does not seem to be able to keep its act together to pull that nation out of its long recession. With the bursting of the economic bubble, Japanese firms are instead turning to America for lessons, from corporate downsizing to discount retailing.[10]

Change is in the wind. What was suitable for Japan during the high-growth era after World War II is no longer true of the low growth, mature economy of today. In the 1950s and 1960s, bank interest was kept artificially low to allow capital to flow easily to factories, and domestic consumer prices were kept artificially high to encourage factories to sell their products abroad, eventually bringing in a huge trade surplus. These practices were desirable at a time when industry needed funds to expand and when Japan was running a trade deficit in the early decades after World War II. Low-interest rates hurt savers, and high prices hurt consumers. The Japanese willingly tightened their belts in the early years in the name of patriotism. However, pressure from foreign governments and a strong *yen* make Japan's continued dependence on exports increasingly difficult and a budding consumers' rebellion demanding lower prices at home will not go unheard by the political leaders. It is clear that Japan's working practices and institutions, which worked so well in the postwar years, have fallen victim to their own success. It is also clear that people everywhere value freedom and individualism more as they become more affluent. Both are evident in the lackluster "Japan model" today. While many founding fathers of America were fired by universalistic ideals, Japan's power as a role model is characterized by an intense nationalism. As the old Japan model began to weaken, many "universalistic" tendencies began to appear. So again, Japan and the United States appear to be moving in the same direction. The opportunities for the United States are immense, the challenge is how best to approach these opportunities.

Another issue of critical importance to U.S.-Japan relations is nuclear nonproliferation in the region. To help maintain regional stability, the United States has a responsibility to see to it that Japan does not go nuclear, and the best way to do this is to continue providing Japan with a nuclear umbrella. A withdrawal of the U.S. nuclear umbrella will surely push Japan down the road of acquiring nuclear weapons of its own, a course of action always popular with a small number of latent ultranationalists who want to see a return of the glory of a militarist Empire of the Sun. Civilian use of nuclear fuel is another aspect of the larger problem. Although experts do not fully agree whether "reactor-grade" plutonium suitable for nuclear power generation can be easily turned into usable "weapons-grade" plutonium for making bombs, there is already real worry that this could be the way for countries at the low end of technological expertise to become nuclear powers.

Japan, depending heavily on nuclear power for the generation of electricity, has numerous nuclear reactors and is building more. These include breed-reactors, the kind from whose used fuel rods plutonium can be extracted, the material for making bombs. Japan has repeatedly argued that the spent nuclear rods of its reactors can be reprocessed to extract only reactor-grade plutonium, not the weapons-grade kind. Reiterating its commitment never to make or possess nuclear weapons, the government has insisted that it does not have the capability to build the bombs. However, there have been conflicting signals. In June 1994, for example, former Prime Minister Tsutomu Hata took the world by surprise when he said "Japan has the capability to possess nuclear weapons but it has not made them."[11] Indeed, information declassified in recent years by the Department of Energy and statements by a number of American weapons designers suggest that Japan's official position is less than reassuring.

In 1962, American weapons laboratories tested a bomb built from reactor-grade fuel. Only a slightly larger amount of reactor-grade plutonium is needed to make a bomb, which normally requires about four kilograms of weapons-grade plutonium to make.[12] Therefore, the proliferation of not only weapons-grade plutonium, but reactor-grade plutonium as well, is a major concern to the United States. Japan has legitimate needs for nuclear fuel and the United States has an interest in curbing nuclear proliferation and preventing nuclear weapons from falling into the hands of international terrorists or rogue governments. In this context, Japan can be seen either as an ally safely under the U.S. nuclear umbrella or a potential source for serious breach of nonproliferation. How to reconcile the conflicting objectives of the United States and Japan poses another challenge for U.S. policy makers.[13]

The foregoing discussion only demonstrates that views on Japan, as on China, can change rather drastically if we confine our vision to narrow and immediate issues and react impulsively. Hence, Japan can be a hated target in America and then fade quickly with changes in the economies of both countries. China can be a land of teeming millions to whom we would pour our hearts out, and then it could turn into our worst enemy for decades with the change of postwar geopolitical and ideological alignment. Short-term views, therefore, are likely to be short-sighted. We need to reach for a firm grasp of the fundamentals that are not easily swayed by momentary changes, such fundamentals as the basic impulses of our capitalist system and our role of global leadership, the potential of China and the industriousness of the Japanese, and the perspective on which to base these fundamentals. With such perspective, we can then proceed to take initiatives in seeking ways to best serve our mutual interests and meet the challenges ahead.

POLICY OPTIONS: PROS AND CONS

It is clear that the United States has vital interests in East Asia, regionally and in global context. Effective policies toward China and Japan will go a long way toward serving these interests. In what ways can the United States make her policies effective? More specifically, what should U.S. policies be regarding issues such as trade and security arrangements with Japan and human rights and Taiwan with China? Depending on the lens through which one views China and Japan, some see friends, others see potential adversaries. Those who see friends naturally would want to resolve minor differences in the interest of greater common good, while those who see potential rivals would see insidious designs and naturally wish their "enemies" ill. Hence, discussions on policy options would run the full political spectrum, from get-tough positions to compromise, from punitive measures to accommodation.

CHINA

Sources of favorable views on China's economy are numerous, despite fresh memories of political repression symbolized by the Tiananmen Massacre of demonstrating students in 1989. Even the most casual visitors to China cannot fail to observe the vibrant, and indeed maddening, pace of growth, in both the cities and the countryside. Construction seems to go around the clock in Beijing or Shanghai, where skyscrapers are going up like bamboo shoots after a spring shower, while newly rich peasants are replacing mud huts with new brick buildings along paved roads busy with tractors loaded with goods. Eyewitness reports are confirmed by government statistics showing sustained high annual growth rates in the post-Mao years, particularly since Deng Xiaoping's economic reform began in 1978.

Chinese government figures, previously known for questionable accuracy, were accorded new respect after the World Bank began to issue glowing reports on the Chinese economy in 1992, which were given prominence in influential publications such as *The Economist* and *Financial Times*. With subsequent World Bank reports and also those by the International Monetary Fund (IMF), the outline of a reassessment emerged: The Chinese economy, already large, was much larger, in fact many times larger than previously assumed, mainly because of the "wrong" method used in past calculations. Both the World Bank and the IMF came to the conclusion that the old method of computing the total worth of the Chinese gross domestic product (GDP) in U.S. dollars based on the official exchange rate tended to vastly understate the size of the Chinese economy, because the official exchange rate was set by governments with no concern for the market. The real purchasing power of Chinese money, World Bank and IMF economists argue, was much greater in an economy that bears little resemblance to the economies in the West. Therefore, using the Purchasing Power Parity (PPP) method would be a much more realistic and accurate way of measuring the total value of the Chinese economy.

The new computing method yielded results that dramatically changed the ranking of the world's largest economies, catapulting China from tenth place to third place, next only to the United States and Japan, with a GDP almost doubling that of many leading G-7 nations, such as Germany and France. Even in terms of per capita GDP, which will be necessarily small compared to those of most developed nations with a much smaller population, there was still an instant four- to six-fold jump, from $370 to $1,450 by IMF computing or to $2,040 according to the World Bank.[14] Although both the World Bank and the IMF used the PPP, they came to substantially different estimates of the size of the Chinese economy in dollar amount, suggesting the unresolved controversy—the difficulty in determining the PPP. However, the controversy did not dampen the euphoria about China's economy with its vast potential as a market. The World Bank anticipates China overtaking Japan and the United States by the year 2010 and, if one refers to Greater China—that is, with Taiwan and Hong Kong thrown in—by the year 2002. The more conservative IMF estimates were quickly revised in subsequent reports, which now rank China as already the world's second largest economy.[15]

Commenting on the rush to reassess China's economic potential, Professor Paul Krugman of Stanford University put his finger on the real issue when he said that the main importance of all this was geopolitical. "It is a reminder that China is a great power already, which is something many people have not quite grasped yet," he said.[16] Of course, Krugman does not suggest that the economic side of the total picture is unimportant. Despite the fact that per capita income is low (about one-eighth of that of G-7 nations), China's overall economy is large. Growing at a prodigious rate, this economy of more than a billion consumers is a huge market that no developed nation can ignore.

It is only natural that reassessment of China's economic might will lead to a new appreciation of China's place in the world, at times in an exaggerated way. Former President Richard Nixon, whose crowning foreign policy success was his dramatic opening of China, is a good example of this. In his last book *Beyond Peace*, completed just days before death, Nixon, ever the pragmatic politician, argues that China's economic power makes U.S. lectures about human rights imprudent. Nixon recalled one of his meetings with the late Soviet leader Leonid Brezhnev in San Clemente in 1984. Brezhnev expressed concern about the growing threat of China. When Nixon said that it would be at least twenty-five years before China became a significant economic and military power, Brezhnev held up both hands with fingers outstretched, which Nixon thought was a sign of surrender. The translator finally interpreted Brezhnev's gesture to mean ten years. According to Nixon, Brezhnev was closer to being right than he was. In his characteristic hyperbole style, Nixon said in his book that the world's largest Communist society could become the world's richest capitalist economy in the next century. Referring to U.S. policy of linking MFN with human rights, a policy he opposed, Nixon writes: "Within a decade, it will make them (human rights lectures by the United States) irrelevant. Within two decades, it will make them laughable." By then, according to Nixon, "the Chinese may threaten to withhold MFN status from the United States unless we do more to improve living conditions in Detroit, Harlem and South Central Los Angeles."[17]

Serious policy debate concerning a proper response to China's human rights abuses continues. The massacre of students demonstrating for democracy in Beijing's Tiananmen Square in 1989 is a bloody memory that will not go away easily. Political persecution of intellectuals, repression in Tibet, and religious persecution worsened at the very time that President Clinton de-linked trade and human rights. Indeed, many believe that Clinton's cave-in to pressure from big business emboldened Beijing in its human rights abuses, as human rights groups and Congressional critics continue to call for selective sanctions against China.

Appreciating China's economic importance and its vast market can lead to apprehension that economic power ultimately may mean a future world dominated by China. This type of apprehension, if widely shared in the high councils, will inevitably have an impact on policy formulation. For example, a senior senate aide, a specialist in Chinese military affairs, has warned that China is the only country in the world that has ICBMs and submarine-based missiles aimed at the United States. It is the only declared nuclear power now seriously building up its military and the only one that continues to test nuclear weapons. It has virtually replaced Russia as our "enemy" at the Pentagon. The Office of Net Assessment of the Defense Department is said to be conducting computerized war games to see how we would fare against a resurgent Chinese military twenty-five years hence and has found out that we would lose.[18]

Amidst the euphoria and at times exaggerated views of China, there are cooler heads too. Among them are Richard Hornik and Gerald Segal, both having recently written widely influential essays bucking the trends. Hornik, formerly *Time* magazine's bureau chief in Beijing (1985–1987) and Hong Kong (1991–1993), points up many trouble spots in what he calls China's "bubble economy," which faces the real danger of bursting, despite often-cited growth rates and apparent signs of prosperity reported by visitors and potential investors. He cites the following factors for why the bubble may burst: capital outflow, capital shortage in rural and interior regions, surplus rural laborers flowing uncontrollably into urban and coastal areas with serious social consequences, lack of fiscal and monetary discipline resulting in runaway inflation and stifling administrative controls and, last but not least, weakening of political controls as a result of new economic freedoms, particularly among the affluent segment of the population.

Some information is not widely known by the public, which tends to see China's phenomenal growth at a time when many parts of the world are in an economic slump. For example, Hornik notes, China's net capital outflow in 1992 topped $30 billion, including a substantial amount funneled through "backdoors" out of the country, indicating a lack of confidence by the very people who are in power. Inflation can hurt both the urban dwellers and the peasants as, for example, when in the summer of 1993 the *yuan* lost half its value in a few months because money supply was up over 50 percent. Inflation rates have been kept at between 20 and 30 percent in recent years, mainly through administrative controls rather than market forces. What China now has, in the words of Hornik, is a "halfway house between the rigidity of a command economy and the chaos of a free market."[19] When it finally comes to a choice between political loyalty and economic competence, Hornik believes Beijing's choice is clear. As long as China's rulers insist on complete political control, it will be difficult for China to replicate the economic success of the "little dragons" of East and Southeast Asia.

Hence, overoptimism about China's economy needs to be tempered by a note of caution. The difficult transition from a centralized system to one based on the market is far from over. The notion of a "socialist market economy," or "socialism with Chinese characteristics," as Beijing calls it, is a novel one, and nowhere in the world has there been a successful case of it yet. Even now, China faces the serious risk of either uncontrolled growth and rampant inflation or excessive economic austerity and slowdown, with fallout far beyond economic confines. Huang Fanzheng, vice president of the Economic Research Center of China's State Planning Commission, admitted that the old planning system had not been fully dismantled nor had the market system matured, thus financial institutions are neither controlled by government nor restrained by markets, creating a dangerous situation that will last for as long as the reform is in progress.[20] Professor Lawrence B. Krause of University of California at San Diego, head of a panel of economists commissioned by the Pacific Economic Cooperation Council, believes that "a risk of serious macroeconomic miscalculation" exists in China.[21]

Environmentalists have pointed out the serious problems of environmental degradation and pollution, including the desertification of arable land, soil erosion, deforestation, industrial pollution of major rivers and air, and depletion of water resources. A leading scholar believes that without radical changes in its ambitious and unrealistic modernization goals and environmental policy, sustainable development in China may well be an illusion.[22]

There are two major aspects to Deng Xiaoping's economic reforms: opening to the West and decentralization of decision-making power. The former, meaning trade and importing modern technology, is better known in the West now that major corporations in the developed nations are competing for a share of the vast China market. But it is the latter that has arguably brought about such a profound change from the Maoist days that even the most ardent reformers have been taken by surprise. *Quanli xiafang*, literally meaning "administrative power transfer downward," was originally designed to move away a bit from the suffocating socialist central planning, giving the local authorities some decision-making power in economic matters in order to stimulate the faltering economy.

This "power transfer" was to be limited to the economic areas—negotiating with the peasants on terms of land lease, local guidelines on foreign investments, etc.: It was not supposed to affect other aspects of life in a controlled society. However, over the years the local authorities have "amplified" this limited economic autonomy in unexpected ways, affecting people of all walks of life and threatening the integrity of a totalitarian state. Increasing outside contacts at the local level and regional disparity in economic development tend to produce centrifugal forces, pulling the "central kingdom" apart. As Beijing gives more leeway to the regions, it grows harder to retain central control. With the death of old ideologies and only a weakening nationalism as the remaining organizing principle to pull the nation together, China is suffering from an "identity crisis" that will only deepen with the passing of the last of the revolutionary generation from the political scene.

Gerald Segal, a senior fellow at the International Institute for Strategic Studies and an editor of *The Pacific Review*, urges that to better understand China's future, Sinologists must abandon the traditional methods and look beyond Beijing. Pointing to the obvious fact that China's regions count for more, Segal lists factors well beyond Beijing's control: burgeoning flows of commerce, decisions by regional and local players, and the powers that accrue to new economic centers. All these, and more, Segal argues, will change "how China is perceived, how it is governed and how the outside world interacts with this rising power in the twenty-first century."[23]

Citing the traditional fear of Asian nations for a strong China and the growing regional support by foreign powers—southern coastal region by Southeast Asian nations and Northeast China by Japan—Segal suggests the likelihood of a messy pattern of "military regionalism" following the economic regionalism in the post-Deng China.[24] While few anticipate a return to the warlordism period of the 1920s, much less the "warring states" of the third century B.C., the increasing trend toward regionalism should be a sober reminder for those who are overtly euphoric about the rosy prospect of unlimited opportunities in a centrally-ruled China, as well as those who are uneasy at the thought of Chinese domination of the world in the twenty-first century.

JAPAN

Turning to U.S.-Japan relations, many revisionists, or Japan-bashers, come to mind. Prominent among them are Lee Iacocca, former chairman of Chrysler Corporation; James Fallows, an editor at *The Atlantic*; Chalmers Johnson, a Japan scholar at Berkeley; Karel von Wolferen, a Dutch journalist and long-time resident of Japan; and Clyde Prestowitz, a former U.S. trade negotiator. The most commonly heard complaint about Japan is that it has gotten a free ride from the United States on its national security since the end of World War II. Critics say the U.S. nuclear umbrella, as well as protection by conventional forces, has cost the United States hundreds of billions of dollars. As U.S. taxpayers shouldered the burden, Japan rode the gravy train of the "biggest U.S. foreign aid program" to great wealth. During the period 1981–1992, the United States spent $3 trillion on defense, or $12,000 per capita, compared to less than $2,000 per capita in Japan. The $10,000 per capita difference thus gave Japan a $1.2 trillion advantage. In this view, Japan not only should have shared the cost, but should also compensate the United States for defense services.[25]

A best-selling book by Japan's most influential politician—Ichiro Ozawa, who was the moving force behind the rebellion against the long-ruling Liberal Democratic Party in 1993—is ostensibly a reply to the charges of Japan's free ride under the U.S. security umbrella. In his *Blueprint for a New Japan*, Ozawa acknowledges the fact that for almost half a century, the United States has assumed Japan's share of the "cost of peace and freedom." "Had Japan borne these costs," he asserts, "it would not have been possible to achieve today's prosperity [in Japan]."[26] With the end of the Cold War, the United States simply no longer has any reason to bear Japan's share. If Japan wants to continue enjoying peace and prosperity, it must shoulder the costs associated with it.

However, Ozawa sees a much larger role for Japan than merely emerging from under the U.S. defense umbrella. He urges a leap from "exclusive defensive strategy" to a dynamic "peace-building strategy" through close cooperation with the United States in peacekeeping missions under the U.N. flag. He believes it is time for Japan to play a greater international role, and he assails the Constitutional restraints that made Japan "unable to cooperate militarily when we were needed." Countering the fear of many people, including no less than Henry Kissinger, that any Japanese role in the security arena conjures up images of a re-armed, militarized Japan, Ozawa writes:

"This is not an issue of militarization or aspiration to military superpower status. It is a question of Japan's responsible behavior in the international community."[27] Understandably, many people remain unpersuaded by Ozawa's passionately nationalistic argument.

Among books that might be regarded as Japan-bashing, the latest is *Looking at the Sun* by James Fallows, a long-time Japan observer. He argues that Japan's success, and that of its East Asian neighbors, is based not on American-style laissez-faire economics but on active government intervention aimed at economic domination. The "paternalistic" business-government collusion that has made Japan such a tough international competitor in the past will continue to pose an ever-greater challenge in the future if the United States does not adopt a more interventionist national economic policy of its own.[28]

The argument of "cultural uniqueness" of Japan, and of East Asian countries in general, is carried further by others, among whom Ian Buruma, another veteran Japan observer, detects a cultural difference between Japanese and German memories of war crimes.[29] He discusses the German concept of *betroffen*, meaning "made speechless by a feeling of guilt." The Japanese can be just as *betroffen* as the Germans, Buruma writes, "But you see it less because in Japan, the war is remembered much more as a misguided military conflict and not in terms of a nation responsible for a huge and horrendous crime."[30] This comes close to the old stereotype: Orientals care only about face, but have no sense of guilt.

The Clinton administration's policy toward Japan is best presented by Roger C. Altman, until late 1994 Deputy Secretary of the Treasury. Writing in the May-June 1994 issue of *Foreign Affairs*, Altman comes to what he believes to be the crux of the problem between the two countries concerning trade, namely, Japan's protectionism.

He outlines four phases of U.S.-Japan relations in the period since the end of World War II. The first was the reconstruction period, running through the early 1950s, when the United States tolerated Japan's protection of home markets while consciously helping to rebuild Japan's industrial capacity devastated by war. The second phase began with the 1952 Mutual Security Assistance Pact, ending the occupation and extending the U.S. nuclear umbrella over Japan as the Asian cornerstone of the Cold War strategy. The early 1970s signaled the beginning of the third stage, which saw growing policy differences and trade friction, even though security considerations remained paramount until the end of the Cold War.

Beginning in 1993, Altman writes, the U.S.-Japan relationship was "jolted into its fourth phase" by the newly elected President Clinton, whose post-Cold War priorities put economic rather than security matters first. In this post-Cold War atmosphere, it is only natural that the public, business, and Congress all clamored for actions to level the playing fields with Japan. Justifying the administration's stance, Altman compares the huge Japanese trade surplus with that of other trading partners of the United States and concludes that the ball is in the court of Japan, which must make the next move to open up the domestic markets and to reduce the trade surplus.[31]

Taking the opposite side in the debate, Professor Jagdish Bhagwati of Columbia University, an advisor to the General Agreement on Tariffs and Trade (now renamed World Trade Organization), writes in the same issue of *Foreign Affairs* that the United States, not Japan, is to blame for the current differences. The demands put forth by the United States—numerical targets for U.S. goods in Japanese domestic markets and managed trade—are simply unacceptable to the new Japan. Numerical targets are nothing more than export protectionism for U.S. business, and managed trade is diametrically opposed to the principle of free trade which all developed nations, including the United States, profess to uphold. Japan, therefore, should not be expected to accept what no other sovereign nation would accept under U.S. pressure. "The Clinton administration simply does not get it," Bhagwati writes, stressing that "the new Japan is trying to be like the old United States, just as the new United States is trying to be like the old Japan."[32] Urging cooperation rather than confrontation, he says that if President Clinton ever fancied the glory of "opening Japan" as a modern-day Commodore Perry, he should be reminded that historical parallels will not work.[33]

During the Cold War, American and Japanese national security interests were identical. This is no longer true in the much changed post-Cold War world, particularly in East Asia. Because of geographical proximity to the Asian mainland and "historic experience," Henry Kissinger sees Japan slowly but unmistakably coming out from under the U.S. nuclear umbrella. He thinks it is vitally important that the United States exercise a moderating influence to forestall a possible resurgence of Japanese militarism. The Japanese defense budget has been creeping upward to become the second largest in the world, and Japan might decide to press its technological and strategic superiority "before China emerges as a superpower and Russia recovers its strength" and go on to pursue "that great equalizer," namely, nuclear weapons. It is against this unseemly scenario that Kissinger believes that close Japanese-American relations will be a vital contribution to Japanese moderation and a significant reassurance to the other nations of Asia, particularly China. Alluding to the bitter memories of a militarist Japan during World War II and looking into the future, Kissinger writes: "Japanese military strength linked to America worries China and the other nations of Asia less than purely national Japanese military capabilities. And Japan will decide that it needs less military strength so long as an American safety net exists."[34]

POLICY RECOMMENDATIONS FOR THE TWENTY-FIRST CENTURY

It should be clear that moderation and cooperation rather than confrontation and hostility should guide the formulation of U.S. policies toward China and Japan in the new era. Although the polarizing ideology and deadly militarism that once threatened the fate of humanity no longer exist, there will continue to be many thorny issues, from human rights and the integrity of Taiwan in China to regional security and trade with Japan. The solution to any of these problems requires not only a global perspective, but also steadfastness in upholding certain fundamental human values.

For the first time since the Opium War ended in 1842, China appears to be set on its way to regain its place in the sun. The long search and humiliation are ending, as China seems to have found the path to greatness. Many factors, external and internal, now converge to create an environment conducive to such a development. China, in short, has reached a historic turning point in its destiny. Among the factors are the following:

- After more than seventy years, the Communist-Nationalist rivalry, which led to civil war and devastation, is abating. Mainland China and Taiwan are talking. Unofficial exchanges between the two, including mounting trade and travels, will help draw the two closer together.

- Despite the disparity in levels of economic development between mainland China and Taiwan, there is a shared emphasis on continued economic growth between them. Given China's phenomenal growth rates in recent years, the gap between China and Taiwan will narrow as the economies of coastal China and Taiwan become increasingly intertwined and interdependent. Economics, in due course, will exert a strong influence on the future course of political relations between China and Taiwan. The great majority of people on both sides of the Taiwan Straits, irrespective of their ethnic origins, prefer stability to political chaos. Stability will only lead to mutually beneficial economic growth and the integration of a greater China.

- The imperialist powers at whose hands China suffered in the past have largely waned or changed, no longer in a position to impose their will on China. In the post-Cold War world, the United States is the only surviving superpower, not without its own problems. The rise of Chinese nationalism under these circumstances is understandable, and nationalism can be a potent force for national growth when properly harnessed.

- The center of gravity of global economy is moving east to the Western Pacific rim, for which China provides the vast hinterland with rich natural resources, a huge labor force, and a market consisting of a quarter of the world's population. Greater China, therefore, can potentially emerge as the place where the action is in the twenty-first century. There is yet another factor in China's favor. For the first time in recent history, China is free of military threat from a neighbor, and this situation in all probability will continue in the foreseeable future.

- Ethnic Chinese in other lands around the world, more than thirty million strong, constitute a powerful force in terms of wealth and knowledge. Not unlike Jews scattered around the world, these Chinese have left their homeland to escape poverty, war, or political repression. Over the centuries, they have assimilated and prospered in their adopted countries but, unlike many racial or ethnic groups, have managed to retain their cultural roots and identity. Few "overseas Chinese" are supporters of the Chinese brand of socialism under Deng

Xiaoping, but all want to see China prosperous, free, and strong, and they can make a significant contribution toward this goal.[35]

To be sure, one can get a bit carried away by one's own logic, overlooking other factors. For example, amidst the economic growth, there is corruption and graft of monumental proportions; the gap between the rich and poor is widening at an alarming rate and so is the disparity between the coastal and inland provinces. All of this is diametrically opposed to the fundamental dictum of socialist egalitarianism by which the Chinese have been conditioned for two generations. The state sector of the economy, consisting primarily of key heavy industries, continues to be a heavy drain on the nation's treasury with thousands of large plants depending on government subsidy. Fifteen years into Deng's reform, these state-owned enterprises are yet to be privatized. Why? The simple answer is that privatization would mean millions of workers losing their "iron rice bowls," creating the potential for social disturbances about which the Beijing leadership has a mortal fear. On top of economic problems, both structural and those resulting from the reform, China is still ruled by a repressive dictatorship. And there is the urgent problem of political succession. When ninety-one-year-old Deng, the last strongman of the Long March generation, passes from the scene, will there be continued political stability? Without a charismatic leader pulling the country together, what are the chances of the nation falling apart, descending into a civil war, and negating the economic gains made in the last decade and half? Finally, despite the absence of a strong neighbor harboring territorial ambitions on China, there remains North Korea, China's ally, which in the past allegedly attempted to develop the ability to engulf the region in a nuclear devastation.

Weighing all the pluses and minuses, what policies should the United States pursue in the years to come that can best serve our short- and long-term interests? To begin with, there should be a basic understanding that a free, prosperous, and democratic China is in the best long-term interest of the United States. Without such a China, regional stability will be absent and global peace will be threatened. Needless to say, U.S. economic interest will be greatly impaired. The promotion of a free, prosperous, and democratic China, therefore, should be the premise on which policies are formulated. It should be seen not as a United States favor to China, but as a mutually beneficial objective.

In his last book, former President Nixon expressed the belief that Sino-American differences could be bridged by discussion behind the scenes but would be exacerbated by red-hot exchanges of public rhetoric. Knowing many world leaders with a degree of intimacy few others did, Nixon recalled that in late 1992 Deng was widely believed to have given the Chinese government the marching orders for dealing with the new administration in Washington: "Increase trust, reduce troubles, develop cooperation, and avoid confrontation." Pointing to the open feud with China on human rights, Nixon criticized the Clinton administration for responding to Beijing by "increasing distrust, stirring up troubles, threatening noncooperation, and fomenting confrontation."[36] In the future, Nixon said, Washington should treat China with the respect a great power deserves and not as a pariah nation. Henry Kissinger, his pragmatic national security advisor and secretary of state, is in substantial agreement with Nixon when he suggests that the United States should refrain from "publicly prescribing conditions," an act viewed in China as a humiliating attempt to convert its society to American values. Kissinger believes that the key to Sino-American relations is a "tacit" cooperation on global and especially Asian strategy.[37]

In the emerging new world order, Kissinger believes that the challenge for America in East Asia is to develop good long-term relations with both China and Japan. He sees a new triangle emerging there, with the United States destined to play the role of a balancer between China and Japan. Between the two, Kissinger makes his view clear that China is more important. "Good American relations with China," he asserts, "are the prerequisite for good long-term relations with Japan, as well as for good Sino-Japanese relations," because China in the coming years will show "the greatest increase in stature among the major powers."[38]

Given America's past involvement in East Asia and the growing economic interest and continued security interest in a region dominated by China and Japan, to mention the emergence of a new triangle would seem to be stating the obvious. And most people would agree with Kissinger that this triangular relationship is quite different from the old one during the Cold War years that involved the United States, the Soviet Union, and China, when security considerations were supreme and ideological lines were clear. In those days, friends and foes were easy to identify. With the prominence of economic issues and the fast disappearance of the great ideological divide, old labels are no longer applicable and there is a good deal of ambiguity with which Americans are not entirely comfortable. How do you cope with friction with two "friends" who are also friends but who have friction between themselves? During the Cold War days, Kissinger was the one who skillfully manipulated the Washington-Moscow-Beijing relationships, playing off Beijing against Moscow to moderate the bipolar balance of terror in the world. That can no longer be done with economic issues, which are by nature far more complicated and do not lend themselves easily to triangular manipulation. When combined with regional security issues, they become even more complex. How, for example, can the United States reduce trade deficits with both Japan and China while at the same time playing an active role in promoting regional security and stability? The following simple, not altogether hypothetical, chain of events may occur: Punitive measures against Japan's trade practices produce a backlash in Japan, which fuels the rise of fanatic nationalism and a drive for re-armament, which then touches off a dangerous arms race between Japan and China.

What this scenario shows is that it is easier to deal with an enemy than it is to deal with two friends involved in a number of interrelated issues. American diplomatic skills will be severely tested, not in achieving unqualified victory, but in reaching accommodation and equilibrium.

Amidst all the rapid changes in the post-Cold War world, there are few guideposts in the search for a new world order other than the general principles of the Wilsonian ideals—peace, stability, progress, and freedom for all mankind. The best minds of the day are not able to offer us anything more concrete. Looking at our failure to predict the rise of fascism after World War I and the failure again to predict the recent dissolution of western communism, Jean Kirkpatrick, U.S. representative to the United Nations for four years (1981–1985), said in August 1994 that she was not impressed with our capacity to predict the future or to perceive even the broad political trends emerging. All we can do, according to her, is to "observe as closely as we can and try to understand what is happening as it happens."[39]

Kirkpatrick's plain words convey essentially the same message as the elegant prose of Henry Kissinger in his massive new book. While seeing world leadership in the coming century as inherent in American powers and values, Kissinger nevertheless cautions that the fulfillment of America's ideals will have to be sought in the "patient accumulation of partial success." Echoing Kirkpatrick about our inability to predict or even to perceive future political trends, Kissinger writes that the convictions needed to master the emerging world order are more "abstract," because a vision of the future cannot be demonstrated and judgments about the relationship "between hope and possibility" are at best conjectural. The journey has no end, Kissinger concludes, quoting a Spanish proverb: "Traveler, there are no roads. Roads are made by walking."[40]

Great pragmatic minds can hardly be faulted for being ostensibly amoral considering the complexities of human events. The challenge ahead lies in how to strike a balance between pragmatism and the moral principles on which the United States is founded and of which the United States is today the sole guardian in the new world order. Moral principles—the profound sense of human decency against which human behavior is ultimately judged—cannot be abandoned without the sad consequence of condemning us all to a lower level of existence.

NOTES

1. James Fallows, "Clinton and Asia: Real Progress, But Trouble Ahead," *International Herald Tribune*, June 7, 1994, p. 6.
2. Patrick Tyler, "Awe-Struck U.S. Executives Survey the China Market," *The New York Times*, September 2, 1994, p. D1.
3. Henry Kissinger and Cyrus R. Vance, "America's China Policy Is Back on Course," *International Herald Tribune*, June 8, 1994, p. 9.

4. Steven Greenhouse, "U.S., Despite Critics, Is to Expand Taiwan Ties," *The New York Times*, September 8, 1994, p. A5.
5. "A Survey of Japan," a special pull-out section in *The Economist*, July 9, 1994, p. 1. Page number refers to the special pull-out section.
6. Ibid., p. 2.
7. Paul T. Welty, *The Asians: Their Evolving Heritage*, 6th ed. (New York: Harper and Row, 1984), p. 11.
8. "The Fading of Japanophobia," *The Economist*, August 6, 1994, p. 21.
9. Ibid.
10. Michael H. Armacost, "Japan Goes to Business School," *The New York Times*, July 28, 1993, p. A23.
11. David Sanger, "Effort to Solve Energy Woes Clashes with Nuclear Safety," *The New York Times*, August 20, 1994, p. 1.
12. Ibid.
13. Novelist Tom Clancy's best-seller, *Debt of Honor* (New York: G.P. Putnam's Sons, 1994), containing a Japan-U.S. war scenario with nuclear threats, is a good illustration of this.
14. Steven Greenhouse, "New Tally of World's Economies Catapults China into Third Place," *The New York Times*, May 20, 1993, p. A1.
15. Gerald Segal, "China's Changing Shape," *Foreign Affairs* 73, no. 3 (May–June 1994): 44.
16. Greenhouse, "U.S., Despite Critics, Is to Expand Taiwan Ties," p. A5.
17. Richard M. Nixon, *Beyond Peace* (New York: Random House, 1994), p. 128.
18. William C. Triplett, II, "Dangerous Embrace," *The New York Times*, September 10, 1994, p. 19.
19. Richard Hornik, "Bursting China's Bubble," *Foreign Affairs* 73, no. 3 (May–June 1994): 40.
20. Michael Richardson, "China Boom: A Two-Edged Sword," *International Herald Tribune*, June 8, 1994, p. 15
21. Ibid.
22. Vaclav Smil, *China's Environmental Crisis* (White Plains, NY: M.E. Sharpe, 1993).
23. Segal, "China's Changing Shape," p. 44.
24. Ibid.
25. Ernest J. Oppenheimer, "Japan Should Pay for Its Own Defense," *The New York Times*, June 25, 1994, p. 22.
26. Ichiro Ozawa, *Blueprint for a New Japan*, as excerpted in *Time*, January 13, 1994, p. 38. The book, already a bestseller in Japan, has just been translated into English.
27. Ibid.
28. Richard Hornik, "Blinded by the Light," *Time*, June 6, 1994, p. 68.
29. Ian Buruma, *The Wages of Guilt* (New York: Farrar, Straus and Giroux, 1994).
30. Scott Veale, "Reduced to Silence," *The New York Times Book Review*, June 26, 1994, p. 3.
31. Roger C. Altman, "Why Pressure Tokyo," *Foreign Affairs* 73, no. 3 (May–June 1994): 2–6.
32. Jagdish Bhagwati, "Samurais No More," *Foreign Affairs* 73, no. 3 (May–June 1994): 9.
33. Ibid., p. 12.
34. Henry Kissinger, *Diplomacy* (New York: Simon & Schuster, 1994), p. 828.
35. Chen Youwei, "China and the World: Impact and Challenges," *Shijie Zhoukan* (World Journal Weekly), July 31, 1994, p. 1.
36. Nixon, *Beyond Peace*, p. 132.
37. Kissinger, *Diplomacy*, p. 837.

38. Ibid., *Diplomacy*, p. 829.
39. Barbara Crossette, "A Warrior, a Mother, a Scholar, a Mystery," *The New York Times*, August 17, 1994, p. Cl.
40. Kissinger, *Diplomacy*, p. 835.

CHAPTER 6

AMERICAN POLICY
TOWARD INDIA AND PAKISTAN

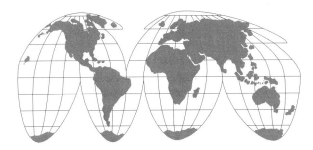

THE SOUTH ASIAN RIVALS

Kul B. Rai

During the Cold War period, American policy toward South Asia, especially India, was often described as ambivalent and marked by ups and downs. It was not based on any inherent U.S. interests, but rather was dictated by international events. On several occasions the United States became deeply embroiled in South Asia, only to find that the money and the energy spent there brought it few results. It never gained much influence in any of the countries in the region, nor did it earn goodwill. That has changed with the end of the Cold War and the occurrence of another significant event—the acquisition of nuclear-weapons capabilities by India and Pakistan. With the worries of the containment of communism gone and the increasing liberalization of economies in South Asia, the vast market of over a billion consumers has become enticing to American corporations for investment and trade. An even more compelling concern is to prevent a nuclear war between India and Pakistan and, if possible, to denuclearize the region.

In order to understand the changed importance of South Asia to the United States and the significance of this region to American interests in the twenty-first century, we first present a historical background of the relations between the United States and South Asian countries.

HISTORICAL BACKGROUND

BEFORE THE COLD WAR

Some years ago a historian wrote: "The United States had no South Asian policy prior to 1947."[1] This is a somewhat exaggerated statement, since immediately preceding 1947, when India and Pakistan emerged as two separate and independent states as a result of the partition of British India, the United States did show interest in the granting of independence to India. Evidence reveals that during World War II President Franklin Roosevelt attempted to gain independence for India from Britain, but was constrained in his effort by his desire to maintain the wartime alliance with Britain.[2] It is true, however, that the United States had no South Asian or rather Indian policy prior to its entry into World War II in December 1941, following the Japanese attack on Pearl Harbor. India was strategically located for a base from which to fight the Japanese forces in Southeast Asia and China. Britain had made India, its largest colony, available to the allies for that purpose. It was also in support of the allied war effort that the United States decided, in 1941, to exchange diplomatic representatives with India. Since India was still a colony, these representatives did not have the rank of ambassador. The Indian representative in Washington, moreover, functioned under the directives of the British embassy there. Prior to these appointments, the British Foreign Office and the embassies working under it conducted all foreign relations for India.

Before World War II, the United States and India had very limited contacts, which often were misunderstood on both sides. India served as a major economic resource for its colonial ruler, Britain, but had insignificant trade or investment opportunities for the United States. The most visible American presence in India during this period was that of missionaries who started arriving in the early nineteenth century. The missionaries "numbered only a few thousand, far fewer than the Americans active in China."[3] The Indian presence in the United States was even less. American laws denied immigration and citizenship to Indians and other Asians. As if immigration laws were not enough to create resentment in India, some popular books published in the United States, notably Katherine Mayo's 1927 publication *Mother India*, vilified India. Indian authors retaliated by publishing negative accounts of the United States.

Although a handful of American academics had studied Indian culture and the classic Indian language, Sanskrit, social scientists had shown virtually no interest in that distant land. W. Norman Brown writes: "Before World War I there was scarcely an American economist, sociologist, modern historian, political scientist, geographer, or anthropologist who was trained in the Indian aspect of his science or knew his way around in it."[4] The next two decades only marginally improved American academic understanding of India. As a result, "in the interwar period a very small number of social scientists, less than a dozen all told, came to qualify as competent on India."[5] Although American governmental as well as scholarly interest in India increased appreciably following the end of World War II and India's independence from Britain, misgivings on both sides lingered and still continue today.

DURING THE COLD WAR

A scholar on India commented in 1984:

> It has been an assumption of American foreign policy that the United

States has no vital strategic interests in South Asia as such. American involvement in the region has been episodic and derivative of other interests—notably containment of the Soviet Union and, earlier, of China, and, more prominently over the past decade, protection of the vital petroleum resources of the Gulf and their access through the sea lanes of the Indian Ocean.[6]

The Cold War had developed even before the birth of the independent states of India and Pakistan, and it initially affected Europe and the Middle East. South Asia seemed remote and of little value. The region had neither the strategic location nor the vital natural resources nor the cultural affinity for the West or the Soviet Union to attract the contending sides. India and Pakistan both entreated the United States for economic as well as military help—no other power was in so strong a position or perhaps appeared as generous as the United States. The U.S. response was ambivalent at first. It needed time to understand the new entities in South Asia and evaluate their value to U.S. interests. Emergence of two new democratic states, especially the much larger India, impressed many Americans. There was also the desire to help the faraway poor, notably with food aid.

Three events in Asia—war between India and Pakistan in 1948 over a disputed territory, Kashmir; establishment of a Communist regime in China in 1949; and the Korean War in 1950—involved the United States in South Asia rather abruptly. India brought the Kashmir issue before the U.N. Security Council in 1948 with a complaint that Pakistan had committed aggression.[7] The decision of the Hindu Maharajah in October 1947 to make his predominantly Muslim state of Kashmir a part of the largely Hindu India instead of Pakistan, which is mostly Muslim, had triggered that conflict. Both warring parties expected American sympathy in the United Nations. India believed that the United States, a founding member of the U.N. Charter, would oppose an act of aggression. Pakistan considered the democratic American tradition to be in its favor. Pakistan wanted Kashmir's political future to be decided by the wishes of the Kashmiris. The Indian Prime Minister Jawaharlal Nehru had, in fact, accepted in 1947 the holding of a plebiscite in Kashmir. The United States supported this solution to the dispute in Kashmir. In 1949 the U.N. Security Council, with the support of the United States (as well as the Soviet Union), voted in favor of a plebiscite. The Indian government reneged on its commitment to hold such a plebiscite on grounds of "completely changed circumstances." Pakistan wanted the United States to put pressure on India. The United States was unwilling to take any drastic steps. As a result, Pakistan was offended. India was not happy either, since it desired the United States to condemn Pakistan's aggression against Kashmir. The issue of Kashmir led to another war in 1965 between India and Pakistan and remains unresolved.

The victory of communism in China added another dimension to the Cold War. The concern in Washington was that communism might spread to other Asian countries, including India and Pakistan, both located along the southern border of China. Of the two, India presented a greater worry, since it was the larger of the two and, more important, it had a well-organized Communist party with a sizeable following. It was suspected that now both the Soviet Union and Communist China would support Communist parties in other countries in the hope of spreading communism. The Soviet actions in Europe and the Middle East provided enough evidence in favor of such concern. The war in Korea in 1950 further indicated that the Soviet Union and China wanted to expand Communist control by bringing the entire Korean peninsula under the umbrella of communism.

The United States spearheaded the collective security action of the United Nations in fighting North Korea in the Korean War. A handful of U.N. members had supplied a small portion of the U.N. troops, but it was principally an American war against communism. Neither India nor Pakistan had offered troops to fight North Korea. Pakistan, however, was far more sympathetic to the American war effort in Korea than India. India instead played its neutral card and tried to improve its regional and possibly international status on the basis of a neutral role in Korea. That proved to American policy makers that India could not be cultivated as an ally.

The United States in its crusade to contain communism still sought India as an ally, in addition to Pakistan. President Eisenhower's secretary of state, John Foster Dulles, wanted to make the two South Asian rivals members of the U.S. alliance system to contain communism. India and Pakistan were invited, along with Middle-Eastern countries such as Iran and Turkey, to join Dulles' "Northern Tier" defense arrangement. Pakistan was receptive. India's Prime Minister Nehru, on the other hand, scoffed at it. Nehru wanted India to become the leader of the newly emerging nonaligned African and Asian nations. Nonalignment to Nehru meant a policy of staying neutral between the competing alliance systems of the United States and the Soviet Union. To Dulles, nonalignment made little sense and was "an immoral and short-sighted conception."[8]

Pakistan sought U.S. military protection and the economic aid that came with it, not to contain communism, but to shore up its strength against India, which it considered the greatest threat to its security. Of course, in public statements and in meetings with American policy makers, Pakistan's officials vigorously advocated their fear of communism and their desire to curb that threat. The United States allayed India's fears of Pakistan becoming a threat as a result of American support by promising (on behalf of Pakistan) that the weapons to be transferred to Pakistan would not be used against India—a promise that, as later events were to show, was broken by Pakistan. American officials perhaps genuinely believed that any American weapons in the hands of Pakistan were exclusively for the purpose of fighting Communist incursions that might be prompted by the Soviet Union and China. Most analysts agree that such officials displayed a poor, if not dismal, understanding of the hostility between India and Pakistan.

The United States and Pakistan signed the Mutual Defense Agreement in May 1954. Four months later Pakistan became a member of the South East Asian Treaty Organization (SEATO) and in September 1955 of the Baghdad Pact (renamed the Central Treaty Organization [CENTO] in 1959). With the American commitment to give military aid and to increase economic assistance, Pakistan became an ally. Alliance with Pakistan was a part of American efforts to contain communism in South Asia, Southeast Asia, and the Middle East. The United States did make it clear that these alliances were created not to help its signatories against any attack, but only against Communist aggression.[9]

Historian Stanley Wolpert has labeled the U.S. military alliance with Pakistan "surely the worst single blunder in U.S. South Asian policy and easily the most costly."[10] Political scientist Robert Hardgrave, a respected authority on South Asia, writes: "With little sensitivity to the impact of American actions on regional stability, the U.S. contributed to deepen Indo-Pakistan enmity and spurred India to seek closer ties with the Soviet Union."[11] The Soviet Union was eager to win India on its side in the Cold War struggle. The Soviet Union not only provided economic and military assistance to India, but also declared its support of India's position on Kashmir. Soviet support of India helped it to negotiate increased economic assistance from the United States. India learned rather well how to exploit its nonalignment policy for aid from both the United States and the Soviet Union. That made Pakistan unhappy. Any increase in India's strength was a threat to Pakistan. A Pakistani scholar notes:

From 1949 to 1971 the United States contributed ten billion dollars to India's economic development. The massive U.S. economic assistance enabled India to divert her own resources to purchase military hardware and, consequently, to maintain her superior military position in the region. The policy of alignment, on the other hand, earned for Pakistan the hostility of the Soviet Union.[12]

If it is considered that India, during the period 1949–1971, had four times as many people as Pakistan, per capita American nonmilitary assistance to the latter was far greater than to the former. India during this period, however, did increase its military strength and remained a threat to Pakistan.

Although U.S.-Indian relations were strained during the first term of President Eisenhower, mainly due to the defense pact between the United States and Pakistan and the American military aid to Pakistan, they improved during his second term. India had enhanced its status in the international arena, in part as a result of its nonalignment policy. The United States grudgingly accepted India's nonalignment as an unavoidable international event. Increased economic assistance to India thawed the coldness on the Indian side. Relations with Pakistan, on the other hand, followed an opposite pattern. Pakistan's disappointment with American aid to India was understandable. The U.S. position on Kashmir did not change in Pakistan's favor. In 1959 Secretary Dulles, a great friend of Pakistan, died. A number of American leaders, including Senator John F. Kennedy, who was elected President in 1960, were impressed by India's democratic record. Pakistan had come under military rule in 1958. By the time Kennedy took office as U.S. President in January 1961, the pendulum of the U.S. policy was swinging away from Pakistan and toward India.

President Kennedy wanted to keep U.S. commitments to its military allies, including Pakistan. He was, however, more in favor of "new alliances for progress" than military alliances. Kennedy's vision was to help the underdeveloped countries with American economic assistance so that they could reduce poverty and become friends of the United States and supporters of its foreign policy. India was at the top of the list of such poor countries. Some key presidential advisors, notably Chester Bowles, a former U.S. ambassador to India and Under Secretary of State Department under Kennedy, Adlai Stevenson, U.S. Ambassador to the United Nations, and John Kenneth Galbraith, U.S. Ambassador to India, were among the greatest supporters of India. As a result, American economic assistance to India increased considerably and reached about $400 million (excluding surplus food) during 1961–1962.

Increased economic assistance to India was also influenced by two other factors.[13] With the development of nuclear technology, especially intercontinental ballistic and submarine-launched missiles, the importance of bases in countries such as Pakistan, which were near the Soviet border, decreased. India's importance, on the other hand, increased because it was perceived to be in a unique position to help the United States contain China's aggressive ambitions in Asia. India was also considered of value to the Soviet Union in controlling China's designs, since the two Communist giants had developed serious ideological and border differences. China had already intervened in East Asia and Southeast Asia. By late 1950s it was threatening India by claiming fifty-five thousand square miles along their common border.

The arguments in favor of a U.S. tilt toward India appeared so strong that minor or even major irritants in the Indo-U.S. relations were ignored.[14] Several accounts reveal that President Kennedy was disappointed by Indian Prime Minister Nehru in their meeting in Washington in 1961 mainly because of the latter's self-righteous attitude. Of greater consequence was India's use of force in taking over Goa, a Portuguese colony within India. India had claimed to be a great advocate of peaceful resolution of international disputes. India's invasion of Goa, therefore, appeared hypocritical to many in the West, including American leaders.

Of greatest help to India in gaining economic as well as military assistance from the United States was the Chinese invasion of India in late 1962.

India was ill-prepared to face superior Chinese military forces. China's military overwhelmed the Indian army and captured a substantial portion of the disputed territory. India almost frantically asked the world for help. Its greatest friend, the Soviet Union, initially showed no sympathy. The United States and Britain, on the other hand, immediately sent military aid to India. China ended the war on its own terms a month after the invasion.

U.S. military assistance to India worried Pakistan. Pakistan's concerns were enhanced by the Soviet Union's resumption of military aid to India following a policy reappraisal in early 1963. India had reaped rather well the benefits of its nonalignment, or "double alignment" as a study describes it.[15] In the meantime, Pakistan had tried to establish friendship with China. In 1963 it signed a border agreement with China, thereby giving up claims to several thousand square miles of territory. Pakistan, concerned about the reliability of the United States as its protector, also cultivated friendly relations with the Soviet Union.

From Pakistan's perspective, the United States proved to be an utterly unreliable ally in the war between India and Pakistan in 1965, again fought over Kashmir. Adopting an even-handed approach in the 1965 war between India and Pakistan, the United States cut off military and economic aid to both. The disruption of military aid did bring the war to an end. The two sides were back again to their prewar positions in Kashmir. The Pakistanis, however, felt betrayed by the United States. Interestingly, the Soviet Union brokered a peace agreement between India and Pakistan in a meeting held in Tashkent in January 1966.

At the same time U.S. interest in South Asia declined. The United States was getting embroiled in Southeast Asia where the threat of the spread of communism appeared much greater than in the subcontinent. American policy makers also started questioning the value of foreign aid in bringing about stability and economic development in the underdeveloped countries.[16] The result was a sharply reduced level of commitment in South Asia. Economic assistance to India and Pakistan was reduced and only the supply of spare parts, but not weapons, was resumed to both in 1967. Pakistan perceived its security as adversely affected, since India remained a serious threat and Pakistan had largely relied upon American weapons. Pakistan, therefore, turned to Europe and China to diversify its weapons supplies and even made overtures to the Soviet Union for arms aid. The Soviet Union exploited the opportunity to reduce American as well as Chinese influence in Pakistan by promising it modest amounts of economic and military assistance. Nevertheless, India remained the primary Soviet ally in South Asia and did not consider the new friendship between the Soviet Union and Pakistan a threat to its security or relations with the Soviet Union.

U.S. indifference toward South Asia was short-lived. Two events again brought a more active American role in the subcontinent—a change in the U.S. policy toward China and the third Indo-Pakistan war in 1971. President

Nixon, elected in 1968, wanted to normalize relations with China and sought the help of China's friend and neighbor, Pakistan, for this purpose. Pakistan's new military ruler, Yahya Khan, who had come to power in March 1969, was all too willing to oblige the United States. Evidence indicates that Yahya Khan was indeed of considerable help to Richard Nixon in establishing relations with China, which led to the U.S. recognition of China in 1979 and close economic ties between the two powers.[17] Yahya Khan's help, however, was returned rather grudgingly by President Nixon during the Indo-Pakistan war of 1971.

The 1971 war between India and Pakistan was over the question of East Pakistan, which seceded and became an independent nation in 1971 thanks to India's support. Elections in East Pakistan held in December 1970 had resulted in the winning of 160 of East Pakistan's 162 seats in the National Assembly by one party, the Awami League, whose undisputed leader was Mujibur Rahman. Yahya Khan did not like Mujibur Rahman's victory. Negotiations between the two sides broke down, which led to a civil war culminating in the war between India and Pakistan and the dismembering of Pakistan. Despite advice from the United States to seek a political solution, Yahya Khan sent the military into East Pakistan to suppress the revolt there. The attempts at repression of the revolt brought chaos to East Pakistan, which started an exodus of refugees across the border into India. By the end of 1971, as many as nine million refugees, virtually all members of the Hindu minority in East Pakistan, had moved into India. India appealed to the international community for economic assistance to care for the refugees. More important, it seized the opportunity to reduce Pakistan's strength permanently, fought a war with Pakistan, inflicting upon it a humiliating defeat, and helped create an independent Bangladesh.

The 1971 war was disastrous for U.S. relations with India, Pakistan, and the newly created Bangladesh. Despite American help to feed the refugees and the American public and media's opposition to Pakistan's repression of East Pakistan, India resented the U.S. tilt toward Pakistan. The U.S. evenhandedness of 1965 had disappeared under President Nixon's administration. In return for the Pakistani president's cooperation in dealing with China, Nixon had personally approved an arms agreement with Pakistan in 1970. Arms supplies to Pakistan were not halted even when intelligence sources indicated that they were being used by Pakistan to control the revolt in East Pakistan, nor were they stopped during the Indo-Pakistan war of 1971. Pakistan, on the other hand, was unhappy with the United States for not helping it enough in the war against India. The United States had moved a part of the Seventh Fleet from Southeast Asia to the Bay of Bengal. This was, however, done toward the end of the war and most scholars agree that the American military presence off India's shores had virtually no impact on the outcome of the war.[18] The leaders of the new nation, Bangladesh, were disappointed that the United States, a great champion of human rights and freedom, had implicitly aided repression in their new land.

U.S. relations with Bangladesh soon improved because the fledgling nation needed American aid. The first aid agreement between the two nations was signed in 1972 and "by the end of 1973 the United States had given about $347 million, amounting to over 27 percent of Bangladesh's total external aid and the largest single contribution."[19] Repairing relations with India was much more complex than resumption of aid. Indians resented President Nixon's tilt toward Pakistan during the 1971 war. Aid to India remained cut off for six years until early 1978 when President Carter resumed it.[20] In February 1974 the United States did, however, write off two-thirds of the loans India owed to the United States in rupees (Indian currency).[21]

Two events further strained Indo-U.S. relations—India's detonation of a nuclear device in May 1974 and the declaration of a national emergency in June 1975 that brought India under the authoritarian rule of Prime Minister Indira Gandhi for the next twenty-one months. Surprisingly, the United States initially reacted mildly, even indifferently, to both events, in part because it had come to accept India's pre-eminent position in South Asia and in part because the subcontinent was again relegated to a status of little interest to the United States. When Jimmy Carter became president, the U.S. policy toward India changed. President Carter had a personal interest in India—his mother had served as a Peace Corps volunteer there. Further, soon after he took office, India reverted back to democracy. Carter was, however, more concerned about nuclear proliferation than Presidents Ford and Nixon. That created differences with India that seemed almost unresolvable.

Pakistan remained uncertain of U.S. support, despite the lifting of the arms embargo in February 1975.[22] India, on the other hand, was unhappy at the American policy change and considered it inimical to its security. Pakistan needed the American weapons to counterbalance Soviet military aid to India. Pakistan also considered U.S. nuclear policy biased toward it. It felt even more threatened by India after the 1974 nuclear test. Pakistan's leader, Zulfikar Ali Bhutto, who had replaced General Yahya Khan at the end of 1971, understandably wanted to develop nuclear weapons to assure protection from India. Pakistan continued its nuclear program, despite Bhutto's ouster from power by a military coup in 1977, led by General Zia-ul-Haq (Bhutto was executed in 1979). As a result of the Symington-Glenn amendment to the International Security Assistance Act of 1977, which aimed at nuclear nonproliferation, U.S. economic and military assistance to Pakistan was cut off in early 1979. When the Soviet Union invaded and occupied Afghanistan late in December that year, President Carter offered $400 million in military assistance to Pakistan, which its leader, General Zia, rather scornfully refused. Indeed, "the Carter administration ended its term with a South Asian policy in shambles."[23]

President Reagan took office in January 1981 and mended relations with Pakistan by offering an attractive five-year $3.2 billion package of military and economic aid. Military aid was now offered on terms different from previous years.[24] The aid was no doubt to contain the Soviet expansion in South Asia. There was, however, no condition in the agreement that military aid was not to be used against India. India was upset by the lack of such a provision and by the delivery of sophisticated American weapons to Pakistan, notably F-16 fighter planes, considered the most advanced in the U.S. inventory. The United States justified aid to Pakistan on grounds of its strategic interests not only in South Asia but also in the neighboring Middle East. American weapons were needed to bolster Pakistan's strength against any possible eastward Soviet incursions and to help the Afghan guerrilla forces fight the Soviet troops from Pakistani territory. Aid was also given to help Pakistan care for the Afghan refugees who in just a few years increased to three million. A less convincing argument used in support of aid to Pakistan was that "a conventionally secure Pakistan would have less incentive to pursue a covert nuclear weapons program."[25]

American aid to Pakistan continued throughout the 1980s at an annual rate of more than $500 million. Opposition to the aid policy, however, had developed in Congress with the knowledge that Pakistan was continuing its nuclear program. In 1985 Senator Larry Pressler of South Dakota was instrumental in getting an amendment (named after him) to the Foreign Assistance Act passed that required the president to certify to Congress every year that Pakistan did not possess a nuclear explosive device. The Bush administration was unable to provide such a certification in 1990. As a result, all economic and military aid to Pakistan was cut off in October 1990. Suspension of aid on the nuclear issue once again soured U.S.-Pakistan relations. "The nuclear issue," according to one source, "is perhaps the most sensitive, recurrent, and disturbing roadblock in the Pakistan-U.S. security relationship."[26]

Pakistan's lobby in Washington tried hard for a resumption of aid. The U.S. Department of State was willing to recommend aid to Pakistan in a reduced amount. In the meantime, the Soviets withdrew from Afghanistan in February 1989, after suffering at least fifteen thousand casualties and leaving that country in disarray. The collapse of communism in the Soviet Union and Eastern Europe further reduced the need for Pakistan as an ally. Relations between the United States and Pakistan in the changed world order had to be based on considerations entirely different from those prevailing in the Cold War.

Relations between the United States and India also had to be established on the basis of changed world conditions. In the 1980s, however, though starting rather ominously with the resumption of military aid to Pakistan, U.S. relations with India gradually warmed up.[27] Development assistance in modest amounts, not exceeding $100 million annually and sometimes much less, was given to India. At the same time the United States sold it some advanced technology and even some military hardware.[28] Of far greater value to the Indian psyche was the U.S. acknowledgment and even Pakistan's acceptance of India's preeminent status in South Asia.

Furthermore, India was moving away from a public-sector-dominated economy toward increased private enterprise. Those changes opened up opportunities for American corporations for investment and profit.

U.S. INTERESTS, CHALLENGES, AND OPPORTUNITIES

U.S. interests, as well as the challenges and opportunities faced by its policy makers, were far different during the Cold War than at present and what is anticipated for the next century. Despite some official pronouncements to the contrary, South Asia was considered of little intrinsic value to the United States during the Cold War. It had no strategic resources, such as oil, and it was far removed from the United States geographically. The Korean War and the resultant American perception that the Soviet threat in Asia could move southward made South Asia important enough in the eyes of the American policy makers to be considered for alliances and substantial foreign aid. The United States, however, wanted to keep its commitments in the subcontinent limited and was anxious for the countries of the region, notably India and Pakistan, to do their share of security and economic development. William Barnds summarizes American interests in South Asia after the Korean War as follows:

> (1) That the subcontinent be militarily secure from external [Communist] attack; (2) that India and Pakistan assume some of the responsibility for the defense of Asia; (3) that the two countries cooperate politically with the United States and the Western powers; (4) that the quarrels between India and Pakistan, and between them and their neighbors, be settled or at least kept under control; (5) that both countries make sufficient political, economic, and social progress to enable their non-Communist governments to continue in power; and (6) that they be willing to provide the United States with transit rights, communications facilities, and perhaps even military bases if necessary.[29]

Neither India nor Pakistan had much to offer to the United States in the areas of trade and investment. Their value to the United States, therefore, was political and strategic, not economic.

In pursuing political and strategic goals, the United States made Pakistan a military ally, provided it weapons and economic assistance, and tolerated military regimes in that country. Although India did not join the U.S.-led alliance system and remained nonaligned, it succeeded in obtaining economic aid and, as a result of the Indo-Chinese war of 1962, military aid from the United States. By providing foreign aid, especially military assistance, to the two rivals, the United States perhaps inadvertently increased hostility between the two. India complained of the growing military threat from Pakistan and the likelihood of Pakistan's use of American weapons against it. Pakistan, on the other hand, resented American aid to India, since even without such assistance India was strong enough to present a threat to Pakistan.

As events outside as well as inside South Asia unfolded during the Cold War period, the United States varied the amounts of military and economic assistance to India and Pakistan, sometimes cut off aid and sometimes simply downgraded the entire subcontinent in its priority scale of foreign policy making. Because of its superpower status, the United States could not altogether ignore the subcontinent. The U.S. tilt toward Pakistan by President Nixon notwithstanding, India began to be considered the preeminent nation in the region, especially after the creation of Bangladesh in 1971 following the dismemberment of Pakistan and the detonation of a nuclear device by India in 1974.[30] When Pakistan started pursuing a nuclear option vigorously, the United States had to permanently elevate South Asia's importance in making foreign policy because of the threat of the spread of nuclear weapons in South Asia. As a result, even after the Soviet withdrawal from Afghanistan, South Asia remained important in the considerations of American policy makers.

The issue of nuclear proliferation is significant indeed for the subcontinent and the American policy in this region. Before considering it at some length, we analyze the changed post-Cold War conditions in South Asia and within India and Pakistan. In comparison to the defunct Soviet Union, its major successor state, Russia, has little influence in South Asia, including India, the former Soviet ally in the region. However, relations between Russia and India are friendly and there is even military cooperation between the two, involving rocket engine technology and naval equipment.[31] On the other hand, Pakistan has attempted to repair its strained relations with the United States, its former protector. As the editor of *The New York Times* wrote in April 1995, "Pakistan wants improved relations, renewed American aid and delivery of 38 F-16 jet fighters it bought in 1988."[32] There is some evidence that the United States may be softening its policy toward Pakistan, despite the latter's continuation of a nuclear program.[33]

The external Islamic factor should also be kept in view for considering the U.S. South Asia policy.[34] Both India and Pakistan have well over one hundred million Muslims, next only to Indonesia, which has the largest Muslim population in the world. Since Pakistan is officially an Islamic country and 97 percent of its 130 million people are Muslims, it tried to befriend Islamic countries of the Middle East during the Cold War period, mainly to increase its outside support against India. The end of the Cold War has increased the importance of the Muslim nations to Pakistan, since the latter cannot count on the United States. In addition to the Middle-Eastern Islamic countries, Pakistan has made overtures to the Central-Asian Islamic countries, which were parts of the Soviet Union.[35] India is aware of such efforts of Pakistan and has counteracted them by playing its secular card (officially, India treats all religions equally, Pakistan does not) and by siding with the Arab nations against Israel in their conflict.

The changed conditions in South Asia do present economic opportunities for the United States. Both India and Pakistan have embraced private enterprise and liberalized their controlled economies, encouraging trade and foreign investment. U.S. Secretary of State Warren M. Christopher commented in a policy statement:

> We increasingly view South Asia as a region of intense economic growth and development.... India's economic reform has cleared the way for unprecedented trade and investment between our two countries, a matter that has certainly been noted by more and more of our business community.... Pakistan, too, has undertaken a long-term economic reform program.[36]

U.S. economic opportunities in South Asia, however, should be considered keeping in view potential political instability in India and Pakistan and the possibility of increased regional economic cooperation.

Despite major economic reforms since 1991, India remains a hotbed of religious and caste rivalries, which often erupt into violence. Demands for secession, especially in Kashmir, also remain strong. The growing gap between the rich and poor is another disruptive factor for India. The Indian government has many a time silenced its opponents by throwing them into jails without trial. India's democracy is indeed tainted by a dose of dictatorial rule and is likely to stay that way in the foreseeable future.[37] The United States, therefore, will have to do business with India, ignoring some of its own values on the rights of the individual in a democracy. Of course, India's poverty (its per capita income is still below $400) makes labor cheap. Indian labor is considered highly skilled and productive, which makes it attractive to American investors.

Pakistan perhaps has finally emerged from its vacillations between democracy and military rule. Charles H. Percy, a former U.S. Senator from Illinois and chairman of the Senate Foreign Relations Committee, wrote in *Foreign Affairs*: "Despite the continuing clout of Pakistan's military, its overt return to power seems unlikely."[38] Pakistan, however, is plagued by ethnic discord that frequently erupts into violence. Pakistan's militant Islamic fundamentalism is a threat to the rights of minorities in the country, and by Western standards, to the rights of Pakistani women as well. Further, "as a conduit for a multibillion-dollar annual traffic in narcotics from Afghanistan, Pakistan has itself fallen victim to widespread drug addiction in its major cities."[39] Some allege that Pakistan has tolerated and possibly encouraged international terrorism. Pakistan is 10 to 15 percent better off than India in per capita income, but it still is a poor country and, like India, has cheap and productive labor. In conducting business with Pakistan, the United States will have to blunt its sensibility on the democratic rights of individuals.

Regional cooperation in South Asia so far has been less pronounced than regional hostilities, especially between India and Pakistan. Despite the existence of the South Asian Association for Regional Cooperation (SAARC) since the mid-1980s, there has been "until recently little economic or political linkage" between its member states.[40] One study argues:

> While economic interdependence has been low in South Asia, especially between India and Pakistan, the increasing regionalization of global trading arrangements, the exclusion of both states from these arrangements, the direction of economic reforms in both states, and the pressures within SAARC from the smaller states presage change. South Asians may be moving toward increasing economic interaction and interdependence.[41]

If indeed the South Asians were to proceed on a path of economic interdependence, they could potentially present a challenge to outsiders, including the United States, and make it harder for them to do business in the region. The prospect of that happening in the near future is, however, dim if not nonexistent.

Since close regional economic interdependence is not likely to occur in South Asia, U.S. interests lie in exploiting the new economic opportunities in the region that have arisen with the liberalization of the economies. Because of the much larger population and workforce, India presents far greater opportunities to the United States for investment and trade than does Pakistan. Travels by U.S. officials and corporate executives to India (as well as to Pakistan) in the 1990s have become considerably more frequent than in the previous decades. Optimism in the United States about economic opportunities in India is such that a *New York Times* reporter headlined a story in April 1995: "India, U.S. Diplomacy Is Sounding a Lot Like Economics."[42] The reporter stated:

> Now the looming issues between the United States and India are not New Delhi's role in the nonaligned movement or its nuclear-weapons program, but the liberalization of its shallow and corrupt financial markets, its reluctance to allow private competition in the insurance business, and its slowness in sweeping away choking regulations that date to British Raj.[43]

The Indians are, however, sensitive to any evidence, real or imagined, of undue Western influence. An Indian economist commented: "If the impression develops, and it has, that America is delving deeply into the details of India's economic policy, it will have a backlash."[44] U.S. officials, therefore, have to be careful in advancing economic interests in India or, for that matter, in Pakistan, since similar considerations exist in that country also. In comparison to some other Asian countries, both are less important to the U.S. interests, notwithstanding the growing American investment and trade in South Asia. If we compare U.S. investments in India to those in China and Thailand in 1992 and 1993, "American companies invested seven times more in China, and six times more in Thailand, a country of 20 million, compared with 900 million in India."[45]

There are, of course, other U.S. interests in South Asia besides economic ones. The familiar argument that restlessness of the poor can disturb the peace enjoyed by the rich is still advanced. A study conducted by the Asia Society wrote the following:

> Another imperative is that South Asian countries develop the capacity to feed their rapidly growing populations; otherwise, the resulting social and political unrest and refugee flows will threaten regional and international peace and stability.[46]

The Asia Society, in the same study, also pointed out the impact of the South Asian pollution on the global ecology. Since increased industrial activity pollutes the environment, unless antipollution controls are exercised, South Asian pollution may adversely affect the global environment.[47] Based on such considerations, this analysis urged the United States to "take a fresh look at South Asia because the region will become more important, even vital, to American welfare and security."[48]

While economic as well as political development in South Asian countries is of value to the United States, the issue of nuclear proliferation in our view is of paramount significance. According to a *New York Times* editorial, "U.S. intelligence predicts that if a nuclear war is going to happen, it will be a war between India and Pakistan."[49] Since the two rivals are determined not to sign the nuclear Nonproliferation Treaty (NPT) and both have nuclear-weapons capabilities, perhaps even a few bombs, and are improving their delivery mechanisms, one of the greatest challenges to the United States is to reduce and, if possible, eliminate the likelihood of a nuclear war in the region. For facing such a challenge and formulating a policy for the rest of this decade and the early next century, we need to understand the motivations behind the efforts of the two countries in acquiring the nuclear option.

Most analysts consider India's defeat by China in the war of 1962 and the latter's first nuclear test in 1964 the catalysts in India's pursuit of the nuclear program. A Carnegie Endowment study, however, claims that "India may have launched its nuclear program after a request for security assurances from the big powers went unheeded."[50] If this claim is correct, then China's nuclear explosion did not influence India's program and India may even have initiated its nuclear efforts before China did. Another view posits that the Indian program was an "energy-to-security-driven phenomenon"; in other words, India was primarily interested in meeting its energy needs through the development of nuclear power and security considerations, such as responding to the Chinese threat, were secondary.[51] There is little doubt that Pakistan developed its nuclear-weapons capability in order to secure its position against the much more powerful India and gave secondary consideration to the energy potential of its nuclear program.

Although India and Pakistan behaved rationally in the three wars between them since 1947 and avoided inflicting damages on each other that lacked military significance, political changes in the two countries have reduced the likelihood of the continuation of such rationality, even during a crisis that may involve the possible use of nuclear weapons.[52] In a 1991 treaty, the two rivals assured each other of nonattack on nuclear facilities in case of a war. That assurance was undoubtedly well-intentioned, but in the frenzy that may be created in a future crisis in the subcontinent, it may not hold. We present such an alarming viewpoint because of the emergence of Hindu fundamentalism in India and the Islamic fundamentalism in Pakistan and their growing political power. At this time the religious fundamentalists do not directly control federal governments, which would make decisions on the use of nuclear weapons in the two countries. However, their strength is increasing and if they were to gain control of government in both countries, the probability of a nuclear war between the two would certainly increase.[53]

POLICY OPTIONS: PROS AND CONS

During the Cold War, the U.S. policy option formulation process for any region, though complex, was based on certain givens, in particular the purported expansionist goals of communism and the Soviet net of economic and military links with the Second- as well as Third-World countries. In South Asia, India maintained close economic and military relations with the Soviet Union, and Pakistan was an American ally. For almost four decades, until U.S. economic and military aid to Pakistan was cut off in 1990 due to the latter's nuclear program, Pakistan was favored over India. In any U.S. policy formulation, Pakistan's role in containing communism in South Asia and in creating a balance in the region by keeping India under check was given prominence. Since India is a much larger and more powerful country, it could not be ignored. Most U.S. policy makers, however, relegated India to a secondary status and found the Indian leaders difficult to work with. Pakistan, on the other hand, was not only viewed with sympathy, its leaders also appeared to American policy makers as friendly and sometimes even pliable. As India gained economic and military strength and enhanced its international status, especially after its first nuclear test in 1974, its position as a preeminent state in South Asia was recognized by the United States. Pakistan, however, still remained the only South Asian country that the United States could count on.

Even during the Cold War, U.S. policy options for South Asia, or for that matter for any other region, were seldom mutually exclusive. They have become even less so in the post-Cold War period. It is not realistic to argue that only one option is the best and should be pursued and that all other options should be ignored. Nor is it advisable to present simplistic options, attractive though they may seem. In an article published in *The New York Times*, a scholar noted:

> Curbing the spread of nuclear arms is a worthy objective, but now that both India and Pakistan, despite our best efforts, have nuclear capabilities, we should leave it to these contending parties to sort out their own affairs. We must count on their own good sense of the dangers of nuclear war to lead them to avoid it.[54]

The U.S. stake in the nuclear issue is such that we cannot wash our hands of South Asia and simply hope that India and Pakistan would never engage in a nuclear war because of its potential dangers.

The most desirable option, in our view, is that the relative importance of India and Pakistan to the United States must change. We must give India greater weight than it had during the Cold War, and we do not need to expend enormous amounts on Pakistan even if aid were to be resumed. This option, however, does not imply that we should flaunt our improved relations with India to the detriment of our relations with Pakistan. Both countries are of value to U.S. interests, and we should not tilt our policy toward one or the other. Such an option is akin to what is often called a "region-wide approach."[55] Some elements of this option are "an impartial but activist approach to pressing issues between Islamabad and New Delhi," measures aimed at peace and stability in the region, including avoidance of arms sales to either country that would aggravate their already tense relations, and even a system of reward and penalty for progress toward or steps against regional stability.[56] A central feature of the regional option is neutrality on the part of the United States between India and Pakistan. *Become a Balanced*

POLICY RECOMMENDATIONS FOR THE TWENTY-FIRST CENTURY

Based on the history of U.S. relations with India and Pakistan, U.S. interests, challenges, and opportunities in the post-Cold War era, and our preference for a regional approach to South Asia, we make the following policy recommendations for the rest of this decade and the next century.

NEUTRAL POLICY

The United States should treat both India and Pakistan similarly and not tilt its policy toward one or the other. Both countries can be useful for advancing American economic and security interests, and the United States should exploit the new opportunities available rather than favor one over the other and increase hostility between them. As an example, the United States signed a military cooperation accord with India in 1995 that provided for "consultations between the Pentagon and India's Defense Ministry, as well as joint military exercises, military training, defense research, and weapons production."[57] Without giving up its stand on nuclear proliferation, the United States should pursue a similar agreement with Pakistan. Treating India and Pakistan equally would help the United States pursue its own goals effectively and harness the two countries' cooperation in combating such international problems as terrorism and drug-trafficking.

FOREIGN AID, INVESTMENT, AND TRADE

U.S. military aid to Pakistan in the Cold War period compelled India to join the Soviet camp. When the United States provided any military aid to India, Pakistan felt threatened. We recommend that military aid as well as arms sales be taken off the U.S. agenda for relations with India and Pakistan. Both countries need economic assistance for development and prefer multilateral over bilateral assistance. The United States should stop all bilateral aid to India, not resume the aid to Pakistan that was cut off in 1990, and instead concentrate on meeting their development requirements through multilateral agencies such as the World Bank and the United Nations. Private U.S. investment in both countries should be increased, since the two countries are much more receptive to such investment than in the past. The United States should also take maximum possible advantage of the improved trade opportunities in the region.

DEMOCRACY AND HUMAN RIGHTS

India will maintain democracy in the foreseeable future. Prospects for the continuation of democracy in Pakistan are better today than they perhaps were at any time in its history of five decades. The United States will have to accept somewhat lower levels of democracy in these countries than democracy in the West. Both countries show far less respect for human rights than do Western societies. While the United States should try to steer both India and Pakistan toward more tolerant and humane societies, it should not expect miracles in either case. In other words, while not ignoring concerns for human rights and democracy, it should set realistic goals for progress in these categories in South Asia.

REGIONAL ISSUES

Regional issues, notably the dispute on Kashmir, will continue to destabilize South Asia. The United States should not only play the role of a neutral on such issues, but it should be more active in goading the hostile parties into negotiations than it was in the past. Seemingly unresolvable conflicts in other regions have sometimes been resolved. Even though the Kashmir dispute appears to defy any solution at this time, it is possible to decrease tension in the area through negotiations and perhaps reach an acceptable resolution in the not too distant future. Indians and Pakistanis, or Hindus and Muslims, of the region do not have any more serious differences than do Arabs and Israelis. Since peace efforts are continuing in the Middle East and some progress has been made to resolve that conflict, we should also remain optimistic about Kashmir.

THE NUCLEAR ISSUE

Since South Asia is the region where a nuclear war is most likely to occur, an overriding goal of U.S. policy toward South Asia in the post-Cold War period should be to make it nuclear-free and if that goal fails, then to contain the growth of nuclear weapons in this region as much as possible. For the success of such a goal, India and Pakistan need credible assurances not only from each other to guarantee their security, but also from the other nuclear powers that reduction of nuclear weapons to minimum levels through a comprehensive test ban treaty and dismantling of nuclear weapons is being pursued. China must be a party to any agreement on South Asia, because India will not descale its nuclear program if it perceives China as threatening to its security. Pakistan's fears against India are quite as legitimate. The United States should, therefore, pursue its leadership role in Asia by bringing China, India, and Pakistan together around a negotiation table on the nuclear and the broader security issues. Unless the United States exerts such leadership in Asia, we cannot expect peace in the Asian continent or the world.

NOTES

1. Stanley Wolpert, *Roots of Confrontation in South Asia* (New York: Oxford University Press, 1982), p. 140.
2. See Dennis Kux, *Estranged Democracies: India and the United States, 1941–1991* (New Delhi: Sage Publications, 1993), pp. 6–38.
3. Ibid., p. 3.
4. W. Norman Brown, *The United States and India, Pakistan, Bangladesh* (Cambridge, MA: Harvard University Press, 1972), p. 393.
5. Ibid.
6. Robert L. Hardgrave, Jr., *India under Pressure: Prospects for Political Stability* (Boulder, CO: Westview Press, 1984), p. 203. See also M. S. Venkataramani, *The American Role in Pakistan, 1947–1958* (New Delhi: Radiant Publishers, 1982), Chapter 1.
7. For a view sympathetic to India on Kashmir, see Srinivas C. Madumbai, *United States Foreign Policy towards India, 1947–1954* (New Delhi: Manohar, 1980), pp. 79–106. For a perspective sympathetic to Pakistan, see Shirin Tahir-Kheli, *The United States and Pakistan: The Evolution of an Influence Relationship* (New York: Praeger, 1982), pp. 12–19.
8. Madumbai, *United States Foreign Policy towards India, 1947–1954*, p. 65.
9. At least one analyst argues that "the United States had promised to help even if the aggression was noncommunist and Indian." See G. W. Choudhury, *India, Pakistan, Bangladesh, and the Major Powers* (New York: The Free Press, 1975), p. 121.
10. Wolpert, *Roots of Confrontation in South Asia*, p. 142.
11. Hardgrave, *India under Pressure*, p. 203.
12. Mohammed Ahsen Chaudhri, "Pakistan and the United States," in *Pakistan-United States Relations*, Rais Ahmad Khan, ed. (Islamabad: Quaid-i-Azam University, 1983), p. 12.
13. See Choudhury, *India, Pakistan, Bangladesh, and the Major Powers*, p. 101.
14. For an analysis of this tilt, see ibid., pp. 100–126.

15. William J. Barnds, *India, Pakistan, and the Great Powers* (New York: Praeger, 1972), p. 182.
16. See ibid., pp. 8–9.
17. See, for example, Wolpert, *Roots of Confrontation in South Asia*, pp. 150–151.
18. See Kux, *Estranged Democracies*, p. 305.
19. Choudhury, *India, Pakistan, Bangladesh, and the Major Powers*, p. 235.
20. See Kux, *Estranged Democracies*, p. 355.
21. The loan amounted to $2.2 billion worth of rupees. Ibid., p. 314.
22. Kux, *Estranged Democracies*, p. 330.
23. Shivaji Ganguly, *U.S. Policy toward South Asia* (Boulder, CO: Westview Press, 1990), p. 237.
24. See Kux, *Estranged Democracies*, p. 384. Also see Hasan-Askari Rizvi, "Pakistan-U.S. Security Relations: Pakistani Perceptions of Key Issues," in *Pakistan-U.S. Relations: Social, Political, and Economic Factors*, Noor A. Hussain and Leo E. Rose, eds. (Berkeley: University of California, 1988), p. 13.
25. Ganguly, *U.S. Policy toward South Asia*, p. 239.
26. Iftikhar H. Malik, "Pakistan's Security Imperatives and Relations with the United States," in *Beyond Afghanistan: The Emerging U.S.-Pakistan Relations*, Leo E. Rose and Kamal Matinuddin, eds. (Berkeley: University of California, 1989), p. 84. See also Iftikhar H. Malik, "The Pakistan-U.S. Security Relationship," *Asian Survey* (March 1990): 297.
27. Kux, *Estranged Democracies,* pp. 416–418. The United States and India did experience some serious differences in this period, especially on trade and the supply of enriched uranium for an Indian nuclear power plant near Bombay. See M. J. Vinod, *United States Foreign Policy towards India* (New Delhi: Lancer Books, 1991), pp. 86–123.
28. See Paul Kreisberg, "The United States, South Asia, and American Interests," *Journal of International Affairs* (Summer/Fall 1989): 89.
29. Barnds, *India, Pakistan, and the Great Powers*, pp. 4–5.
30. In a memorandum written by nine South Asia experts, including this author, and submitted on November 30, 1979 to Mr. Harold H. Saunders, Assistant Secretary of State, Bureau of Near Eastern and South Asian Affairs, the preeminent position of India in South Asia was considered a given.
31. See Lawrence E. Grinter, "The United States and South Asia: New Challenges, New Opportunities," *Asian Affairs, An American Review* (Summer 1993): 104.
32. *The New York Times*, April 13, 1995, p. A24. The jet fighters purchased by Pakistan from the United States were not delivered due to the cut off of American military and economic aid to Pakistan in 1990 on the issue of nuclear weapons.
33. See *The New York Times*, April 12, 1995, pp. A1, A5.
34. See Raju G. C. Thomas, "South Asian Security in the 1990s," *Adelphi Papers* (July 1993): 14–18.
35. Ibid., p. 15.
36. *U.S. Department of State Dispatch*, October 3, 1994, p. 656.
37. See Kul B. Rai, "India's Democracy Is Stained by a Dose of Dictatorial Rule," *Hartford Courant*, February 23, 1995, p. A17.
38. Charles H. Percy, "South Asia's Take-Off: The Region Turns to Market Economics," *Foreign Affairs* (Winter 1992–1993): 168.
39. Selig S. Harrison, "South Asia and the United States: A Chance for a Fresh Start," *Current History* (March 1992): 100.
40. Gowher Rizvi, *South Asia in a Changing International Order* (New Delhi: Sage Publications, 1993), p. 147. Members of the SAARC are Bangladesh, Bhutan, India, the Maldives, Nepal, Pakistan, and Sri Lanka.
41. Kanti P. Bajpai and Stephen P. Cohen, "Introduction," in *South Asia after the Cold*

War, Kanti P. Bajpai and Stephen P. Cohen, eds. (Boulder, CO: Westview Press, 1993), p. 5.
42. *The New York Times*, April 23, 1995, p. A12.
43. Ibid.
44. Ibid.
45. Ibid.
46. *South Asia and the United States after the Cold War* (New York: The Asia Society, 1994), p. 4.
47. Ibid.
48. Ibid.
49. *The New York Times*, March 29, 1994, p. A22.
50. *India Abroad*, May 12, 1995, p. 10, in a report on the Carnegie study, *Security Assurances*.
51. Thomas, "South Asian Security in the 1990s," p. 63.
52. For the display of rationality by the two sides in wars, see ibid., p. 67.
53. See Kul B. Rai, "Indian, Pakistani Tensions Could Explode in Nuclear War," *New Haven Register*, December 13, 1992, p. B3.
54. Nathan Glazer, "Why Arm Pakistan?" *The New York Times*, April 13, 1994, p. A21.
55. Grinter, "The United States and South Asia," p. 115.
56. Ibid.
57. *The New York Times*, January 13, 1995, p. A12.

CHAPTER 7

AMERICAN POLICY
TOWARD LATIN AMERICA

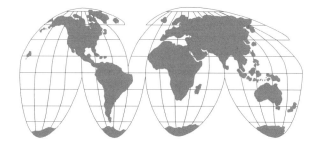

JAMES W. DULL

With faded memories of the first Pan-American Conference in 1889 in the background, President Bill Clinton opened the Summit of the Americas in Miami, Florida, in December 1994. Its goal, said one administration official, was "to create a new post-Cold War mature hemispheric partnership for peace, democracy, mutual growth, and shared prosperity."[1] The summit and the start of the North American Free Trade Agreement in 1994 marked important steps toward formation of a hemispheric trade bloc and closer coordination of American states.

No sooner had the summit ended, however, than a new crisis challenged the proposed partnership as Mexico devalued its peso, forcing the United States to swiftly organize a rescue package for the Mexican government. Simultaneously, in early 1995, the U.S. military intervention in Haiti was phased out, replaced by a multinational force including U.S. personnel under a U.N.-sponsored resolution. The counterpoint of these events raised serious questions about the future form and character of a "mature partnership" and the nature of U.S. leadership in the hemisphere.

Although a noted scholar argues that "the end of the Cold War marked the end of the Monroe Doctrine,"[2] recent events suggest that the Monroe Doctrine remains very much alive and it continues to sustain the U.S. role in the Americas. The Monroe Doctrine has been the basis of U.S. foreign policy in the hemisphere for nearly two centuries. Buttressed by subsequent policies, such as the Roosevelt Corollary, the "big stick," "dollar diplomacy," gunboat diplomacy, and the Good Neighbor Policy, the Doctrine was "fundamentally the assertion of an American (U.S.) sphere of influence in the hemisphere."[3]

The Monroe Doctrine, promulgated in 1823, gave notice of U.S. opposition to additional European colonization and to expansion of existing colonies in the hemisphere.[4] More than the intention to exclude or expel European influence, it was a clear signal of U.S. hegemony once and for all, and while it has often been challenged (most recently by the Soviet Union), it survives in U.S. thinking despite the end of the Cold War and the disintegration of the Soviet Union. However, other important changes in the global system and in the hemisphere have caused recent U.S. presidents to reassess the fundamental relationships in the Americas and the specific U.S. foreign policies necessary to pursue the national interests of the United States.

Even before the end of the Cold War, for example, new power centers had emerged in Europe and Asia, creating dynamic competition in the global economy. The expansion of the European Union, the strength of Germany and Japan, the rising force of China, and the potential power of a reconstituted Russia form the backdrop of global change. Within Latin America, the transitions to democracy and market economies have created a new promise of political stability and economic development.

In this changing framework, the United States remains the most powerful state in the global system and in the hemisphere. Other states look to it for leadership and accept its primacy, and at the end of the century the United States remains committed to its leadership role and the costs and responsibilities that go with it. However, the effort to reshape U.S. policy raises a number of important questions, such as the following: What are U.S. national interests in the hemisphere? Have they changed? Is a new relationship necessary? How is it to be defined? Is it possible to achieve? What forms should it take?

As the Clinton administration and the Americas struggle with these issues, this chapter explores the complex framework in which U.S. foreign policy is made and implemented. First, the United States conducts foreign policy on at least five levels of roles and responsibilities: global, hemispheric, regional, bilateral, and domestic. Each level imposes its own opportunities and constraints in the service of U.S. national interests. Second, policy functions along four major tracks, which are distinct yet interconnected: political, economic, military, and cultural.[5] All levels and tracks must be effectively coordinated to achieve maximum benefits for the national interest. Third, policy makers must accommodate the enormous diversity, pluralism, and dynamics of Latin America and adapt policy to the often-turbulent history of American relations. Finally, defining and confronting complex and changing issues encountered in common by the Americas are indispensable elements in the policy process.

THE NATURE OF LATIN AMERICA

A vast territory occupying the continent of South America, parts of North America, and numerous islands of the Caribbean, Latin America is a most heterogeneous region, which some observers question calling "Latin" America at all because of the extraordinary blend of cultures living there.[6] Home of the ancient Olmec, Mayan, Inca, Toltec, Aztec, and other native civilizations, the area became colonies of Spain and Portugal following the voyages of Columbus. In the next three centuries, more than 5 million African slaves were imported to work in the development of the area.[7] Gradually, other Europeans migrated to the region, including, British, Germans, French, and Italians. In addition, long before the independence of the United States, North Americans pursued commercial interests in the West Indies, Mexico, and Central America.[8] Meanwhile, intermixtures of races and ethnic groups led to the formation of complex social groups: creoles, mestizos, mulattos, pensulares, blacks, and native Indians.

The long history of colonization contributed to the varied geographical and political shapes found in the Latin American states of the late-twentieth century: a blend of thirty-four independent countries of widely-varying size plus French departments, Dutch territories, British associate states, and possessions of the United States.

An authoritative source categorizes the states of Latin America in four regions: North America, Central America, South America, and the Caribbean.[9] Mexico is part of North America, while Central America includes Belize, Costa Rica, El Salvador, Guatemala, Honduras, Nicaragua, and Panama. The countries of the Caribbean are the following: Antigua and Barbuda, the Bahamas, Barbados, Cuba, Dominica, the Dominican Republic, Grenada, Haiti, Jamaica, St. Kitts-Nevis, St. Lucia, St. Vincent and the Grenadines, and Trinidad and Tobago. In South America are Argentina, Brazil, Bolivia, Chile, Colombia, Ecuador, Guyana, Paraguay, Peru, Suriname, Uruguay, and Venezuela.

On the more complex scales measuring levels of democracy, political stability, and social justice, the character of Latin America is less easily defined. Moreover, the scope and magnitude of poverty, so visible even in major Latin American cities, scar every country. Relatively small oligarchies continue to own a substantial portion of land, capital, and leadership, backed by military forces often among the most highly trained and disciplined elites in many countries. The middle class, the presence of which usually is regarded as a prerequisite for democracy, varies in size from country to country. The rural peasantry usually constitutes the broad mass of the social structure characterized by limited power and even less ownership of land.

The obstacles to creation of future U.S. foreign policy in Latin America are formidable, and lurking always in the background is the suspicion, mistrust, and fear of the United States and its private sector left over from nearly two centuries of U.S. hegemony in what it has always considered its sphere of influence.

HISTORICAL BACKGROUND

Long before independence from Great Britain, North American merchants, often in violation of British law, traded in the West Indies as exporters and shippers. After independence, U.S. interests still encountered British, French, and Spanish obstacles to freedom to trade. The Napoleonic Era opened the way for the Louisiana Purchase in 1803 (which more than doubled the size of the United States) and for the independence of former Latin American colonies of Spain and Portugal. With the fall of Napoleon, the United States moved to limit Russian and French claims, and the British sought to prevent the restoration of Spanish control in the Americas. For once, U.S. and British interests coincided and formed the backdrop for a bold initiative by the U.S. government: The Monroe Doctrine.

On December 2, 1823, President James Monroe delivered to Congress the proposal that much later became known as the Monroe Doctrine. It made three major points: (1) no further colonization of the Americas by "any European powers"; (2) no further expansion of European colonies already in the hemisphere; and (3) noninvolvement by the United States in European affairs.[10] It was a clear U.S. claim to its own sphere of influence and to its own position as hegemonic, or dominant, power. European powers continued to either ignore or challenge the Doctrine, but, ironically, the British navy gave it some credibility. Nonetheless, it has remained the foundation of U.S. foreign policy in Latin America up to the present.

U.S. continental expansion proceeded rapidly in the early nineteenth century, and by 1830 an estimated fifteen thousand settlers had moved into the Mexican province of Texas. Their agitation against Mexican authorities led to the confrontation at the Alamo in 1835 and to eventual independence. Texas' support for annexation to the United States increased tensions with Mexico, and President James K. Polk used Mexico's refusal to negotiate as a basis for a declaration of war in 1846. U.S. military victories led to the Treaty of Guadalupe Hidalgo and the surrender of massive territories in a region that now encompasses the states of California, Nevada, Utah, Arizona, New Mexico, and parts of Colorado. Texas was also annexed by the United States.

The appeal of expansion, known by the mid-nineteenth century as "manifest destiny," gained strength in the United States, especially in Southern states hoping for an extension of slavery into new areas. During and after the Civil War, manifest destiny also remained intense in the North, reflected in the views of Secretary of State William Seward in the 1860s. He envisioned "a coordinated empire tied together by superior American institutions and commerce" and speculated that Mexico City would make "a fine imperial capital."[11] In 1865 Seward sought unsuccessfully to buy the Danish West Indies. The deal was finally completed in 1917, and they became the U.S. Virgin Islands; but in 1867, Seward was more successful in buying Alaska from Russia. Much of the rest of his imperial vision came to nothing at the time.

During the U.S. Civil War, France sought control of Mexico by attempting to install Austrian Archduke Ferdinand Maximilian as emperor. Mexican revolutionaries led by Benito Juarez, French troubles at home, and U.S. threats persuaded France to recall its troops, leaving Maximilian to a Mexican firing squad.

The dream of a canal in Central America flourished in the post-Civil War United States, especially after the successful construction of the Suez Canal in Egypt. In 1850 the United States and Britain had concluded the Clayton-Bulwar Treaty, creating a partnership to build a canal; but U.S. leaders increasingly explored ways to do it alone. "A canal under American control, or no canal," said President Rutherford B. Hayes in 1880.[12] However, it was to be another quarter century before the canal became a reality.

The 1890s marked a period of expanded U.S. intervention in Latin America. Involvements in disputes with Chile in 1891 and in the settlement of a border conflict between Britain and Venezuela in 1895 provided the background for another blatant claim of U.S. hegemony. In the Venezuelan matter, Secretary of State Richard Olney asserted: "The United States is practically sovereign on this continent, and its fiat is law upon the subjects to which it confines its interposition."[13] The conclusion of the dispute led to what one historian regards as "a self-conscious British decision to permit the United States to govern Caribbean affairs."[14]

If the British were prepared to accept U.S. dominance in the hemisphere by the end of the century, Spain was not. Repeated Cuban revolts and Spanish repressions threatened human decency and U.S. interests, and efforts to modify Spanish tactics proved unsuccessful. In 1896 President William McKinley sent the warship *Maine* to Havana Harbor to demonstrate U.S. pressure. When explosions, never fully explained, sank the *Maine* in February, reaction in the United States led to a declaration of war by Congress. When the war ended with a U.S. victory and the collapse of the Spanish empire, the United States annexed Hawaii, gained control over the Philippines, Guam, and Puerto Rico, and liberated Cuba. Debate over the fate of Cuba produced the Teller Amendment prohibiting annexation of Cuba, but the Platt Amendment to a military spending bill in 1901 proclaimed the right of the United States to intervene in Cuba to protect its interests. Although Cubans protested vigorously, the act established a protectorate status for Cuba for some time to come, until the revolution of 1958.

Following the assassination of William McKinley in 1901, Theodore

Roosevelt became president. Embodying the spirit of expansionism, Roosevelt focused his attention on building a canal. Just as important in the long term was another initiative: the Roosevelt Corollary to the Monroe Doctrine in 1904. It asserted the right of the United States to use "international police power" to prevent European intervention in the Americas and to permit U.S. regulation of Latin American affairs.[15] Despite U.S. approval of German and British military interventions to enforce financial claims, concerns increased in Washington about hemispheric interference from abroad.

When a canal project of a French-based company failed in 1888, the United States moved to renegotiate with Great Britain the Clayton-Bulwar Treaty of 1850, which had provided for joint ownership and the absence of fortifications of a future canal. The result was the Hay-Pauncefote Treaty, which, in its final form in 1902, established exclusive authority as well as the right of fortification for the United States. When consideration of Colombia or Nicaragua as possible sites for a canal encountered insurmountable problems, the Roosevelt administration focused on the territory of Panama, then under the control of Colombia. With encouragement by the United States, revolution erupted and produced a new provisional government that was promptly recognized by the U.S. government. Within two weeks a treaty with the new government, the Hay-Bunau-Varilla Treaty, provided authority for the United States to proceed with construction. The project began in 1904 and the new Panama canal opened ten years later in 1914.

The Roosevelt policies, called the "Big Stick," based on his admonition to "speak softly but carry a big stick," underwent some changes by his successor, William Howard Taft. "Dollar diplomacy" became the catchword for the use of investment as a preferable tool of policy to achieve stability and development in Latin America. One example found the United Fruit Company exercising broad influence in a number of countries, but unrest in Nicaragua led to a military intervention in 1912 that lasted until 1925 and another in 1926 that continued until 1933.

The election of Woodrow Wilson produced a change in U.S. rhetoric toward Latin America, but little evidence of a change in practice. Interventions in the Dominican Republic, Haiti, and Mexico continued the pattern. Revolution and rapid governmental turnovers in Mexico during the Wilson presidency prompted military intervention, but the threat of German and Japanese alliances with Mexico, just as World War I was approaching led Wilson to recognize the government of Venustiano Carranza. Mexico remained neutral in the war.

After the war, U.S. investments in Latin America more than doubled during the 1920s, and U.S. interests gained control of copper resources in Chile and oil in Venezuela. According to historian Walter LaFeber, one survey of the 1920s showed that "of the twenty Latin American nations, all but six were controlled or heavily influenced by U.S. Marines, U.S. bankers, or both."[16] Military interventions in the Dominican Republic, Nicaragua, and Haiti extended well into the decade, contributing to the rise of authoritarian rulers who were to last for years. Rafael Trujillo came to power in the Dominican Republic and ruled until his assassination in 1961. In Nicaragua, the return of U.S. forces in 1926 to combat a revolution led by Augusto Sandino resulted in the authoritarian rule of the Somoza family for another half century.

Nineteen years of U.S. occupation of Haiti failed to produce a democratic political order and instead left conditions ripe for the dictatorship of the Duvalier family—Dr. Francis "Papa Doc" and his son "Baby Doc." In Cuba, political instability resulted in the rise of the power of the military, led directly and indirectly by Fulgencio Batista until the 1958 revolution of Fidel Castro.

When Franklin Roosevelt took office in 1933, he offered a less interventionist theme for Latin America: the Good Neighbor Policy. Instead of force, the policy emphasized close economic ties and massive economic dependence on the United States for trade, credit, and investment as the best means to deal with the hemisphere. However, the Good Neighbor Policy ran afoul of the worldwide economic depression of the 1930s, with devastating effects on the United States and its neighbors. Although industrialism was not widespread in Latin America, a drastic drop in demand for the region's primary crops and materials cut foreign earnings, expanded debt, and crippled economies. Roosevelt responded by gaining congressional approval of the Reciprocal Trade Agreement, designed in part to keep U.S. markets open to Latin American goods. Congress also created the Export-Import Bank to encourage inter-American trade. The results were regarded in Latin America as inadequate, but as the 1930s continued, the prospects of world war again loomed before the hemisphere.

The decade produced considerable political and economic instability in Latin America and a whirlpool of contradictory ideologies and passions: nationalism, socialism, communism, fascism, Catholicism, and capitalism. Germany and Italy saw Latin America as a promising source of allies, military bases, and raw materials, but Roosevelt sought hemispheric unity. In 1938, American governments meeting in Lima, Peru formed the Lima Pact, creating new consultative machinery. Then, meeting in Panama in 1939, foreign ministers of hemispheric countries pledged mutual cooperation to protect their neutrality rights. At their meeting in 1940, the United States and the Latin American governments issued the Havana Declaration, pledging to defend any hemispheric lands owned by non-Americans against seizure by others, such as Germany.

When the United States entered World War II in December 1941, nearly all of the Latin American states, with the exception of Argentina (until 1944), joined the allied cause. Historian Walter LaFeber observes that "U.S.-Latin American relations were never closer than during World War II."[17] He notes that $450 million in lend-lease aid went to Latin America, 80 percent of it to Brazil, which provided transit bases for U.S. aircraft heading for North Africa and Europe.[18] Fifty percent of Latin exports went to the United States, providing valuable raw materials. Latin America also provided military bases and alliances.

When the war ended, a new one began: the Cold War—the often dangerous conflict between the U.S.-led western bloc and the Soviet bloc. The containment doctrine, designed by the United States to deter expansion by the Soviet Union and communism in Europe, at first provided little for Latin America, where disillusionment with the benefits from World War II cooperation intensified social unrest.[19] Recognizing the potential Soviet threat to the hemisphere, the administration of Harry S. Truman sought the severing of diplomatic relations with the Soviet Union by Latin states, and only Mexico, Argentina, and Uruguay declined. Efforts to persuade Latin governments to outlaw domestic communist parties were also widely successful. In 1947, the United States initiated the Rio Pact, defining external attacks as attacks on all members.[20] Then, in 1948, at Bogota, Colombia, the Organization of American States (OAS) was formed, providing regular consultation and common action against threats to the hemisphere.[21] Yet all was not well in Latin America. Scholars have noted:

> Latin American poverty was stark; illiteracy rates were high; health care was inadequate; a population explosion was underway; productivity showed minuscule growth; profits from raw materials like sugar and oil flowed through American companies to the United States; and Washington had taken the region for granted.[22]

Meanwhile, private U.S. investment and trade increased rapidly. U.S. government aid had come to include military assistance to allies committed to resisting Soviet expansion, and this assistance included weapons, training, and money. In 1951, the United States extended its Military Security Program to include Latin America and linked military elites to Washington through training, equipment, spare parts, and ammunition.

Despite all of the military aid provided to Latin American military professionals, the United States found few allies when the United Nations authorized military action in Korea in 1950. Only Colombia sent a battalion of infantry.

When the Eisenhower administration came into office in 1953, it viewed most of the troubles of Latin America as Soviet-inspired and brought an intense free-market, free-enterprise ideology to the United States and to its Latin American neighbors.[23] The intended result was far less governmental economic assistance from Washington and an increased reliance on the private sector for investment. Growing revolutionary ferment focused on Washington as often as it did on national governments. The growth of neo-imperialist ideology and the so-called Dependency Theory strengthened the view that the United States shared the responsibility for deplorable standards of living in most of Latin America.[24]

Reformists of all stripes emerged throughout the region, and when one of them, Jacobo Arbenz, came to power in Guatemala, the Eisenhower administration decided to act quickly. A U.S. initiative led by the CIA helped to oust Arbenz and install Carlos Castillo Armas. Arbenz had initiated a policy of expropriation and nationalization of private lands, including some held by the United Fruit Company.[25]

Later in the 1950s, an eight-nation Latin American tour by Vice President Richard Nixon encountered violent protests and a threat to Nixon's life. However, a broader challenge to the United States emerged in 1958 from another event of considerable importance: the Cuban Revolution and the rise of Fidel Castro.

Castro gained a powerful ally—the Soviet Union, whose interests in penetrating the hemisphere and counterbalancing U.S. global power made Cuba and Castro unexpected allies against the United States. By 1960 the Eisenhower administration began serious planning for Castro's removal through an invasion by Cuban exiles and an expected uprising of the Cuban people against Castro. After John F. Kennedy won the presidency, the new administration took over the plan, revised it to remove the appearance of U.S. involvement, and moved ahead. The result was the Bay of Pigs disaster in 1961, humiliating the United States, weakening the Kennedy administration, and leaving over 1,200 prisoners in Castro's jails. Negotiations later engineered a deal for their release, but the Soviets perceived inept leadership in Washington. This proved to be a dangerous miscalculation, but it set in motion the plan for the most deadly threat of the Cold War: the Cuban Missile Crisis.

Determined to reduce the disparity in the global nuclear balance, Soviet leadership decided to install medium-range missiles in Cuba capable of striking the United States. The effort was discovered and confirmed in October 1962, and Kennedy demanded that the missiles be removed, ordered a naval "quarantine" of Cuba, and hinted at escalation. Ultimately, secret negotiations led to Soviet agreement to remove the missiles in return for a U.S. pledge to remove some missiles from Italy and Turkey and not to overthrow Castro.

Meanwhile, the idea for a massive aid program for Latin America had been evolving in the Kennedy administration—the Alliance for Progress. As early as March 1961, Kennedy discussed it with Latin American diplomats, and in an August meeting in Punta del Este, Uruguay, the plan was announced. It was a ten-year program providing $100 billion, 20 billion of it by the United States. It proposed tax reform, land reform, and, in effect, a redistribution of political power from ruling oligarchies to the masses. The Alliance, however, failed for numerous reasons: the assassination of Kennedy;

the attention to Vietnam by his successor, Lyndon B. Johnson; and, most importantly, the unwillingness of Latin elites to relinquish land, money, and power.[26]

For President Johnson, Vietnam became the dominant U.S. foreign policy issue. U.S. support for the Latin American military increased and contributed to the removal of a civilian president in Brazil, Joao Goulart, inaugurating a twenty-year period of military rule. Then instability in the Dominican Republic, following the 1961 assassination of dictator Rafael Trujillo, occurred. President Juan Bosch and the military struggled for power. When a split occurred in the military, Bosch sought to regain office, at which point Johnson decided to send troops to restore order.

Shortly after his inauguration in 1969, Richard Nixon faced the valid election of a socialist, Salvador Allende, as President of Chile. With massive U.S. corporate investment in Chile, especially in the copper industry, the Nixon administration had taken action to prevent Allende's election, and when Allende's victory led to expropriation of foreign-owned property, the United States encouraged Chilean middle- and upper-class opposition to resist. Ultimately, a military coup removed Allende, and he died in the violence that followed. Under General Augusto Pinochet, the military junta remained in power until 1989 when, emboldened to run an election, Pinochet lost.

Richard Nixon resigned the presidency in August 1974 because of the Watergate affair and was succeeded by Gerald Ford. In turn, Ford lost the 1976 election to Jimmy Carter, but had set in motion efforts to respond to increasing protests and demonstrations in Latin America over the Panama Canal. Carter moved quickly to renegotiate U.S. use of the canal. Despite intense opposition in the country and in the U.S Senate, Carter negotiated the Canal Treaty and worked diligently for its passage. Actually, two treaties were approved. The first provided that Panama could assume control of the canal in the year 2000 and that the United States would retain rights of passage. The second treaty assured that the United States had the right of intervention in case the canal was threatened.

However, another major hallmark of the Carter presidency was an insistence on the observance of human rights by allies and enemies alike. Exercising pressure upon the military governments of Latin America, Carter promoted a transition to democracies, but in El Salvador and Nicaragua, Carter confronted immediate and complex challenges.

In El Salvador, a repressive military government, often supported by the United States, came under attack from a leftist revolutionary movement. A moderate leader, Jose Napolean Duarte, came to power, but when four American churchwomen were killed by military "death squads," Carter cut off U.S. aid, and the war continued for another decade. In Nicaragua, broad-based unrest convinced Somoza to flee, and the new government, including the well-organized Sandinista movement, sought U.S. aid. When Sandinistas gradually forced others out of the government, the Carter administration ceased assistance.

Carter also sought improved relations with Cuba and removed some travel and economic restrictions. One result was the Mariel boat lift, when 125,000 Cubans fled to the United States, provoking angry debate within the United States. However, this was only one of many issues that led to Carter's defeat in 1980 by Ronald Reagan.

For the Reagan administration, Latin America was a battleground of the Cold War against an "evil empire."[27] Moreover, Latin American states had accumulated massive debts, threatening the entire global monetary system. On another front, Cuban troops served abroad in an effort by Castro to assist his Soviet ally. The Reagan administration, therefore, went on an economic, military, and political offensive in the 1980s, turning first to continuing conflicts in Nicaragua and El Salvador. The United States continued to support the Duarte government of El Salvador and its efforts to reduce the power of the most radical military leaders and to negotiate with the guerrillas. In Nicaragua, the Reagan policy emphasized the development of the "contras," opponents of the Sandinista regime willing to use force against the government. By mid-1987, several Latin American governments, under the leadership of President Oscar Arias Sanchez of Costa Rica, proposed a peace plan that included a cease fire, negotiations, a cut-off of outside aid, and elections. Reagan opposed the plan and provided more aid for the contras. When Congress prohibited further military aid (the Boland amendments), the Reagan team sought financial support elsewhere, including proceeds from sales of weapons to Iran in exchange for help in getting U.S. hostages released from Lebanon. The whole scandal came to be called the Iran-Contra affair and promoted extensive investigations by Congress and by a special prosecutor.[28] Elections were eventually held in Nicaragua, and the Sandinistas were voted out of office. Also, a settlement was negotiated among warring factions in El Salvador.

The Baker plan, offered by Secretary of the Treasury James Baker in 1985, eased the credit problem for the moment, and earlier in the administration, the president proposed the Caribbean Basin Initiative (CBI) to open the U.S. market more favorably to exports from Latin states.[29]

Through the 1980s, a U.S. offensive against the international drug trade failed to stop drug cartels from shipping increased volumes of narcotics to the United States. In addition, domestic efforts to reduce the demand for drugs appeared to make no better progress.

One clear-cut victory for the Reagan administration was the invasion of Grenada. Convinced that Cuba and the Soviet Union were preparing the eastern Caribbean Island as a base, Reagan used a sizeable force to create conditions for the election of a government satisfactory to the United States.[30] Another Reagan administration initiative with the possibility of longer-term benefits was the preliminary development of the idea of a trade bloc within the western hemisphere.[31]

This idea carried over into the presidency of George Bush. Embodied in the broad "Enterprise for the Americas" plan announced in June 1990, the core of the North American Free Trade Agreement took shape with the passage of the free-trade agreement between Canada and the United States.[32] Mexico came into the partnership later.

The Bush administration took office during one of the most profound transitions in world history: the end of the Cold War, the disintegration of the Soviet bloc and the Soviet Union itself, and the emergence of several new power centers in the global system. Massive change was also underway in Latin America. Several states turned away from military government to democracy in one form or another. State-run economies gave way to increasing reliance upon the free market and the privatization of business, although military elites remained in the background. The United States promoted the Brady Plan, proposed by the Secretary of the Treasury, to recycle and reduce Latin American debt. In the midst of these changes, however, Bush decided to invade Panama. Angered by the actions of General Manuel Noriega to overturn a democratic election, as well as infuriated by the continuing drug trafficking of the Panamanian leader, the Bush administration sent in the troops in December 1989.[33] Noriega was captured and returned to the United States for trial, but the incident demonstrated again that the United States would intervene unilaterally when it concluded that its interests were sufficiently threatened.

Another threat developed in Haiti when its military overthrew the democratically elected president, Jean Bertrand Aristide, and thousands fled to sanctuary in the United States. Before Bush could deal with the situation, he lost the 1992 election to Democrat Bill Clinton.

Clinton resolved all doubt in September 1994 by sending U.S. forces into Haiti.[34] A diplomatic solution worked out by former President Jimmy Carter, former Chairman of the Joint Chiefs of Staff Colin Powell, and Senator Sam Nunn prevented a violent and hostile intervention and led to the restoration of Aristide to the presidency. In this case, action was authorized by the United Nations and it was carried out by a coalition of forces from the United States, Latin America, and elsewhere.[35] Earlier, Clinton agreed to discussions with the Castro government over the latest flood of refugees from Cuba, raising speculation that the administration might move to expand contacts with Cuba prior to the eventual departure of Fidel Castro from power. However, at the moment, the Cuban issue remains fluid.[36]

In addition to a peaceful restoration of a democratic government in Haiti, the major Clinton achievement regarding Latin America was the completion and operation of the NAFTA trade pact.[37] At the end of 1994, the Summit of the Americas, the first since 1967, produced important tangible agreements as well as what President Clinton called the "Spirit of Miami" reflecting a new era of cooperation in the Americas.[38] Thirty-four leaders agreed to proceed toward the formation of a Free Trade Area of the Americas by 2005, and the NAFTA countries invited Chile to become the next member of the bloc.[39] The plan for a hemispheric trade area includes a timetable for coordinating the five major free-trade hemispheric agreements already in place. The meeting also explored such topics as "good governance and civil society, the collective defense of democracy, regional integration, trade expansion, and sustainable development and poverty alleviation."[40]

The euphoria of the Summit of the Americas was quickly shaken when, shortly after the conference, the Mexican government devalued the peso, causing a severe economic crisis, which the Clinton administration moved rapidly to stabilize by organizing a massive credit plan. The president acted despite major opposition in Congress and in U.S. public opinion, but by early spring 1995 the Mexican crisis had subsided.[41] Ripple effects of the Mexican monetary crisis affected other Latin American states, foreign investors, and major global institutions, such as the International Monetary Fund, emphasizing again the interdependence of the global economy and the Americas. Moreover, it raised new questions about the possibilities for a "new mature partnership" as a basis for U.S. foreign policy.

U.S. INTERESTS, CHALLENGES, AND OPPORTUNITIES

The United States has exercised hegemonic power throughout the Americas for much of the past two centuries. Ranging from "hard" control in some places to "soft" control in others, U.S. foreign policy has customarily been comprised of pressure on and/or inducements for most Latin American governments to accept the preferences, decisions, and initiatives flowing from Washington. Ten years before the Monroe Doctrine of 1823, for example, Thomas Jefferson expressed the core of hegemonic claims:

> America [the United States] has a hemisphere to itself. It must have a separate system of interest which must not be subordinated to those of Europe.[42]

From Washington came a steady stream of policies, actions, and proclamations: the Monroe Doctrine, manifest destiny, war with Mexico, the Roosevelt Corollary, the Spanish-American War, the Platt Amendment, the Panama Canal, "dollar diplomacy," military interventions, the Good Neighbor Policy, Pan-Americanism, containment and the Cold War, the Alliance for Progress, covert action by the CIA, the Caribbean Basin Initiative, the Enterprise for the Americas, NAFTA, and now, a "new mature partnership." Past U.S. behavior has variously been characterized as imperialistic, neo-imperialistic, mercantilist, paternalistic, dominant, exploitative, interventionist, arrogant, or unilateral. Therefore, proposals for a new partnership raise doubts about whether they merely mask continued U.S. hegemony or whether they genuinely reflect the "new architecture" suggested by President Clinton at the 1994 Summit of the Americas. For a mature partnership among the Americas to progress, several conditions must be met. First, the national interests of the United States and of the states of Latin America must be identified and accommodated. For the United States, the Monroe Doctrine and the Roosevelt Corollary reflected the political objective to expel, exclude, and replace European power and control from the hemisphere. In recent years, this led to broad-based actions to resist Soviet intervention and the threat of Communist revolution. In the post-Cold War period, U.S. national interests in the Americas have been defined as maintenance of political stability through establishment of democracy, protection of human rights, good governance, and effective government. Moreover, even with the goal of a "mature partnership," the continuation of the United States as "senior" partner exercising political leadership is an explicit part of the plan. In addition, on specific policies, the United States has made clear its interests in stopping the drug trade based in Latin America; in managing the flow of illegal immigrants to the United States; in deterring corruption in government; and in discouraging the military from seizure of power.

In the economic track, U.S. interests have always included reliable access to Latin American markets, minerals, materials, manpower, and monetary linkages. At present, the United States sees Latin America's economic growth and reduction of poverty as essential interests. In the military track, U.S. interests include access to bases, facilities, allies, and common commitments against perceived foreign threats. In addition, U.S. interest also was defined as support for military governments willing to follow its leadership. The United States also retained the prerogative to intervene militarily in Latin America when it decided its vital interests were at stake.

Until the twentieth century clashes with foreign ideologies such as fascism, communism, and socialism, the cultural track required only a general recognition of U.S. political hegemony. Today, with expanding intercommunication among the Americas, U.S. national interests encompass the idea of an integrated, interdependent American community facing common challenges through democracy, the free market, and open trade.

From the perspective of Latin America, despite thirty-four separate sets of national interests, some *common* interests can be identified. Politically, despite centuries of division and weakness, the power of nationalism, national identity, and national independence remain dominant forces in relations with the United States. Tinged by mistrust and fear of the power of their northern neighbor, Latin Americans have nevertheless demonstrated continued interest in political association with the United States and, within limits, acceptance of its political leadership. Economically, the search for economic growth and effective solutions to the massive poverty that touches virtually every country inevitably underscores a high level of economic dependence upon the United States for credit, markets, investment (both multinational corporations and portfolio), aid, trade, tourism, and cooperation. Despite active trade with Europe and Japan and expanding intraregional coordination, Latin America still relies on the U.S. economy for its primary support. In the military track, Latin American interests include continued U.S. protection from foreign threats, especially nuclear ones. They also include access to training, arms, and funds, since, even in the larger nations, Latin America is being redefined and reshaped to adjust to an era of new democracies. Culturally, the historic pursuit of a sense of equality, dignity, and independence continues. In the struggle for a dominant ethos, Latin Americans turn to democratic and free market values and an accommodation with socialist principles as a guide to identity. In the search, many Latin Americans have increasingly identified their interests as a sense of shared community and cooperation with the United States. Overall, their interests historically have included opposition to unilateral U.S. intervention along all the tracks of policy, but recent events strongly suggest an openness to the concept of mature partnership among the Americas.

If the foregoing sketch represents a reasonable and fair summary of U.S. and Latin American interests, the search for a partnership, if it is to replace past practice, necessitates the effort to transform as many national interests as possible to mutual interests. In doing so, the Americas face a number of additional problems. First, the asymmetrical power and wealth of the United States cast doubt upon the legal, psychological, and operational equality essential to a genuine partnership. On this point, the experience of many international organizations, alliances, and blocs of which the United States is a member indicates that superior U.S. power has not prevented successful shared decision making. In itself, asymmetry is not an insurmountable obstacle to an increase in the capabilities for economic growth and political stability in most Latin American states. Second, though still reliant on the United States for support, many Latin American states have formed their own trade blocs and actively trade with Europe and Asia. A third important factor in forming a U.S.-Latin America partnership is the global competition provided by Europe and Asia for goods and services produced in the Americas. The challenge underlying this development strengthens the case for expanded *interdependence*,[43] with its common opportunities. Fourth, machinery through which partners can share decision making and produce effective action is readily available. Although perceived as generally ineffective in the past,[44] the Organization of American States is targeted for revitalization, and the expanded NAFTA structure and ongoing negotiations on the Free Trade Area of the Americas provide new machinery for expanding coordination. In addition, the Inter-American Bank affords expertise and resources for the evolving community. Finally, perhaps the most critical element in forging a strengthened partnership is the nature of future U.S. leadership. Facing the probability that hegemony as it has been exercised in the past is no longer feasible in the Americas, the United States faces a choice between its historic claim to unilateral intervention in pursuit of its interests and the continued exercise of leadership through multilateralism and collective action. Although some recent U.S. actions have enjoyed bipartisan support, considerable opposition to any change in the U.S. posture persists. This view was succinctly expressed by candidate Ronald Reagan in 1980 in reference to revision of the Panama Canal Treaty: "We bought it. We paid for it. It's ours. And we should keep it."[45]

In the mid-1990s, the appeal of U.S. dominance and of the Monroe Doctrine remains very much in play. In addition, opponents of hemispheric trade integration, such as organized labor and some consumer interests, have also joined the effort to block any change in U.S. policy.[46] Despite opposition, the Clinton administration has moved forward on the principle of partnership. In the Haitian crisis of 1994, the United States relied on the authority of the United Nations and the support of many Latin American states to intervene to restore the democratically elected government of Jean Bertrand Aristide.[47] In dealing with the Mexican peso crisis, the Clinton administration organized a credit package that included the international community as well as contributions of $1 billion from several Latin American states. However, while the foundations of a mature partnership may be in place, its solidity will be tested the first time an American president considers unilateral intervention in Latin America when a vital U.S. interest is believed to be at stake. If the nature and quality of U.S. leadership is central to the concept of partnership in the formation of its foreign policy, so, too, is the character of *political stability* among its American partners. The concept of political stability refers to conditions of nation-states or multilateral systems related to continuity, predictability, orderliness in governance, and the transference of power. Implicit in the concept is the belief that political stability is an indispensable factor in achieving economic development, social progress, and other goals. Moreover, of multiple mechanisms available for achieving stability, the United States has promoted *democracy*. Its essential principles include government based on the consent of the governed, expressed through free and fair elections with genuine political opposition, free speech,and free press involved; the rule of law and the guarantee of human rights; and the separation of powers among governmental units. While the form and substance of democracy practiced throughout Latin America vary considerably in the 1990s, and, in some cases, are regarded as fragile, all states but Cuba have democratically elected governments as of the mid-1990s.

However, more than democracy is required to maintain political stability and public confidence: Efficiency and effectiveness of democratic governments in meeting social and political challenges is also needed. In this area, U.S. foreign policy is now designed to provide support. For fiscal year 1995 the president proposed spending several million dollars to support projects in Latin America related to civil rights; political, organizational, and social improvements; aid for court administration, judicial training and police development; and projects aimed at emphasis of civilian control of the military, human rights education, and professionalism in administrative management.[48] Yet, the problems facing Latin America remain formidable. United States Assistant Secretary of State for Inter-American Affairs, Alexander F. Watson, put it this way before Congress:

> Corruption remains a critical concern. The cry for social equity is growing; income inequality in the region ranks among the worst in the world. The disparities between wealth and poverty are increasingly apparent and breed political volatility. By U.N. estimate, 45 percent of Latin America's people live in poverty, and per capita income in 1992 was still 7 percent below that of 1991.[49]

The appalling level of poverty throughout Latin America remains a primary economic issue, but its potential *political* consequences cannot be ignored. The Zapatista rebellion in the Chiapas state of Mexico and the rebellion of the Shining Path guerrillas in Peru demonstrate that political instability associated with poverty is a perennial phenomenon in Latin America, and revolution remains a persistent threat.

On another level, the threat of military coups d'etat hovers over political change in Latin America. Usually among the most highly trained and disciplined sectors of society, military elites have seized power many times throughout most of the region's history.

It makes no difference whether political stability is threatened by rebellion from below or military takeover from above. It is the perpetuation of mass poverty and stratified class structure that causes political tensions and conflict between dominant oligarchies controlling the bulk of the wealth, land, and power and the masses of peasants and the powerless. U.S. policies aimed at education and expansion of the middle class through economic growth and development may help, but the failure of a previous U.S. policy promoting social reform—John F. Kennedy's Alliance for Progress—demonstrates the difficulty of the task and the limits of U.S. capabilities in directly remedying the problems of Latin America.

Apart from continuing class conflict and the threat of revolution, the most threatening issue faced by all American states is the drug trade.[50] Drug cartels operating in several countries, including the United States, use immense profits to challenge governments; to corrupt public officials; to use terrorism to expand operations; and to increase the economic dependency of peasants, farmers, and other workers who benefit from the growth and processing of narcotics. Political cooperation among governments has been inadequate thus far in successfully destroying the drug trade. The Clinton administration's policy includes de-emphasis on interdiction, replacing it with a commitment to "building, strengthening, and professionalizing host nations' counter-narcotics institutions, such as judicial systems, prosecutors, and law enforcement agencies."[51] The change in strategy carries no guarantees of increased success in countering the narcotics industry in the Americas, but foreign policy aimed at maintaining political coordination of the issue remains a top priority of the United States.

The persistent flow of illegal immigrants from Latin America into the United States also remains a source of conflict in the hemisphere. The 1994 California referendum banning services to illegal immigrants symbolized the conflict from the U.S. perspective, and Latin American leaders at the Summit of the Americas expressed their perspective by criticizing the California action.[52] U.S. foreign policy aimed at promoting economic development in the Americas is cited as the most effective policy in reducing the illegal flow of people into the United States.

In 1994 Cuba again added to the flow of Latin American emigration when Fidel Castro permitted thousands of citizens to take to the sea in an effort to reach the United States.[53] The sudden flow of refugees led to discussions between the two governments, but little progress toward reopening formal relations occurred. Cuba remains the only nondemocratic government in the region and was absent from the Summit of the Americas. Fidel Castro gives no indication of stepping down from power and opening the country to democratic elections, and so, U.S. foreign policy in Cuba remains unchanged.

Two other major issues of concern to the United States—the environment and labor policy—arose at the Summit.[54] The Clinton administration added agreements on these issues to NAFTA and sought hemispheric support for commitments to protect the environment and to improve the wages and rights of workers.[55] The Summit decision to proceed on a hemispheric trade agreement included a broad statement that trade policy and environmental and labor issues are "mutually supportive"[56] but strengthening this initiative remains a task for future foreign policy.

POLICY OPTIONS: PROS AND CONS

The transition of most Latin American states toward the principles of capitalism and liberalism and away from socialist concepts of state-directed, protectionist economics has been energetically promoted by the foreign policy of the United States and, despite numerous difficulties, the movement toward economic privatization has continued. However, there is wide disparity within and among Latin American states in their levels of development. Moreover, the effort of many governments to satisfy aggregate popular demands for better living standards continues to lead to excessive spending, uncontrollable budget deficits, borrowing, printing money, and inflation.

Also, where implemented, free-market policies can lead to unemployment, labor unrest, and declining wages in some sectors, but, in others, to new jobs in new businesses and increased government revenues. In addition, massive poverty continues in most countries, and however well-intentioned, the U.S. role remains suspect because of past policies. Finally, given the political environment in the United States, there is no assurance of continuity of U.S. policy. The next president could change direction again.

Nonetheless, U.S. foreign policy in the economic track centers on long-term interests involving Latin American markets and resources, trade, credit, investment, monetary linkages, and aid.

For illicit drug dealers, Latin America is a major source of supply, and for drug cartels, the U.S. market is the largest in the world. For the U.S. government, controlling the drug trade "continues to be a top foreign policy priority."[57] The Clinton administration has shifted from a policy based on interdiction to a broader-based approach focusing on building counternarcotics institutions such as judicial systems, prosecutors, and law enforcement agencies in drug-producing states.

While Latin America at present is a small part of total U.S. commerce, U.S. administrations recognize increasing interdependence among the countries of the region. The formation of NAFTA and the commitment to the start of a trade bloc from Alaska to Argentina mark a new dimension of U.S. foreign policy in the Americas, and, together with the dynamics of new trade agreements among several Latin American regions, promise a new era of hemispheric relations.

NAFTA took effect on January 1, 1994, with the United States, Canada, and Mexico joining to create a trade area. Then, in December 1994, they agreed to admit Chile and to set the conditions for admission of other states, such as Argentina and Brazil, in the foreseeable future.[58] In addition, thirty-four American states agreed to proceed with formation of a hemispheric bloc. At the Summit of the Americas held in Miami, Florida, the American states set the year 2005 as a target for a framework and for progress in coordinating other major trade blocs in the hemisphere with the proposed "Free Trade Area of the Americas." Others have suggested the designation "Western Hemispheric Free Trade Area"[59] or simply dropping the term "North" from NAFTA to make it "AFTA," the Americas Free Trade Area. Whatever name and acronym emerge, the new initiative is just one in which American states pursue economic development by expanding trade. At the Summit of the Americas, hemispheric leaders also explored ways to combat the drug trade by confiscating drug fortunes; to free economies to accept foreign investment; to liberalize and integrate capital markets; to establish an investment code for the region; and to encourage private investment in such sectors as telecommunications, highways, and electricity.[60]

The Clinton administration also pressured Latin American governments for policies to improve conditions for workers, for environmental protection, for protection of investments in services and intellectual property, and for assurances against dumping of exports. (Dumping is the practice of selling goods abroad below cost in order to gain a share of the market.)[61]

In addition to efforts to expand hemispheric trade, the Clinton administration has embarked on an initiative to organize an Asian-Pacific trade bloc in which several Latin American states would participate.

Over the past few decades, Latin American states have also been active in developing their own regional and subregional trade groups.[62] The Latin American Free Trade Association was reformed in 1980 to become the Latin American Integration Association (ALADI). Its members include Argentina, Bolivia, Brazil, Chile, Colombia, Ecuador, Mexico, Paraguay, Peru, Uruguay, and Venezuela. The Andean Pact group includes Bolivia, Colombia, Ecuador, Peru, and Venezuela, and the Central American Common Market (CACM) includes Costa Rica, El Salvador, Guatemala, and Nicaragua. A group of states in the Caribbean operate the Caribbean Community and Common Market (CARICOM). Its members are Anguilla, Antigua and Barbuda, the Bahamas, Barbados, Belize, Dominica, Grenada, Guyana, Jamaica, Monserrat, Sts. Christopher and Nevis, St. Lucia, St. Vincent and the Grenadines, and Trinidad and Tobago. In addition, seven of the smaller states form the East Caribbean Common Market, part of the Organization of East Caribbean States.

The most recently formed and potentially the most important of the regional trade groups is Mercosur with Argentina, Brazil, Paraguay, and Uruguay in the southern cone of the continent.[63] Chile has also joined.

For many Latin American countries, participation in multi-level trade structures signaled an end to a long period of import substitution industrialization, a model devoted to protectionism of national markets against foreign exports. Increasing liberalization of trade policies to encourage intraregional and intrahemispheric trade is one of the dominant features of Latin American economies.

Trade protectionism, of course, has worked both ways in the Americas. In the past, the United States applied tariffs on some products of greatest value and importance to Latin American exporters.[64] According to one scholar, tariff rates imposed by the United States have remained comparatively high for some consumer goods and textiles, product areas in which Latin states often have comparative advantage. Moreover, the General System of Preferences (GSP) often failed to provide adequate access to the U.S. market in the same general product areas.[65] In the application of antidumping legislation (ADD) and countervailing duties (CVD), Latin American states accounted for 47 percent of U.S. actions against imports.[66] In the late 1980s, these actions were concentrated on products from Argentina, Brazil, and Mexico, including textiles, apparel, and footwear.[67]

On the other hand, the Caribbean Basin Initiative proposed by

President Reagan opened the U.S. market to some exports from the region duty-free. Nevertheless, at the Summit of the Americas in December 1994, Prime Minister Owen Arthur of Barbados, in closing remarks, used the occasion to urge expanded U.S. imports of bananas from the Caribbean region.[68]

Although NAFTA has produced positive results so far, according to all three members, there are no guarantees of continued success of NAFTA or future success for hemispheric efforts to expand trade. Nor can all groups be guaranteed benefits from expanded trade. Domestic concerns expressed in the United States by organized labor and consumer groups that increased trade will cost jobs echoes domestic concerns in Latin America that the new agreements will mainly benefit the United States. But U.S. foreign policy is bound to the principle of expanded trade as a major instrument to help attain political stability and economic growth for all sides.

Open and integrated markets, however, depend in some measure upon the availability of investment in all of its forms. In November 1994, AT&T, the giant U.S. phone company, announced plans to enter a joint venture with Grupo Alfa of Mexico to compete for the potentially lucrative communications market with Telefonos de Mexico (Telmex).[69] The new group is the latest to join the chase for the Mexican market. MCI, Sprint, and GTE have also formed partnerships with Mexican firms. As a result of the government's decision to privatize the telecommunications industry, Mexico has opened its market to other firms when the Telmex monopoly expires in 1997. Although the Mexican government has yet to explain how other companies will be allowed to compete, the rush of the largest U.S. phone companies to enter Latin American markets can also be expected in other states privatizing their industries.[70] Even as partnership agreements emerge, the level of U.S. securities investment in Latin America and other developing countries also rapidly increases, at least before the Mexican peso crisis of 1994.

These two forms of investment—direct and portfolio—provide a growing base of economic development. Direct foreign investment (DFI) in the form of multinational corporations, joint ventures, branches, affiliates, and partnerships has been an essential part of U.S. foreign policy for more than a century. The United Fruit Company, for example, is an early case of a company formed by entrepreneurs from the United States operating in several countries in Latin America, developing markets in bananas and other agricultural products.[71] By the late twentieth century, U.S. banks, auto manufacturers, steel companies, electronics firms, and many other sectors developed varied business arrangements throughout Latin America.

On the positive side, multinational corporations contribute money, jobs, taxes, credit, skills, training, modern technology, export opportunities, and ties with the global economy to host countries throughout the hemisphere.[72] However, critics have argued that there is a downside to foreign investments: exploitation of local capital and labor, a brain-drain of local talent, tax avoidance and transference, unusual advantages over local companies, and distorted pricing of imports.[73]

Whatever the pros and cons of direct foreign investment, massive portfolio investments from the United States have poured into Latin America through the stock, bond, futures, and options markets. Brokers, individual investors, mutual funds, and pension funds in the United States have committed large blocs of money to Latin American companies open to privatization.[74] Telecommunications, manufacturing, banking, insurance, and other service industries have been regarded as attractive opportunities for investors.[75]

U.S. foreign policy of opening the markets of Latin America to all forms of investment has remained constant. For Latin America, it poses immense opportunities but embodies a lingering fear that Latin economies will be absorbed and controlled by outside forces, especially those based in the United States. Without easily perceived mutual benefits, the temptation to once again restrict markets and investment could become irresistible and future U.S. policy is needed to promote success.

Foreign aid takes several forms. Direct allocation of funds by the United States government in its budgeted foreign aid program provides one source of support for Latin America. For example, the Clinton administration proposed $839 million for Latin America in its fiscal year 1995 foreign-aid program.[76] For projects in El Salvador, Haiti, Nicaragua, Peru, and Guatemala, $75 million of economic assistance has been requested. An additional $430 million was included for the "Promoting Sustainable Development" program, and $199 million for PL 480 Title II Food Assistance. In the past, large amounts of military aid were included to support facilities, equipment, personnel, and supplies. However, the Clinton administration has given less emphasis to this portion of the aid program.

Additional aid is provided through the Agency for International Development and the Peace Corps. Emergency aid in cases of destructive weather, earthquakes, or other natural disasters has been an important part of U.S. foreign aid to many countries. In the recent involvement in Haiti, the U.S. military role was supplemented by allocation of substantial aid funds to sustain security and economic stability pending the removal of U.S. forces.

In the past, U.S. aid has been inconsistent, varying widely depending upon the political ideology of different administrations or the governments of particular countries. For many years, aid was heavily weighted toward *military support* for governments aligned with the United States in the Cold War.

U.S. connections with the Haitian military proved useful, for example, as negotiations continued to remove the military junta without hostilities. The effort paid off in a peaceful intervention and a return of Aristide.[77]

Under a U.S. coalition, a transition continues at this time with the gradual withdrawal of U.S. forces.

Although skeptics have suggested that the Haitian operation amounted to U.S. unilateralism with a facade of U.N. legitimacy easily engineered by the United States, the Clinton administration contends that it marked a new approach by the United States toward a genuine multilateral partnership in the decision to use military force in the hemisphere. It wasn't the first time, however. Over the past decade or more, military cooperation between the United States and Latin American countries formed the basis of the effort to interdict the production and transport of illegal drugs between drug-producing countries and the U.S. market. The Clinton administration has taken a different approach, as already noted.[78]

In Brazil, the military is being used to combat the drug trade for the first time. Former President Itmar Franco announced in late 1994 that the army would join in the effort to combat drug trafficking.[79] Speaking to senior Brazilian officers in Rio in November 1994, U.S. Defense Secretary William J. Perry noted that "both the United States and Brazil have assigned a role to their military in supporting civilian law enforcement agencies in fighting the drug trade."[80] To this end, the United States has provided $1.5 million in aid for computers, vehicles, and communications equipment to the Brazilian government.

The United States has also provided funds throughout Latin America for defense training in logistics, management, and respect for human rights. According to one U.S. official, these efforts "serve to encourage concepts such as civilian control over the military" and constitute the only military aid proposed by the Clinton administration in fiscal year 1995.[81]

In Argentina, civilian leaders have downsized the military and reduced its budget, and they have decided on creation of a smaller professional volunteer force.[82] Government officials have indicated that the future role for the military will be limited to guarding the country's 2,150-mile border and participating in international peacekeeping missions.[83] In some of the Andean region countries, like Colombia, the armed forces have also been used to combat the drug trade.

The United States retains its options for actions considered in its own vital interests. For example, no president could avoid action in case of an attack on the Panama Canal or a threat to shut it down. Furthermore, the possibility that Latin states may not always share U.S. views about common threats complicates the problem of producing collective action. In any case, the path to multilateralism and collective security is filled with obstacles, doubts, and complexities, yet the machinery is available. The Charter of the United Nations, the Rio Treaty, the Organization of American States, and numerous bilateral treaties provide workable instruments of collective security.

The emphasis of future U.S. foreign policy on collective security can be viewed as an essential prerequisite for a "mature hemispheric partnership." Fear of the possibility of U.S. unilateralism inevitably intrudes upon the mutual trust essential for a mature partnership, but the deepening of trust depends upon the expansion of shared ideas, ideals, and ideologies. That is the basis of the cultural track.

In the 1990s, two U.S. presidents have now taken steps to change the cultural foundation for the transition from hegemony to a new mature partnership. The efforts by the Bush and Clinton administrations, although generally applauded, nonetheless face considerable skepticism, mistrust, and outright opposition in the Americas, including the United States. Although some scholars believe that "the end of the Cold War marked the end of the Monroe Doctrine,"[84] powerful political forces in the United States committed to the principles of the Monroe Doctrine and the untrammeled right of U.S. intervention argue the counterpoint. More complex than the basic liberal-conservative split in U.S. ideological thinking, belief in U.S. supremacy in the hemisphere dates from the prerevolutionary period through the long period of U.S. global leadership and the Cold War. With conservatives in control of Congress following the 1994 U.S. elections, withdrawal from the posture of hegemony may be more troublesome than first thought. Underlying the debate are questions relating to what form future U.S. leadership should take.

The struggle continues in each country over fundamental cultural values, beliefs, and ideologies and over relations with the United States. One scholar contends that "most Latin American governments and many opposition movements in Latin America today want stronger links with the United States."[85] It wasn't always so. Given the history of relations in the Americas, the United States was often seen in cultural terms as arrogant, domineering, condescending, hateful, and dangerous.[86] Leaders in the United States often spoke of Latin Americans with disdain, disrespect, or disinterest.[87] Although attitudes on all sides appear to be changing, Latin American societies continue to evolve with considerable speed. From religion to the arts, from political ideology to the family, Latin Americans are grappling with adjustments of ancient cultures to twentieth century modernity, a process accelerated by the mass media that pervade societies everywhere. If they are now somewhat less suspicious of the motives and politics of the United States and are open to closer links, a fundamental change in the cultural track may be partly responsible. Latin American attitudes toward the United States have been ambivalent and even contradictory. The intense belief of U.S. citizens in national independence, democracy, and autonomy inspired the long struggle for independence in Latin America. Anticolonialism intensified, however, as foreign countries, including the United States, sought to exploit Latin America. From the struggle for independence emerged the passion for nationalism, national identity, and national dignity and equality. Underlying the struggles for nationhood, independence, and autonomy, however, the colonial tradition of authoritarianism survived. Democrats struggled to win and then to keep power, mostly without success. Belief in strong authoritarian governments, military or civilian, flourished until the 1980s, and many scholars doubt that it has entirely disappeared.[88] With the broad transition to democracy in the past two decades, Latin America has made an apparent commitment to the cultural concepts of free and genuinely competitive elections, human rights, limited government, and other aspects of democratic ideology. In this sense, Abraham F. Lowenthal argues that "there is greater convergency in the Americas, North and South, on political values and economic fundamentals than ever before, but a hemispheric political community is far from achieved."[89]

POLICY RECOMMENDATIONS FOR THE TWENTY-FIRST CENTURY

Forging a community in which the national interests of all parties are maximized by their pursuit of mutual interests involves several factors: the continued leadership of the United States under a foreign policy committed to partnership; an active role by leaders and elites throughout the Americas to educate and persuade their publics about changing conditions; expanded intercommunication among leaders; utilization of mass media for accelerated dissemination of communication; active participation by multinational corporations; expanded cultural exchange and tourism; and usefulness of acceptable immigration/emigration policies.

In terms of leadership, President Clinton has provided consistent commitment to the concept of mature partnership, and all of the democratically elected leaders of the Americas have joined in the process. Detailed negotiations and coordination symbolize community efforts to deal with hemispheric issues such as trade, investment, drug-trade control, political stability, and economic growth. Given the widespread availability of mass media, the opportunity for leaders to shape public opinion and cultural attitudes is substantial.

Multi-channel cable and satellite systems provide a vast exchange of communication in all relevant languages. CNN, MTV, and Latin American language networks televise simultaneously in many countries. Beyond private firms, government-supported communications also reach tens of millions of people. U.S. government agencies, such as the United States Information Agency, the Voice of America, and Radio Marti, tailor many of their efforts toward Latin America.

Of immense importance in the process of intercultural communication are multinational corporations whose personnel exchange a wide range of ideas, techniques, and political and economic values. Since multinational

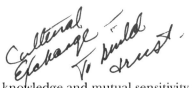

business requires expanded cultural knowledge and mutual sensitivity to languages, arts, religions, and traditions and also supports constant travel among countries, these firms are among the most vibrant cultural forces in the Americas.

Another key element of cultural development is the broad field of cultural exchange. Governments sponsor the formalized exchange of students, scholars, scientists, athletes, and others. Private businesses move executives from country to country. However, the most massive form of cultural exchange is embodied in the emigration/immigration process. The Americanization of Latin America and the Hispanicization of North America are unmistakable legacies of four centuries of intermixture in the hemisphere. Hispanic culture spread into North America long before the United States existed, and large parts of Hispanic America became part of the United States through U.S. expansion and colonization. Puerto Rico and the U.S. Virgin Islands became part of the United States long after the U.S. absorbed territories that are now the southwest and southeast of the country. Massive immigration, legal and illegal, has formed huge Hispanic populations in California, Texas, Florida, New York, and numerous other states. Growing intermixture of languages, styles, food, music, and arts makes up much of the culture of the Americas in the 1990s.

A final form of cultural exchange that expands communication and connects cultures is tourism. The largest or second-largest business in many Latin American countries, it is important to all in attracting visitors. Moreover, the tourist industry connects countries to vast multinational leisure industry firms in the global system.

CONCLUSION

In a rapidly changing global environment, Latin America has become more important than ever to the national interest of the United States, and the most effective U.S. foreign policy of the future rests on recognition and expansion of the mutual interests of the Americas.

If it is to serve the interests of the United States most effectively, U.S. foreign policy in Latin America needs the imagination and flexibility to provide hemispheric leadership without creating the perception of dominance and exploitation. Policy makers have to walk a fine line between these options and remain consistent from one presidency to another. Both tasks may be exceedingly difficult.

The immediate post-Cold War period provides a fertile time for reconstruction of relationships. The absence of foreign threats to the hemisphere for the first time in the twentieth century provides the chance to rethink and redefine the American community. Setbacks are inevitable. Political and economic growth will be neither consistent nor uniform, and global responsibilities will occasionally divert the attention of the United States from the rest of Americas, but there is considerable optimism that the Americas are on the right track. Former Secretary of State Henry Kissinger recently commented that "after a series of ups and downs, the Western Hemisphere seems on the verge of turning into a key element of a new and humane world order."[90] That, of course, has been defined in the 1990s as one of the fundamental objectives of U.S. foreign policy in Latin America, and a mature partnership has been proposed here as the best way to achieve it.

NOTES

1. Testimony by Alexander F. Watson, Assistant Secretary of State for Inter-American Affairs, before the subcommittee on Western Hemisphere Affairs of the House Committee on Foreign Affairs, March 9, 1994, p. 5.
2. Gaddis Smith, *The Last Years of the Monroe Doctrine* (New York: Hill and Wang, 1994), pp. 7–8.
3. Ibid., p. 8.
4. Thomas G. Paterson, J. Garry Clifford, and Kenneth Hagan, *American Foreign Policy: A History* (Lexington, MA: D.C. Heath and Company, 1977), pp. 94–95.
5. The four-track concept was an effective organizational method in James W. Dull, *The Politics of American Foreign Policy* (Englewood Cliffs, NJ: Prentice-Hall, 1985), pp. 204–205.
6. Thomas E. Skidmore and Peter H. Smith, *Modern Latin America*, 3rd. ed. (New York: Oxford University Press, 1992), p. 5.
7. Ibid., p. 21.
8. Paterson, Clifford, and Hagan, *American Foreign Policy*, pp. 7, 26–29, 85.
9. Paul Goodwin, Jr., *Global Studies: Latin America*, 6th ed. (Guilford, CT: The Dushkin Publishing Group, Inc., 1994), p. 41.
10. Smith, *The Last Years of the Monroe Doctrine*, pp. 21–24; Paterson, Clifford, and Hagan, *American Foreign Policy*, pp. 97–98.
11. Paterson, Clifford, and Hagan, *American Foreign Policy*, p. 192.
12. Ibid., p. 180.
13. Ibid., p. 180; see also Smith, *The Last Years of the Monroe Doctrine*, pp. 24–25.
14. Paterson, Clifford, and Hagan, *American Foreign Policy*, p. 192.
15. Walter LaFeber, *The American Age: United States Foreign Policy at Home and Abroad since 1750* (New York: W. W. Norton and Company, 1989), pp. 232–233.
16. Ibid., pp. 340–341.
17. Ibid., p. 463.
18. LaFeber, *The American Age*, p. 463; see also James Brooke, "Brazil's Glory Days of B-25s and Boogie-Woogie," *The New York Times*, April 26, 1994, p. A4.
19. LaFeber, *The American Age*, p. 463.
20. Skidmore and Smith, *Modern Latin America*, p. 358.
21. Ibid.
22. Paterson, Clifford, and Hagan, *American Foreign Policy*, p. 508.
23. Skidmore and Smith, *Modern Latin America*, p. 361.
24. Ibid., pp. 363–364.
25. Ibid., pp. 339–343, 364.

26.   LaFeber, *The American Age*, pp. 557–559.
27.   Ibid., p. 668.
28.   Ibid., pp. 690–692.
29.   Robert A. Pastor, *Whirlpool: U.S. Foreign Policy toward Latin America and the Caribbean* (Princeton, NJ: Princeton University Press, 1992), pp. 177–179.
30.   Ibid., pp. 111–112; see also LaFeber, *The American Age*, pp. 686–687.
31.   LaFeber, *The American Age*, p. 676.
32.   Skidmore and Smith, *Modern Latin America*, pp. 377–378.
33.   Pastor, *Whirlpool*, pp. 89–94.
34.   Douglas Jehl, "Haitian Military Rulers Agree to Leave: Clinton Calls Off Plans for Invasion," *The New York Times*, Sept. 19, 1994, p. 1.
35.   Richard D. Lyons, "U.N. Authorizes Invasion of Haiti to Be Led by U.S.," *The New York Times*, August 1, 1994, p. 1.
36.   "Cubans Meet U.S. Aides on Refugee Crisis," *The New York Times*, September 2, 1994, p. 1.
37.   Smith, *The Last Years of the Monroe Doctrine*, p. 229.
38.   Address to the closing session of the Summit of the Americas, on C-SPAN, December 11, 1994.
39.   Helene Cooper and Jose DeCordoba, "Chile Is Invited to Join NAFTA as U.S. Pledges Free-Trade Zone for Americas," *The Wall Street Journal*, December 12, 1994, p. A3.
40.   Richard E. Feinberg, Special Assistant to the President for Inter-American Affairs, National Security Council, remarks at the Latin American Studies Association, Atlanta, Georgia, March 10, 1995, p. 8.
41.   "I.M.F. Chief Says Mexican Crisis Has Eased," *The New York Times*, May 23, 1995, p. D21.
42.   Paterson, Clifford, and Hagan, *American Foreign Policy*, p. 86.
43.   Charles W. Kegley and Eugene R. Wittkopf, *World Politics: Trend and Transformation*, 4th ed. (New York: St. Martin's Press, 1993), p. 214; Robert Keohane and Joseph S. Nye, Jr., *Power and Interdependence*, 2nd ed. (Boston, MA: Scott, Foresman and Company, 1989), pp. 8–11.
44.   Cooper and Cordoba, "Chile Is Invited to Join NAFTA as U.S. Pledges Free-Trade Zone for Americas," p. 3.
45.   Pastor, *Whirlpool*, p. 9.
46.   David E. Sanger, "Chile Is Admitted as North American Free Trade Partner," *The New York Times*, December 12, 1994, p. 8; John T. Rourke, *International Politics on the World Stage*, 4th ed. (Guilford, CT: Dushkin Publishing Group, 1993), pp. 542–544.
47.   Eric Schmitt, "U.S. Gets Caribbean Backing for Possible Invasion of Haiti," *The New York Times*, August 31, 1994, p. 8.
48.   Watson, Senate testimony, p. 6.
49.   Ibid.
50.   Abraham F. Lowenthal, "Latin America: Ready for Partnership?" *Foreign Affairs, America and the World, 1992–93*, vol. 72, no. 1 (New York: Council on Foreign Relations, 1993), p. 90; see also Watson, Senate testimony, pp. 11–12.
51.   Watson, Senate testimony, p. 11.
52.   Remarks by Ernesto Zedillo, President of Mexico, at the Summit of the Americas, Miami, Florida, televised on C-SPAN, December 11, 1994.
53.   "Cubans Meet U.S. Aides on Refugee Crisis."
54.   Cooper and Cordoba, "Chile Is Invited to Join NAFTA as U.S. Pledges Free-Trade Zone for Americas," p. 3.
55.   Ibid.
56.   Ibid.

57. Watson, Senate testimony, p. 10.
58. Cooper and Cordoba, "Chile Is Invited to Join NAFTA as U.S. Pledges Free-Trade Zone for Americas," p. 3.
59. Roberto Bouzas, "U.S.-Latin American Trade Relations: Issues in the 1980s and Prospects for the 1990s," in *The United States and Latin America in the 1990s: Beyond the Cold War,* Jonathan Hartlyn, Lars Schoultz, and Augusto Varas, eds. (Chapel Hill: University of North Carolina Press, 1992), p. 153.
60. James Brooke, "U.S. and 33 Hemisphere Nations Agree to Create Free-Trade Zone," *The New York Times,* December 11, 1994, p. 1.
61. Ibid.
62. *Atlas of the United States Foreign Relations* (Washington, D.C.: U.S. Department of State, 1985), p. 33.
63. Lowenthal, "Latin America: Ready for Partnership?" p. 87; see also James Brooke, "Brazil's Horizons Widening with New Common Market," *The New York Times,* January 4, 1995, p. 8.
64. Bouzas, "U.S.-Latin American Trade Relations," pp. 152–180.
65. Ibid., pp. 163–164.
66. Ibid., pp. 164–168.
67. Ibid., p. 164.
68. Closing session, Summit of the Americas, December 11, 1994, Miami, Florida, televised on C-SPAN.
69. "AT&T Corp. and Grupo Alfa Plan Venture," *The Wall Street Journal,* November 10, 1994.
70. Allan Myerson, "PEMEX Chief Sees Sale of Units Soon," *The New York Times,* February 9, 1995, p. D6.
71. Skidmore and Smith, *Modern Latin America,* pp. 316–317, 325–326, 331, 340–342.
72. Kegley and Wittkopf, *World Politics,* pp. 189–193.
73. Ibid.
74. Kathryn Jones, "Steamy Brazil Helps Emerging Markets," *The New York Times,* October 3, 1994, p. D11. The story summarizes the experience of leading investment funds in the global emerging markets, with an emphasis on Latin America.
75. Continuing daily reports in *The Wall Street Journal, The New York Times,* and CNBC.
76. Watson, Senate testimony, p. 6.
77. Jehl, "Haitian Military Rulers Agree to Leave."
78. Watson, Senate testimony, p. 11.
79. James Brooke, "Brazil's Army Joins Battle against Drugs," *The New York Times,* November 20, 1994, p. 4.
80. Ibid.
81. Watson, Senate testimony, p. 8.
82. Calvin Sims, "Argentina Demotes Its Once-Powerful Armed Forces," *The New York Times,* November 24, 1994, p. 3.
83. Ibid.
84. Smith, *The Last Years of the Monroe Doctrine,* p. 7.
85. Lowenthal, "Latin America," p. 76.
86. Paterson, Clifford, and Hagan, *American Foreign Policy,* passim; see also LaFeber, *The American Age,* passim; Frederick Pike, *The United States and Latin America: Myths and Stereotypes of Civilization and Nature* (Austin: University of Texas Press, 1992); and Roland H. Ebel, Raymond Trax, and James D. Cochrane, *Political*

Culture and Foreign Policy in Latin America (Albany: State University of New York Press, 1994).

87. Paterson, Clifford, and Hagan, *American Foreign Policy,* passim.
88. Lowenthal, "Latin America," pp. 82–85.
89. Ibid.
90. Henry Kissinger, *Diplomacy* (New York: Simon & Schuster, 1994), p. 832.

CHAPTER 8

AMERICAN POLICY
TOWARD THE MIDDLE EAST

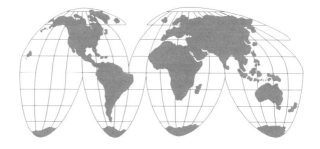

GHASSAN E. EL-EID

Throughout the centuries, the Middle East has figured prominently in the strategic calculations of major powers. Its strategic location at the hub of Africa, Asia, and Europe, in addition to its wealth in resources, made it the focal point of the great powers' attention. Furthermore, the world's major religions of Judaism, Christianity, and Islam all originated in the area: The holiest shrines of these monotheistic faiths are located there.

The United States, like France, Great Britain, and Turkey before it, found itself deeply involved in that region of the world. The Turks controlled the area for almost four centuries while France and Great Britain established presence in the Levant (Syria, Lebanon, and Israel) in the aftermath of World War I. The United States' active involvement in the Middle East began with the end of World War II when it inherited the position of France and Britain as the guardian of Western interests. This chapter will focus on the U.S. policy toward the region, its past, present, and future. The origins, objectives, and options of American foreign policy vis-a-vis the Middle East will be analyzed. To accomplish this goal, we construct a conceptual framework with the following components:

1. The domestic environment and the interplay between domestic and foreign policies
2. The decision-making process
3. Economic variables
4. Geopolitical factors
5. Personal characteristics of American presidents

In order to understand the motives, tactics, and objectives of the United States in the Middle East, however, it is important to examine the evolution of American policy toward the region over the last five decades.

HISTORICAL BACKGROUND

Prior to World War II, the United States had few interests in the Middle East. Great Britain and France, having established their presence after World War I, were the dominant players in the region. America's interests were primarily cultural, through the activities of missionaries in Lebanon, Palestine, and other parts of the Levant. The Holy Land had always been the object of Christian concerns since the days of the Crusaders centuries ago. Furthermore, there were economic interests: in the 1920s Washington supported American oil companies in their efforts to explore for oil. By the end of the 1930s, the oil companies acquired important concessions in Saudi Arabia and the Persian Gulf. Indeed, President Franklin D. Roosevelt established contacts with the Saudi monarch Abdul Aziz Ibn Saud in the mid-1930s that enabled American companies to exploit oil in the Arab peninsula.[1]

By the mid-1930s, however, another issue was emerging: the question of Palestine. In 1917, the leaders of the Zionist movement (a Jewish nationalist movement committed to the establishment of a Jewish homeland in Palestine) succeeded in getting the support of the British government, which controlled Palestine at that time, for the establishment of a Jewish state in Palestine. This was in a letter sent by Lord Balfour, Britain's Secretary of State for Foreign Affairs, to Chaim Weizmann, a prominent Zionist leader and chemist who contributed to the British war effort:

> His majesty's Government views with favor the establishment in Palestine of a National Home for the Jewish people, and will use their best endeavors to facilitate the achievement of this object, it being clearly understood that nothing shall be done which may prejudice the civil and religious rights of existing non-Jewish communities in Palestine....[2]

President Woodrow Wilson responded to the Balfour declaration by appointing the King-Crane Commission to gather facts and make recommendations concerning the Palestine question. The commission urged that Greater Syria (which included Lebanon and Palestine) should remain united and that the wishes and desires of the region's people must be taken into consideration.[3] This, of course, was compatible with the main theme in American foreign policy at that time that supported self-determination for people and independence for colonized territories. In this case, however, the United States failed to dissuade Britain from pursuing its divide-and-conquer strategy in the region. Congress was sympathetic to the Zionist movement and played a major role in President Wilson's strategy which seemed to ignore

British policy in the Levant as long as American oil companies were given a free hand in exploring for oil resources in Iraq and Saudi Arabia.

The deference to Britain remained unchanged until President Franklin D. Roosevelt promised the Saudi monarch Ibn Saud in 1943 that any solution in Palestine must take into consideration both Arab and Jewish aspirations.[4] The United States, however, adopted a hands-off approach to the Palestinian issue, accepting the fact that the area was within the British sphere of influence.

When Harry Truman ascended to the presidency in 1945, he faced a tense situation in Palestine. The British were trying to limit Jewish immigration, arguing that it would inevitably lead to war, and American Zionist leaders were putting pressure on him to intervene with the British to lift the immigration restrictions on Jews. Furthermore, Jewish extremists in Palestine under the leadership of Menachem Begin, were waging a war against the British with the intention of forcing them out of the country.

On October 4, 1946, Truman appealed to the British in an open letter for substantial Jewish immigration into Palestine and expressed his support for a Zionist entity in part of Palestine.[5] The British bitterly criticized Truman for making this letter public, claiming that it might jeopardize efforts to reach a compromise between Arabs and Zionists.

In analyzing the shift from noninvolvement to an active pro-Zionist policy, we can identify several factors. Domestic politics is certainly a source of foreign policy, and in Truman's case, lobbying by pro-Zionist groups was intense. The President's daughter, Margaret, recalls an episode when, in October 1948, a group of prominent Democratic Party leaders from New York visited her father and urged him to offer Israel *de jure* recognition, lift the arms embargo, and support the widest possible boundaries for Israel. They warned him that failure to do this would result in the loss of New York State in the upcoming elections.[6] It should be mentioned that earlier in his presidency, Truman assured Egyptian Prime Minister Nokvashy Pasha that he was pursuing the policy that was articulated by his predecessor, Franklin D. Roosevelt, which emphasized consultation with both Arabs and Jews.[7]

Electoral politics aside, we must take into consideration Truman's personal beliefs and convictions. He seemed to be sympathetic to the Zionist demands, particularly after the horrors of the Holocaust were revealed. Hence, he supported the Jewish state on humanitarian grounds. Furthermore, he saw the Balfour declaration as being compatible with the principle of self-determination that both he and his predecessors supported. The problem with the British pledge was that it created a situation where two peoples were vying for the same territory. Nevertheless, Truman ignored the advice of his Department of State advisors that a pro-Zionist policy could antagonize Arab states and could harm American economic interests in the region. Instead, he became convinced of the congruence of support for Israel with U.S. interests in the region and that Saudi Arabia and the other Gulf states were unlikely to cut off economic ties with America.[8] On May 15, 1948, Israel declared its independence. President Truman recognized the new state eleven minutes after the declaration.

Truman's policy toward the Middle East disappointed many Arab leaders who felt betrayed by promises that were never kept. To be sure, Arab leaders admired the United States, which fought its own battle for independence and self-determination. Unlike other Western powers, America was not burdened by colonialism, and its image was not tarnished, at least not in the Middle East.

The end of World War II significantly changed the global power configuration. The number of major powers had been reduced to two—the United States and the Soviet Union. A tight bipolar system emerged in which the two superpowers were competing for influence and leverage. Ideological rivalries and competition, in addition to the distrust that plagued bilateral relations, made peaceful coexistence almost impossible. Hence, a Cold War began in which each side sought to enhance its position by undermining and weakening the other. For the United States, containing Soviet/Communist expansion became the major theme in its foreign policy. This policy of containment emerged gradually in the postwar years, but it was Truman who laid its foundation. The Truman Doctrine was promulgated in response to developments in Greece and Turkey where the Communist movement was gaining momentum. On March 12, 1947, President Truman went before Congress to pledge that the United States was willing to help people throughout the world in their struggle for freedom and against oppression. In his speech, he linked totalitarianism to aggression and promised that his administration was

> willing to help free peoples to maintain their institutions and their national integrity against aggressive movements that seek to impose upon them totalitarian regimes. This is no more than a frank recognition that totalitarian regimes, imposed on free people by direct or indirect aggression, undermine the foundations of international peace and hence the security of the United States.... At the present moment in world history nearly every nation must choose between alternative ways of life. The choice is often not a free one.... I believe that we must assist free peoples to work out their own destinies in their own way.[9]

Certainly, Truman delivered one of the most important speeches in the history of the United States. In essence, he pledged American support to any nation threatened by totalitarianism (communism) and aggression. The United States was emerging as the "policeman of the world." Whether the United States had the resources or the resolve to play such a role, however, was a different question. The President did manage to persuade Congress to appropriate $400 million for economic and military aid to Turkey and Greece.[10]

The United States sought to contain communism by forming military alliances. Hence, the North Atlantic Treaty Organization (NATO) was formed in 1949 to contain Soviet expansionism in Europe. In 1954, President

Eisenhower formed the Southeast Asia Treaty Organization (SEATO) as a warning to both the Soviet Union and China. Overtures were made to many Middle-East states to join the United States in an anti-Soviet alliance. Most countries refused to join in such a pact, preferring a more neutral stance vis-a-vis the superpowers. This type of nonalignment was defined by a scholar as a "refusal to view international life from the perspective of the Cold War."[11] Arab states were more concerned with issues of nation-building and modernization than they were with Cold War rivalries.

By the mid-1950s, the United States did manage to extend the wall of containment to the Middle East. In 1955, the Eisenhower administration succeeded in persuading Britain to establish the Baghdad Pact, also known as the Middle East Treaty Organization (METO). In addition to Britain, the pact included Turkey, Iran, Iraq, and Pakistan.[12] Iraq was the only Arab country to join METO. In the summer of 1958, the new Iraqi government decided to withdraw from the alliance system, which was later renamed the Central Treaty Organization (CENTO), but in the following years, CENTO became totally ineffective.[13]

While the United States was preoccupied with building the Northern Tier, the Soviet Union was achieving considerable success in establishing a foothold in Egypt, the most powerful Arab state. Hence, Moscow managed to "leap frog" the containment line drawn by Washington. The Eisenhower administration antagonized Egypt by withdrawing its offer of economic support to build the Aswan Dam. Furthermore, Egyptian President Nasser saw the Baghdad Pact as an instrument to further Western interests in the region and to protect corrupt regimes. Indeed, the pact helped draw Egypt closer to Moscow, which was eager to offer Nasser the economic and military aid he needed to enhance Egypt's position in the Arab world. So, while Washington was pursuing containment as a strategy, Egypt was engaged in a political, and sometimes military, struggle on two fronts: against Israel, which was perceived as an alien entity established by Western imperialism and against the conservative Arab regimes that were viewed as puppet governments that facilitated the exploitation of Arab resources by imperialist powers. In addition, the Soviet Union traditionally viewed the Middle East as a vital region because of its geographic location and wealth in resources. It offered the Soviet Union an opportunity to outflank and neutralize NATO and to possibly control the oil resources that were vital to Western economies.

Soviet advances in the Middle East prompted President Eisenhower to proclaim the Eisenhower Doctrine in January 1957. The President pledged to help friendly Middle-East states both economically and militarily and to provide

> assistance and cooperation (which would) include employment of the armed forces of the United States to secure and protect the territorial integrity and political independence of such nations requesting such aid, against overt armed aggression from any nation controlled by international communism.[14]

The major problem with the Eisenhower Doctrine was that it focused almost exclusively on containing Soviet and Communist expansionism. It demonstrated little interest in the aspirations and goals of Arab states. The Soviet Union, on the other hand, was willing, and sometimes eager, to support the Arab states economically and militarily and was generally sympathetic to the Arab position in the confrontation with Israel.[15] U.S. policy antagonized Arab states and led to the radicalization of Arab nationalist regimes in Egypt, Syria, and Iraq. By the late 1950s, all three states were allied with the Soviet bloc.

The Suez Canal crisis of 1956 marked the beginning of dynamics that planted the seeds of regional alliances and shaped the superpowers' policies toward the region. On July 26, 1956, Egypt nationalized the Suez Canal, which was run by the British. Britain retaliated by launching an invasion with French forces that enabled them to secure the canal by November 7, 1956. By that time, Israeli forces had already crossed the border and were in control of the Sinai Peninsula.

The tripartite invasion of Egypt provided the United States with an opportunity to improve its position in the Arab world. Despite its close relationship with Britain and France, the American government criticized the invasion on the grounds that the use of force could not be justified as a means to settle disputes. Washington was instrumental in forcing the invading forces to withdraw from Egyptian territories. By March 1957, all forces were withdrawn.[16]

While the Suez conflict enhanced Egypt's position politically, it did little to alter the regional balance of power. The Soviets capitalized on the crisis by strengthening their military and political alliance with Egypt and by replacing the military hardware lost by Egypt during the war. The invasion of Egypt further radicalized Arab regimes and increased their hostility toward Israel. Nasser's stature was enhanced, and he emerged as the most popular Arab leader, which helped him to successfully promote his ideas of Arab nationalism, socialism, unity, and anticolonialism.

In 1958, Eisenhower found an opportunity in Lebanon to implement his doctrine. The country had been plagued by violence and factional fighting for months. President Camille Shamoun, who had pursued a pro-Western policy, triggered the latest war between the predominantly Muslim leftist forces opposed to his regime and progovernment, mostly Christian, forces who supported him and were in favor of renewing his term as president (the Lebanese constitution prohibited renewal of the president's six-year term). The leftist forces were supported by Nasser. The Lebanese government claimed that the United Arab Republic (comprised of Egypt and Syria) was intervening in Lebanon by sending fighters and military hardware to help the insurgents. The Lebanese government sought American aid to counterbalance the alleged intervention in its internal affairs. The Eisenhower administration responded by invoking the Eisenhower Doctrine on the grounds that the Lebanese government was being threatened by armed aggression. The United States dispatched fourteen thousand troops to Lebanon. The message was clear: The United States was willing to use force to support its allies and to maintain the line of containment. The Soviets, on the other hand, having made promises to send volunteers to oppose the Western "imperialists" in the Middle East, failed to deliver. The failure of the Soviet Union to do more than criticize the American intervention made it clear that there were limits to Soviet willingness to help their Arab allies.[17]

The intervention in Lebanon proved to be the last major American action in the region for nearly a decade. The Eisenhower administration focused its attention on other parts of the world, notably Europe and Cuba. In general, we can argue that Eisenhower was less sympathetic to Israel than Truman. Indeed, the Israelis resented American pressure, which had forced them out of the Sinai desert in 1957. While the United States failed to diminish Soviet influence, it did demonstrate strong resolve and commitment to help its allies by its actions in Lebanon.

When John F. Kennedy was inaugurated as president in January of 1961, the Middle East was relatively quiet. The new president was preoccupied with the Cuban Missile Crisis, the arms race with the Soviet Union, and the deteriorating situation in Vietnam. Arab nationalists, however, were making significant gains in Syria and Iraq. By the mid-1960s, both of these countries were controlled by anti-Western regimes with close ties to the Soviet Union. The Kennedy years witnessed the end of America's reluctance to provide Israel with weapons. Heretofore, Israel had relied on European powers, mainly France, as major weapons suppliers. Also, the Kennedy administration backed a United Nations Conciliation Commission to devise a plan to repatriate or resettle Palestinian refugees. Both Israel and the Arab states refused to cooperate with the commission.[18]

The peace that seemed to have settled over the Middle East in the early 1960s was an illusion. By 1967 intra-Arab rivalries and tensions on the Israeli-Syrian borders were prompting Egypt's Nasser to reassert his leadership of the Arab world. For years the Egyptian leader wooed the Arab masses by his charisma and tough anti-Zionist rhetoric. When the Syrians pleaded for his help in May 1967, claiming that Israel was poised to attack, Nasser was compelled to act. He demanded the withdrawal of U.N. peacekeeping forces from the Egyptian-Israeli border and blockaded the Gulf of Aqaba, which was a vital waterway for Israel. These were viewed by Israel as provocative acts. On June 5, 1967, Israel launched a preemptive strike that destroyed the Egyptian air force. In a few days, Israel was able to capture the Sinai Peninsula from Egypt, the West Bank from Jordan, and the Golan Heights from Syria.

The June 1967 war was a crushing defeat for the Arabs. It shattered the myth of Arab superiority and created new realities. Arab nationalists were embarrassed and humiliated. In Egypt, Nasser offered to resign. In Syria and Iraq the governments were overthrown. The Soviet Union's hopes for establishing hegemony in the region were dashed. Had the Soviets succeeded in the Middle East, Western vital interests would have been seriously threatened. Throughout that short war, the United States' main concern was to make sure that the Soviet Union did not intervene on the side of Egypt and Syria in a way that would result in a confrontation between the two superpowers. There were exchanges between Washington and Moscow over the "hot line" that convinced the Johnson administration that the Soviet Union had no interest in going to war with the United States over the Middle East.[19] Furthermore, the American public, particularly the Jewish community, was strongly behind Israeli actions. This explains Johnson's strong support of Israel. Israel, however, was concerned that Johnson would do what Eisenhower did in 1957: ask for withdrawal from occupied territory.[20] Instead, President Johnson, seeking to preempt a Soviet move in the U.N. Security Council demanding an Israeli withdrawal, proposed a peace plan to end the Arab-Israeli conflict. Johnson's principles of peace stressed peaceful coexistence of all states in the region, justice for refugees, freedom of navigation, control of the regional arms race, and, finally, peace based on recognized borders.[21]

Johnson's plan failed to gain momentum. One problem had to do with the view that many Arab leaders held about the President. He was perceived to be biased toward Israel and was accused of basing U.S. Middle-East policy on the requirements of Israel rather than on the interests of the United States.[22] Many were convinced that Johnson gave tacit approval to Israel to attack Egypt.[23] One author suggested that the Johnson administration facilitated the Israeli actions against Egypt by shipping military hardware and ammunition to Israel on May 23, 1967.[24] In effect, Johnson was the founder of the "special relationship" policy with Israel. This seriously hampered his efforts in bringing peace to the region. Nevertheless, he inaugurated the peace process and established conflict resolution as an American foreign policy objective.[25]

On November 22, 1967, the United States supported a British motion in the Security Council, later known as Resolution 242, that proclaimed the following principles for a peaceful settlement of the Arab-Israeli conflict:

1. Withdrawal of Israeli forces from territories occupied in the recent conflict

2. Termination of all claims or states of belligerency and respect for sovereignty, territorial integrity, and political independence of every state in the region and their right to live in peace within secure and recognized boundaries

3. Freedom of navigation through international waters

4. Just settlement of the refugee problem

5. Territorial inviolability and political independence of every state in the area through measures including the establishment of demilitarized zones[26]

Resolution 242 failed to generate momentum for peace in the Middle East. The Arabs criticized it on the grounds that it was not comprehensive enough and that it did not specify which territories Israel was supposed to relinquish. Israel, on the other hand, having achieved an overwhelming victory over its Arab foes, saw no need for compromise and emerged as the region's superpower.

In evaluating Johnson's policy toward the Middle East, we can argue that it heavily favored Israel and that it was generally geared to satisfy Israeli interests. In seeking to explain Johnson's policy, we must focus on politics within the United States, that is, domestic political factors. As we have indicated above, the American public was generally more sympathetic to Israel than it was to the Arabs. Second, pro-Israeli votes and donations by Zionist sympathizers figured prominently in Johnson's political calculations. Third, he was influenced by those who argued that Israel's military performance and effectiveness was more important than containing Soviet advances in the region. Israel was viewed as a strategic asset. Fourth, Johnson disliked Egypt's Nasser and viewed him as a "windbag" whose tough rhetoric and inflammatory speeches contributed to regional instability. Thus, the President did not mind seeing Nasser punished. Fifth, Johnson was heavily influenced by his close advisors who were very sympathetic to Israel. Those included Eugene Rostow, Arthur Goldberg, Harry McPherson, and others. Finally, the Americans were convinced that the so called "moderate" Arab states would not risk jeopardizing their relationship with the United States despite Washington's strong support of Israel.

Richard Nixon showed an interest in the Middle East even before he was inaugurated as president in 1969. In November 1968, when he was president-elect, Nixon dispatched William Scranton to the Middle East to investigate the situation and to make recommendations regarding future American strategy there. Scranton advised a more "even-handed" approach:

> America would do well to have a more even-handed policy.... We are interested, very interested, in Israel and its security, and we should be. But it is important to point out in the Middle East and to people around the world that we are interested in other countries in the area and have friends among them.[27]

Scranton's statement engendered criticism and hostility in Israel and among its sympathizers in Washington. Soon after taking office, Nixon realized that this new approach of "evenhandedness" was politically risky. He abandoned this policy after his first year in office.

To be sure, Nixon assumed the presidency at a difficult time: The United States was bogged down in Vietnam, and the arms race with the Soviet Union was escalating. In the Middle East, the war of attrition between Egypt and Israel was raging on. Six Arab states (Algeria, Egypt, Iraq, Sudan, Syria, and Yemen) broke diplomatic relations with the United States in protest of

American support to Israel. Nixon, however, came to power determined to make a fresh start in American foreign policy toward the Middle East. Achieving peace in the area became a top priority for him.

Initially, Nixon focused on the Persian Gulf region, which contained the largest oil resources in the world. While the United States was not dependent on Middle-Eastern oil at that time, countries in that area provided Western Europe and Japan with the bulk of their oil. Britain was withdrawing from that region after maintaining a presence there since the mid-nineteenth century. The United States, however, after its Vietnam experience, was not eager to fill the power vacuum left by the British. Therefore, Iran, Washington's closest ally in the Gulf and the area's most powerful state, was called upon to safeguard Western interests and to ensure stability in the area. Furthermore, the Iranians played an important role in destabilizing pro-Soviet Iraq.[28]

In deciding his policy toward the Middle East, Nixon sought to launch a unilateral effort aimed at ending the Arab-Israeli conflict. On December 9, 1969, Secretary of State William Rogers outlined a comprehensive peace plan to achieve peace. It was inspired by U.N. Security Council Resolution 242, which we discussed previously. The plan called on Israel to withdraw from the occupied territories and urged the Arabs to recognize the Jewish state. "Our policy is to encourage the Arabs to accept a permanent peace based on a binding agreement and to urge the Israelis to withdraw from occupied territory when their territorial integrity is assured as envisaged by the Security Council resolution.... We do not support expansionism. We believe troops must be withdrawn as the resolution provides."[29]

The Rogers plan represented a significant departure from Johnson's policy. It sought a more "evenhanded" approach. The Israelis criticized the plan and rejected "outside attempts to determine boundaries."[30] While the plan was comprehensive and dealt with a number of relevant issues (including refugees and the status of Jerusalem), it did not become a genuine and official peace proposal. In his memoirs, Nixon stated:

> I knew that the Rogers plan could never be implemented, but I believed that it was important to let the Arab world know that the United States did not automatically dismiss its case regarding the occupied territories or rule out a compromise settlement of the conflicting claims. With the Rogers plan on record, I thought it would be easier for the Arab leaders to propose re-opening relations with the United States without coming under attack from the hawks and pro-Soviet elements in their own countries.[31]

The civil war in Jordan in September 1970 threatened regional peace and influenced American policy in the area. King Hussein, traditionally a pro-Western leader, was having difficulty controlling Palestinian armed activities in his country. The situation deteriorated into a full-scale war between Palestinian fighters and the Jordanian army. Neighboring Syria sent troops into Jordan in support of the Palestine Liberation Organization (PLO) guerrillas. Israel, in response, threatened to intervene in defense of the moderate Jordanian regime. Eventually, the Jordanian army prevailed, the PLO was expelled from Jordan, and the Syrians withdrew. Israel's actions enhanced its value as a key American ally and as a "strategic asset." Had the PLO succeeded in toppling Hussein, a radical regime would have ascended to power in Jordan posing a serious threat to American interests in the area.

On October 6, 1973, Egypt and Syria launched a surprise attack against Israel. This time, it was the Arabs who struck first. Egyptian and Syrian forces crossed Israeli fortifications and advanced into the Sinai and the Golan Heights. As the war raged on, however, Israel was able to reverse the tide. In the meantime, the Nixon administration had arranged for a massive airlift of American weapons to Israel, providing it with thousands of tons of war material. Israel received large numbers of sophisticated warplanes, tanks, and a total of more than twenty-two thousand tons of military equipment. In addition, Nixon asked Congress to appropriate $2.2 billion in emergency aid to Israel, including $1.5 billion in outright grants.[32] Furthermore, he put America's strategic forces on alert.[33]

Nixon's decisions outraged the Arab world. For years, Arab leaders accused the United States of favoring Israel. Nixon's behavior confirmed their suspicions. In retaliation for what they considered to be hostile American actions, Arab oil-producing countries meeting in Kuwait proclaimed a total oil embargo against the United States. The embargo was later lifted, but it eventually led to quadrupling of oil prices. The Arabs, for the first time, were using oil as a weapon. The impact of the oil embargo on the world economy was dramatic, since most Western economies were dependent on Middle-Eastern oil.

The Arab oil embargo forced Nixon and his close advisors to put top priority on dealing with the Arab-Israeli conflict. Resolving the Middle-East conflict was treated as a critical foreign policy issue. As Steven Spiegel put it: "Never had an administration felt more pressure to resolve the conflict."[34]

The Nixon administration responded to the crisis by inaugurating what was later referred to as "shuttle diplomacy" by Secretary of State Henry Kissinger. He made numerous trips between Israel and its Arab neighbors that resulted in a six-point cease-fire agreement on November 11, 1973, that was signed by Egyptian and Israeli military representatives. Later that year, the Geneva conference on the Middle East was convened in accordance with U.N. Security Council Resolution 338.[35] The conference was co-chaired by the United States and the Soviet Union and attended by Israel, Egypt, and Jordan, but boycotted by Syria.

The Geneva Conference was an important event, but it was clear that neither the United States nor Israel was enthusiastic about it. Israel has always resisted collective negotiations with the Arabs, and the United States wanted to see the Soviet Union excluded from peacemaking efforts in the Middle

East. Nevertheless, the Geneva Convention was seen as a triumph for American, not Soviet, diplomacy.

The Arab oil boycott demonstrated, as we mentioned earlier, international dependency on Middle-Eastern oil and sharpened awareness worldwide to the dangers that regional conflicts can pose to global stability. Hence, it became a top priority for Nixon to end this embargo. He pledged to King Faisal of Saudi Arabia that the United States would endeavor to establish a just and comprehensive peace in the area. But it was the Arab leaders, notably Sadat of Egypt, who convinced Arab states to lift the embargo. On July 11, 1974, oil ministers of seven Arab states, meeting in Cairo, agreed to remove all restrictions on oil exports.[36]

In evaluating the Nixon policy toward the Middle East, it is interesting to note that while he pledged to follow a balanced policy toward Israel and the Arabs, his actions clearly showed preferential treatment to Israel. He provided Israel with massive aid and dramatically broadened the American-Israeli relationship.

President Gerald Ford took office on August 9, 1974 after Nixon resigned in the wake of the Watergate scandal. Kissinger, who was retained by the new president as Secretary of State, continued his shuttle diplomacy to secure an agreement between Israel and Egypt. Israel was not inclined to give territorial concessions. Israeli Prime Minister Yitzhak Rabin argued that the aim of Israel should be to gain time in order to delay an agreement that could require Israel to give up land to the Arabs. With time, he hoped that the United States would become less dependent on Arab oil and less disposed to pressure Israel.[37] This attitude infuriated Ford, who sent Rabin a cable in which he stated:

> I wish to express my profound disappointment over Israel's attitude in the course of the negotiations.... Failure of the negotiations will have a far-reaching impact on the region and on our relations. I have given instructions for a re-assessment of United States policy in the region, including our relations with Israel, with the aim of ensuring that overall American interests are protected. You will be notified of our decision.[38]

Ford's warning succeeded in forcing Israel and Egypt to conclude an interim agreement in September 1975, that resulted in a pullback of Israeli troops in the Sinai.[39] Nevertheless, the policy of reassessment was not abandoned and toward the end of Ford's presidency, U.S. Ambassador to the United Nations William Scranton supported a Security Council resolution criticizing Israel for building settlements in the occupied territories and rejecting Israel's annexation of East Jerusalem, which it conquered from Jordan in 1967.[40] Although Ford tried to adopt a more balanced approach to the Middle East, it was clear that he was constrained by the Nixon-Kissinger strategy that focused on strengthening Israel as a "strategic asset" and on diminishing the Soviet influence in order to force the Arabs to accept an exclusive American role in the peace process. In fact, the Ford administration gave Israel specific assurances that any American peace proposal would have to be acceptable to Israel and it pledged not to recognize the Palestine Liberation Organization or to negotiate with it without Israeli consent until the PLO formally recognized Israel and renounced violence.[41]

Overall, an argument can be made that while Ford intended to broker a comprehensive peace agreement, he never developed a concrete plan for resolving the conflict. In an election year, it was very difficult for him to inaugurate an American initiative without antagonizing the powerful pro-Israeli lobby. Hence, he was forced to endorse Kissinger's policy that accommodated most Israeli demands but alienated the Arab states and harmed American interests in the Middle East. Indeed, during the Ford era, Israel received massive supplies of weapons. By early 1977, Israel's air force was the third strongest in the world.[42]

President Jimmy Carter sought to reactivate the peace process in the Middle East. Unlike his predecessors, who ignored the Palestinian factor and focused on peace between Israel and its Arab neighbors, Carter spoke of the plight of the Palestinian people. "There has to be a homeland for the Palestinian refugees who have suffered for many, many years."[43] In trying to understand Carter's ideology, we must consider his personal characteristics. As one scholar put it, "Carter combined profound religious devotion, attachment to high moral principles, and patriotism enhanced by service in the navy."[44] Indeed, Carter portrayed himself as an honest public servant, uncorrupted by special interests. In the wake of the Watergate scandal and Kissinger's Machiavellian politics, Carter's unblemished past and high moral standards set him apart as a man of integrity and honesty.

In the area of foreign policy, the new president was inexperienced and sometimes appeared to be overwhelmed by global events. Like his predecessors, however, Carter strove to counteract the Communist threat. Carter introduced a new theme in foreign policy: promotion of human rights.[45] He even linked American aid to the recipient state's record on human rights. The message was clear: Regimes that violated human rights of their nationals will not be eligible for American aid. On U.S. policy toward the Middle East, Carter's support for Israel was ironclad. He generally subscribed to the view that Israel should be viewed as a strategic asset and as a key American ally in the area.

Early in his presidency, Carter decided to make conflict resolution in the Middle East a central theme in American foreign policy. Carter and his advisors were critical of the step-by-step approach to peacemaking that was pursued by Kissinger. Instead, they sought a comprehensive settlement of the Arab-Israeli dispute. One of the President's key advisors, George W. Ball, argued that Kissinger's policy had emphasized tactics over strategy and that it failed to deal with the core of the problem: the plight of the Palestinians. Ball maintained that "Secretary Kissinger has pursued a practice that most medical doctors would deplore: he has sewn up part of the wound, leaving a raging infection inside."[46]

Carter's emphasis on human rights reflected on his Middle-East policy. He pressured the Soviet Union to relax restrictions on Jewish emigration. The Soviets agreed, and as a result, the number of Jewish emigrants quadrupled to 51,320 from 1976 to 1979.[47] Also, the President's commitment to basic human rights meant that he was sympathetic to Palestinian demands for a homeland.[48]

The Carter administration also strove to normalize relations between Israel and its Arab neighbors. However, two events shaped U.S. policy toward the region. The first was the election of Menachem Begin as Prime Minister of Israel in 1977. As a member of the Likud party, he was less likely to compromise with the Arabs. He was convinced that the West Bank (which was conquered in 1967) was part of Greater Israel and, therefore, was not subject to negotiations. He authorized building more Israeli settlements in the area, which President Carter viewed as "obstacles to peace." Clearly, Begin and his cabinet were committed to Israeli control over all of the West Bank. The second event was the surprise visit by Egyptian President Sadat to Israel in November 1977. The visit was an important event. Sadat was the first Arab leader to visit Jerusalem, where he delivered a speech in the Knesset, Israel's parliament, in which he offered Israel recognition and peace based on territorial concessions. The visit provided a convincing demonstration that Egypt was prepared to negotiate peace with Israel.

In July 1977, Carter had already outlined to Begin his peace proposal for the Middle East. It consisted of five points:

1. Comprehensive peace between Israel and its Arab neighbors
2. Peace to be based on U.N. Security Council Resolution 242
3. Peace would involve open borders and free trade
4. Withdrawal of Israeli forces from occupied territories to secured borders
5. Creation of a Palestinian entity[49]

While Begin objected to the idea of a Palestinian entity, subsequent negotiations, especially after Sadat's visit to Jerusalem, paved the way for the establishment of agreed upon frameworks that would later produce the Camp David Accords.[50]

The Camp David approach was a departure from the Geneva meetings in 1975 that included representatives from Israel, Egypt, Jordan, the Soviet Union, and the United States. It was a bilateral agreement, an approach favored by the Israelis. In the eyes of the supporters of Camp David, there were two major accomplishments:

First, it was a peace treaty between Egypt and Israel in which Egypt regained control of the Sinai Peninsula and normalized its relationship with the Jewish state. The agreement stated that "The parties agree that the normal relationship between them will include full recognition, diplomatic, economic, and cultural relations, termination of economic boycotts and discriminatory barriers to the free movement of people and goods, and will guarantee the mutual enjoyment of citizens of the due process of law."[51]

The second point emphasized in the agreement was the need to continue the efforts to achieve a comprehensive peace for the area:

> The parties are determined to reach a just, comprehensive, and durable settlement of the Middle East conflict through the conclusion of peace treaties based on Security Council Resolutions 242 and 338 in all their parts.... They recognize that, for peace to endure, it must involve all those who have been most deeply affected by the conflict.[52]

In evaluating the Camp David agreement we can argue that while it was successful in ending the state of belligerency between Egypt and Israel, it failed to bring peace to the region. The treaty was bitterly opposed by most Arabs, who accused Sadat of betraying the Palestinians. The accords, they maintained, tilted the balance of power in favor of Israel by isolating Egypt, the most powerful Arab state, from the Arab camp. Furthermore, critics argued that the agreement did not press Israel to withdraw from occupied territories other than the Sinai desert. So while the agreement was hailed as a triumph for American diplomacy in the West, the rest of the world viewed it as a separate peace treaty that failed to take into account the core problem in the Arab-Israeli conflict: the fate of the Palestinian people. The Carter administration, however, felt that by getting the Egyptians and the Israelis to agree to involve the Palestinians at a later stage, it had obtained their commitment to resolve the Palestinian issue.

While Carter was the first U.S. President to oversee an Arab-Israeli peace treaty, he suffered a major setback in Iran, a traditional American ally. Late in 1979, the Shah of Iran was overthrown and the American Embassy in Tehran was seized and its employees were held hostage by militant students. The hostage crisis that ensued, in addition to the Soviet invasion of Afghanistan in December 1979, severely hurt the Carter administration's prestige and projected an image of weakness.

When Ronald Reagan was elected president in November 1980, he promised to enhance America's prestige and to get tough on communism. Rather than focusing on the Arab-Israeli conflict as a central issue in foreign policy, his administration tended to view the Middle East as a component of America's global policy framework. Once again, the emphasis was on containment. Reagan tended to blame insurrections and international instability on Moscow. In fact, he referred to the Soviet Union as an "evil empire."

Early in his administration, Reagan promulgated the Reagan Doctrine. It legitimized American military, economic, and political support for those who were fighting repressive regimes. It supported the view that armed revolt was justified where the rights of citizens were systematically violated.[53] The doctrine was used to support insurgents in Nicaragua and anti-Communist Islamic fighters in Afghanistan. The intention was to bleed target governments into submission.[54] The strategy was successful in both states. By the early 1990s, the Sandinistas were out of power in Nicaragua and the Soviets were forced to withdraw from Afghanistan.

In June 1982, Israel invaded Lebanon with the intention of destroying the infrastructure of the Palestine Liberation Organization (PLO) that had managed to establish a state within a state in that country. Israel also wanted to bring to power a friendly government in Lebanon that would eventually sign a peace treaty with it. As the fighting intensified, the United States sought to play a key role in resolving the conflict. An American-sponsored plan led to the evacuation of the PLO fighters from Lebanon and the election of Bashir Gemayel, Israel's key ally, as President of Lebanon. It was at that time when Reagan announced his "peace plan" to resolve the Arab-Israeli dispute. In a televised speech from the White House in September 1982, the President called for a "fresh start" to reinvigorate the peace process. He argued that the Camp David agreement remained the basis of his policy and stressed negotiations as a means to resolve the dispute. He urged Israel to accept Resolution 242 and called on the Palestinians and the Arab states to recognize Israel. He also acknowledged that the United States had a special responsibility to be the main peace broker in the Middle East. The United States, he maintained, "will support positions that seem to the United States fair and reasonable compromises, and likely to promote a sound agreement."[55] Reagan's plan offered nothing new, and both Israel and the Arabs rejected it. Israeli Prime Minister Menachem Begin bitterly criticized the plan, arguing that it was not compatible with Camp David. In addition, the assassination of Lebanon's President-elect Bashir Gemayel on September 14, 1982 led to the rapid deterioration of the situation. Israeli troops, in violation of the American-sponsored agreement, moved into West Beirut, avowedly to prevent chaos and bloodshed. A few days later, thousands of Palestinians were massacred in refugee camps by Israel's Lebanese allies—Gemayel's phalangist militia.

Certainly, the events in September were a setback for Reagan's policy. In the next few years, Americans were kidnaped in Lebanon and taken as hostages by the pro-Iranian Hezbollah fighters. In 1983, the United States suffered a serious blow when the Marine headquarters in Beirut International Airport was destroyed by a suicide car bomb, resulting in the death of 241 marines. Eventually, Reagan was forced to "redeploy" American forces from Lebanon. During 1984 and 1985, nine Americans were kidnaped in Beirut. The Reagan administration was faced with a dilemma: The President had bitterly criticized the Carter administration for its "weakness and lack of competence" in dealing with the Iranian hostage crisis. Yet, in Lebanon, Reagan had discovered the limit of power. Like Carter before him, Reagan was bitter and frustrated. The mightiest nation in the world could not obtain the release of a few hostages held by terrorists. Eventually, Reagan resorted to secret negotiations with Khomeini's government in Iran, in what was later known as the Iran-Contra scandal.

In January 1986, President Reagan authorized secret negotiations with Iran. The plan was to sell Iran (a state that supported anti-Western groups in Lebanon) weapons and ammunition. The money was to be forwarded to the Contras, America's allies in Nicaragua, and the Iranians were to persuade their allies in Lebanon to release American hostages. This secret agreement was publicized in November 1986 by a Lebanese magazine. Reagan first denied the story, but later admitted that contacts were established with Iran.

The Iran-Contra scandal seriously undercut America's policy of no negotiations with terrorists or states that supported them. At a time when Washington was criticizing European states, especially Italy and France, and accusing them of being soft on terrorism, the Reagan administration was secretly negotiating with the Ayatollah Khomeini's government. This significantly weakened American credibility and undermined its efforts to combat international terrorism.

Toward the end of his second term, Ronald Reagan authorized a dialogue with the PLO. Back in 1975, Kissinger had pledged to the Israelis that the United States would not negotiate with the PLO until the Palestinian organization renounced terrorism and acknowledged Israel's right to exist. In 1988, Yassir Arafat, Chairman of the PLO, informed U.S. Secretary of State George Shultz that he was prepared to recognize Israel and renounce violence. Consequently, in December 1988, the Reagan administration announced that it was prepared to establish a dialogue with the PLO.[56]

In the Gulf area, the Reagan administration, in a clear signal to Iran, which was threatening to disrupt the flow of oil, authorized American naval escorts of Kuwaiti ships. Some Kuwaiti oil tankers were even "reflagged," where an American flag was flown instead of the Kuwaiti flag. The message to Iran was clear: The United States was prepared to use force to ensure the flow of oil from the Gulf. There were several confrontations that resulted in the destruction of a few Iranian boats, and on July 3, 1988, an Iranian airliner was shot down by an American warship. The navy claimed that it mistook the Airbus for an Iranian warplane.[57]

George Bush took office in 1989 with impressive credentials in foreign policy. As a former U.S. Ambassador to China and a former representative to the United Nations, he had gained extensive experience in foreign affairs. In addition, he was Reagan's vice president for two terms. Hence, there were expectations that he would continue Reagan's policy toward the Middle East. But it became evident that Bush and his foreign policy advisors would be less patient with Israel than Reagan had been. In a speech to the American-Israeli Public Affairs Committee (AIPAC), a powerful pro-Israeli lobby, Secretary of

State James Baker urged Israel to "lay aside, once and for all, unrealistic vision of a greater Israel.... Forswear annexation; stop settlement activity; allow schools to reopen; reach out to the Palestinians as neighbors who deserve political rights."[58] While Baker's comments angered Israel's supporters, they did not signal any change in American policy. Previous American administrations also viewed Jewish settlements on occupied territories as being illegal and obstacles to peace.

Some Israeli writers lamented what they considered "pro-Arab inclinations" of the Bush administration.[59] Moshe Arens, who was a member of the Likud-led government in the early 1990s, criticized the "perfidious" conduct of Secretary Baker, accusing him of interfering in the internal affairs of Israel.[60] In reality, the Bush administration tried to adopt a balanced approach toward the two sides. Hence, when the PLO's Yassir Arafat failed to condemn a terrorist attack in 1990, Bush decided to suspend the U.S. dialogue with the Palestinian organization. Overall, the Bush administration tried to play the role of an impartial peace broker by demonstrating toughness with both sides.

The Iraqi invasion of Kuwait in August 1990 seriously threatened regional and global stability and the balance of power in the Middle East. For years, the Iraqis made territorial claims against their oil-rich neighbor. Some Iraqis even argued that Kuwait was an integral part of the Basra, Iraq's southernmost province.[61] In fact, immediately after Iraqi troops gained control of Kuwait, the Baghdad government began referring to the conquered country as Iraq's nineteenth province.

The invasion and occupation of Kuwait presented the Bush administration with a serious challenge: how to repel aggression while protecting American vital interests in the Gulf area? The Bush administration responded by taking two steps. The first was to work with Congress to deploy American troops in Saudi Arabia. Secondly, a diplomatic initiative at the United Nations was launched in order to authorize military sanctions against Iraq. In a major speech on August 8, 1990, in which he announced his decision to deploy troops in Saudi Arabia, the President stated:

> First, we seek the immediate, unconditional, and complete withdrawal of all Iraqi forces from Kuwait. Second, Kuwait's legitimate government must be restored to replace the puppet regime [imposed by the Iraqis]. Third, my administration, as has been the case with every president from President Roosevelt to President Reagan, is committed to the security and stability of the Persian Gulf.[62]

Most Americans supported Bush's decision to dispatch troops to Saudi Arabia and to use force in dislodging the Iraqi army from Kuwait. A *New York Times*-CBS News poll in 1991 revealed that 66 percent of Americans approved President Bush's Persian Gulf policy. Later, as the military campaign against Iraq intensified, polls indicated that the approval rate was close to 82 percent.[63] Clearly, Iraq's act of aggression was blatant, and America's vital economic interests (oil) were threatened. In addition, Washington sought to coordinate with major powers, including the Soviet Union and regional powers, in responding to Iraqi aggression.

The United States was able to pass resolutions through the U.N. Security Council that authorized the use of force against Iraq. The Soviets were no longer in a position to challenge the United States after the collapse of the Communist system. Therefore, it was unlikely that Moscow would risk antagonizing the United States in support of Iraq. As a result, the U.N. Security Council passed several resolutions authorizing military sanctions against Iraq. This enabled the United States to obtain legitimacy for its military actions against Saddam Hussein. In January 1991, the American-led coalition forces began their campaign to expel Iraqi forces out of Kuwait. By the end of February, Kuwait was liberated.

While the Persian Gulf War was a brilliant military operation, questions lingered about Bush's decision to let Saddam stay in power. The United States, however, did not have a U.N. mandate to enter Baghdad. Nevertheless, there were those who blamed the United States for leading the Iraqis to believe that the United States was not obligated to defend Kuwait, and hence did not deter Saddam Hussein from invading the country.[64]

The Gulf War greatly altered the regional balance of power in the area. Prior to 1991, Iraq was the dominant Arab state in the area. Its battle-hardened army of one million men posed the most serious threat to Israel and to pro-Western Arab states. The war greatly reduced Iraq's military strength, but Saddam remained in power. In order to force the Iraqi government to comply with the U.N. resolutions (which include paying war reparations to Kuwait and abandoning efforts to develop weapons of mass destruction, including nuclear and chemical weapons), the United Nations continues to maintain economic sanctions against Iraq.

The United States emerged from the Gulf War with its prestige and influence greatly enhanced. To be sure, with the end of the Cold War the United States was the only remaining superpower. President Bush often talked about "the New World Order," a new era where power politics and ideological rivalries will take a back seat to global cooperation and the quest for collective security. The fact that the United Nations was able to authorize military sanctions for the first time since the Korean War was only possible because of Soviet cooperation.[65]

After the Gulf War, the United States focused its attention once again on the peace process. Within weeks after the war, Secretary of State James Baker made several trips to the region to persuade Israel and the Arab states to attend an international peace conference to negotiate a settlement for their dispute. Eventually, Baker was successful and the first conference was held in Madrid, Spain, on October 30, 1991. This was a triumph for U.S. diplomacy, even though comprehensive peace remains elusive in the Middle East.

With the election of Bill Clinton to the presidency in 1992, there were concerns as to whether the new president had the credentials or the expertise to be a credible mediator in the Middle East. From the beginning, however, Clinton made it clear that obtaining peace in the Middle East was a top priority. In a speech on September 13, 1993, at the signing of the Israeli-Palestinian agreement on Palestinian self-rule, Clinton remarked:

> Ever since Harry Truman first recognized Israel, every American president, Democrat and Republican, has worked for peace between Israel and her neighbors. Now the efforts of all who have labored before us bring the U.S. to this moment.... When we dare to pledge what for so long seemed difficult even to imagine: that the security of the Israeli people will be reconciled by the hopes of the Palestinian people and there will be more security and more hope for all.[66]

In the same speech, Clinton outlined his administration's policy toward the region. He promised that the United States would be committed to the security of the region and to its economic well-being.[67]

In 1994, the Clinton administration was successful in brokering a peace agreement between Israel and Jordan, a moderate Arab country that maintained secret relations with Tel Aviv for a long time. In September 1995, Israel and the PLO signed a peace accord that expanded Palestinian self-rule in the West Bank. Syria and Lebanon are the only remaining Arab states among Israel's neighbors that have not signed a peace agreement with Israel. Broadening peace in the Middle East remains a top priority in Clinton's foreign policy.

U.S. INTERESTS, CHALLENGES, AND OPPORTUNITIES

As we have seen from the analysis of U.S. foreign policy in the Middle East since World War II, there were three major themes:

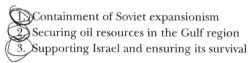

1. Containment of Soviet expansionism
2. Securing oil resources in the Gulf region
3. Supporting Israel and ensuring its survival

There were, of course, other interests. Containing radical Arab regimes and coping with nationalist movements and Islamic fundamentalism were also important foreign policy goals. In general, we can discuss five phases in the evolution of American foreign policy priorities in the region:

Phase 1 (1945–1948)

1. Establishing friendly relations in Middle-Eastern states and extension of influence in the region
2. Protecting economic interests (oil) in the Arab peninsula and Gulf region

Phase II (1948–1967)

1. Containing the Soviet threat by establishing regional alliances (the Baghdad Pact)
2. Supporting Israel
3. Protecting its economic interests in the Gulf region

Phase III (1967–1974)

1. Strengthening commitment to Israel (the United States became the major weapons supplier and political backer of Israel)
2. Undertaking an active role in conflict resolution in the area
3. Coping with the 1973 Arab oil embargo
4. Containing communism

Phase IV (1974–1990)

1. Resolving the Arab-Israel conflict (Camp David)
2. Diminishing Soviet influence in the region
3. Reversing the tide of Islamic fundamentalism
4. Combating terrorism
5. Ensuring the flow of oil from the Gulf (reflagging of Kuwaiti ships)

Phase V (1990–Present)

1. Resolving the Arab-Israeli conflict
2. Supporting Israel and "moderate" Arab regimes
3. Maintaining regional peace
4. Containing "radical" regimes (Iran, Iraq, Libya)
5. Stopping the proliferation of weapons of mass destruction
6. Protecting oil production in the Gulf
7. Responding to Islamic fundamentalism and ultranationalism

As illustrated in phase V, the challenges facing the United States in the Middle East today are enormous. While progress has been made in the peace process (Egypt, Jordan, and the PLO have signed peace agreements with Israel), forces of extremism continue to challenge America. While conflict with the former Soviet Union was resolved, proponents of Islamic fundamentalism and Jewish extremism pose the greatest challenge to the peace process. As evidenced by the assassination of Israeli Prime Minister Yitzhak Rabin, who was shot by a member of a Jewish extremist organization, these groups will not hesitate to use violence to accomplish their goals.

It is clear that the Middle East is a vital region for the United States and the West. The importance of the region's oil resources will compel the United States to maintain a presence there. America's military superiority cannot be questioned. However, it does not mean that its presence in the region will not be challenged. The U.S. relations with Iraq, Iran, Libya, and Syria are less than cordial. American nationals are still prohibited from visiting Lebanon (for security reasons) and American installations continue to be targeted by anti-Western groups. Nevertheless, the United States continues to play the role of a mediator and the guarantor of the security of Israel and the moderate Arab states.

The end of the Cold War and the consequences of the Gulf War created new realities in the region:

1. The Soviet Union lost its superpower status in the region. States like Libya, Syria, and Iraq, which relied on Soviet weapons, have to look for other suppliers of weapons.

2. The myths of Arab unity and the pro-Arab nationalist ideas were shattered. The Gulf War pitted Arab against Arab and demonstrated that Arab states were more concerned about promoting their own interests rather than pursuing the ideas of Arab unity and pan-Arabism.

3. Arab states became increasingly indifferent to the plight of the Palestinian people. This explains, in part, the PLO's decision to pursue direct negotiations with Israel. By siding with Iraq during the Gulf War, the PLO alienated its wealthy backers in the Gulf region.

4. Pro-American regimes in the oil-rich states emerged as the key players in Arab politics after the war.

5. The United States strengthened its ties with the Gulf states and enhanced its role as their protector.[68]

POLICY OPTIONS: PROS AND CONS

Before evaluating the U.S. foreign policy options in the Middle East, it is useful to analyze the determinants of U.S. foreign policy. To this end, we sought to construct a conceptual framework composed of five variables:

1. Domestic politics and the societal variables
2. The decision-making process
3. Economic variables
4. Geopolitical variables
5. Personality traits of American presidents

It has been argued that a state's foreign policy is an extension of its domestic political environment. Certainly, the interplay between domestic and foreign policies cannot be underestimated.[69] Obviously, in a democracy public opinion is a key factor in influencing leaders' decisions. In the case of the United States, the president is influenced by his close advisors, cabinet members, Congress, interest groups, the media, and public opinion.[70] In evaluating America's Middle East policy, we can argue that interest groups and Congress play a key role in shaping and influencing it. The American-Israeli Public Affairs Committee (AIPAC), one of the most powerful lobbying groups in the United States, plays an instrumental role in lobbying both the president and Congress for increased economic and military aid for Israel. On the Arab side, the American-Arab Anti-Discrimination Committee, among other groups, seeks to represent the Arab view.

The role of Congress in making America's foreign policy is significant. It fills a number of important tasks. First, it appropriates funds for foreign aid. Second, it legislates laws that often guide U.S. foreign policy. Third, it oversees foreign policy decisions by holding hearings. Fourth, it has the power to reject treaties signed by the president. Indeed, in order for a treaty to be binding, it must be ratified by the Senate. Finally, Congress plays an important role in debating foreign policy issues and in educating the public about such issues.[71] AIPAC has been very successful in lobbying Congress on behalf of Israel. For the past decade, Israel has been receiving $3 billion annually in grants from the U.S. government. In 1993, total contributions to Israel from the United States (including special deals and loan guarantees) totaled $6.3 billion.[72] In 1995, despite delays in congressional approval of the foreign appropriations bills, House Speaker Newt Gingrich promised Israeli Ambassador Itamar Rabinovich to "speed up" approval of Israel's aid package.[73]

The media plays a critical role in influencing not only the public views but also views of decision makers. The American media traditionally gave considerable attention to Israel, which has often been portrayed as a key ally, a strategic asset, and the only democracy in the Middle East. Thomas Friedman suggests that Israel receives so much attention because of cultural and religious factors (Israel is in the Bible) and that "the whole notion of Israel is deeply embedded in the American psyche and consciousness.... Israel gets widely reported in the American media which creates a sense of familiarity.... We like whom we know and we know the Israeli."[74] Certainly, supporters of the Arabs have often complained about the pro-Israeli bias in the American media.

The decision-making process is a useful tool in analyzing foreign policy behavior. In making decisions, leaders are often influenced by the views and ideas of their close advisors. In addition, decisions are usually a result of compromises along competing organizational interests and bureaucratic pressures.[75] Ultimately, however, decision makers are influenced by the interaction of structure and process and by their perception of the situation. Hence, with a pro-Israeli Congress, AIPAC, media attention to Israel, and close advisors sympathetic to Israel, it is unlikely that a president will adopt an anti-Israeli stance.

Economic variables are important determinants of foreign policy. In the Middle East, protection of petroleum production has been a top priority in American foreign policy. Ever since Franklin D. Roosevelt established contacts with Ibn Saud in the mid-1930s, the United States has sought to ensure the flow of oil. Indeed, the Persian Gulf War was fought to prevent a hostile power (Iraq) from gaining control of the region's oil resources.

At the geopolitical level, containing Soviet communism was also a major foreign policy objective for the United States. In the mid-1950s, Washington was instrumental in establishing a British-led anti-Soviet alliance in the Middle East—the Baghdad Pact. The pact, however, was short-lived, since most Arab countries refused to join, claiming that their problems were not with Soviet expansionism, but with Zionism and Western imperialism.

Washington's close commitment to Israel alienated many Arab states and pushed them to the Soviet camp.

Finally, we cannot ignore the importance of the character of the president as well as his predispositions. One way to explain President Eisenhower's view of Israel is his background as a general. He revealed during his presidency that had he been president in 1948, he might not have recognized Israel. Johnson expressed his admiration of Israel by telling visitors that he read about the Jewish state in Sunday school and that he equated Israelis with Texans and Arabs with Mexicans.[76] To be sure, Jimmy Carter's religious devotion and attachment to high moral principles explain his position on the right of the Palestinian people to live in peace and dignity.

From the previous discussion, we can conclude that domestic politics, economic variables, and geopolitical considerations were the most important determinants of U.S. policy toward the Middle East during the Cold War. In the post-World War II era, the United States was preoccupied with fighting communism. Clearly, Washington does not have to worry about this Soviet threat today.

The Clinton administration put forth four major principles for the United States in the New World Order: First, to lead the world in order to promote international stability; second, to seek productive political and economic relations with major powers; third, to build strong and stable international institutions to enhance cooperation among states; and finally, to support human rights and democratic values.[77]

The United States is certainly attempting to lead in the Middle East. Secretary of State Warren Christopher made it clear that the United States will continue to protect its allies and its vital interests from threats posed by "rogue" states such as Iran, Iraq, and Libya.[78] Hence, containment shifted from containing the Soviet Union to containing mischievous regional powers. Being the foremost military power in the world today, the United States is tempted to use its formidable fighting force not only to defend its vital interests (*a la* the Gulf War), but to enforce peace (the deployment of twenty thousand American troops in Bosnia). While Clinton's Bosnian policy has been criticized, even the administration's critics agree that America, as the only global power, must lead. Furthermore, few would disagree with Clinton's goal in the Persian Gulf—to maintain access to oil.[79]

Concerning the Arab-Israeli conflict, the United States must continue to urge the disputing parties to negotiate and to seek peaceful settlements for their disputes. Previous administrations have focused on the Soviet threat, Israel's security, and oil. Today, the United States must endeavor to adopt a coherent foreign policy that promotes regional peace and stability. While progress has been made, much work has to be done in promoting peace between Israel and the rest of the Arab world. In addition, states like Iran continue to oppose the peace process and to support extremist groups that seek to undermine it.

The United States must continue to play the role of the peacemaker in the Middle East. It is the only power that can play such a role. As one senior administration official put it: "Without the United States' constant nurturing of the peace process, that process would not go forward…. A lot of reassurance is needed, and they have looked to the United States for that reassurance."[80] One of the important goals of the United States should be to promote economic growth in the Middle East. While Secretary of State Christopher argued that promoting sustainable growth is a strategic American principle,[81] the Palestinian Authority in Gaza and the West Bank has not received promised and much-needed funds. For peace to work, it has to be augmented with economic and political support.

Recently, the Clinton administration has articulated a policy on Islam and Islamism. The crux of this policy is that Islam is not a threat to American or Western interests. Clinton rejected the argument that Islam is incompatible with the West. America's quarrel, the President maintained, is with those extremists "who cloak themselves in the rhetoric of religion and nationalism, but behave in ways that contradict the very teachings of their faith."[82] The President's national security advisor Anthony Lake reiterated Clinton's position by rejecting the notion that traditional Islamic values contradict western democratic principles.[83] We believe that this is a prudent approach to the question of Islam. In the Western media, there is a tendency to associate acts of violence committed by fanatics in the name of Islam to the Islamic culture. The fact is that the vast majority of Muslims renounce terrorism and violence. The administration, however, has to balance its support to its traditional allies, particularly Egypt, with the need to focus on the aspirations of disenchanted and alienated segments of the population that see in Islamic organizations alternatives to repressive regimes.

POLICY RECOMMENDATIONS FOR THE TWENTY-FIRST CENTURY

As we approach the twenty-first century, the United States faces new realities in the Middle East. The Soviet empire has collapsed, and no other major power seems to be capable or willing to challenge the United States in the region. It is easy for the United States to become complacent, basking in the glory of its victory over communism in the Cold War and over Iraq in the Gulf war. In reality, there is much work to be done in order to maintain progress toward peace and democratization. For the post-Cold War era and the years to come, we outline some policy recommendations.

PEACE PROCESS

The United States must continue its efforts to resolve the Arab-Israeli conflict and to bring peace to the region. While progress has been made, the momentum for peace must be maintained. So far, the United States has been acting as a mediator, but it may be called upon to play a more active role on the Israeli-Syrian front. In the ongoing negotiations between the two countries, there are suggestions to deploy American troops on the Golan Heights to act as a "buffer" between the two states. The United States must pursue peace with determination and vigor, since it is the only country that has the resources and the will to lead. U.N. Security Council Resolutions 242 and 338 offer the best formula for peace. If peace is to be achieved, the Arabs must offer Israel peace and recognition, and Israel must relinquish control of the territories it conquered in the 1967 war. Most people in the area are yearning for peace, and the United States can help make peace a reality.

STRENGTHENING THE UNITED NATIONS

The United States will do well to strengthen the United Nations. With the end of the Cold War, there was a great deal of optimism that a new era of cooperation will replace the ideological antagonism of the bipolar world. Unfortunately, the world today is not necessarily more stable than it was prior to 1990. The United States must endeavor to empower international organizations to promote collective security and economic and social welfare of all peoples. The United Nations can play an important role in helping the Palestinian Authority in Gaza and the West Bank and can help states make better use of their resources. Strengthening the United Nations is compatible with the Clinton administration's goal of building lasting global and regional institutions.[84]

DETERRING WARS OR REGIONAL CONFLICTS

America's ability to deploy troops in the Middle East and to project military power there put it in an advantageous position to deter aggression by hostile forces. It is clear that the confrontation is between forces of moderation and extremism (whether Arab or Israeli). The true clash, a Pentagon official said, is "within civilizations, between extremists and moderates."[85] The containment strategy is now applied to Iran, Iraq, and Libya. Hence the new strategy is "triple containment." The United States should work hard to promote democracy within these states. This, however, may not be an easy task to accomplish. Some argue that Bush's decision to dispatch troops to the Gulf was motivated by strategic, not economic, factors: to stop an aggressive, radical, and anti-American regime from gaining control over oil supplies.[86]

SUPPORTING ALLIES AND PROMOTING ECONOMIC PROSPERITY

The United States must demonstrate its commitment to support its allies. This can be military (against aggressor states) and/or economic. With the collapse of the Soviet Union, there will be less need for military build-up in the region. The fact that Iran is buying weapons from China and North Korea should not compel the United States to escalate the arms race in the region.

Rather, a policy of containment and deterrence, coupled with sustained economic support of friendly regimes, will best promote American interests.
While the United States must maintain its commitment to aid its allies economically, it is necessary to support new arrangements that will promote free
trade. Enhancing the General Agreement on Tariffs and Trade (GATT),
recently replaced by the World Trade Organization (WTO), which is
designed to reduce tariffs and promote international trade, is a step in the
right direction. More importantly, the Arab League must be empowered to
deal with the region's economic, as well as political, problems. A redistribution of wealth is in order in a region where there is a huge disparity between
the oil-rich states and the rest of the Arab world. In the long run, the objective should be to develop a regional balance of power that will protect
America's allies and maintain the flow of oil. In its recent meeting in Muscat,
Oman, in November 1995, the six-nation Gulf Cooperation Council, which
includes Saudi Arabia, Kuwait, Oman, Qatar, Bahrain, and the United Arab
Emirates, expressed concerns about regional security.[87] The United States
must aim for a policy of regional self-reliance in the Gulf.[88] Eventually, this will
allow it to play the role of a balancer and conciliator rather than protector.

PROMOTING DEMOCRATIC VALUES

Recognizing the fact that democracy is not a value-free concept, the United
States must expend efforts to promote democratic principles. This must be
done while acknowledging cultural differences and sensitivities. Islam as a religion promotes democracy, consensus, and cooperation. In the Islamic political thought, an ideal ruler must demonstrate justice, compassion, and benev-
olence. These principles are not incompatible with Western democratic values. The Clinton administration is on the right track when it emphasizes that
it has no quarrel with Islam. Indeed, the problem is with extremists, whatever
their religious persuasion may be. Those who reject compromise and accommodation are the real obstacle to peace and democracy. In the final analysis,
peace and democracy are interconnected: You cannot have peace without
democracy and, conversely, you cannot have democracy without peace. As
Boutros Boutros-Ghali, the United Nations Secretary-General, put it:

> Peace is a pre-requisite to development; democracy is essential if devel-
> opment is to succeed over the long term. The real development of a state
> must be based on participation of its population.... Without peace, there
> can be no development and there can be no democracy.[89]

CONTROLLING THE ARMS RACE

Over the past few decades, hundreds of billions of dollars have been spent on
armaments. The Arab-Israeli conflict and the Iran-Iraq war, in addition to
regional rivalries, escalated the arms race and enhanced the probability of
wars and military conflicts as a means to resolve disputes. During the Cold

War era, both superpowers provided sophisticated weapons to the belligerent states. With the collapse of the Soviet empire, the crippling of Iraq's military capability, and the progress in the peace process, conditions are ripe for a policy of arms control and counterproliferation of weapons of mass destruction. America's "dual containment" policy against Iraq and Iran is intended to deter aggressive behavior and to discourage attempts to acquire weapons of mass destruction by these two states. In fact, the United States has threatened to retaliate against states that might contemplate the use of weapons of mass destruction.[90] This threat, of course, is intended to deter Iraq and Iran from using such weapons. Our recommendation, however, is that the United States should pursue an objective of a nuclear-free Middle East. Only one state in the region has nuclear capability (Israel), and as long as Israel retains this capability, other states may be tempted to acquire it. Israel has refused to sign the Nuclear Non-proliferation Treaty, which compelled other states, including Egypt, to threaten rejection of the treaty as well.[91] With progress in the peace process, it is more likely for states to agree on guidelines for arms control.

In a dynamic and ever-changing world, the United States, as the sole superpower, must be prepared to assert its leadership. With leadership, however, comes responsibility. Hence, America must resist the temptation to act as the gendarme of the world, but should bring its power to bear against aggression, whether in the Middle East or elsewhere. In this new post-Cold War era, we face new challenges and problems: extremism, intense nationalism, terrorism, dwindling resources, regional conflicts, underdevelopment, environmental and ecological problems. As countries become increasingly interdependent, America must use its resources and resolve to help shape a more peaceful, democratic, and prosperous world.

NOTES

1. See George Lenczowski, ed., *United States Interests in the Middle East* (Washington, D.C.: American Enterprise Institute, 1968).

2. As cited in John N. Moore, ed., *The Arab-Israeli Conflict: Readings and Documents* (Princeton, NJ: Princeton University Press, 1977), p. 884.

3. See Richard Cottam, "The United States and Palestine," in *The Transformation of Palestine*, Ibrahim Abu Lughod, ed. (Evanston, IL: Northwestern University Press, 1971).

4. Evan Wilson, "The Palestine Papers, 1943–1947," *Journal of Palestine Studies* 2, no. 4 (Summer 1973).

5. Daniel C. Diller, "The Middle East," *Congressional Quarterly* (Washington, D.C.: 1994), p. 62.

6. Quoted in George Lenczowski, *American Presidents and the Middle East* (Durham, NC: Duke University Press, 1990), p. 28.

7. Ibid., p. 24.

8. Joe Stark, "U.S. Policy and the Palestine Question," in *The United States and the Middle East*, Hooshang Amirahmadi, ed. (Albany: State University of New York Press, 1993), p. 130.

9. Cited in John Spanier and Steven Hook, *American Foreign Policy since World War II* (Washington, D.C.: Congressional Quarterly Inc., 1995), p. 42.
10. Ibid., p. 43.
11. Fayez Sayegh, ed., *The Dynamics of Neutralism in the Arab World* (San Francisco, CA: Chandler Press, 1964), p. 5.
12. Spanier and Hook, *American Foreign Policy since World War II*, p. 113.
13. Alan Taylor, *The Superpowers and the Middle East* (Syracuse, NY: Syracuse University Press, 1991), p. 59.
14. Cited in Lenczowski, *American Presidents and the Middle East*, p. 52.
15. Taylor, *The Superpowers and the Middle East*, p. 60.
16. Diller, "The Middle East," p. 64.
17. Spanier and Hook, *American Foreign Policy since World War II*, p. 118.
18. Stark, "U.S. Policy and the Palestine Question," p. 132.
19. See T. G. Fraser, *The U.S.A. and the Middle East since World War II* (New York: St. Martin's Press, 1989), p. 81.
20. Ibid., p. 82.
21. Ibid., p. 83.
22. See Taylor, *The Superpowers and the Middle East*, p. 77.
23. William Quandt, *Decade of Decisions: American Policy toward the Arab-Israeli Conflict, 1967–1976* (Berkeley: University of California Press, 1977), pp. 57–59.
24. Stephen Green, *Taking Sides: America's Secret Relations with a Militant Israel* (New York: William Morrow, 1984), p. 199.
25. Taylor, *The Superpowers and the Middle East*, p. 79.
26. For the field text of U.N. Resolution 242, see William Quandt, *Camp David: Peacemaking and Politics* (Washington, D.C.: The Brookings Institution, 1986), pp. 341–342.
27. Cited in Ralph H. Magnus, ed., *Documents on the Middle East* (Washington, D.C.: American Enterprise Institute, 1969), p. 223.
28. See Henry Kissinger, *White House Years* (Boston, MA: Little, Brown, 1979), p. 224.
29. See *The New York Times*, December 11, 1969.
30. Lenczowski, *American Presidents and the Middle East*, p. 123.
31. Richard Nixon, *The Memoirs of Richard Nixon*, vol. 1 (New York: Warner Books, 1978), p. 593.
32. Lenczowski, *American Presidents and the Middle East*, p. 128.
33. Ibid., p. 131.
34. Steven L. Spiegel, *The Other Arab-Israeli Conflict: Making America's Middle East Policy, from Truman to Reagan* (Chicago, IL: The University of Chicago Press, 1985), p. 220.
35. U.N. Security Council Resolution 338 (Oct. 22, 1973) called upon the parties to terminate all military activity immediately and to implement Resolution 242. See full text in Quandt, *Camp David*, p. 342.
36. Lenczowski, *American Presidents and the Middle East*, p. 135.
37. Edward Sheehan, *The Arabs, Israelis, and Kissinger: A Short History of American Diplomacy in the Middle East* (New York: Readers Digest Press, 1976), p. 68.
38. Cited in Lenczowski, *American Presidents and the Middle East*, p. 149.
39. See text of agreement in Sheehan, *The Arabs, Israelis, and Kissinger*, pp. 245–250.
40. Taylor, *The Superpowers and the Middle East*, p. 90.
41. I. Fahmy, *Negotiating for Peace in the Middle East* (London: Croom Helm Press, 1983), p. 164.
42. Lenczowski, *American Presidents and the Middle East*, p. 153.
43. Quoted from Taylor, *The Superpowers and the Middle East*, p. 92.
44. Lenczowski, *American Presidents and the Middle East*, p. 157.

45. Jimmy Carter, *Keeping Faith: Memoirs of a President* (New York: Bantam Books, 1982), p. 277.
46. Cited in Fraser, *The U.S.A. and the Middle East since World War II*, p. 141.
47. Carter, *Keeping Faith*, p. 149.
48. Ibid., p. 290.
49. Ibid., p. 291.
50. For the text of the Camp David Accords, see Quandt, *Camp David*, pp. 397–401.
51. Ibid., p. 399.
52. See Harold Sanders, "American Diplomacy and Arab-Israeli Peace since 1977," in *Security in the Middle East*, Samuel Wells and Mark Bruzonsky, eds. (Boulder, CO: Westview Press, 1987), p. 292.
53. See Jean Kirkpatrick and Allan Gerson, "The Reagan Doctrine, Human Rights, and International Law," in *Right v. Might: International Law and the Use of Force*, Lewis Henkin, et al., eds. (New York: Council on Foreign Relations, 1991), p. 20.
54. Spanier and Hook, *American Foreign Policy since World War II*, p. 207.
55. For the full text of Reagan's speech, see William Quandt, *Peace Process* (Washington, D.C.: The Brookings Institution, 1993), pp. 476–483.
56. Diller, "The Middle East," p. 85.
57. Ibid., p. 83.
58. Ibid., p. 85.
59. Leon T. Hadar, *Quagmire: America in the Middle East* (Washington, D.C.: The Cato Institute, 1992), p. 141.
60. See Moshe Arens, *Broken Covenant* (New York: Simon & Schuster, 1995).
61. For more information on the Gulf War, see M. L. Sifrey and Christopher Cerf, eds., *The Gulf War Reader: History, Documents, Opinions* (New York: Random House, 1991). See also Ghassan E. El-Eid, "Roots of the Gulf War: Historical Factors, Personality Traits, and Ideological Variables." Paper presented at the Gulf War Conference, University of Hartford, Hartford, CT, March 1991.
62. Cited in Diller, "The Middle East," p. 89.
63. Bruce W. Jentleson, "The Pretty Prudent Public: Post-Vietnam American Opinion on the Use of Military Force," in *The Domestic Sources of American Foreign Policy*, Eugene R. Wittkopf, ed. (New York: St. Martin's Press, 1994), p. 71.
64. See Michael Gordon and Bernard Trainor, *The General's War: The Inside Story of the Conflict in the Gulf* (Boston, MA: Little, Brown, and Co., 1995), p. 34.
65. For a discussion of the role of the United Nations in the post-Cold War era, see Ghassan El-Eid, "The UN in the Post-Cold War Era: The Quest for Collective Security," in *Democracy and New International Order in the 21st Century*, J Yill Ra, ed. (Seoul, South Korea: Center for the Reconstruction of Human Society, 1993), pp. 322–334.
66. Cited by David Makovsky, *Making Peace with the PLO: The Rabin Government's Road to the Oslo Accord* (Boulder, CO: Westview Press, 1996), p. 228.
67. Ibid., p. 229.
68. See Barry Rubin, "America and the Middle East in the Post-Cold War World," in *Eagle in New World: American Grand Strategy in the Post-Cold War Era*, Kenneth Oye, et al., eds. (New York: Harper Collins, 1992), p. 424.
69. See James N. Rosenau, *The Scientific Study of Foreign Policy* (New York: The Free Press, 1971).
70. Eugene R. Wittkopf, *The Domestic Sources of American Foreign Policy* (New York: St. Martin's Press, 1994), p. 146.
71. Raymond Wolfinger, "Structural and Generational Changes in Congress, and the Role of Congress in U.S. Foreign Policy," in *U.S. Middle East Policy: The Domestic Setting*, Shai Feldman, ed. (Boulder, CO: Westview Press, 1988), pp. 8–9.

72. *Middle East International,* July 21, 1995, p. 8.
73. *The Jerusalem Post,* November 29, 1995, p. 2.
74. Thomas Friedman, "The U.S. Media and the Middle East," *U.S. Middle East Policy,* Feldman, ed., p. 36.
75. Graham Allison, *The Essence of Decision: Explaining the Cuban Missile Crisis* (Boston, MA: Little, Brown, and Co., 1971), p. 6.
76. Steven Spiegel, "The Presidency and the NSC Staff," in *U.S. Middle East Policy,* Feldman, ed., p. 12.
77. Warren Christopher, "America's Leadership, America's Opportunity," *Foreign Policy* 98 (Spring 1995): 6.
78. Ibid., p. 7.
79. Bob Dole, "Shaping America's Global Future," *Foreign Policy* 98 (Spring 1995): 35.
80. *The New York Times,* September 26, 1995, p. A1.
81. Christopher, "America's Leadership, America's Opportunity," p. 16.
82. See *The Economist,* August 26, 1995, p. 25.
83. Ibid., p. 26.
84. See Christopher, "America's Leadership, America's Opportunity," p. 13.
85. *Middle East International,* August 4, 1995, p. 16.
86. Rubin, "America and the Middle East in the Post-Cold War World," p. 428.
87. *Al-Sharq Al-Awsat,* December 4, 1995.
88. See Charles W. Maynes, "A Workable Clinton Doctrine," *Foreign Policy* 93 (Winter 1993–94): 10.
89. Cited in Bruce Russett and Harvey Starr, *World Politics: The Menu for Choice* (New York: W. H. Freeman & Co., 1996), p. 466.
90. *Middle East International,* August 4, 1995, p. 17.
91. *The New York Times,* March 9, 1995, p. 3.

CHAPTER 9

AMERICAN POLICY
TOWARD AFRICA

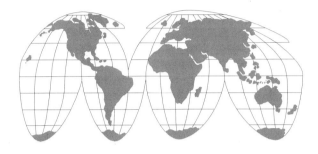

WALTON L. BROWN

America is uniquely brought closer to Africa by historical ties.
Cheikh Anta Diop, 1985

The end of the Cold War has compelled a rethinking and reformulation of the American role in the international system. The fundamental question is: How have the end of the Cold War and the collapse of the Soviet Union altered the definition of U.S. interests in the international system? Additionally, questions arise as to the principal regions and nations that will threaten or advance U.S. interests in the international system; and, what strategies and instruments of policy will be necessary for the United States to defend and advance its interests? The instruments of U.S. foreign policy—economic, diplomatic, and military—used during the Cold War may not be equally effective in the post-Cold War international system. The answers to these questions and more will determine the future direction of U.S. policy. As U.S. grand strategy in the international system is reassessed and formulated, so too will be U.S. policy toward the nations on the continent of Africa.

In general, the process of U.S. foreign policy making is affected by several major factors: the external environmental factors (bipolar, multipolar, etc.), societal factors (interest groups, culture, values, ideology, etc.), governmental (bureaucracies, legislatures) and individual factors (personality of the actors, especially presidents).[1] The relative impact that each factor has upon the decision making process depends upon the level of importance attached to the issue. Foreign policy is not made in a vacuum, nor is it implemented in a vacuum. There are both causes and consequences of policy formulation and implementation.

Readily identifiable factors have determined the U.S. approach to the formulation and implementation of its Africa policy. These factors have worked together over time to stultify the development of policies that will lead to a lucid set of U.S. goals and interests in Africa and the development of cohesive strategies to foster those goals and interests in the post-Cold War era. They are as follows:

1. National security bureaucracies have been the primary institutional forces driving U.S. Africa policies. Africa policy is generally entrenched in the State Department, National Security Agency, and the CIA due to the neglect of Congress and the president during non-crisis situations.

2. The role of executive/presidential influence in the formulation and implementation of U.S. Africa policies occurs most frequently during crisis situations—crisis situations that involve strategic interests or the interests of other allies, mainly European, in the region.

3. U.S. Africa policies have depended upon the following set of factors:

   a. The existing role and interests of the European powers—U.S. allies—during colonialism and after decolonization

   b. The level of Soviet influence in Africa during the Cold War

   c. Prevailing perceptual problems such as lack of clarity as to who Africans are and what Africa is[2] and pessimism about Africa's past and future

4. The level of domestic interest group participation in the formulation of U.S. Africa policy depends upon the amount of media attention given to the issue and the prolonged nature of the issue. The anti-apartheid movement in the United States or the famine in Ethiopia and Somalia, for example, gained momentum not only because of the amount of media attention given to them, but the prolongation of the crises.

If U.S. relations with the nations on the continent of Africa are to withstand the uncertainties of the post-Cold War transformation of the international system, the nature of U.S.-Africa relations before and during the Cold War must be revisited. This chapter covers the historical background of U.S. Africa policy, U.S. interests in Africa, the challenges and opportunities of U.S. Africa policy, the pros and cons of policy options, and some recommendations for the twenty-first century. The following questions underlie the discussion in the chapter: What factors have most influenced the development and implementation of U.S. Africa policy? What have been the patterns of U.S. Africa policy during and immediately after the end of the Cold War? What was the nature of U.S. Africa policy during the Carter, Reagan, Bush, and Clinton administrations? What are the possible policy directions for U.S. Africa policy in the future? The chapter discusses in detail one case of U.S. Africa policy during the Cold War—Zaire, 1960; and one case of U.S. post-Cold War Africa policy—the Horn of Africa—especially U.S. intervention in Somalia in 1992.

HISTORICAL BACKGROUND

Despite the historic cultural and human linkages to Africa that date before the founding of the republic in 1789, for most U.S. citizens and policy makers Africa has never assumed a high level of importance, except during moments in which large-scale human catastrophe or major political upheavals capture the attentions of the American press and public.[3] Apart from those periods of catastrophe and political upheaval, U.S. policy toward Africa is best characterized as indifferent; at worst, nearly nonexistent.

During the last three decades of the nineteenth century the international economic system, centered in Europe, was near collapse—resources and profits were unstable. The European "scramble" for African colonies accelerated. The colonization process incorporated Africa into the "global order" of the nineteenth century and first half of the twentieth century as an appendage of Europe. European hegemony in Africa marginalized the continent's position in the international system. Despite its long participation in the African slave trade and the establishment of Liberia as a solution to its free slave "problem," after the Civil War the United States maintained little if any direct involvement in Africa. Africa was considered to be a primarily European area of interest and influence. This attitude toward Africa led the United States to follow the lead of Africa's colonial powers—mainly Britain, France, Germany, the Netherlands, Belgium, Spain, and Portugal.

The Second World War left the majority of European colonial powers unable to maintain control of their colonial empires. Most of the colonial powers extracted resources, human and natural, from their colonies in order to support their war efforts. African troops were essential to the French in their military campaigns in Southeast Asia. U.S. strategic interests in Africa during the war included stemming the tide of Italian expansionism into Ethiopia and the Nazi campaigns in the Sahara. Liberian airfield facilities were used in the U.S. war effort against the Nazis in North Africa.

At the end of World War II, the United States was ill-prepared for the rising tide of independence that was to eventually alter the international status quo between the nations in the north and those in the south; the status quo between colonizer and colonized. The United States continued to view Africa as a primarily European sphere of influence. For fear of "radical" political movements in the international system, the United States was initially not a vociferous proponent of the emerging independence movements in Africa or other areas of the colonial world after the war. The level of direct U.S. interest in Africa began to change, however, at the onset of the Cold War. At that point, U.S. policy makers began to consider Africa in terms of the prospects for the development of ideological and strategic allies on the continent.

In 1957, U.S. Vice President Richard Nixon recommended the creation of a separate Bureau of African Affairs in the State Department: It was created in 1958. The Bureau made a significant decision that defined the U.S. concept of Africa. It placed North African issues within the auspices of the bureau responsible for Mideastern affairs and defined the rest of the continent as "sub-Saharan."[4] This concept of Africa rejected the view that the continent should be approached as a whole and, therefore, placed limitations on the ability of policy makers to make a full assessment of the intracontinental forces and factors influencing change in Africa.

In 1957, Senator John F. Kennedy also warned of Africa's impending importance to the United States: "The only real question is whether these new nations will look West or East—to Moscow or Washington—for sympathy, help, and guidance in their effort to recapitulate in a few decades the entire history of modern Europe and America."[5] At that point in U.S. foreign policy, Africa was about to experience its few moments of glory in the U.S. policy agenda, but only as the United States undertook to formulate a global strategy to counter Soviet initiatives on the continent.

THE COLD WAR AND U.S. POLICY

The direction of U.S. foreign policy during the Cold War was a reflection of both U.S. values and interests. Adherents of political realism and the "reason of the state" schools of thought believe that policy actions were based solely and strictly on the pursuit of tangible interests. This theoretical position, however, does not explain in total U.S. foreign policy behavior. Ethical principles and values also affect the decision-making processes that lead to the identification of interests as well as the way in which policy makers justify and seek to legitimize their policy decisions.[6] During the Cold War, U.S. policy toward the nations on the African continent was linked to its interests and relations with its European allies before and after World War II; its Cold War geostrategic interests; and its ethical beliefs about the "evils" of communism, the spread of Soviet influence, and "revolutionary" regimes. The principle of containing the Soviet Union both dominated and simplified U.S. policy choices and behavior for forty-five years.

The post-World War II global order was a bipolar configuration that legitimized the continued competition for the control of African resources and influence over African governments. The post-World War II superpower rivalry in Africa led to the bolstering of corrupt dictatorships and military regimes by the Western powers and the reliance of many nations upon the political and economic support of the Soviet Union and Eastern European bloc. For more than four decades after World War II, the superpowers were involved, directly and indirectly, in African domestic and regional politics.

The restructuring of the global system and the decline of Europe after World War II raised the political and economic hopes of the newly independent African nations. During the 1960s, the decade of independence, Africa's political visibility in the international system increased. The fervor of political independence was, however, quickly dashed by the new realities of the Cold War and the emergence of neocolonial ties that continued to bind

African nations to the economies of the former colonial powers, other Western industrialized nations, and international lending institutions.

Few nations on the continent attempted to completely overhaul the political and economic institutions and structures left to them by the colonial powers. Some nations, such as the former French colonies, consciously chose to continue neocolonial ties with France.[7] All, however, entered the web of the restructured post-World War II global political and economic system with political and economic vulnerabilities. The onset of the Cold War between the two superpowers also legitimized the continuation of European influence in Africa. In retrospect it is clear that: "...with the development of the Western strategy of containment, the Europeans were able to obtain not only the tacit consent of the United States for their continued presence in Africa but their involvement in it."[8]

In order to limit Soviet expansion in Africa the United States used economic and political incentives to seek influence in the emerging nations of the continent. The emphasis upon the Cold War blurred the ability of U.S. policy makers to distinguish the internal political forces of nationalism as the cause of domestic instability from external Soviet pressure. The pattern of U.S. involvement in the changing politics of the continent was fully established during the Congo (Zaire) crisis in 1960.

THE CONGO CRISIS: A CASE OF U.S. COLD WAR AFRICA POLICY

Five days after Zaire's (the Belgian Congo) independence in July 1960, the Zairian military began to mutiny against their Belgian commanders. Riots and unrest spread throughout the nation, and Belgian troops intervened. The wealthiest territory, Katanga (Shaba) province, declared independence and attempted to secede from the country; another province, South Kasai, also declared independence one month later. The attempted secession of Katanga province was aided by the Belgian economic interests that maintained control of the copper mines in the region. In essence, the newly independent state of Zaire was in the process of disintegrating five days after its independence and was once again occupied by Belgian troops. Neither the United Nations nor the new government of Zaire was able to tolerate the immediate crisis of national disintegration.

In response to this postcolonial crisis, Zaire's new leaders, Patrice Lumumba and Joseph Kasavubu, appealed to the United Nations to provide protection against Belgian reoccupation. Initially, the United States did not respond to the crisis, leaving it to Belgium because of the latter's historical role in the region. U.S. attention to the crisis heightened after Lumumba and Kasavubu broke relations with the United Nations and announced their intention to seek help from the Soviet Union to expel the Belgian troops. In August 1960, Lumumba followed through on the announced intention and formally broke ties with the United Nations because of the inability of its forces to drive the Belgians out of Zaire.

The prospect of a Soviet presence in Central Africa gained the attention of U.S. policy makers. The crisis became one of major importance to the United States. Patrice Lumumba, especially, was of concern to policy makers (Kasavubu was eventually cultivated by the CIA and broke with Lumumba). He came to be viewed as the next "Castro." This image of Lumumba prevailed in the national security bureaucracies of the CIA and the State Department. Soviet technicians arrived in Zaire shortly after Lumumba's official break with the United Nations, and the United States immediately labeled Lumumba a Soviet client. Covert U.S. actions in the nation eventually led to the ouster, arrest, and assassination of Lumumba, and the eventual installation of the present (1996) U.S.-supported leader, Mobutu Seso Seko.[9]

THE CONSEQUENCES OF THE ZAIRIAN CASE

The Zairian case established several elements of U.S. policy in Africa that would continue throughout the Cold War: the avoidance of direct military intervention and the reliance on covert/indirect forms of intervention; containment of the Soviet Union; and the cultivation of pro-American leaders in Africa. The pattern of U.S. indirect support of seemingly pro-Western and anti-Soviet leadership in Africa continued throughout the Cold War. The United States did not become directly involved in military conflicts on the continent, choosing instead to extend military and economic aid to pro-Western, anti-Soviet actors in crisis after crisis.

In cases where there was no immediate Soviet threat, the United States supported policy actions that favored either the use of third parties to resolve the conflict or other actions that were considered to be preventative in nature. This policy approach often had dire consequences for the nations and peoples involved. The decision to support Ethiopian control of Eritrea sparked a civil war that lasted for thirty years, until Eritrean independence in 1993, for example. U.S. support of the apartheid regime in South Africa as the "only" bulwark of democracy in Africa not only prolonged the viability of the regime, but helped to prolong the level of domestic repression and violence of the regime against the majority population.

Throughout the Cold War, the United States continued to support Portugal against the anticolonial movements in Angola and Mozambique that had adopted a Marxist political orientation. In Angola, the United States continued to back Jonas Savimbi and UNITA (National Union for the Total Independence of Angola), which waged a civil war (1974–1995) against the Marxist government that had come to power in 1974. U.S. support of UNITA and the civil war hindered Angola's development potential for two decades. This did not change until the Clinton administration formally recognized the Marxist Angolan government in 1992, but congressional support for UNITA still lingered.

The emphasis upon Cold War global strategy and security issues in the formulation of U.S. policy prevented the development of long-term sustainable interests in Africa that the U.S. could continue to pursue after the cessation of the Cold War. Strategy based on the Cold War required that Washington support African regimes that were antithetical to basic American democratic values, and the United States developed a reputation as an opponent of political change and social-economic progress in Africa. The legacy of Washington's Cold War policies of expediency, in the name of Soviet containment, limited the development of stable African political regimes and prosperous economies.

FROM CARTER TO REAGAN

The Carter administration attempted to abandon the postwar containment approach in its formulation of U.S. Africa policy. Although labeled a moralist, Carter's approach was based upon practical and realistic assumptions about the limits of U.S. power in Africa. The underlying logic of the Carter approach was

> ...that the costs of United States intervention to frustrate political change were too high; that radical governments were usually established in response to internal conflicts and problems and that their economic and national interests were more important than their ideologies; that the United States and other Western countries would gain strategic advantages in working with these countries, given Western markets, technology, and capital; that the United States' interest in certain areas, from export markets to access to vital raw materials, involved the need for more cooperative relationships; and that the United States' image as an opponent of political and social change and a supporter of "friendly" authoritarian governments was detrimental to the interests of the United States and had corrosive political consequences for American institutions and behavior.[10]

Unlike his predecessors, Carter welcomed African heads of state in Washington and traveled to the continent. The Carter approach toward Africa significantly changed the U.S. view of the apartheid government in South Africa. Carter and members of his executive branch sent clear signals to John Vorster, the South African Prime Minister, that as a result of apartheid the United States could not be counted on for support in a crisis. The Carter administration's support for political and social change in South Africa, however, did not include support for the ANC (African National Congress) and other movements in the region aimed toward the removal of white minority rule in the nation.

Carter's policies toward Africa initially sought to advance the cause of human rights and economic development on the continent. The administration was ridiculed and criticized for this perspective and in essence was blamed for the advancement of radical Marxist regimes whose leaders and policies were inimical to American interests. It was argued that the Carter administration's emphasis upon human rights punished "friendly" and reformable authoritarian regimes that were of strategic value to the United States. Carter was accused, by his critics, of alienating the apartheid regime of South Africa.

By 1979, events external to Africa—the overthrow of the Shah of Iran, the seizure of American hostages in Tehran, the Soviet invasion of Afghanistan, and the escalation of U.S. fears of Soviet expansion in the Persian Gulf—worked to alter the Carter administration's policy approach. The Cold War climate returned. The administration revived the strategic-based formulation of Africa policy, especially in the Horn of Africa. Between 1977 and 1979, the presence of Soviet and Cuban troops in Ethiopia increased significantly. The intervention of the Soviet Union on the side of Ethiopia during the 1977 Somalian-Ethiopian war in the Ogaden radically shifted the pattern of superpower alliances in the region. The Soviet Union shifted its allegiance away from Somalia, toward Ethiopia. Initially, Carter was unwilling to counter the new Soviet-Ethiopian alliance by backing Somalia, despite persistent overtures from Somalia. However, by the end of his term in office, U.S.-Somali relations began to warm up.

The success of Carter's approach toward Africa and his attempt to raise African issues to a higher level on the foreign policy agenda were thwarted by the divisions between his Secretary of State, Cyrus Vance, and his National Security Advisor, Zbigniew Brzezinski. The competition between these two foreign policy bureaucrats was one that pitted Cyrus Vance's position, which advocated "progressive" policies in Africa, against Zbigniew Brzezinski's position, which advocated the more traditional anti-Communist approach. The latter prevailed; the United States returned to the habit of supporting reactionary and repressive regimes in Africa, as long as those regimes professed to be anti-Communist.

When Ronald Reagan took office in 1981, the reversal of Carter's ideal of insulating Africa from the U.S.-Soviet competition was endorsed. The Reagan approach to foreign affairs in general revitalized the principles of the Cold War. The Reagan doctrine advocated the policy of assisting anti-Communist guerrillas in the Third World. In Africa, Doe of Liberia, King Hassan of Morocco, Siad Barre of Somalia, and Mobutu of Zaire were perceived by the administration to be the "guardians" of U.S. interests on the continent.[11] Reagan also restored U.S. relations with the white minority apartheid regime in Pretoria.

Reagan's complete revival of Cold War politics encouraged his Assistant Secretary of State for African Affairs, Chester A. Crocker, to advance a policy of "constructive engagement" toward the white minority regime in South Africa. The intent was to regain the confidence of the regime and reward a "friendly" regime of strategic importance to U.S.–anti-Soviet strategy. The policy of "constructive engagement" piggy-backed the efforts of the right-wing in the Republican party, which previously had consistently sought to end the sanctions against the minority Rhodesian regime.[12] "Constructive engagement" bought time for the pro-apartheid forces in South Africa to buttress and reinforce their position.

The Reagan administration's willingness to support the "constructive engagement" approach toward South Africa was not only motivated by strategic interests, but U.S. economic issues as well. U.S. economic interests in South Africa were no less important and were at the root of Reagan's aversion to economic sanctions and Congressional support of divestiture and disinvestment policies. By 1983 the South African economy accounted for the largest U.S. economic holding on the entire continent—$3 billion in private direct capital investments and $4 billion in annual trade.[13]

The return to Cold War politics altered Washington's view of the Namibian independence movement. While the Carter administration formally recognized SWAPO (South West African People's Organization) as the legitimate representative of Namibian public opinion, the Reagan administration deliberately linked the U.S. position on Namibian independence to Cuban/Soviet withdrawal from Angola.[14] The official policy positions of the Reagan administration on southern African issues sent a message to the world that the United States indirectly supported South African occupation of Namibia, and its military intervention in southern Angola. Both South African actions were recognized as illegal by the majority of the members of the United Nations. Finally, as a part of this reversal of policy toward South Africa, the United States signalled its support of South African involvement in the organization and military support of RENAMO (also known as the MNR, Mozambique National Resistance), the insurgency force in Mozambique, and its efforts to weaken the proclaimed Marxist regime in that nation, through civil war.

The Reagan administration also sought to repeal the 1976 Clark Amendment, which prohibited U.S. support of the anti-Marxist movements in Angola. In 1985, the amendment was repealed and weapons began to flow freely to Jonas Savimbi's UNITA forces. Reagan's Secretary of State, George Shultz, claimed that the support of Savimbi was not intended to overthrow Dos Santos and the MPLA (Popular Movement for the Liberation of Angola)—but to force the MPLA to negotiate with UNITA. The policy prolonged the Angolan Civil War.

At the opposite end of the continent, the Reagan administration targeted Libya and Quadhafi. The administration apparently approved plans to target Quadhafi during the U.S. bombing of Quadhafi's Tripoli headquarters in retaliation for a terrorist bombing in Europe. The action demonstrated U.S. willingness to use direct military force against an African regime.[15] In some ways, it can be taken as a reversal of the tendency on the part of U.S. policy makers to avoid direct military involvement in Africa.

By the end of the 1980s and the wane of the Reagan administration, the Soviet Union sent signals of fatigue in its Africa policy to Washington. Gorbachev's "new realism" of the late 1980s altered the Soviet view of its involvement in Africa. The reorientation of Soviet policy toward Africa was signaled by Moscow as early as 1985, when it indicated to Washington that it was willing to cooperate with the United States to resolve conflicts in the Third World.[16] The United States and the Soviet Union had both pursued their own national strategic and economic interests in Africa; neither superpower based its policies on how they affected the welfare, progress, and development of Africa. In 1987 the Soviets declared Africa to be of low priority to Moscow.

The first fruits of the Soviet policy change were reaped from the tripartite accord in southern Africa, which led to the withdrawal of South African and Cuban troops from Angola. The quid pro quo for the change was the withdrawal of U.S. support of South African troops in Namibia. Ironically, the convergence of the U.S. and Soviet interests in Africa resulted in the independence of Namibia in 1990. The tripartite accord, however, did not lead to the reversal of U.S. support for Savimbi.

Indications of the Cold War's end precipitated in Africa. Gorbachev's "new realism" and Soviet/Cuban withdrawal from Africa signaled the end of an era. The United States and the Soviet Union no longer had an interest in competing for allies in the region and cultivating the cooperation of African leaders. It is unlikely that the Reagan administration would have made the first move toward Cold War disengagement in Africa. The Soviet decision to withdraw from Africa, in essence, hurled Africa into the uncertainties of the post-Cold War international environment. The major area of uncertainty was, of course, the future of U.S. policy in Africa.

THE END OF THE COLD WAR

During the Cold War the United States had a clear vision of its purpose in the international system. International interests and goals were simply defined and solutions were implemented with relative ease because both were determined by the Cold War imperative—the containment of the Soviet Union. The Cold War afforded the United States many opportunities to expand its global presence and pursue its international interests. U.S. actions in the international system, however, were limited by the strategic imperatives of the Cold War and constraint of the bipolar global order. Visions of the global order became less lucid at the Cold War's end: Problems could not be easily defined and policy choices could not be easily made. However, the end of the Cold War eased the conditions that constrained U.S. international behavior. Now, the United States had the opportunity to pursue its international goals and objectives without the constraints imposed by the existence of an equally powerful adversary.

The previously predictable and stable external international system disappeared. Major changes in the post-World War II international order were set in motion because of the implosion of the Soviet state, the restructuring of Europe through the efforts to integrate the former Eastern bloc nations into the economic and political sphere of the West, and the intensification of conflict within and among nations in the Third World.[17] As a result, the major Cold War strategic interests affecting the formulation of U.S. policy toward African nations declined in importance.

Before the end of the Cold War, the superpowers became less willing or unable to continue their involvement or establish new levels of involvement in the resolution of political or military conflicts on the African continent. Strategic considerations were no longer motivations for superpower military involvement and "...reductions in U.S. assistance demonstrate[d] one effect of the changes in the international system on U.S. policy."[18] Several cases epitomize the change in superpower attitudes toward Africa. One important case is the unwillingness of the United States to make significant commitments to the resolution of the Liberian civil war. Instead of direct U.S. military intervention, it supported the intervention of a five-nation force—comprised of troops from Ghana, Nigeria, Sierra Leone, Gambia, and Guinea. U.S. policy makers took the position that Africans should solve their own regional problems with limited U.S. involvement.[19] On the part of the Soviet Union, its inability to support its ally in Ethiopia, Mengisthu Mariam, is also an example of the effects of the reduction of Cold War hostilities.

The major flashpoints of Cold War tensions in Africa were now viewed from a different perspective—no longer viewed as simply the extensions of superpower competition. The Gorbachev era (1985–1990) in Soviet foreign policy brought an end to the support of the regime in Angola. By the end of the Gorbachev era, Namibia gained its long awaited and long fought for independence; the Soviet-backed Dergue in Ethiopia fell to the Tygrean opposition forces; Eritrea gained independence from Ethiopia; the Somalian government collapsed and Somaliland (formerly British Somalia) declared its independence in 1991; and the ANC (African National Congress) gained legitimacy in 1990 and was elected as the majority party in the postapartheid South African legislature in 1993.

The antagonisms of the East and West during the Cold War were played out in Africa. The long civil wars in Angola and Mozambique, the collapse of Somalia, and the prolonged survival of the apartheid regime in South Africa were all the result of the Cold War strategic policy imperatives of the two superpowers. But the end of the Cold War did not mean the end of violence and military conflict in Africa.[20] African nations suffered from the collapse of the Cold War in two ways: Intracontinental rivalries supported by the Cold War interests of the two superpowers were not resolved when the superpowers decided to call it quits; and, the fragile political stability that the many regimes, supported by one or the other superpower, enjoyed during the Cold War was no longer sustainable. Additionally, the postcolonial ties between African nations and the former colonial powers continued to acerbate intercontinental conflicts. The French arms trade in the Chad crisis and in Rwanda, for example, heightened the intensity levels of those conflicts.[21]

THE BUSH ADMINISTRATION

The Bush administration was the last Cold War, as well as, the first post-Cold War administration. The policies of the Bush administration began the post-Cold War foreign policy transition toward Africa. The Bush administration attempted to moderate Reagan's policies toward Africa during the initial years of its tenure. The collapse of the Soviet Union and the formal end of the Cold War did not come to fruition until the end of the Bush administration. Ironically, it was during the Bush administration that for the first time in the post-World War II era the opportunity to develop Africa policy, insulated from the Cold War and advocated earlier by Carter, emerged. While the "strategic imperative" of U.S. Africa policy faded, a new rhetoric in which the United States pledged to support the process of democratization and democratic movements taking place on the continent emerged. In reality, however, it was during this period that the United States began its attempts to extricate itself from its responsibilities in Africa.

In August 1990, Bush's Assistant Secretary of State for African Affairs, Herman Cohen, traveled to Kenya in response to the increased repression of prodemocratic forces by the Moi government. Instead of altering Moi's position, Cohen's visit strengthened his resolve, because it was clear that the United States would not unilaterally repudiate or punish Moi's regime for its human rights violations. It was only after the United States and Kenya's other major international donors, convinced by Moi's major opponent, Paul Muite, suspended foreign aid to Kenya that Moi reversed his opposition to multiparty elections.[22] Without the carrot of military assistance and the specter of Soviet expansionism on the continent, the U.S. approach moved away from unilateral toward multilateral responses to problems in Africa.

Fear of the spread of Marxist ideology in Africa was replaced by concern for the activities of secondary powers and mobilizing ideologies. In the wake of the Gulf War, the Bush administration labeled Islamic fundamentalism the next "worrisome trend for Africa in the post-Cold War era."[23] Attention turned toward the potential spread of Islamic fundamentalist regimes, which were labeled threats to the secular political and cultural values of the West. Iran was cited by members of the Bush administration to be the major source of Islamic fundamentalism in Sudan, for example.[24]

During the war against Iraq (Gulf War, 1990–1991), U.S. citizens were encouraged to evacuate Mauritania and Sudan—the two African nations that aligned with Iraq. Additionally, in Nigeria and South Africa, Muslim populations demonstrated against U.S. involvement in the Gulf War. Demonstrations also occurred in Uganda, Tanzania, and Mauritius—the latter expressing opposition to the use of Diego Garcia as a launching point for U.S. strategic bombers in the Gulf. During the Gulf War, U.S. policy makers linked U.S. African policy objectives to U.S. policy objectives in the Middle East. (After all, the majority of Islamic nations and Arab populations in the world are also in Africa, or closely tied to Africa. As long as this is the case and the Middle East remains a region of U.S. policy priority, the United States will not be able to completely extricate itself from the affairs of the African continent.)

The Bush administration continued to support the previous administration's policy toward Liberia—the noninterventionist policy. A spokesperson for the State Department announced that "the administration believes that it's not our role to intervene, to engage in peacekeeping, or to impose a government or political system in Liberia," and Assistant Secretary of State Herman Cohen argued in 1990 that the United States bore no responsibility for the Liberian tragedy.[25] The Bush administration continued to back the use of Nigerian-led ECOWAS (Economic Community of West African States) troops in Liberia. Finally, the administration offered safe passage out of the country to the beleaguered Samuel Doe. The decision to aid Doe was in part the result of the fact that during the Reagan administration, Liberia was the only country in West Africa where U.S. planes could land with twenty-four hours notice and served as a landing base for the U.S. supply network to Jonas Savimbi in Angola.[26]

Bush lacked the dogged Cold War loyalties that Ronald Reagan had for South Africa's apartheid regime. Although opposed to the sanctions against the apartheid regime, Bush was unable to reverse Congress's endorsement of the sanctions against South Africa. In 1990, the release of Nelson Mandela and de Klerk's turnaround in his support of apartheid policies diminished the visibility of the United States in the remaking of South Africa; the impetus for change in South Africa had become internally generated.

The major change in the Bush administration's Africa policy occurred at the end of his term in office. The decision to intervene in Somalia can be viewed as the first act of U.S. post-Cold War Africa policy.

THE HORN OF AFRICA: A CASE OF U.S. POST-COLD WAR POLICY

The Horn of Africa is comprised of nations that became of major strategic importance to the United States during World War II because of Fascist Italy's presence in the region. During the Cold War, the region became a major area of U.S.-Soviet competition. For most of the Cold War, the United States supported Ethiopia and the Soviets supported Somalia. Relations between Ethiopia and Somalia were strained during the Cold War, especially due to the territorial claims that each placed on the Ogaden. The demarcation of superpower alliances in the region only widened the chasm and intensified the level of conflict between Somalia and Ethiopia, as both received technical military support and arms.

U.S.-Ethiopian relations began to deteriorate in 1974 after the overthrow of the Ethiopian monarchy and the successful establishment of a Marxist-oriented military junta, the Dergue. While the United States attempted to maintain ties with the Dergue, the formal relationship between the United States and Ethiopia ended in 1977 after a series of diplomatic events that led to the final expulsion of U.S. personnel from Ethiopia. Concomitant with the dissipation of the U.S.-Ethiopian relations, the Somali government began to distance itself from its long relationship with the Soviets.

Soviet intentions to build relations with the Ethiopian Dergue damaged its relationship with Somalia. Somalia retaliated by making overtures to the United States, the West, and the Arab world. In order to maintain its influence in the Horn of Africa, the United States eventually responded to Somali overtures; the pattern of superpower alliances in the region "reversed" during the Carter administration. Shortly thereafter, Somalia invaded the Ogaden and the war between Ethiopia and Somalia began—a war that proved embarrassing to the United States because its newly-found ally, Somalia, was the indisputable aggressor.[27]

The 1977–1978 war in the Ogaden did not lead to U.S. military intervention. But it did lead to the massive deployment of Soviet and Cuban troops in Ethiopia—a deployment that would remain a major source of tension between the United States and Soviet Union until the end of the Cold War. From 1977 until the late 1980s, U.S.-Somali ties were strengthened through large sums of military and economic aid. During this period, U.S.-Ethiopian relations were altered briefly as the United States responded with food and humanitarian aid to the victims of the Ethiopian famine of 1983–1985. In 1988, Ethiopia and Somalia signed a peace accord—both agreeing to re-establish diplomatic relations and withdraw troops from the Ogaden (this occurred at nearly the same time that the Soviet Union signaled its willingness to work with the United States to resolve conflicts in Africa).

The dissipation of both the Ethiopian and Somali governments began after the signing of the Ethiopia-Somali accord. The stability of the Somali regime was fragile to start with, as the Somali National Movement (SNM) in the North, the United Somali Congress (U.S.C), and the Somali Patriotic Movement (SPM) were each associated with 'clan/family' allegiances, which the regime of Siad Barre had been unable to unify. In Ethiopia, despite the revolution of 1974, the Dergue was unable to undermine the threats of the Ethiopian People's Revolutionary Democratic Front (EPRDF), dominated by the Tygrean People's Liberation Front (TPLF), the Oromo Liberation Front(OLF), and the Eritrean People's Liberation Front(EPLF).[28]

As Somalia's internal politics rapidly disintegrated into civil war, congressional and bureaucratic battles raged over the future of the U.S.-Somali relationship. The civil war displaced large populations and led to a famine on the scale of, if not greater than, the earlier famine in Ethiopia. The Somali crisis severely undermined U.S. support for Siad Barre's leadership, as charges of human rights violations against his government surfaced in the United States. There were increased calls for disengagement from Somalia in the U.S. Congress. At the same time a major debate was being waged over the future of U.S.-Ethiopian relations. Between 1989 and 1990, the Bush administration attempted to disengage from Somalia and negotiate an end to the Ethiopian civil war. By 1990, the leader of the Ethiopian government, Mengistu Mariam, announced that he was abandoning his commitment to Marxism (the same year that the Soviet Union formally announced that it would not renew its military agreement with Ethiopia).

In 1991, the political tides changed radically for both Somalia and Ethiopian governments. Both governments collapsed, Siad Barre fled Somalia, and, shortly thereafter, so too did Mengistu Mariam from Ethiopia.

For Somalia, the collapse of the central government resulted in the total breakdown of the law, civil society, and domestic stability. The civil war between the competing parties and clans worsened the scale of population displacement—the refugee crisis—and famine. One faction, the SNM in the north, declared its independence in 1991, but the fighting in southern Somalia continued. The self-proclaimed independence of Somaliland resulted in the return to the 1960 border divisions between northern and southern Somalia. To date (1995), Somaliland is not recognized by the United States as an independent nation.

In Ethiopia, the collapse of the Mengistu regime led to the victory of the Tygrean People's Liberation Front, which quickly established a coalition government with the other contending parties in Ethiopia. Eritrea was able to successfully achieve its independence, unlike Somaliland. While the Bush administration was willing to intervene and facilitate the transfer of power in Ethiopia and the independence of Eritrea via the United Nations, the U.S. position on Somaliland was not an unfamiliar one. Since Great Britain and Italy were the former colonial powers in Somalia, the Bush administration favored the intervention of those two nations in the resolution of Somalia's civil war.

The collapse of the Cold War occurred at the same time that major political upheavals in the Horn of Africa took place. Given that there was no longer a significant Soviet presence or threat in the region, U.S. Africa policy was under the management of the foreign policy bureaucracies rather than the executive. It was a matter of routine. Neither the Horn of Africa nor Africa was on the front burner of the Bush administration's agenda.

Bush's "quiet detachment" from Africa took an abrupt turn at the end of his administration when he authorized the deployment of U.S. troops in Somalia. Initially the deployment of U.S. troops was labeled a humanitarian mission aimed toward the stabilization of the nation in order to facilitate the distribution of food to the Somali population by the United Nations and international relief agencies.

THE CONSEQUENCES OF SOMALIA

The decision to send U.S. troops to Somalia was the last major Africa policy of the Bush administration. The consequences of this decision were left to the Clinton administration; chief among them was the need for the clarification of U.S. policy goals in Somalia. The Somali case was the first post-Cold War test of U.S. Africa policy and the scale of the deployment of U.S. troops to that nation was a radical break with past U.S. Africa policy. It was the first time that U.S. troops were deployed in such large numbers in an African crisis situation.

The U.S. "peacekeeping" role in Somalia became a military one by the ninth month of the Clinton presidency. Congressional and public pressures for the withdrawal of U.S. troops escalated in the fall of 1993, after U.S. forces suffered thirteen casualties during maneuvers to capture General Mohammed Aidid in southern Mogadishu. The goals of U.S. policy in

Somalia became the subject of acute public and congressional scrutiny. A secondary issue arising from the controversy was the question of the U.S. role in U.N. peacekeeping missions—since U.S. troops in Somalia were ostensibly under the command of the United Nations.

In the fall of 1993, the Clinton administration announced plans for total withdrawal from Somalia by the first of April, 1994. Clinton's Secretary of State, Warren Christopher, announced the U.S. position on conflict resolution in Africa. The policy was consistent with the Bush administration policy toward the Liberian crisis—the "African Solution."[29] The "African Solution" to the Somali crisis on the one hand supported the involvement of nations in the region—Ethiopia, Kenya, and Egypt—and the OAU (Organization of African Unity); on the other hand, the policy approach again signaled U.S. desire to disengage from military involvement on the continent.

Although the United States had officially disengaged from Somalia, U.S. military presence remained in the region. U.S. troops remained in Kuwait after the Gulf War. The United States had also lent military equipment to the remaining United Nations forces in Somalia—equipment that was returned to the United States. On December 16, 1994, President Clinton approved the redeployment of U.S. troops to aid the withdrawal of U.N. troops from Somalia, and UNOSOM (United Nations Operation in Somalia) forces were withdrawn by the spring of 1995.

Somalia will not be recorded in history as a major military or diplomatic success for the Bush and Clinton administrations. It will be remembered as a demonstration of the limits of U.S. post-Cold War Africa policy. It is possible that the results of U.S. policy in Somalia will be used by some policy makers during the 1990s as justification for further U.S. disengagement from Africa. One can only speculate that if the Somali mission had been successful, the United States may have attempted to intervene in the Rwandan civil war, which led to the destruction of nearly a half million lives during 1992–1994.

THE CLINTON ADMINISTRATION: BEYOND SOMALIA

Somalia dominated the U.S. policy agenda at the beginning of the Clinton administration but it was not the only African issue that the administration had on its plate. When Clinton assumed the office of the U.S. presidency, he was given the awesome task of redefining the role of the United States in the post-Cold War international system. Clinton, elected on a platform that emphasized a U.S. domestic agenda, was left to articulate a new *raison d'etre* for U.S. foreign policy. His State Department foreign policy team included some veterans of the Carter administration's foreign policy apparatus.[30] Hopes were that he would be able to provide strategic coherence to U.S. foreign policy in the making of the "new world order." The "new world order" began with more than thirty civil wars and conflicts raging throughout the world; thirteen were in Africa, including those in Sudan, Somalia, Liberia, Zaire, Togo, Cameroon, Angola, Chad, Rwanda, Burundi, and Mozambique.

Concern for the potential spread of Islamic fundamentalism in Africa also continued to permeate the formulations of U.S. policy. In the summer of 1993, the State Department placed Sudan on its list of states sponsoring terrorism, sharing the designation with Iraq, Libya, Cuba, North Korea, and Syria. The decision was made when intelligence reports verified Sudanese support of terrorist Muslim organizations operating throughout the region and the world. The decision was also supported by evidence in the 1993 New York City World Trade Center bombing case that tied Sheik Omar Rahman and at least one of the suspects in the bombing to the Sudanese government.[31]

The Clinton administration expressed its support of the democratization movements occurring in many African nations. Secretary of State, Warren Christopher, made it clear that

> [a]s the world's oldest democracy we have an enduring interest in the success of the new democracies in Africa.... The Clinton administration will provide a strong and visible support for the movement of freedom in Africa—to democracies and free markets. We will work with the nations of Africa to address the health, environmental, and population issues that threaten life and imperil sustainable development. And we will help Africa build its capacity for preventative diplomacy and conflict resolution, so that the people of that continent can live free of the terror of war.[32]

Christopher's definition of democracy included the benchmarks of elections, free and open debate, the rule of law, and the existence of a civic culture. With these criteria it is clear that the Clinton administration would pursue policies that would base U.S. relationships in Africa upon American political ideology and structures. African nations would be compelled to conform to U.S. and Western standards of democratic governance—standards that include human rights and women's rights, as well. On May 21, 1993, Secretary of State, Warren Christopher stated:

> The Clinton Administration will provide strong and visible support for the movement toward freedom in Africa—the movement toward democracies and toward free markets.... At the heart of our new relationship will be an enduring commitment to democracy and human rights—that includes women's rights.[33]

Democratization and economic liberalization became the new post-Cold war foreign policy imperatives.

Past efforts to apply policies consistent with U.S. values have often led to major policy inconsistencies. In January 1992, for example, the Bush administration supported the cancellation of the Algerian elections when it was clear that the Islamic fundamentalist party, the Islamic Salvation Front(FIS), would win. A state of emergency was declared in 1992 when the military seized power and thousands of FIS supporters were detained. The FIS as well as other opponents of the military regime turned to armed resistance in response to the military crackdown on FIS party activities, and numerous deaths and arrests occurred. However, in reaction to the actions of the Babangida regime's nullification of the results of the presidential elections in the summer of 1993, the United States suspended $1 million of its nonrelief aid to Nigeria. Finally, in the case of Angola, though the Clinton administration officially recognized the election of the Dos Santos government in May of 1993, nothing was done to compensate for the years that the United States supported the armed resistance of the UNITA forces.

The troubling messages sent in these cases might be that the United States would support nondemocratic actions in cases in which the democratic process (elections) leads to undesirable outcomes—the election of Islamic fundamentalist parties, for example; and the United States holds no responsibility for the past destabilization of democratically elected regimes that were in reality, or had been perceived to be, ideologically incompatible with the United States.

While the Clinton administration made promises to renew relations with African nations, the U.S. Congress trimmed the African aid fund of the Agency for International Development (AID) as well as contributions to international lending institutions, such as the World Bank. Additionally, the State Department's Bureau of African Affairs lost seventy posts, a 9 percent cut within a year. Consulates have been closed in several nations in order to accommodate the need to fill positions and increase budgets to establish diplomatic relations with the new East European nations. The U.S. Agency for International Development reduced its Africa staff and the African Affairs Bureau in the National Security Council lost six directors between 1988 and 1992.[34]

U.S. INTERESTS, CHALLENGES, AND OPPORTUNITIES

The end of the Cold War has significantly blurred perceptions of U.S. interests in Africa. While Washington and Moscow competed for influence on the continent during the Cold War years, the United States has been unable to clearly define its interests in Africa outside of the Cold War paradigm. In addition, the political volatilities and economic vulnerabilities facing nearly every African nation complicate the ability of U.S. policy makers and the public to clearly identify strategic and economic interests in Africa. Much of Africa's future will depend upon the perceptions of those nations in the international system, which have the wealth and resources to help African nations effectively address their problems.

Therefore, a major challenge to the United States will be to identify the endogenous perceptual barriers that prevent it from looking at Africa in realistic terms and to focus on the opportunities that Africans themselves create for effective U.S. involvement. Two cases demonstrate the success of the latter approach: the effective role of the United States in the resolution of conflict in Ethiopia at the end of the Mariam regime in 1991 and in the transition of South Africa from apartheid to a multiracial democracy in 1993. In both cases, the opportunities for U.S. involvement were guided by the goals that Ethiopians and South Africans defined for themselves, rather than goals defined by the United States.

More than any other region in the world, Africa's contemporary economic and political realities are products of international politics. International competition among the major powers interfered with the development of appropriate African systems of governance and economics. Reformulating U.S. Africa policy without taking into account the impact that U.S. Cold War policies had on the contemporary realities of Africa will lead to a formula for disaster. It is imperative that the reformulation of U.S. Africa policy begin with a realistic discernment of post-Cold War African political and economic realities. Africa is neither hopeless nor helpless. It is, however, a continent with a series of complex problems that have no facile solutions.

AFRICAN POLITICAL AND ECONOMIC REALITIES

For the most part, Africa's contemporary realities are not of its own making. Centuries of exploitation, colonial rule, and the international slave trade deprived African nations of the ability to preserve and develop the tools necessary for economic development. The imposition of colonial boundaries—which arbitrarily separated nations and forged new multinational units in which peoples, some of whom were traditionally hostile toward one another, were forced to develop new national identities—inhibited the development of stable civil societies and political units.

Africa, at the end of the Cold War, was left in a condition of political and economic crisis that may prove to be near fatal for many nations. U.S. policies during the Cold War did not adequately address the needs of African economic development. Economic aid packages, emanating either directly from the United States and/or from U.S.-supported international lending institutions, were devised without regard for the international factors leading to African economic problems (primarily the rapid decline in terms of trade for African agricultural products and raw materials, currency fluctuations, increased oil prices, etc.).[35]

Africa is one of the most distressed regions in the world. In 1993, Africa's economic output decreased while the aggregate measure of global economic output actually increased. The decline in Africa's economic output is demonstrated in the figures for individual nations; Cameroon's GDP declined 5.2 percent in 1992, Madagascar's 6.3 percent, Malawi's 7.7 percent, and Zaire's 10.6 percent. Inflation in Africa averaged 36.1 percent compared to 13.9 percent globally. Africa's export sector has remained stagnant, but imports rose 11.6 percent. The rising cost of manufactured goods—the bulk of Africa's imports along with food—rose 3.7 percent. The result was a major increase in the level of foreign debt for the continent—$128.3 billion in 1992.[36]

The average per capita income for Africans is $340. Statistics on Africa's social development also paint a bleak picture. Adult literacy is 50 percent, and mortality rates are 15 times higher than in the United States. A grim consequence of social decline in African nations is prolonged political turmoil. Starvation and famines are frequent phenomena across the continent, as well as devastating plagues, such as the rapid spread of AIDS in Central Africa.

The combination of economic decline and political instability has led to increased state repression, rather than democracy, in many nations on the continent. During 1983–1991, many African nations began to implement reforms required by the IMF and World Bank—reforms that were meant to transform African economies. However, it is clear that

> these transformations indicate a marked decline in the relative impor-
> tance of agriculture and industry and a substantive proportional increase
> in the service sector. There was virtual collapse of much of the formal sec-
> tor of the economy, along with an expansion of the informal sector. The
> period also saw a significant adjustment in incomes and economic activi-
> ties of skilled and unskilled wage earners and of social groups in both sec-
> tors of the economy.... The adoption of structural adjustment programs
> as a major governmental response to the crisis also tended to exacerbate
> social problems.[37]

More than half of the nations on the continent have been forced by pressures from external lenders to adopt radical structural adjustment programs that favor privatization. Some nations recognized the inefficiency of their economic systems before the imposition of reforms by the World Bank and IMF; Benin was among the first to begin voluntary economic reforms. The absence of indigenous entrepreneurs at independence, and until recently, led to the development of state-controlled enterprises—called parastatals—that encouraged the importation of capital through foreign investments.

The role of the state in industrialization and capital generation proved to be inefficient for many reasons, including corrupt government officials, poor planning, the lack of supportive infrastructure, high external debt, and low capital generation. Compounding the problem were the numerous poor policy decisions that redirected capital investments away from agriculture and toward industrial/urban sectors of African economies. This, in most cases, diminished the productivity of domestic food producers (Africa's overall agricultural output has declined since the 1950s). The failure of African agriculture has weakened its future growth potential.

The adoption of structural adjustment programs because of the external pressures from international lending institutions worsened the level of economic and social crises in most nations on the continent. The efforts made to reform African economies and political systems in order to attract foreign capital have deepened the condition of dependency and instability. Without government subsidies, fuel and food prices have inflated beyond the means of the poor and rural peasants who have been the hardest hit.

The belief that political stability is promoted by economic development assumes a one-directional causal relationship between the two when, in fact, the economic reforms advocated by the IMF can be directly linked to economic problems that undermine the legitimacy of government. Even in advanced economic nations, problems such as domestic market dislocations, price distortions, high rates of unemployment, diminished infrastructural development, and declining agricultural and manufacturing productivity lead to the decline in the public's confidence in government. In those nations, economic crises lead to the election of new leadership. In developing economies with fragile political systems, economic crises more frequently lead to military coups, revolutions, or prolonged violence.

Another consequence of economic reform has been the high level of unemployment—created by privatization policies. The privatization of parastatals, for example, raises the level of unemployment among sectors of the labor force that have high levels of education, political expectations, and the ability to politically mobilize against government policies. The decline in manufacturing and agricultural productivity displaces lower or unskilled labor in urban areas and rural areas. Rural populations often respond to declining agricultural productivity by migrating to urban areas, therefore increasing the ranks of the urban unemployed and demands for government services—services the governments are unable to provide.

Not only have African nations paid extraordinarily high interest rates on debt, which has drained the foreign capital accounts of most nations, but also their debt payments have helped to finance the very lending agencies that have imposed restructuring policies that became inimical to their economic progress and political stability. The debt crisis in Africa in many ways mortgaged the futures of African economies. Without appropriate debt relief, successful economic programs will not bring substantial or immediate benefits to African populations. There are those in the U.S. State Department who view the misery of Africa as so dire that Africans will be begging to be recolonized. From the African perspective, restructuring programs have been intentionally designed to make African nations vulnerable to recolonization efforts.[38] This view is reinforced by the fact that, as a result of structural adjustment programs in Africa, IMF and World Bank officials have taken over the running of national economic policy from local civil servants, bureaucrats, and policy makers in Africa.[39]

WEIGHING THE REALITIES

African governments are constrained in the number of options available to them. They will more than likely have to adjust to the continued intervention of the IMF and the World Bank in their economies in the near future. If U.S. goals in Africa, even in the post-Cold War environment, remain centered around its basic commitment to the promotion of democracy, then any efforts by the United States to pursue these goals in Africa are destined to fail. U.S. strategies must carefully consider the African political, social, and economic factors that can inhibit the development of stable and sustainable democracy. The opportunities for positive U.S. involvement would depend greatly upon how well U.S. policy makers and other actors encourage African nations to develop their resources to deal with the problems of the continent. "Instead of developing high profile initiatives … U.S. officials and other Americans concerned about the continent should undertake to strengthen the various groups that comprise African civil society…."[40]

The promotion of U.S. market interests will also depend greatly upon the encouragement of market forces in African economies. The process of privatization has begun in many nations. But African economic development is far behind the economic development occurring in Asia and some parts of Latin America. If the United States redefines its overall global strategy as one that is exclusively based upon economic and market interests, U.S. investments will be encouraged to flow to nations with healthy stable markets. African nations will become marginal to U.S. global economic interests. The persistence of economic marginalization will impede African democratization.

POLICY OPTIONS: PROS AND CONS

The development of future Africa policy will not be the result of academic discourse. The policy process is one that is highly political and does not occur within a vacuum. Since the end of the Cold War, at least three different views of future post-Cold War U.S. interests in Africa have emerged. Each view has a different definition of the nature and importance of the U.S. economic, strategic, and humanitarian interests in Africa.

The most conservative of these views advocates disengagement from Africa on the grounds that the United States no longer has any real interests in Africa, other than South Africa, since the end of the Cold War. From this perspective, U.S. economic interests on the continent are marginal because trade between Africa and the United States is insignificant; Africa is not a large market for U.S. products and vice versa; and trade will probably not increase significantly in the future. The lack of success associated with past levels of U.S. assistance to Africa justifies a shift in U.S. aid to areas that are of more importance. South Africa, however, remains an important source of strategic minerals: It has an industrial base and should continue to receive aid.

Similarly, this argument concludes that the United States does not need access to the African continent in order to maintain its geostrategic position after the Cold War. It no longer matters what type of regimes govern in Africa because they will not threaten the United States. Political instability and violence in Africa do not affect U.S. interests. The United States, being incapable of assuring human and civil rights in Africa or any other part of the world, should limit its humanitarian assistance to African countries.

At the end of the Cold War, the United States, like other developed nations, began to emphasize the development of strong economic ties in the international system. The United States began to seek greater involvement in the rapidly growing Asian markets and the development of a Western hemispheric trade bloc, beginning with NAFTA (North American Free Trade

Agreement). The international economic policy approach emphasized the development of economic ties with those nations that were perceived to be "good risks" for American investments and would stimulate growth and productivity in the U.S. market. African economies are not viewed to be good investment risks.

The sweeping victory of the Republican party in the U.S. House of Representatives and the Senate midterm elections of 1994 led to major changes in Congressional leadership—leadership that seems to favor this first school of thought about the U.S. Africa policy in the post-Cold War era. The new leader of the Senate Foreign Relations Subcommittee on Foreign Operations, Senator Mitch McConnell (R-Kentucky), sent signals at the end of 1994 about the new Republican majority's view of U.S. foreign aid, especially U.S. aid to Africa. McConnell proposed the abolition of the Development Fund for Africa and the slashing of aid for African population programs. He suggested that: "Africa could no longer expect an automatic annual entitlement of $800 million."[41] Senator Jesse Helms, Chair of the Senate Foreign Relations Committee, compared foreign aid to throwing money down a "rathole."[42]

The second school of thought argues for limited engagement in Africa. The United States should direct its attention to situations that best serve U.S. interests. The United States should select a few nations in Africa that can best serve its interests and nations that face serious humanitarian crises: Somalia, and potentially Angola, Mozambique, Liberia, Sudan, and Zaire. The United States has an interest in increasing investments in Africa in order to access resources such as oil, natural gas, and strategic metals. The United States should promote economic development in order to increase demand for U.S.-produced goods in African markets. The United States should target only those nations that meet the criteria of democratic politics, accountability, human and civil rights, and the existence of a stable private sector. The United States should promote the peaceful resolution of conflicts in Africa and provide limited quantities of military assistance to friendly African states. Any military involvement in Africa should involve European allies and existing international institutions.

The third school of thought argues that the United States should seek a new activism in Africa. The United States should take an active role in the support of African democratization, development, and economic initiatives. Military assistance should be replaced with an increase in economic and development assistance. The United States has a vital interest in promoting stable and sustainable economic growth in Africa because many nations are important, or potentially important, trading partners and markets for U.S. goods. This position advocates the development of U.S. aid programs that resemble those of the Marshall Plan in Europe after World War II. This position also advocates the promotion of peaceful conflict resolution in Africa.[43] If this option is chosen, it would certainly require a high level of fiscal and human commitment to Africa. Of all of the policy options, this is the most unlikely, given the competing interests of U.S. domestic needs, the deficit, and public resistance to spending U.S. monies abroad—especially after the public's negative reaction to the 1995 U.S. Mexican peso "bailout plan."

It is unlikely that any one of these three policy options will emerge as the dominant U.S. Africa policy for the future. The future of U.S. policy will be greatly affected by the perceptions that U.S. policy makers and the public hold about Africa, as well as by the manner in which the overall strategy of the United States in the international system is reformulated.

POLICY RECOMMENDATIONS FOR THE TWENTY-FIRST CENTURY

The debate about future U.S. relations with the nations on the continent of Africa will likely center around the ways in which the United States can best relate to the patterns of political and economic development on the continent. Without the Cold War strategic imperatives of the past, the United States can freely develop relations with states on the continent that genuinely support values that are compatible with U.S. values and interests. The United States can choose to develop relationships with nations that support its conception or compatible notions of human rights and civil liberties, for example, rather than choosing relations on the basis of political ideology. It is also possible for the United States, at this point, to demilitarize its relations with African governments, and pursue policies that do not fan the flames of domestic or international conflict on the continent.

There are at least three policy directions that the U.S. policy makers and the public might take toward Africa in the future. They include the expansion of societal and nongovernmental linkages, accepting boundary transformations, and strengthening the creation of regional organizations.

EXPANSION OF SOCIETAL AND NONGOVERNMENTAL LINKAGES

There is a need for U.S. policy to encourage the expansion of contacts and linkages with African nations outside of official governmental channels. The creation of networks of association and linkages between the informal sectors of African and American societies—those societal and nongovernmental organizations such as small businesses, universities, professional associations, humanitarian organizations, and churches—would diversify the level of contacts between Africans and Americans.[44] Some of these networks already exist and have proven to be resilient and sustainable, even during periods of major political changes in the international system or relations between the U.S. government and specific African governments.

The promotion of nongovernmental networks and relations between Africans and Americans can facilitate the transfer of skills, technology, social linkages, and organizational skills. These types of networks have more potential for the effective development of African populations through the direct transfer of a wide range of skills to rural and urban populations. Economic development skills, such as small business development among rural and urban populations, have proven to be effective. "NGOs (Nongovernmental Organizations) are encouraging rural as well as urban dwellers to generate income from their agricultural products by making credit available to them. Quite a number of beneficiaries are getting credit to work on horticulture, beekeeping, weaving, fuel stove making, poultry development ... the NGOs help the target groups to market their products...."[45] This approach will also create new opportunities for development initiatives in which the true development needs of populations can be appropriately identified.

The creation of nongovernmental networks between Africans and Americans might also lead to the strengthening of African civil society and civic culture—two areas that are essential for successful democratization. The promotion of linkages between African and American organizations at the community, state, and national levels could potentially benefit both the United States and African nations through the development of new and durable channels of interaction.

For the majority of Americans, Africa has not been an area of high priority, despite the fact that a significant percentage of Americans are of African descent, not to mention the significant numbers of African descendants in the Western hemisphere—the Caribbean and Latin America. The level of interest mobilization that develops among Americans of African descent will make the difference in the level of priority that U.S. foreign policy decision makers give to U.S. relations with Africa. Substantial efforts have been made by African-American organizations to create permanent and useful economic ties to African nations. In May 1993, for example, an African-American/African summit was held in Libreville, Gabon. The conference was intended to boost economic relations between African and African-American entrepreneurs. The first conference of this sort was held in 1991, in Abijan, Ivory Coast.

The African-American-based lobbying organization, TransAfrica, has also effectively worked to advocate African interests in Congress, the State Department, and the executive office. In fact, without the efforts of TransAfrica, the issue of U.S. economic sanctions against South Africa most likely would have faded away. In Congress, the Congressional Black Caucus began in the late 1960s to increase the visibility of African issues in Congress. In the future, the visibility and priority given to African issues may greatly depend upon the advocacy efforts of African Americans, as well as other interests within American society.

TransAfrica has spearheaded an initiative to affect change in Nigeria through the mobilization of American public opinion against the Nigerian military's annulment of the democratic presidential election of June 1993; the imprisonment of the winning candidate, Chief Abiola, and other elected civilian governors; the disbanding of the national and state legislatures; press censorship; and the banning of all political activity. The organization has effectively mobilized American civil rights advocates, legislators, university presidents, actresses and actors, and church leaders in its effort to pressure the Abacha military government to move forward with the redemocratization of the Nigerian political system.

Other public interest and professional organizations, like the Carter Center, Atlanta, Georgia, and the African Studies Association (ASA) will become more and more important for their lobbying efforts and influence on African issues in Washington. The Carter Center, a nonprofit, nonpartisan public policy institute, founded in 1982 and named for former President Jimmy Carter, has been very active in developing programs and initiatives in many nations in Africa. Many of the programs are aimed toward the development of democratic governance, human rights, and conflict resolution in African nations.

The African Studies Association, the largest constituency of academicians with expertise on African issues, suffered from isolation from Washington policy making circles, especially during the 1970s and 1980s.[46] But the academic community will continue to be a major source of policy innovation and influence now that the Cold War has ended. Other public interests groups like Africare, Oxfam, National Council of Negro Women, World Vision, Americares, and the numerous church-based relief organizations will be essential to the future of U.S. policy.

ACCEPTING BOUNDARY TRANSFORMATIONS

The United States must also be prepared to recognize the changes in the present borders that designate African nations. The cases of Eritrea and Somaliland may be harbingers of future changes that may occur on the continent. The emergence of new national secessionist movements is highly probable in the post-Cold War politics of Africa. The inability of the existing nations to manage internal ethnic conflicts will more than likely continue to produce instability. As boundary changes occur, however, the potential for regional political and economic integration may increase—as the smaller political units become incapable of economic or political survival without the formation of cooperative ties with other units in the region or continent. While the United States may be unable to directly involve itself in the process of African political reorganization, its policies toward Africa will be conditioned by the emergence of newer political and economic units.

STRENGTHEN THE CREATION OF REGIONAL ORGANIZATIONS

A stable prosperous continent of Africa is in the best interest of the United States. Future U.S. policy initiatives must continue to focus on Africa's basic problem areas. Existing initiatives in these areas may be reassessed, but not abandoned. There are at least four major problem areas: food, conflict resolution, ecological integrity, and economic development—areas in which Africans have expressed the need for assistance. In most instances, these problems are transnational on the continent; the management of or solution to each will require multilateral cooperation.

U.S. policy could focus on providing the resources, financial as well as technical, to existing regional and continental organizations like the OAU (Organization of African Unity) or the regional economic organizations like ECOWAS (Economic Community of West African States). African nations may benefit from the creation of organizations modeled after the European OECD (Organization for Economic Cooperation and Development), EEC (European Economic Community), or the more recently formed, EU (European Union).[47]

LOOKING TOWARD THE TWENTY-FIRST CENTURY

The recommendations suggested here are merely a few of many suggestions that will emerge as the question of the future of U.S.-Africa relations is debated among U.S. policy makers, foreign policy specialists, Africanists in academia, interest groups, and individuals with concerns about Africa. It is hazardous to attempt to predict the future of African politics, given the dynamic fluidity that exists on the continent; old problems remain unresolved and new ones emerge. The United States will be unable to fully ignore or save Africa.[48] The inclination to let Africans find solutions to African problems should not be used as a reason for U.S. policy makers and the public to neglect the continent.

The process of coming up with a new and creative role for the United States in Africa's future will be challenging. However, the development of U.S. policy based upon the areas of need that Africans define for themselves is the most realistic approach to take. This approach will open the way for the manner in which the United States can reformulate and redefine its interests in Africa.

NOTES

1. See Charles Kegley and Eugene Wittkopf, *American Foreign Policy: Pattern and Process*, 4th ed. (New York: St. Martin's Press, 1992), for detailed discussion of the sources of American foreign policy.
2. Africa is obscured in the American image of the world for two major reasons: (1) It is a continent, not a country, so, unlike specific nations to which Americans relate, Africa does not exist; (2) regions of the continent as well as the people, languages, and cultures differ, which makes it difficult for Americans to form stable and consistent images of the continent. The relationships between the nations in the north of Africa and other nations on the continent are of importance to the understanding of intercontinental relations. The fact that Egypt receives one of the largest U.S. foreign aid allocations— since the Camp David accords—has made it a potential leader in development

for Africa. But Egypt is not viewed as an African nation. It is viewed as a Middle Eastern nation and its role in Africa has been deemphasized. Fortunately, Egypt has expressed interest in working with other nations on the continent. See Marguerite Michaels, "Retreat from Africa," *Foreign Affairs: America and the World 1992/93*, pp. 93–108. See also Michael Clough, *Free at Last? United States Policy toward Africa at the End of the Cold War* (New York: Council on Foreign Relations, 1992) p. 22.

3. Sanford Ungar and David Gergen, "Africa and the American Media," Occasional Paper #9 (New York: The Freedom Forum Media Center, 1991). In addition, despite the American involvement in the transatlantic slave trade and the fact that 12 percent or more of the population is of some African ancestry, Africa remains obscure and unimportant to most of the American public and the majority of foreign policy makers. African Americans have a long history of involvement in the policy making process affecting Africa, contrary to popular belief. See Elliot Skinner, *African Americans and U.S. Policy toward Africa: 1850–1924* (Washington, D.C.: Howard University Press, 1992).

4. John F. Kennedy, "The Challenges of Imperialism in Algeria," in *Let the Word Go Forth: The Speeches, Statements, and Writings of John F. Kennedy*, Theodore C. Sorensen, et al., eds. (New York: Delacorte Press, 1988), pp. 331–337. See also Peter Schraeder, *United States Foreign Policy toward Africa: Incrementalism, Crisis, and Change* (New York: Cambridge University Press, 1994), p. 1.

5. Schraeder, *United States Foreign Policy toward Africa*, p. 1.

6. Miroslav Nincic, et al., "Values, Interests, and Foreign Policy Objectives," paper prepared for the American Political Science Association Annual Meeting, 1994.

7. Francis Terry McNamara, *France in Black Africa* (Washington, D.C.: National Defense University, 1989).

8. See Donald Rothchild, "U.S. Policy Styles in Africa," in *Eagle Entangled: U.S. Foreign Policy in a Complex World*, Kenneth Oye, ed. (New York: Longman, 1979), pp. 307–309.

9. See Schraeder, *United States Foreign Policy toward Africa*, Chapter 3, for detailed discussion of the Congo Crisis.

10. Jon Kraus, "American Foreign Policy in Africa," *Current History* (March 1981): 97–98.

11. During the Reagan administration, Siad Barre's regime in Somalia received more than $700 million in economic and military aid. See Michael Clough, "The United States and Africa: The Policy of Cynical Disengagement," *Current History* (May 1992): 193–198.

12. Jesse Helms, Republican Senator from North Carolina, was a major ally of the Botha regime in South Africa in the U.S. Senate. See Kraus, "American Foreign Policy in Africa," p. 129.

13. Naomi Chazan, et al., *Politics and Society in Contemporary Africa* (Boulder, CO: Lynne Rienner, 1992), p. 404.

14. The general belief was that the Cuban presence in Angola was at the request of the Soviet Union rather than the result of independent Cuban foreign policy decision making.

15. Libya was probably viewed to be an Arab rather than African nation, therefore the policy was viewed to be one that would demonstrate U.S. Middle-Eastern, not African, policy.

16. Winrich Kuhne, "Africa and Gorbachev's New Realism," in *Conflict Resolution in Africa*, Francis Deng and William Zartman, eds. (Washington, D.C.: Brookings Institution, 1991), p. 51.

17. The term "Third World" is at risk of becoming obsolete in its description of nations that are not economically industrialized and in political transition. The

diversity among these nations was more or less repressed during the Cold War. These nations were able to identify common interests and thus coalesce under the rubric Third World. The end of the Cold War and the likely competition for development aid and attention from the developed nations like the United States could loosen the bonds between developing nations established during the Cold War. See Sean Lynn-Jones and Steven Miller, *America's Strategy in a Changing World* (Cambridge, MA: MIT Press, 1992), p. 22.

18. Kuhne, "Africa and Gorbachev's New Realism," pp. 42–57.

19. The reluctance of the United States to become involved in the Liberian civil war is a stark demonstration of U.S. withdrawal from Africa. Liberia was first established as an independent nation in 1847. The American Colonization Society established it as a fledgling colony for freed Black American slaves in 1822. See J. Gus Liebcnow, *Liberia: Quest for Democracy* (Bloomington: Indiana University Press, 1987) for history of U.S.-Liberian relations.

20. See Deng and Zartman, *Conflict Resolution in Africa*.

21. Even after decolonization, France remained very active in African affairs, especially in its former colony, Chad, and the formerly Belgian-ruled Rwanda, where its arms sales and military support continued. For discussion of French colonization, see McNamara, *France in Black Africa*.

22. Clough, "The United States and Africa," p. 195.

23. *The New York Times,* January 1, 1992, section I, 3, p. 1.

24. This concern was not new. Carter was convinced, for example, that an independent Western Sahara would be inimical to U.S. interests after the fall of the Shah of Iran in 1979 and the creation of the Islamic Republic. It was feared that Iran would become a source of support for Islamic fundamentalist movements in Africa.

25. "U.S. Explains Reluctance to Intervene," *Washington Post,* July 31, 1990, p. A18. See also Michael Clough, *Free at Last?* pp. 89–95.

26. William O'Neill, "Liberia: An Avoidable Tragedy," *Current History* (May 1993): 124.

27. Somalia laid claims to the Ogaden because of the large population of Somali nationals living in the region. The Barre regime supported the local insurgency force, the Western Somali Liberation Front, in its efforts against Ethiopian territorial claims to the region, until the 1988 peace accord between Barre and Mengistu Mariam, in which both leaders pledged not to support each other's rebels. See Robert Patman, *The Soviet Union in the Horn of Africa* (New York: Cambridge University Press, 1990); and for a detailed history of U.S. policy in the region, see Schraeder, *United States Foreign Policy toward Africa*.

28. Both Somalia and Ethiopia are nations that have diverse populations in ethnic and political ideological terms. The divisions that developed among the Somali people are reflections of the decisions made by the colonial powers before independence in which the Somalis were divided among the British, Italians, and the French. French Somaliland was not reunified with the rest of Somalia after independence and became the independent nation of Djibouti in 1977. The contemporary division and implosion of the Somali state between the north and the south is essentially a return to the pre-independence configuration of Italian Somaliland in the south and British Somaliland in the north. Ethiopia, on the other hand, was a historically imperial nation that extended its rule over the Eritrean, Tygrean, and Oromo people. Its contemporary political instability is a reflection of that historical past.

29. The notion of the "African solution" was the conceptual foundation for the creation of the Nigerian-led ECOWAS peacekeeping force deployed to Liberia. Ironically, in Somalia the concept was advocated by General Aidid. In December

1993, General Aidid agreed to attend the Somali peace conference in Ethiopia as long as it was exclusive to key African nations. Even more ironic is the fact that the U.S. military provided his transportation to the conference. General Aidid is the same person that the U.S. military sought to capture and prosecute in southern Mogadishu a few months earlier.

30. *The New York Times,* January 19, 1993, section A, 5, p. 1.

31. The response of the Sudanese government was that the United States had targeted it because of its "deep-rooted animosity" of Islam. In reaction, Sudanese Premier, Omar Hassan Bashir, "threatened" to reject the 1993 allocation of $50 million in U.S. humanitarian aid. His belief was that U.S. humanitarian aid was tantamount to a U.S. intelligence presence in Sudan.

32. Warren Christopher, "A New Relationship," *Africa Report* (July/August 1993): 36–37.

33. Warren Christopher, "The United States and Africa: A Relationship," pp. 2–5, quoted from Larry Diamond, "Promoting Democracy in Africa," in *Africa in World Politics,* John Harbeson and Donald Rothchild, eds. (Boulder, CO: Westview Press, 1995), p. 259.

34. Michaels, "Retreat from Africa," p. 93.

35. The United States has controlled nearly one-fourth of the voting power in the World Bank, for example.

36. Although this figure is lower than the U.S. national debt, for African economies the debt repayment has led to an accumulated balance of payments deficit that averaged $8.8 billion in 1992.

37. Zenebeworke Tadesse, "Beyond Authoritarian Rule," *Africa Demos* (July/August 1991): 5.

38. See Michaels, "Retreat from Africa."

39. Peter Lawrence and David Seddon, "What Price Economic Reform?" *Review of African Political Economy* 47 (Spring 1990): 6.

40. Clough, *Free at Last?* p. 112.

41. Steven Greenhouse, "G.O.P. Senate Bill Would Slash Foreign Aid for Africa," *The New York Times,* December 13, 1994, p. A9.

42. T. Masland, "Going Down the Aid Rathole?" *Newsweek,* December 5, 1994, p. 39. See also *The New York Times,* November 13, 1994, section I, 12, p. 3.

43. See *Access: Security Spectrum,* July 1993, Washington, D.C., for a detailed discussion of the three policy positions.

44. Emphasis here is placed upon domestic nongovernmental organizations, rather than international nongovernmental organizations.

45. Zenebworke Bissart, "The Role of Non-Governmental Organizations (NGOs) in the Development of the Informal Sector in Ethiopia," *Africa Update* (Winter 1993): 6–9.

46. For details on the rift between the Africanist academic community and policy makers, see Clough, *Free at Last?* pp. 26–29.

47. See Walton Brown, "The 1992 European Community and Africa," *TransAfrica Forum* (Fall 1992); and Karl Magyar, "Sub-Saharan Africa: Political Marginalization and Strategic Realignment," in *U.S. Foreign Policy in Transition,* James Winkates, et al., eds. (Chicago, IL: Nelson-Hall Publishers, 1994).

48. Clough, *Free at Last?* pp. 111–112.

INDEX

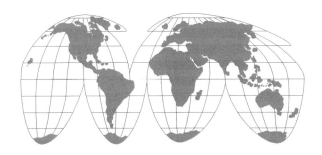